New Perspectives on

The Internet

6th Edition

Gary P. Schneider
University of San Diego

Jessica Evans

THOMSON

COURSE TECHNOLOGY

Australia • Canada • Mexico • Singapore • Spain • United Kingdom • United States

W9-BIL-964

New Perspectives on The Internet, 6th Edition—Introductory

is published by Thomson Course Technology.

Senior Managing Editor:
Rachel Goldberg

Senior Editor:
Amanda Shelton

Senior Product Manager:
Kathy Finnegan

Product Managers:
Katherine T. Pinard, Brianna Hawes

Associate Product Manager:
Shana Rosenthal

Editorial Assistant:
Janine Tangney

Marketing Manager:
Joy Stark

Developmental Editor:
Katherine T. Pinard

Production Editor:
Kelly Robinson

QA Manuscript Reviewer:
Ken Ryan

Text Designer:
Steve Deschene

Cover Designer:
Nancy Goulet

Cover Artist:
Ed Carpenter
www.edcarpenter.net

Composition:
GEX Publishing Services

Proofreader:
Kathy Orrino

Indexer:
Alexandra Nickerson

Preface

Real, Thought-Provoking, Engaging, Dynamic, Interactive—these are just a few of the words that are used to describe the New Perspectives Series' approach to learning and building computer skills.

Without our critical-thinking and problem-solving methodology, computer skills could be learned but not retained. By teaching with a case-based approach, the New Perspectives Series challenges students to apply what they've learned to real-life situations.

Our ever-growing community of users understands why they're learning what they're learning. Now you can too!

See what instructors and students are saying about the best-selling New Perspectives Series:

"First of all, I just have to say that I wish that all of my textbooks were written in the style of the New Perspectives series. I am using these titles for all of the courses that I teach that have a book available."
— Diana Kokoska, University of Maine at Augusta

"The New Perspectives format is a pleasure to use. The Quick Checks and the tutorial Review Assignments help students view this complex topic from a real work perspective."
— Craig Shaw, Central Community College, Hastings

...and about New Perspectives on The Internet:

"This book is very well rounded and covers a wide variety of topics related to the Internet. It would be an excellent choice for anyone teaching an Introductory to mid-level course on the Internet."
— Debbie Huffman, North Texas Central College

Review

Apply

Reference Window

Task Reference

Reinforce

Student Edition
Labs

Why *New Perspectives* will work for you

Context
Each tutorial begins with a problem presented in a "real-world" case that is meaningful to students. The case sets the scene to help students understand what they will do in the tutorial.

Hands-on Approach
Each tutorial is divided into manageable sessions that combine reading and hands-on, step-by-step work. Large screenshots for enhanced readability help guide students through the steps. **Trouble?** tips anticipate common mistakes or problems to help students stay on track and continue with the tutorial.

Review
In New Perspectives, retention is a key component to learning. At the end of each session, a series of Quick Check questions helps students test their understanding of the concepts before moving on. Each tutorial also contains an end-of-tutorial summary and a list of key terms for further reinforcement.

Assessment
Engaging and challenging Review Assignments and Case Problems have always been a hallmark feature of the New Perspectives Series. Colorful icons and brief descriptions accompany the assignments, making it easy to understand at a glance both the goal and level of challenge a particular assignment holds.

Reference
While contextual learning is excellent for retention, there are times when students will want a high-level understanding of how to accomplish a task. Within each tutorial, Reference Windows appear before a set of steps to provide a succinct summary and preview of how to perform a task. In addition, a complete Task Reference at the back of the book provides quick access to information on how to carry out common tasks. Finally, each book includes a combination glossary/index to promote easy reference of material.

Student Edition Labs
These interactive labs help your students review and extend their knowledge of Internet concepts through observation, step-by-step practice, and review questions. Student Edition Labs are tied to individual chapters and cover different subject areas, including the history of computing, an overview of using a browser, searching on the Web, e-mail, computer ethics, and computer viruses.

Student Online Companion
This book has an accompanying online companion Web site designed to enhance learning. This Web site includes:
- All of the links—completely updated for currency—necessary for completing the tutorials, Review Assignments, and Case Problems.
- Student Data Files.
- Additional resources for topics in each tutorial.
- Links to the Student Edition Labs for hands-on reinforcement of selected topics.

www.course.com/NewPerspectives

New Perspectives offers an entire system of instruction

The New Perspectives Series is more than just a handful of books. It's a complete system of offerings:

New Perspectives catalog
Our online catalog is never out of date! Go to the catalog link on our Web site to check out our available titles, request a desk copy, download a book preview, or locate online files.

Coverage to meet your needs!
Whether you're looking for just a small amount of coverage or enough to fill a semester-long class, we can provide you with a textbook that meets your needs.
- Brief books typically cover the essential skills in just 2 to 4 tutorials.
- Introductory books build and expand on those skills and contain an average of 5 to 8 tutorials.
- Comprehensive books are great for a full-semester class, and contain 9 to 12+ tutorials.
- Power Users or Advanced books are perfect for a highly accelerated introductory class or a second course in a given topic.

So if the book you're holding does not provide the right amount of coverage for you, there's probably another offering available. Go to our Web site or contact your Course Technology sales representative to find out what else we offer.

Instructor Resources
We offer more than just a book. We have all the tools you need to enhance your lectures, check students' work, and generate exams in a new, easier-to-use and completely revised package. This book's Instructor's Manual, ExamView testbank, PowerPoint presentations, data files, solution files, figure files, and a sample syllabus are all available on a single CD-ROM or for downloading at www.course.com.

How will your students master Computer Concepts and Microsoft Office?
Add more muscle and flexibility to your course with SAM (Skills Assessment Manager)! SAM adds the power of skill-based assessment and the award-winning SAM classroom administration system to your course, putting you in control of how you deliver exams and training.

By adding SAM to your curriculum, you can:
- Reinforce your students' knowledge of key computer concepts and application skills with hands-on exercises.
- Allow your students to "learn by listening," with access to rich audio in their training.
- Build hands-on computer concepts exams from a test bank of more than 200 skill-based concepts, windows, and applications tasks.
- Schedule your students' training and testing exercises with powerful administrative tools.
- Track student exam grades and training progress using more than one dozen student and classroom reports.

Teach your introductory course with the simplicity of a single system! You can now administer your entire Computer Concepts and Microsoft Office course through the SAM platform. For more information on the SAM administration system, SAM Computer Concepts, and other SAM products, please visit www.course.com/sam.

Distance Learning
Enhance your course with any of our online learning platforms. Go to www.course.com or speak with your Course Technology sales representative to find the platform or the content that's right for you.

www.course.com/NewPerspectives

About This Book

Students gain in-depth knowledge of beginning to advanced Internet concepts through a practical, step-by-step approach.

- Contains coverage of Internet Explorer and Firefox.
- Shows students how to conduct research on the Internet (including the deep Web), evaluate Internet research resources, and cite online works.
- Contains coverage of the ethics of downloading media and copying copyrighted material from the Web.
- Includes an appendix that discusses the history of the Internet and the World Wide Web.
- Online Student Edition Labs and new Lab Assignments help reinforce learning Internet concepts, including using a browser, e-mail, computer ethics, and computer viruses.
- Additional Research Assignments allow students to use their Internet research skills to demonstrate what they've learned.
- The Student Online Companion provides a centralized and constantly updated launching pad for students to find all the links they'll explore in their studies.

Acknowledgments

Creating a textbook is a collaborative effort in which authors and publisher work as a team to provide the highest quality book possible. We want to acknowledge the major contributions of the Course Technology editorial team members: Rachel Goldberg, Managing Editor; Katherine Pinard, Product Manager; Shana Rosenthal, Associate Product Manager; and Kelly Robinson, Production Editor. We thank Burt LaFountain and his team of Quality Assurance testers for their work as well. All of these Course Technology staff members are terrific, positive, and supportive members of a great publishing team. We also want to thank Course Technology Executive Editor Mac Mendelsohn; his vision for this book focused on the Internet, rather than on specific software applications, and he encouraged us to undertake this project.

We also thank our Developmental Editors Judy Adamski and Katherine Pinard. Their sharp eyes caught many mistakes and they contributed excellent ideas for making the manuscript more readable. We offer our heartfelt thanks to the Course Technology organization as a whole. The people at Course Technology have been, by far, the best publishing team with which we have ever worked.

We want to thank the reviewers for their insightful comments and suggestions at various stages of the book's development: J. Human, Lexington Community College; Rebecca Lawson, Lansing Community College; and Marcia Strand, College of the Desert. Special thanks go to Becky Holmes, Brian Morgan at Marshall University, Rebecca Lawson at Lansing Community College, and Dave Nuscher for their contributions to the Additional Research Assignments.

Finally, we want to express our deep appreciation for the continuous support and encouragement of our spouses, Cathy Cosby and Richard Evans. They demonstrated remarkable patience as we worked to complete this book on a very tight schedule. We also thank our children for tolerating our absences while we were busy writing.

Gary P. Schneider

Jessica Evans

Dedication

To the memory of my brother, Bruce. – G.P.S.

To Hannah and Richard. – J.E.

Brief Contents

Internet

Internet—Level I Tutorials   WEB 1

Tutorial 1 Browser Basics . . . . WEB 3
Introduction to the Web and Web Browser Software

Tutorial 2 Basic Communication on the Internet: E-Mail . . . . WEB 71
Evaluating an E-Mail Program and a Web-Based E-Mail Service

Internet—Level II Tutorials   WEB 153

Tutorial 3 Searching the Web . . . . WEB 155
Using Search Engines and Directories Effectively

Tutorial 4 Information Resources on the Web . . . . WEB 201
Finding, Evaluating, and Using Online Information Resources

Tutorial 5 Downloading and Storing Data. . . . . WEB 245
Using FTP and Other Services to Transfer and Store Data

Internet—Appendix A   APP 1

Appendix A The Internet and the World Wide Web . . . . APP 3
History, Structure, and Technologies

Additional Research Assignments   ADD 3

ARA 1 Locating and Evaluating Health Care Information on the Internet   ADD 4

ARA 2 Telemedicine. . . . . ADD 6

ARA 3 Advances in Distance Learning . . . . ADD 8

ARA 4 The Future of Semantic Web . . . . ADD 9

Glossary/Index . . . . REF 1

Task Reference . . . . REF 17

Table of Contents

Preface v

The Internet

Level I Tutorials . . . . WEB 1

Read This Before You Begin . . . . WEB 2

Tutorial 1   WEB 3

Browser Basics . . . . WEB 3

Introduction to the Web and
Web Browser Software . . . . WEB 3

Session 1.1 . . . . **WEB 4**

Understanding the Internet and the World
Wide Web . . . . WEB 4

The Internet . . . . WEB 4

The World Wide Web . . . . WEB 4

Hypertext, Links, and Hypermedia . . . . WEB 5

Web Site Organization . . . . WEB 7

Addresses on the Web . . . . WEB 8

Domain Name Addressing . . . . WEB 8

Uniform Resource Locators . . . . WEB 9

Main Elements of Web Browsers . . . . WEB 11

Title Bar . . . . WEB 12

Scroll Bars . . . . WEB 12

Status Bar . . . . WEB 13

Menu Bar . . . . WEB 13

Page Tab . . . . WEB 13

Home Button . . . . WEB 13

Finding Information on the Web Using Search Engines and
Web Directories . . . . WEB 14

Returning to Web Pages Previously Visited . . . . WEB 15

Using Favorites and Bookmarks . . . . WEB 15

Using the History List . . . . WEB 15

Cookies . . . . WEB 15

Reloading a Web Page . . . . WEB 16

Stopping a Web Page Transfer . . . . WEB 16

Printing and Saving Web Pages . . . . WEB 16

Printing a Web Page . . . . WEB 16

Saving a Web Page . . . . WEB 16

Examining Additional Web Browser Choices . . . . WEB 17

Mozilla Project . . . . WEB 17

Mozilla Suite . . . . WEB 17

Browsers for Hire: Opera and iRider . . . . WEB 18

Reproducing Web Pages and Copyright Law . . . . WEB 21

Session 1.1 Quick Check . . . . WEB 21

Session 1.2 . . . . **WEB 22**

Starting Microsoft Internet Explorer . . . . WEB 22

Status Bar . . . . WEB 23

Menu Bar . . . . WEB 24

Hiding and Showing the Internet Explorer Toolbars . . . . WEB 24

Entering a URL in the Address Bar . . . . WEB 25

Hyperlink Navigation Using the Mouse . . . . WEB 27

Returning to Previously Viewed Web Pages . . . . WEB 28

Using the Favorites List . . . . WEB 28

Organizing Favorites . . . . WEB 31

Using the History List . . . . WEB 32

Refreshing a Web Page . . . . WEB 33

Returning to the Home Page . . . . WEB 33

Printing a Web Page . . . . WEB 34

Changing the Settings for the Page Setup . . . . WEB 35

Checking Web Page Security . . . . WEB 36

Getting Help in Internet Explorer . . . . WEB 37

Using Internet Explorer to Save a Web Page . . . . WEB 38

Saving a Web Page . . . . WEB 38

Saving Web Page Text to a File . . . . WEB 39

Saving a Web Page Graphic to a Disk . . . . WEB 41

Session 1.2 Quick Check . . . . WEB 43

Session 1.3 . . . . **WEB 43**

Starting Mozilla Firefox . . . . WEB 43

Using the Navigation Toolbar . . . . WEB 45

Using the Location Bar . . . . WEB 45

Hyperlink Navigation Using the Mouse . . . . WEB 47

Returning to Web Pages Previously Visited . . . . WEB 48

Creating a Bookmark for a Web Site . . . . WEB 48

Using the History List . . . . WEB 52

Reloading a Web Page . . . . WEB 52

Returning to the Home Page . . . . WEB 52

Printing a Web Page . . . . WEB 54

Checking Web Page Security . . . . WEB 55

Managing Cookies . . . . WEB 56

Getting Help in Firefox . . . . WEB 58

Using Firefox to Save a Web Page . . . . WEB 59

Saving a Web Page . . . . WEB 59

Saving Web Page Text to a File . . . . WEB 60

Saving a Web Page Graphic to a Disk . . . . WEB 62

Session 1.3 Quick Check . . . . .WEB 64

Tutorial Summary . . . . .WEB 64

Key Terms . . . . .WEB 64

Review Assignments . . . . .WEB 65

Case Problems. . . . . WEB 66

Lab Assignments . . . . WEB 68

Quick Check Answers . . . . WEB 69

Tutorial 2   **WEB 71**

Basic Communication on the Internet: E-Mail . . WEB 71

Evaluating an E-Mail Program and a Web-Based

E-Mail Service . . . . .WEB 71

Session 2.1 . . . .**WEB 72**

What Is E-Mail and How Does It Work? . . . . .WEB 72

Common Features of an E-Mail Message . . . . .WEB 73

    To, Cc, and Bcc . . . . .WEB 74

    From . . . . .WEB 75

    Subject . . . . .WEB 75

    Attachments . . . . .WEB 75

    Message Body and Signature Files . . . . .WEB 76

    Internet Etiquette (Netiquette) . . . . .WEB 77

Common Features of E-Mail Programs . . . . .WEB 78

    Sending Messages . . . . .WEB 78

    Receiving and Storing Messages . . . . .WEB 79

    Printing a Message . . . . .WEB 79

    Filing a Message . . . . .WEB 79

    Forwarding a Message . . . . .WEB 79

    Replying to a Message . . . . .WEB 81

    Deleting a Message . . . . .WEB 81

Maintaining an Address Book . . . . .WEB 81

E-Mail Programs . . . . .WEB 81

    Mozilla Thunderbird . . . . .WEB 82

    Opera M2 Client . . . . .WEB 90

Web-Based E-Mail Services . . . . .WEB 95

    Gmail from Google . . . . .WEB 96

Web Logs . . . . .WEB 97

"You've Got Spam!" . . . . .WEB 98

Session 2.1 Quick Check . . . . .WEB 100

Session 2.2 . . . .**WEB 100**

Microsoft Outlook Express . . . . .WEB 100

Configuring E-Mail . . . . .WEB 102

Sending a Message Using Outlook Express . . . . .WEB 104

Receiving and Reading a Message . . . . .WEB 107

Viewing and Saving an Attached File . . . . .WEB 108

Replying to and Forwarding Messages . . . . .WEB 110

    Replying to an E-Mail Message . . . . .WEB 110

    Forwarding an E-Mail Message . . . . .WEB 111

Filing and Printing an E-Mail Message . . . . .WEB 112

Deleting an E-Mail Message and Folder . . . . .WEB 114

Maintaining an Address Book . . . . .WEB 115

    Adding a Contact to the Address Book . . . . .WEB 115

    Adding a Group of Contacts to the Address Book . . . . . .WEB 117

Session 2.2 Quick Check . . . . .WEB 119

Session 2.3 . . . .**WEB 119**

Hotmail . . . . .WEB 119

Creating a Hotmail Account . . . . .WEB 120

Sending a Message Using Hotmail . . . . .WEB 129

Receiving and Reading a Message . . . . .WEB 132

Viewing and Saving an Attached File . . . . .WEB 133

Replying to and Forwarding Messages . . . . .WEB 134

    Replying to an E-Mail Message . . . . .WEB 134

    Forwarding an E-Mail Message . . . . .WEB 135

Filing and Printing an E-Mail Message . . . . .WEB 136

Deleting an E-Mail Message and Folder . . . . .WEB 137

Maintaining an Address Book . . . . .WEB 138

    Adding a Contact to the Address Book . . . . .WEB 138

    Adding a Group to the Address Book . . . . .WEB 140

Session 2.3 Quick Check . . . . .WEB 143

Tutorial Summary . . . . .WEB 143

Key Terms . . . . .WEB 143

Review Assignments . . . . .WEB 144

Case Problems . . . . .WEB 145

Lab Assignments . . . . .WEB 150

Quick Check Answers . . . . .WEB 151

The Internet

Level II Tutorials . . . . **WEB 153**

    Read This Before You Begin . . . . **WEB 154**

Tutorial 3   **WEB 155**

Searching the Web . . . . **WEB 155**

Using Search Engines and Directories Effectively . .WEB 155

Session 3.1 . . . . .WEB 156
Types of Search Questions . . . . .WEB 156
Web Search Strategy . . . . .WEB 158
    Using Search Engines .WEB 159
    Understanding Search Engines . . . . .WEB 159
    Using More Than One Search Engine . . . . .WEB 162
Understanding Search Engine Databases . . . . .WEB 164
    Search Engine Features .WEB 165
    Using Directories and Hybrid Search Engine Directories . .WEB 166
    Using Metasearch Engines . . . . .WEB 173
    Using Other Web Resources . . . . .WEB 175
Session 3.1 Quick Check . . . . .WEB 177

Session 3.2 . . . .**WEB 178**
Boolean Logic and Filtering Techniques . . . . .WEB 178
    Boolean Operators . . . . .WEB 178
    Other Search Expression Operators . . . . .WEB 179
    Wildcard Characters . . . . .WEB 180
    Search Filters . . . . .WEB 180
Complex Searches . . . . .WEB 180
    Using AltaVista Advanced Search . . . . .WEB 181
    Filtered Search in Ask Jeeves . . . . .WEB 183
    Filtered Search in Google . . . . .WEB 186
    Search Engines with Clustering Features . . . . .WEB 189
    Future of Web Search Tools . . . . .WEB 190
    Using People to Enhance Web Directories . . . . .WEB 191
Evaluating the Validity and Quality of Web
Research Resources . . . . .WEB 191
    Author Identity and Objectivity . . . . .WEB 192
    Content . . . . .WEB 193
    Form and Appearance . . . . .WEB 193
    Evaluating the Quality of a Web Site . . . . .WEB 193
Session 3.2 Quick Check . . . . .WEB 195
Tutorial Summary . . . . .WEB 196
Key Terms . . . . .WEB 196
Review Assignments . . . . .WEB 196
Case Problems . . . . .WEB 197
Quick Check Answers . . . . .WEB 200

Session 4.1 . . . . .WEB 202
Current Information on the Web . . . . .WEB 202
Getting the News . . . . .WEB 209
Weather Reports . . . . .WEB 213
Obtaining Maps and Destination Information . . . . .WEB 216
Finding Businesses and People on the Web . . . . .WEB 220
    Finding Businesses . . . . .WEB 220
    Finding People and Related Privacy Concerns . . . . . . .WEB 222
Session 4.1 Quick Check . . . . .WEB 223

Session 4.2 . . . .**WEB 223**
Online Library, Text, and Multimedia Resources . . . . .WEB 223
    Library Resources . . . . .WEB 223
    Text and Other Archives on the Web . . . . .WEB 225
Citing Web Research Resources . . . . .WEB 227
Copyright Issues . . . . .WEB 229
    Copyrights and Ideas . . . . .WEB 230
    Copyright Protection and Internet Technologies . . . . . .WEB 230
    Ethical Issues: Fair Use and Plagiarism . . . . .WEB 230
Images and Graphics on the Web . . . . .WEB 232
Sound, Music, and Video on the Web . . . . .WEB 236
    WAV Audio File Format . . . . .WEB 236
    MIDI Audio File Format . . . . .WEB 236
    AU Audio File Format .WEB 236
Video File Formats . . . . .WEB 237
    Audio from Video: The MP3 File Format . . . . .WEB 237
    Ethical and Legal Concerns: Sharing Audio Files . . . . .WEB 237
    Legal MP3 File Distribution . . . . .WEB 238
Future of Electronic Publishing . . . . .WEB 239
    E-Zines . . . . .WEB 239
    Blogs (Web Logs) . . . . .WEB 239
Session 4.2 Quick Check . . . . .WEB 240
Tutorial Summary . . . . .WEB 240
Key Terms . . . . .WEB 240
Review Assignments . . . . .WEB 241
Case Problems . . . . .WEB 241
Lab Assignments . . . . .WEB 244
Quick Check Answers . . . . .WEB 244

Tutorial 4   **WEB 201**
Information Resources on the Web . . . . WEB 201
Finding, Evaluating, and Using Online
Information Resources . . . . .WEB 201

Tutorial 5   **WEB 245**
Downloading and Storing Data . . . . WEB 245
Using FTP and Other Services to Transfer
and Store Data . . . . .WEB 245

Session 5.1 . . . . .WEB 246

Understanding File Transfer Protocol . . . . .WEB 246

    File Transfer Modes . . . . .WEB 246

    File Types and Extensions . . . . .WEB 246

Connecting to an FTP Server . . . . .WEB 248

    FTP Using an FTP Client Program . . . . .WEB 248

    FTP Using a Web Browser . . . . .WEB 249

Levels of Access for FTP Servers . . . . .WEB 250

    Anonymous FTP . . . . .WEB 251

    Full-Privilege FTP . . . . .WEB 252

    Using a Public Directory . . . . .WEB 252

Using a Web Browser to Navigate an FTP Site . . . . .WEB 253

Checking Files for Viruses . . . . .WEB 256

Session 5.1 Quick Check . . . . .WEB 258

Session 5.2 . . . . .WEB 259

Visiting and Using a Download Site . . . . .WEB 259

Downloading Programs . . . . .WEB 261

    Using a Web Browser to Download an

    FTP Client Program . . . . .WEB 262

    Using an FTP Client Program to Download WinZip . . . . .WEB 265

Compressing and Decompressing Files . . . . .WEB 269

Tracing an Internet Route . . . . .WEB 272

Session 5.2 Quick Check . . . . .WEB 275

Session 5.3 . . . . .WEB 275

Using Online Storage Services . . . . .WEB 275

Online Storage Providers . . . . .WEB 276

Collaborative Authoring on the Web . . . . .WEB 280

Session 5.3 Quick Check . . . . .WEB 287

Tutorial Summary . . . . .WEB 287

Key Terms . . . . .WEB 287

Review Assignments . . . . .WEB 288

Case Problems . . . . .WEB 289

Lab Assignments . . . . .WEB 295

Quick Check Answers . . . . .WEB 295

The Internet
Appendix A
Title Page . . . . APP 1

Appendix A   **APP 3**
The Internet and the World Wide Web . . . . **APP 3**
History, Structure, and Technologies . . . . .APP 3

The Internet and the World Wide Web:

Amazing Developments . . . . .APP 3

Exploring Uses for the Internet . . . . .APP 4

    New Ways to Communicate . . . . .APP 4

    Information Resources and Software . . . . .APP 4

    Doing Business Online . . . . .APP 8

    Entertainment . . . . .APP 8

Computer Networks . . . . .APP 9

    Client/Server Local Area Networks . . . . .APP 9

    Connecting Computers to a Network . . . . .APP 10

Origins of the Internet . . . . .APP 12

    Connectivity: Circuit Switching vs. Packet Switching . . . .APP 13

    Open Architecture Philosophy .APP 15

    Birth of E-Mail: A New Use for Networks . . . . .APP 15

    More New Uses for Networks Emerge . . . . .APP 16

    Interconnecting the Networks .APP 16

    Commercial Interest Increases .APP 17

Growth of the Internet . . . . .APP 18

    From Research Project to Information Infrastructure . . . . .APP 18

    New Structure for the Internet .APP 19

IP Addressing . . . . .APP 20

World Wide Web . . . . .APP 21

    Origins of Hypertext . . . . .APP 21

    Hypertext and Graphical User Interfaces Come to the

    Internet . . . . .APP 22

    The Web and Commercialization of the Internet . . . . . . .APP 24

Business of Providing Internet Access . . . . .APP 25

    Connection Bandwidth . . . . .APP 26

Appendix Summary . . . . .APP 30

Key Terms . . . . .APP 30

Glossary/Index .... .REF 1

Task Reference .... .REF 17

The Internet
Additional Research Assignments
Title Page .... ADD 1

Additional Research Assignments   ADD 3

Additional Research Assignment 1
Locating and Evaluating Health Care Information
on the Internet .... .ADD 4

Additional Research Assignment 2
Telemedicine .... .ADD 6

Additional Research Assignment 3
Advances in Distance Learning .... .ADD 8

Additional Research Assignment 4
The Future of the Semantic Web .... .ADD 9

New Perspectives on
The Internet

Tutorial 1   WEB 3
Browser Basics
Introduction to the Web and Web Browser Software

Tutorial 2   WEB 71
Basic Communication on the Internet: E-Mail
Evaluating an E-Mail Program and a Web-Based E-Mail Service

Appendix A   APP 3
The Internet and the World Wide Web
History, Structure, and Technologies

Read This Before You Begin: Tutorials 1–2

To the Student

Data Files

To complete the Level I Internet Tutorials (Tutorials 1 and 2), you will need the starting student Data Files. Your instructor will either provide you with these Data Files or ask you to obtain them yourself.

The Level I Internet tutorials require the folders shown in the next column to complete the Tutorials, Review Assignments, and Case Problems. You will need to copy these folders from a file server, a standalone computer, or the Web to a drive and folder where you will be storing your Data Files. You instructor will tell you which computer, drive letter, and folder(s) contain the files you need. You can also download the files by going to *www.course.com*; see inside the back cover for more information on downloading files, or ask your instructor or technical support person for assistance.

If you are storing your Data Files on floppy disks, you will need **one** blank, formatted, high-density disk for these tutorials. Label your disk as shown, and copy the folders indicated onto it.

▼ **Internet Data Disk 1**

    Tutorial.01

    Tutorial.02

When you begin a tutorial, refer to the Student Data Files section at the bottom of the tutorial opener page, which indicates the folders and files you need for the tutorial. Each end-of-chapter exercise also indicates the files you need to complete that exercise.

Student Edition Labs

The Level I Internet tutorials feature three interactive Student Edition Labs to help you understand the following concepts: Getting the Most Out of the Internet, E-Mail, and History of Computing (in Appendix A). You can access the labs by going to the Student Online Companion page for the tutorial in which each one appears, and then clicking the Student Edition Labs link.

To the Instructor

The Data Files are available on the Instructor's Resource CD for this title. Follow the instructions in the Help file on the CD-ROM to install the files to your network or standalone computer.

See the "To the Student" section above for information on how to set up the Data Files that accompany this text. To complete the tutorials in this book, students must have a Web browser, an e-mail account, and an Internet connection.

You are granted a license to copy the Data Files to any computer or computer network used by students who have purchased this book.

System Requirements

If you are going to work through this book using your own computer, you need:

- **Computer System** Microsoft Internet Explorer 6.0 or higher, or Firefox 1.07 or higher, and Windows 2000 or higher must be installed on your computer. Note that the figures and steps in this edition were written using Windows XP, so Windows 2000 users may notice minor differences in the figures and the steps. This book assumes a complete installation of the Web browser software and its components, and that you have an existing e-mail account and an Internet connection. Because your Web browser might be different from the ones used in the figures in the book, your screens might differ slightly at times.

- **Data Files** You will not be able to complete the tutorials or exercises in this book using your own computer until you have the Data Files.

- **Student Edition Labs** The Student Edition Labs are available through the Student Online Companion for this book.

www.course.com/NewPerspectives

Objectives

Session 1.1
- Learn about the Internet and the World Wide Web
- Learn how Web browser software displays Web pages
- Learn how Web page addresses are constructed
- Become familiar with Web browsers and the main functions found in this type of software

Session 1.2
- Configure and use the Microsoft Internet Explorer Web browser to navigate the Web
- Save and organize Web addresses using Internet Explorer
- Save Web page text and graphics using Internet Explorer

Session 1.3
- Configure and use the Mozilla Firefox Web browser to navigate the Web
- Save and organize Web addresses using Mozilla Firefox
- Save Web page text and graphics using Mozilla Firefox

Lab

Getting the Most Out of the Internet

Student Edition Labs

Student Data Files

There are no student data files needed for this tutorial.

Browser Basics

Introduction to the Web and Web Browser Software

Case

Danville Animal Shelter

The Danville Animal Shelter is an organization devoted to helping improve the welfare of animals, particularly unwanted pets, in the local Danville area. Trinity Andrews is the director of the Danville Animal Shelter and she is always looking for ways to improve the services it offers to the community.

The shelter is a charitable organization that is supported mainly by contributions from the local community. Trinity tried to budget the funds that the shelter receives to do the most good with the limited available money. One of the critical needs of the shelter is to let people in the community know about pets that are available for adoption. Trinity has placed some advertising in local newspapers and television stations, but advertising is very expensive, even when the local media outlets provide reduced rates or offer to run stories about the shelter.

The problem with using newspapers and television is that the pets available for adoption change from day to day and, by the time a news story or ad runs, the pet that is featured often has been adopted. Trinity has decided that although newspaper and television advertising and promotion can be a good way for the Shelter to get its general message out to the community, these outlets are not the best way to let people know about specific pets that are available for adoption.

You have served as a volunteer at the shelter for several years and Trinity heard that you were learning to use the Internet. Trinity would like you to help identify ways that the shelter can use the Internet to let the community know about the shelter and, in particular, about specific pets that are available for adoption.

Understanding the Internet and the World Wide Web

As you start to consider how you might use the Web to help the shelter, you remember that one of your college friends, Maggie Beeler, earned her degree in library science. You meet with Maggie at the local public library, where she is working at the reference desk. She is glad to assist you.

The Internet

Maggie explains to you that computers can be connected to each other in a configuration called a **network**. If the computers are near each other (usually in the same building), the network is called a **local area network** or a **LAN**. Networked computers that are not located near each other form a **wide area network**, or a **WAN**. When networks are connected to each other, the system is called an **interconnected network** or **internet** (with a lowercase "i"). The **Internet** (with an uppercase "i") is a specific internet that connects computers all over the world using a common set of interconnection standards. Although it began as a large science project sponsored by the U.S. military, the Internet today allows people and businesses all over the world to communicate with each other in a variety of ways.

The part of the Internet known as the **World Wide Web** (or the **Web**) is a subset of the computers on the Internet that use software to make their contents easily accessible to each other. The Web has helped to make information on the Internet easily accessible by people who are not computer scientists. The Internet and the Web give people around the world new ways to communicate with each other, obtain information resources and software, conduct business transactions, and find entertainment. You can read Appendix A to learn more about the history of the Internet and about the technologies that make it work.

The World Wide Web

Maggie begins by explaining that the Web is a collection of files that reside on computers, called **Web servers**, that are located all over the world and are connected to each other through the Internet. Most files on computers, including computers that are connected to the Internet, are private; that is, only the computer's users can access those files. The owners of the computer files that make up the Web have made those files publicly available by placing them on the Web servers. Anyone who has a computer connected to the Internet can obtain access to those files.

When you use your Internet connection to become part of the Web, your computer becomes a **Web client** in a worldwide client/server network. A **Web browser** is the software that you run on your computer to make it work as a Web client. The Internet connects many different types of computers running different operating system software. Web browser software lets your computer communicate with all of these different types of computers easily and effectively. Figure 1-1 shows how this client/server structure uses the Internet to provide multiple interconnections among the various kinds of client and server computers.

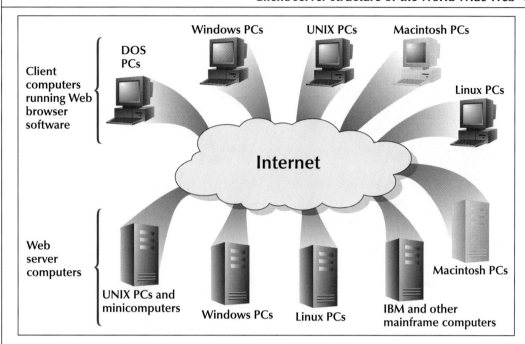

Hypertext, Links, and Hypermedia

The public files on Web servers are ordinary text files, much like the files created and used by word-processing software. To enable Web browser software to read these files, however, the text must be formatted according to a generally accepted standard. The standard used on the Web is **Hypertext Markup Language (HTML)**. HTML uses codes, or **tags**, that tell the Web browser software how to display the text contained in the text file. For example, a Web browser reading the following line of text

```
<B>A Review of the Book <I>Wind Instruments</I></B>
```

recognizes the <B> and </B> tags as instructions to display the entire line of text in bold and the <I> and </I> tags as instructions to display the text enclosed by those tags in italics. Different Web clients that connect to this Web server might display the tagged text differently. For example, one Web browser might display text enclosed by bold tags in a blue color instead of displaying the text in bold. A text file that contains HTML tags is called an **HTML document**.

HTML provides a variety of text formatting tags that can be used to indicate headings, paragraphs, bulleted lists, numbered lists, and other text enhancements in an HTML document. The real power of HTML, however, lies in its anchor tag. The **HTML anchor tag** enables Web designers to link HTML documents to each other. Anchor tags in HTML documents create **hypertext links**, which are instructions that point to other HTML documents or to another section of the same document. Hypertext links also are called **hyperlinks** or **links**. Figure 1-2 shows how these hyperlinks can join multiple HTML documents to create a web of HTML documents across computers on the Internet. The HTML documents shown in the figure can be on the same computer or on different computers. The computers can be in the same room or an ocean away from each other.

Figure 1-2	Hyperlinks create a web of HTML text across multiple files

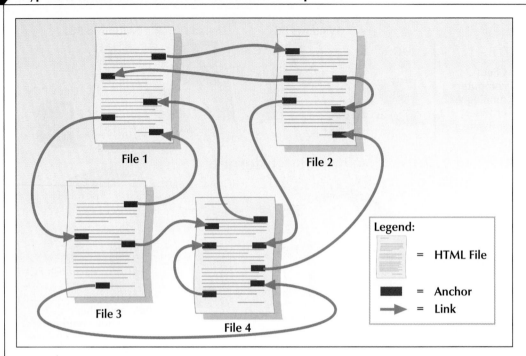

Most Web browsers display hyperlinks in a color that is different from other text in an HTML document and also underline the hyperlinks so they are easy to distinguish. When a Web browser displays an HTML document, it is often referred to as a **Web page**. Maggie shows you a Web page at the World Wide Web Consortium (W3C) Web site. See Figure 1-3. The hyperlinks on this Web page are easy to identify because the Web browser software that displayed this page shows the hyperlinks as blue, underlined text.

Figure 1-3	W3C Web page

Each of the hyperlinks on the Web page shown in Figure 1-3 enables the user to connect to another Web page. In turn, each of those Web pages contains hyperlinks to other pages, including one hyperlink that leads back to the first Web page. Hyperlinks can also lead to computer files that contain pictures, graphics, and media objects such as sound and video clips. Hyperlinks that connect to these types of files often are called **hypermedia links**. You are especially interested in learning more about hypermedia links, but Maggie suggests you first need to understand a little more about how people organize Web pages on their Web servers.

Maggie tells you that the easiest way to move from one Web page to another is to use the hyperlinks that the authors of Web pages have embedded in their HTML documents. Web page authors often use a graphic image as a hyperlink. Sometimes, it is difficult to identify which objects and text are hyperlinks just by looking at a Web page displayed on your computer. Fortunately, on most Web pages, when you move the mouse pointer over a hyperlink in a Web browser, the pointer changes into an icon that resembles a hand with a pointing index finger. For example, when you move the mouse pointer over the Finding Your Way at W3C hyperlink, as shown in Figure 1-4, the shape of the pointer changes to indicate that if you click the Finding Your Way at W3C text, the Web browser will open the Web page to which that hyperlink points.

Mouse pointer hovering over a hyperlink ◀ **Figure 1-4**

mouse pointer changes to pointing finger when moved over a hyperlink

Web Site Organization

Maggie explains that people who create Web pages usually have a collection of pages on one computer that they use as their Web server. A collection of linked Web pages that has a common theme or focus is called a **Web site**. Most Web site's store all of the site's pages in one location, either on one computer or on one LAN. Some large Web sites, however, are distributed over a number of locations. In fact, it is sometimes difficult to determine where one Web site ends and another begins. One common definition of a Web site is any group of Web pages that relates to one specific topic or organization, regardless of where the HTML documents are located.

The main page that all of the other pages on a particular Web site are organized around and link back to is called the site's **home page**. Maggie warns you that the term *home page* is used at least three different ways on the Web and that it is sometimes difficult to tell which meaning people intend when they use the term. The first definition of home page indicates the main page for a particular site. This home page is the first page that opens when you visit a particular Web site. The second definition of home page is the first page that opens when you start your Web browser. This type of home page might be an HTML document on your own computer. Some people create such home pages and include hyperlinks to Web sites that they frequently visit. If you are using a computer on your school's or employer's network, its Web browser might be configured to open the main page for the school or firm. The third definition of home page is the Web page that a particular Web browser loads the first time you use it. This page usually is stored at the Web site of the firm or other organization that created the Web browser software. Home pages that meet the second or third definitions are sometimes called **start pages**.

Addresses on the Web

Maggie reminds you that there is no centralized control over the Internet. Therefore, no central starting point exists for the Web, which is a part of the Internet. However, there is a system for locating a specific computer on the Web.

Domain Name Addressing

Each computer on the Internet has a unique identification number, called an **IP (Internet Protocol) address**. IP addressing is a way of identifying each unique computer on the Web, just like your home address is a way of identifying your home in a city. (You can learn more about IP addressing by reading Appendix A.) Most people do not use the IP address to locate Web sites and individual pages. Instead, the browsers use domain name addressing. A **domain name** is a unique name associated with a specific IP address by a program that runs on an Internet host computer. This program, which coordinates the IP addresses and domain names for all computers attached to it, is called **DNS (domain name system) software**, and the host computer that runs this software is called a **domain name server**. Domain names can include any number of parts separated by periods; however, most domain names currently in use have only three or four parts. For example, the domain name gsb.uchicago.edu is the computer connected to the Internet at the Graduate School of Business (gsb), which is an academic unit of the University of Chicago (uchicago), which is an educational institution (edu). No other computer on the Internet has the same domain name.

Domain names follow a hierarchical model that you can follow from top to bottom if you read the domain names from right to left. The last part of a domain name is called its **top-level domain (TLD)**. For example, DNS software on the Internet host computer that is responsible for the "edu" domain keeps track of the IP address for all of the educational institutions in its domain, including "uchicago." Similar DNS software on the "uchicago" Internet host computer would keep track of the academic units' computers in its domain, including the "gsb" computer.

Since 1998, the **Internet Corporation for Assigned Names and Numbers (ICANN)** has had responsibility for managing domain names. In the United States, the six most common TLDs have been .com, .edu, .gov, .mil, .net, and .org. Although a seventh TLD, the "us" domain, is approved for general use by any person within the United States, it is most frequently used by state and local government organizations in the United States and by U.S. primary and secondary schools (because the "edu" domain is reserved for post secondary educational institutions). Internet host computers outside the United States often use two-letter country domain names instead of, or in addition to, the six general TLDs. For example, the domain name uq.edu.au is the domain name for the University of Queensland (uq), which is an educational institution (edu) in Australia (au).

In 2000, ICANN added seven new TLDs to the general domain category. These were the first new general domains to be added since 1988. Although ICANN chose these new domain names after much deliberation and considering more than 100 possible new names, a number of people were highly critical of the selections. In 2005, ICANN again began the process of adding several new TLDs. One of the proposed domains, a .xxx domain for Web sites with adult content, raised considerable controversy. You can learn more about these criticisms and controversies by going to the Student Online Companion Web page for this tutorial at *www.course.com/newperspectives/internet6*, clicking the Tutorial 1 link, and then following the links in the Additional Information section under the heading "ICANN and Controversy Over Its Rulings." Figure 1-5 presents a list of the general TLDs, including the seven additions made in 2000, and some of the more popular country TLDs.

Common top-level domains (TLDs) | Figure 1-5

Original General TLDs		Country TLDs		General TLDs Approved in 2000	
TLD	**Use**	**TLD**	**Country**	**TLD**	**Use**
.com	U.S. Commercial	.au	Australia	.aero	Air-transport industry
.edu	U.S. Four-year educational institution	.ca	Canada	.biz	Businesses
.gov	U.S. Federal government	.de	Germany	.coop	Cooperatives
.mil	U.S. Military	.fi	Finland	.info	General use
.net	U.S. General use	.fr	France	.museum	Museums
.org	U. S. Not-for-profit organization	.jp	Japan	.name	Individual persons
.us	U.S. General use	.se	Sweden	.pro	Professionals (accountants, lawyers, physicians)
		.uk	United Kingdom		

Uniform Resource Locators

The IP address and the domain name each identify a particular computer on the Internet, but they do not indicate where a Web page's HTML document resides on that computer. To identify a Web page's exact location, Web browsers rely on Uniform Resource Locators. A **Uniform Resource Locator (URL)** is a four-part addressing scheme that tells the Web browser:

• The transfer protocol to use when transporting the file
• The domain name of the computer on which the file resides
• The pathname of the folder or directory on the computer on which the file resides
• The name of the file

The **transfer protocol** is the set of rules that the computers use to move files from one computer to another on an internet. The most common transfer protocol used on the Internet is the **hypertext transfer protocol (HTTP)**. You can indicate the use of this protocol by typing http:// as the first part of the URL. People do use other protocols to transfer files on the Internet, but most of these protocols were used more frequently before the Web became part of the Internet. Two protocols that you still might see on the Internet are the **file transfer protocol (FTP)**, which is indicated in a URL as ftp://, and the **Telnet protocol**, which is indicated in a URL as telnet://. FTP is just another way to transfer files, and Telnet is a set of rules for establishing a connection between two computers over the Internet that allows a person at one computer to control the other computer.

The domain name was described in the preceding section. The pathname describes the hierarchical directory or folder structure on the computer that stores the file. Most people are familiar with the structure used on Windows and DOS PCs, which uses the back slash character (\) to separate the structure levels. URLs follow the conventions established in the UNIX operating system that use the forward slash character (/) to separate the structure levels. The forward slash character works properly in a URL, even when it is pointing to a file on a Windows or DOS computer.

The filename is the name that the computer uses to identify the Web page's HTML document. On most computers, the filename extension of an HTML document is either .html or .htm. Although many PC operating systems are not case-sensitive, computers that use the UNIX operating system *are* case-sensitive. Therefore, if you are entering a URL that includes mixed-case and you do not know the type of computer on which the file resides, it is safer to retain the mixed-case format of the URL.

Not all URLs include a filename. If a URL does not include a filename, most Web browsers will load the file named index.html. The **index.html** filename is the default name for a Web site's home page on most computer systems. Figure 1-6 shows an example of a URL annotated to show its four parts.

| Figure 1-6 | Structure of a Uniform Resource Locator (URL) |

The URL shown in Figure 1-6 uses the HTTP protocol and points to a computer that is connected to the Web (www) at the Boston Symphony Orchestra (bso), which is a not-for-profit organization (org). The Boston Symphony's Web site contains many different kinds of information about the orchestra. The path shown in Figure 1-6 includes two levels. The first level indicates that the information is about the orchestra's summer home at Tanglewood (tangle), and the second level indicates that the page will contain information about the orchestra's performances (perfs) at Tanglewood. The filename (index.html) indicates that this page is the home page in the Tanglewood performances folder or directory.

You might encounter an error message when you enter a URL in a Web browser. Two common messages that you might see are "server busy" and "DNS entry not found." Either of these messages means that your browser was unable to communicate successfully with the Web server that stores the page you requested. The cause for this inability might be temporary—in which case, you might be able to use the hyperlink later—or the cause might be permanent. The browser has no way of determining the cause of the connection failure, so the browser provides the same types of error messages in either case.

Another error message that you might receive appears as a Web page and includes the text "Error 404: File not Found." This error message usually means that the Web page's location has changed permanently or that the Web page no longer exists.

You tell Maggie how much you appreciate all of the help she has given you by explaining how you can use Internet addresses to find information on the Web. Now you understand that the real secret to finding good information on the Web is to know the right URLs. Maggie tells you that you can find URLs in many places; for example, newspapers and magazines often publish URLs of Web sites that might interest their readers. Friends who know about the subject area in which you are interested also are good sources. The best source, however, is the Web itself.

You are eager to begin learning how to use a Web browser, so Maggie explains some elements common to all Web browsers. Most Web browsers have similar functions, which make it easy to use any Web browser after you have learned how to use one.

Main Elements of Web Browsers

Now that you know a little more about Web sites, you start to wonder how a particular computer can communicate with other computers over the Internet. Maggie tells you that there are a number of different Web browsers. Web browser software turns your computer into a Web client that can communicate through an Internet service provider (ISP) or a network connection with Web servers all over the world. The two most popular browsers in use today are **Microsoft Internet Explorer**, or simply **Internet Explorer**, and **Mozilla Firefox**, or simply **Firefox**. You will learn more about these and other Web browsers later in this tutorial.

Maggie reminds you that most Windows programs use a standard graphical user interface (GUI) design that includes a number of common screen elements. Figures 1-7 and 1-8 show the main elements of the Internet Explorer and Firefox program windows, respectively. These two Web browsers share many common Windows elements, such as a title bar at the top of the window, a scroll bar on the right side of the window, and a status bar at the bottom of the window.

Main elements of the Internet Explorer program window   ◀ **Figure 1-7**

Figure 1-8	Main elements of the Firefox program window

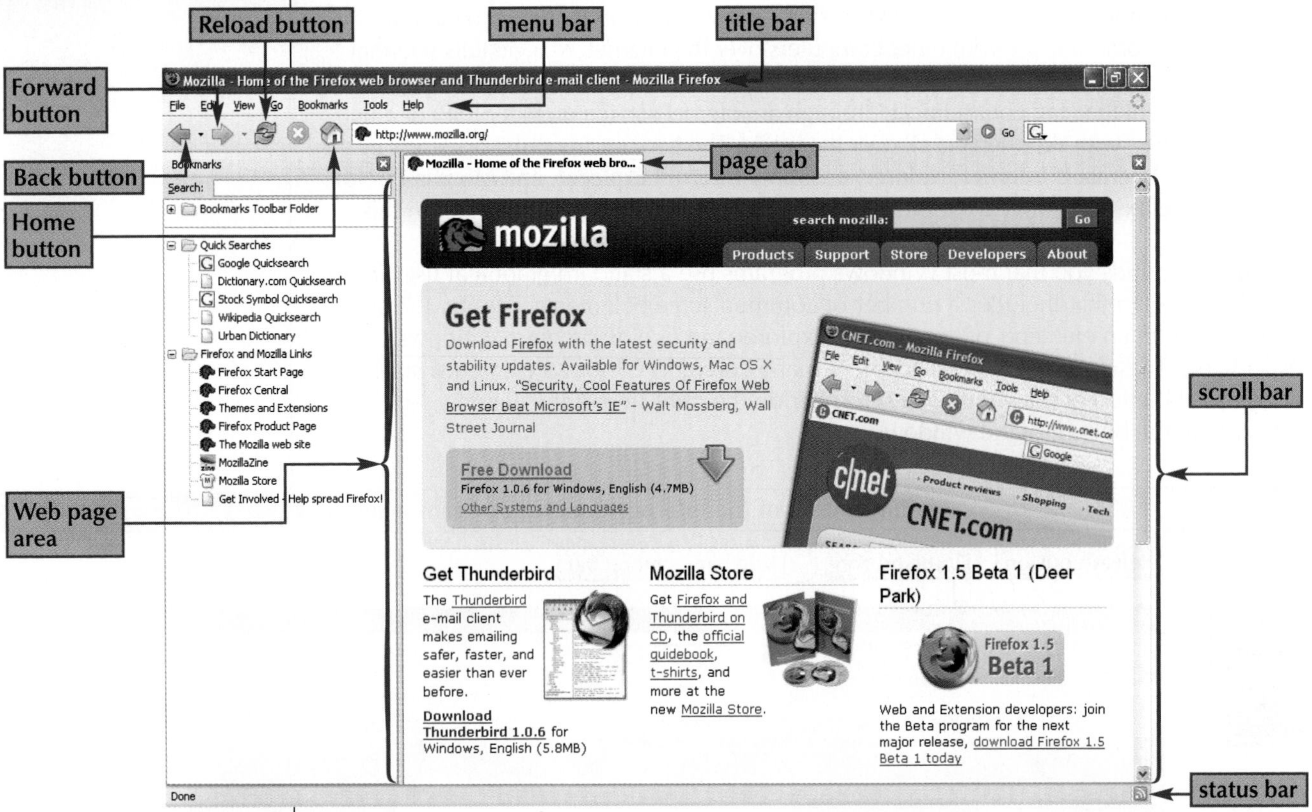

In each program window, the menu bar appears below the title bar, and below the menu bar is a toolbar. Next, Maggie describes the common browser window elements.

Title Bar

A Web browser's **title bar** shows the name of the open Web page and the Web browser's program name. As in all Windows programs, you can double-click the title bar to resize the window quickly. The right side of the title bar contains the **Minimize**, **Restore Down**, and **Close** buttons when the window is maximized to fill the screen. When the window is not maximized, the Restore button is replaced by a **Maximize** button; to expand such a browser window so it fills the screen, you click the Maximize button.

Scroll Bars

A Web page can be much longer than a regular-sized document, so you often need to use the **scroll bar** at the right side of the program window to move the page up or down through the document window. You can use the mouse to click the Up scroll button or the Down scroll button to move the Web page up or down through the windows **Web page area**. You can also use the mouse to click and drag the scroll box up and down in the scroll bar to move the page accordingly. Although most Web pages are designed to resize automatically when loaded into different browser windows with different display areas, some Web pages can be wider than your browser window. When this happens, the browser places another scroll bar at the bottom of the window above the status bar, so you can move the page horizontally through the browser.

Status Bar

The **status bar** at the bottom of the browser window includes information about the browser's operations. Each browser uses the status bar to deliver different information, but generally, the status bar indicates the name of the Web page that is loading, the load status (partial or complete), and important messages, such as "Document: Done." Some Web sites send messages as part of their Web pages that are displayed in the status bar as well. You will learn more about the specific functions of the status bar in Internet Explorer and Firefox in Sessions 1.2 and 1.3, respectively.

Menu Bar

The browser's **menu bar** provides a convenient way for you to execute typical File, Edit, View, and Help commands. In addition to these common Windows command sets, the menu bar also provides specialized commands for the browser that enable you to navigate the Web.

Page Tab

Some Web browsers, including Firefox, can show multiple Web pages within the Web page area. These Web browsers display a **page tab** for each Web page that shows the title of the Web page. The current version of Internet Explorer does not offer tabbed windows, but many industry observers expect Microsoft to include this feature in that browser in its next version.

Home Button

Clicking the **Home button** in Internet Explorer or in Firefox displays the home (or start) page for the browser. Most Web browsers let you specify a page that loads automatically every time you start the program. You might not be able to do this if you are in your school's computer lab because schools often set the start page for all browsers on campus and then lock that setting. Some companies do the same thing on their employees' computers. If you are using your own computer, you can choose your own start page. Some people like to use a Web page that someone else has created and made available for others to use. One example of a start page that many people use as their start page is the refdesk.com Web page, shown in Figure 1-9.

| Figure 1-9 | **Refdesk.com Web page** |

Pages such as the one shown in Figure 1-9 offer links to pages that many Web users frequently visit. The people and organizations that create these pages often sell advertising space on their pages to pay the cost of maintaining their sites.

Finding Information on the Web Using Search Engines and Web Directories

Web search engines are Web pages that conduct searches of the Web to find the words or expressions that you enter. The result of such a search is a Web page that contains hyperlinks to Web pages that contain matching text or expressions. These pages can give new users an easy way to find information on the Web. Internet Explorer and Firefox each include a toolbar button that opens search engines and Web directories chosen by the companies that wrote the browser software. However, many people prefer to select their own tools for searching the Internet.

Sometimes the number of results from a search conducted using a search engine is overwhelming, and you find that you need to sort through links to pages that only vaguely match your criteria. Maggie explains that using a **Web directory**, a Web page that contains a list of Web page categories, such as education or recreation, can narrow the results returned for a particular search. The hyperlinks on a Web directory page lead to other pages that contain lists of subcategories that lead to other category lists and Web pages that relate to the category topics. Instead of relying on a computer to categorize the pages, Web directories employ Web directory editors to categorize Web pages. These editors can weed out the pages that do not fit in a particular category.

Returning to Web Pages Previously Visited

Web addresses can be long and hard to remember, even if you are using domain names instead of IP addresses. You can store the addresses of specific Web pages in most browsers, and then open the pages by clicking the stored address. You can also return to a page you have visited in the past by using the browser's history feature. You realize that using the browser to remember important pages will be a terrific asset as you start collecting information for the shelter, so you ask Maggie to explain more about how to return to a Web page.

Using Favorites and Bookmarks

In Internet Explorer, you can save the URL of a site you would like to revisit as a **favorite** in the Favorites folder. In Firefox, you can use a **bookmark** to save the URL of a specific page so you can return to it. You can use Internet Explorer's Favorites feature or a Firefox bookmark to store and organize a list of Web pages that you have visited so you can return to them easily without having to remember the URL or search for the page again. Internet Explorer favorites and Firefox bookmarks work very much like a paper bookmark that you might use in a printed book: They mark the page at which you stopped reading.

You can save as many Internet Explorer favorites or Firefox bookmarks as you want to mark all of your favorite Web pages, so you can return to pages that you frequently use or pages that are important to your research or tasks.

Keeping track of many favorites and bookmarks requires an organizing system. You store favorites or bookmarks on your computer, but different browsers store them in slightly different ways. Internet Explorer stores *each* favorite as a separate file on your computer, and Firefox stores all bookmarks in one file on your computer. Storing each favorite separately, instead of storing all bookmarks together, offers somewhat more flexibility but uses more disk space. You can organize your favorites or bookmarks in many different ways to meet your needs. For example, you might store all of the favorites or bookmarks for Web pages that include information about pet adoption in a folder named "Pet Adoption Information."

Using the History List

As you click the hyperlinks to go to new Web pages, the browser stores the location of each page you visit during a single session in a **history list**. You click the **Back button** and the **Forward button** in either Internet Explorer or Firefox to move through the history list.

When you start your browser, both buttons are inactive (dimmed) because no history list for your new session exists yet. After you follow one or more hyperlinks, the Back button lets you retrace your path through the hyperlinks you have followed. Once you use the Back button, the Forward button becomes active and lets you move forward through the session's history list.

In most Web browsers, you can right-click either the Back or Forward button to display a portion of the history list. You can reload any page on the list by clicking its name in the list. The Back and Forward buttons duplicate the functions of commands on the browser's menu commands. You will learn more about the history list in Sessions 1.2 and 1.3.

Cookies

Another issue that Web users should know about is the use of cookies. A **cookie** is a small file that a Web server writes to the disk drive of the client computer (the computer on which the Web browser is running). Cookies can contain information about the user such as login names and passwords. By storing this information on the user's computer, the Web server can perform functions such as automatic login, which makes it easier to quickly return to favorite Web pages. However, the user often is unaware that these files are being written to the computer's disk drive. Internet Explorer allows the user to choose to accept all cookies, to accept only cookies from the current site, or not to accept any cookies. Internet Explorer also allows users to delete the individual files that contain specific cookies if the user can identify the files to delete, which can be difficult. Other browsers, such as Firefox, give users more comprehensive tools for managing the cookies that have been stored on their computers. You will learn how to manage cookies using Firefox in Session 1.3.

Reloading a Web Page

When you use your browser to access a Web page, your browser downloads the page to your computer from the Web server on which it is stored. The browser stores a copy of every Web page it displays on your computer's hard drive in a **cache** folder, which increases the speed at which the browser can display pages as you navigate through the history list. The cache folder lets the browser reload pages from the cache instead of from the remote Web server.

Clicking the **Refresh button** in Internet Explorer or the **Reload button** in Firefox loads the same Web page that appears in the browser window again. When you click the Refresh or the Reload button, the browser contacts the Web server to see if the Web page has changed since it was stored in the cache folder. If it has changed, the browser gets the new page from the Web server; otherwise, the browser loads the cache folder copy. If you want to force the browser to load the page from the Web server, hold down the Shift key as you click the Refresh or Reload button.

Stopping a Web Page Transfer

Sometimes a Web page takes a long time to load. When this occurs, you can click a toolbar button in Internet Explorer or Firefox to halt the Web page transfer from the server. You can then click the hyperlink again; a second attempt may connect and transfer the page more quickly. You also might want to abort a transfer when you accidentally click a hyperlink that you do not want to follow.

Printing and Saving Web Pages

As you use your browser to view Web pages, you might find some pages that you want to print or store for future use. You can use a Web browser to print a Web page or to save either an entire Web page or just parts of the page, such as selections of text or graphics.

Printing a Web Page

When you execute a print command, the current page (or part of a page, called a **frame**) that appears in the Web page area of the browser is sent to the printer. Most browsers also provide a print preview command that lets you see how the printed page will look. If the page contains light colors or many graphics, you might consider changing the printing options so the page prints without the background or with all black text. You will learn how to change the print settings for Internet Explorer and Firefox in Sessions 1.2 and 1.3, respectively.

Saving a Web Page

Although printing an entire Web page is often useful, there are times when you will want to save all or part of the page to disk. All Web browsers allow you to save copies of most Web pages as files that you can store on your computer's hard disk, a floppy disk, or other storage medium. Some Web pages are written to make copying difficult or impossible; those pages cannot be saved easily. Internet Explorer and Firefox each perform the save operation somewhat differently, thus you will learn more about saving a Web page and its graphics in Sessions 1.2 and 1.3.

Examining Additional Web Browser Choices

After several years of a stable market for Web browsers, many changes occurred in 2004 and 2005. Internet Explorer, which was used by more than 90% of all Web surfers in 2004, began to see other browsers begin to make a dent in its dominant position. Security flaws in Internet Explorer were exploited by virus and worm writers with increasing frequency. Many organizations and individuals began to doubt whether relying on a single browser was a good idea. Earlier in this Tutorial, you learned about Internet Explorer and Firefox. In this section, you will learn about other Web browsers that people are now using instead of or in addition to these popular choices.

Mozilla Project

Mosaic was one of the first Web browsers developed in the early 1990s. A group of researchers who had helped develop Mosaic left their jobs at the University of Illinois Supercomputing Center to form a new company called Netscape and launched the first commercially successful Web browser, **Netscape Navigator**. Because they wanted to replace Mosaic, they named their development project Mozilla, which was short for "Mosaic Killer." When Navigator was first introduced in 1994, Netscape charged a small license fee for corporate users, but the fee was waived for individuals and academic institutions. During this time, Microsoft began distributing Internet Explorer with its Windows operating system at no additional cost, therefore Netscape was forced to drop its license fee in response and was no longer able to earn a profit on its browser business. AOL bought Netscape's other business assets in 1999, but donated the Netscape browser software to a non-profit organization that continued developing the browser software and distributing it to users at no cost. The nonprofit group named the browser software development project "Mozilla" in a revival of the browser's original name.

When the Mozilla project started work in 1999, the team focused on a complete rebuild of the internal workings of the browser, called the **browser rendering engine**. In the Mozilla project, the browser rendering engine, which is named the **Gecko engine**, is used in Netscape Navigator, the Mozilla browser, and the Mozilla Firefox browser.

The Mozilla project continues to develop the Gecko engine and the interfaces for the three browsers based on that engine. In addition, the project coordinates work on a variety of other software development activities, including the Camino Web browser (for Macintosh computers), the Thunderbird e-mail client (which you will learn about in Tutorial 2), and the Sunbird calendar.

The Mozilla project has been operated on a volunteer basis by programmers working in their spare time since its inception in 1999. In 2003, the Mozilla Foundation was created with an initial contribution of $2 million from Time Warner's AOL division. AOL also contributed equipment, domain names, trademarks, and employees to help with the foundation's initial organization activities. Other corporate supporters of the foundation include Sun Microsystems and Red Hat Software. The foundation will help ensure that the Mozilla project continues into the future.

Mozilla Suite

The **Mozilla Suite** is a combination of software applications that the Mozilla open source project has developed. It includes a Web browser that runs on the Gecko engine, an e-mail client and newsreader (Mozilla Messenger), an HTML editor (Mozilla Composer), and an instant messaging chat client (ChatZilla). The Mozilla Suite is the software that Time Warner's AOL division distributes as Netscape Navigator.

The Mozilla Suite's Web browser offers tabbed windows (including an option to make your start page a set of multiple tabbed windows), a pop-up ad blocker, an image manager (that lets you set the browser so it does not load images until you click the Images button on the toolbar), and a "find as you type" page navigation option.

The Mozilla browser allows you to download and install themes that can give the browser a different look. Figure 1-10 shows the Mozilla browser with the Toy Factory theme installed.

Figure 1-10 | **Mozilla browser with Toy Factory theme installed**

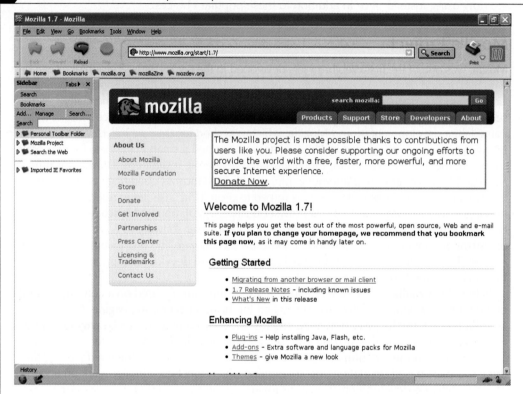

Browsers for Hire: Opera and iRider

Internet Explorer, Firefox, Navigator, and Mozilla, are all available at no cost. There are, however, several browsers available today that charge a license fee. The two that are most widely used are Opera and iRider.

Opera started out in 1994 as a research project at Telenor, which is Norway's state telecommunications company. One year later, an independent development company (Opera Software ASA) was formed to continue work on the Opera project. This company continues to develop and sell the Opera Web browser and related software. The Opera browser (which includes an e-mail client that you will learn about in the next section and a chat client) currently sells for $39, with a student license available for $20. Because Opera's program code was written independently and does not use any elements of the Gecko engine or Internet Explorer, Opera is not affected by any security flaws that might be exploited by those attacking any of the Gecko-based browsers or Internet Explorer. Figure 1-11 shows the Opera browser main screen.

Opera Web browser in main screen ◄ Figure 1-11

In 2000, Opera began offering a free version of its browser that is supported by advertising. The advertising messages are displayed in the toolbar area of the screen. Advertisers can buy a banner ad that runs in a 460 × 60 pixel area of the toolbar or a 225-character text message that scrolls across the top of the screen in its own toolbar area. More than 10 million users worldwide have downloaded the free version of Opera.

Opera was the first Web browser to offer tabbed browsing, a button to toggle on and off the download of images with a Web page, and a search window that the user could configure to run searches in specific search engines automatically. All of these features are currently available in Navigator, Mozilla, and Firefox. Opera also includes a toolbar control that lets users adjust the size of the displayed text in the browser window. Other browsers today provide this same function, but the choices are buried in a menu or submenu.

Opera for Mobile is another Opera software program that gives mobile device users a fully functional Internet browser. Opera for Mobile lets users view any Web site (not just those that are designed to display on mobile devices) using a mobile phone, PDA, or similar device.

Another Web browser that charges a license fee is Wymea Bay's **iRider** browser. The current fee is $29, with a discount available for academic users. The iRider browser is designed for power users, such as the person who has six browsers open at once as he shops for the best deals on airfares, compares products being auctioned on eBay, or looks up a series of different addresses on Yahoo! Maps. The iRider browser helps power users by allowing them to open and manage multiple Web pages at once. Although other browsers provide this functionality, they either open the Web pages in separate windows or in separate tabs within a window. Either way, the user only sees a tiny icon and (perhaps) a part of each Web page name. With iRider, the user can view thumbnail images of all open Web pages displayed in a hierarchical map called a Page List.

More important, iRider keeps all open Web pages in memory until the user deletes them, allowing the user to click any thumbnail image in the Page List to open a Web page and review its contents. Most power users find using the Page List to be much easier than using the Back and Forward buttons or a history list because the page thumbnails are displayed as a hierarchy (all Web pages that are linked from a single Web page are shown indented under that page's thumbnail image) instead of being listed in the order in which they were opened (as they would be in a history list). Figure 1-12 shows iRider being used to search for books about Christmas on Amazon.com and Barnes and Noble.com. The user ran searches on each site, opened three product pages on each site, and returned to the Amazon.com start page.

| Figure 1-12 | Multiple searches in the iRider Web browser |

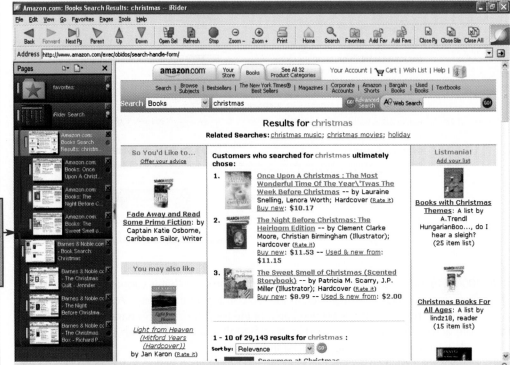

hierarchy of thumbnail images (one for each Web page visited)

Many experienced Web surfers open pages in new windows as a matter of course, but the Web site does not always allow new windows to open, or in some cases, to stay open. In iRider, any window that is opened in the browser remains in the Page List (and thus it is available to be opened again) until the user closes it.

Most airline and travel sites take a few moments to search through all possible flights (or car rentals or hotel rooms) before they return a page of search results. When the search results page appears, a user might decide to try a flight leaving a day earlier or later. Travel sites generally require the user to run the search again, which removes the results of the first search. With iRider, the user can run several searches simultaneously and compare the results, going from page to page as necessary because all of the pages remain available in the Page List. Once again, iRider gives the user more control over which pages remain available and which are closed.

Another useful feature of iRider is that users can select multiple links on a page and iRider will begin to download the pages simultaneously. Each page appears in the Page List when its download is complete so the user can select pages that have downloaded more quickly rather than waiting for a specific page to download, using the Back button to revisit the search page, clicking and waiting for another page to download, and so on.

Reproducing Web Pages and Copyright Law

Maggie explains that there can be significant restrictions on the way that you can use information or images that you copy from another entity's Web site. Because of the way a Web browser works, it copies the HTML code and the graphics and media files to your computer before it can display them in the browser. Just because copies of these files are stored temporarily on your computer does not mean that you have the right to use them in any way other than having your computer display them in the browser window. The United States and most other countries have copyright laws that govern the use of photocopies, audio or video recordings, and other reproductions of authors' original work. A **copyright** is the legal right of the author or other owner of an original work to control the reproduction, distribution, and sale of that work. A copyright comes into existence as soon as the work is placed into a tangible form, such as a printed copy, an electronic file, or a Web page. The copyright exists even if the work does not contain a copyright notice. If you do not know whether material that you find on the Web is copyrighted, the safest course of action is to assume that it is.

U.S. copyright law has a **fair use** provision that allows students to use limited amounts of copyrighted information in term papers and other reports prepared in an academic setting. The source of the material used should always be cited. Commercial use of copyrighted material is much more restricted. You should obtain permission from the copyright holder before using anything you copy from a Web page. The copyright holder can require you to pay a fee for permission to use the material from the Web page.

It can be difficult to determine the owner of a source's copyright if no notice appears on the Web page; however, many Web pages provide a hyperlink to the e-mail address of the person responsible for maintaining the page. That person, sometimes called a **Webmaster**, usually can provide information about the copyright status of materials on the page. Many Web sites also include the address and telephone number of the company or organization that owns the site, although that information can be hard to find on some Web sites.

Now that you understand the basic functions of a browser, you are ready to start using your browser to find information for the shelter. If you are using Internet Explorer, your instructor will assign Session 1.2; if you are using Firefox, your instructor will assign Session 1.3. The authors recommend, however, that you read both sessions because you might encounter a different browser on a public or employer's computer in the future.

Session 1.1 Quick Check

1. True or False: Web browser software runs on a Web server computer.
2. True or False: You can format text using HTML tags.
3. The Web page that opens when you start your browser is called a(n) _____ or a(n) _____.
4. The general term for links to graphic images, sound clips, or video clips that appear in a Web page is _____.
5. A local political candidate is creating a Web site to help in her campaign for office. Describe three things she might want to include in her Web site.
6. What is the difference between IP addressing and domain name addressing?
7. Identify and interpret the meaning of each part of the following URL: http://www.savethetrees.org/main.html.
8. What is the difference between a Web directory and a Web search engine?

Session 1.2

Starting Microsoft Internet Explorer

Microsoft Internet Explorer is Microsoft's Web browser that installs with all recent versions of Windows operating system software. This introduction assumes that you have Internet Explorer installed on your computer. You should have your computer turned on so the Windows desktop is displayed.

To start Internet Explorer:

1. Click the **Start** button on the taskbar, point to **All Programs**, and then click **Internet Explorer**. After a moment, Internet Explorer opens.

    Trouble? If you cannot find Internet Explorer on the All Programs menu, check to see if an Internet Explorer shortcut icon appears on the desktop, and then double-click it. If you do not see the shortcut icon, ask your instructor or technical support person for help. The program might be installed in a different folder on your computer.

2. If the program does not fill the screen entirely, click the **Maximize** button on the Internet Explorer program's title bar. Your screen should look like Figure 1-13.

Figure 1-13	Internet Explorer main program window

Trouble? Figure 1-13 shows the MSN.com home page, which is the page that Internet Explorer opens the first time it starts. Your computer might be configured to open to a different Web page or no page at all.

Trouble? If you do not see the toolbars shown in Figure 1-13, click View on the menu bar, point to Toolbars, and then click the name of the toolbar that is not displayed on the screen. A toolbar that is displayed has a check mark to the left of its name.

Internet Explorer includes a **Standard Buttons toolbar** with a number of buttons, as shown in Figure 1-14. Many of these buttons execute frequently used commands for browsing the Web. The toolbar on your Internet Explorer browser might contain different icons or additional icons to the right of the icons shown in Figure 1-14. Other software programs installed on your computer have placed those icons on your toolbar so that those programs can be used from within Internet Explorer. You will learn about the functions of the most important of these buttons in this session.

Standard Buttons toolbar ◀ **Figure 1-14**

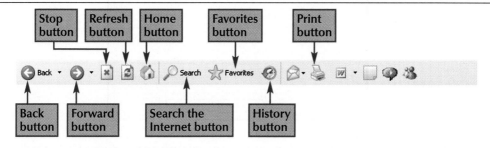

Now that you understand how to start Internet Explorer, you want to learn more about components of the Internet Explorer program window.

Status Bar

The status bar at the bottom of the window includes several panels that give you information about Internet Explorer's operations. The first panel—the **transfer progress report**—presents status messages that show, for example, the URL of a page while it is loading. When a page is completely loaded, this panel displays the text "Done" until you move the mouse over a hyperlink, at which time this panel displays the URL of the hyperlink. While Internet Explorer is loading a Web page from a Web server, a second panel opens and displays a blue **graphical transfer progress indicator** that moves from left to right to indicate how much of a Web page has been loaded. This indicator is especially useful for monitoring progress when the browser is loading large Web pages.

Another status bar panel displays a locked padlock icon when the browser loads a Web page that has a security certificate. You can double-click on the padlock icon to open a dialog box that contains information about the security certificate for a Web page.

The last (rightmost) status bar panel displays the **security zone** to which the page you are viewing has been assigned. As part of its security features, Internet Explorer lets you classify Web pages by the security risk you believe they present. You can open the Internet Security Properties dialog box shown in Figure 1-15 by double-clicking the last (rightmost) status bar panel.

Figure 1-15 ▶ Internet Security Properties dialog box

This dialog box lets you set four levels of security-enforcing procedures: High, Medium, Medium-Low, and Low. In general, the higher the level of security you set for your browser, the slower it will operate. Higher security settings also disable some browser features. You can click the Custom Level button to configure the way each security level operates on your computer.

Menu Bar

In addition to the standard Windows commands, the menu bar also provides access to favorites. The Favorites menu command lets you store and organize URLs of sites that you have visited and want or need to return to on a regular basis.

Hiding and Showing the Internet Explorer Toolbars

Internet Explorer lets you hide its menu bar and toolbars to show more of the Web page area. To hide the menu bar, you can select the Full Screen option on the View menu. When the window is in **Full Screen**, the menu bar is no longer visible, and a smaller version of the Standard Buttons toolbar appears at the top of the screen. To hide the small Standard Buttons toolbar, right-click the toolbar and click Auto-Hide to give you additional room for displaying the Web page. To restore the screen and display both the menu bar and Standard Buttons toolbar, press the F11 key. The F11 key is a toggle. A **toggle** is like a push button switch on a television set; you press the button once to turn on the television and press it a second time to turn it off.

Hiding and Restoring the Toolbars in Internet Explorer

- To hide a toolbar, click View on the menu bar, point to Toolbars, and then click the name of the toolbar you want to hide; or right-click the toolbar, and then click the toolbar name on the shortcut menu.
- To hide the small Standard Buttons toolbar that appears at the top of the screen in Full Screen, right-click the toolbar, and then click Auto-Hide on the shortcut menu.
- To restore a toolbar, click View on the menu bar, point to Toolbars, and then click the name of the toolbar you want to restore; or right-click the toolbar, and then click the toolbar name on the shortcut menu.
- To temporarily restore the small Standard Buttons toolbar in Full Screen, move the mouse to the top of the screen until the toolbar displays.
- To restore the small Standard Buttons toolbar in Full Screen, move the mouse to the top of the screen until the toolbar displays, right-click the toolbar, and then click Auto-Hide on the shortcut menu.

You will switch to Full Screen and try hiding and then restoring the small Standard Buttons toolbar.

To use the Full Screen and Auto Hide commands:

1. Click **View** on the menu bar, and then click **Full Screen**.

2. Right-click the small Standard Buttons toolbar that appears at the top of the screen to open the shortcut menu, and then click **Auto-Hide** on the shortcut menu if it is not already checked.

3. If the toolbar does not immediately roll up out of view, move the mouse pointer away from the top of the screen for a moment. Now, you can see more of the Web page area.

4. Return the mouse pointer to the top of the screen. The toolbar scrolls back down into view.

5. With the toolbar displayed, right-click the toolbar and then click **Auto-Hide** on the shortcut menu. This removes the check mark from the Auto-Hide entry on the menu and turns the toolbar on again.

6. Click the **Restore** button to return to the normal Internet Explorer window. As mentioned earlier, you could also press F11 key to restore the normal window.

You can use the Customize command on the View Toolbars menu to change the appearance of the toolbars. For example, you can choose to show the Standard Buttons toolbar buttons with large icons or small icons.

You may have noticed that there is another option on the shortcut menu that opens when you right-click a toolbar—Lock the Toolbars. If there is a check mark next to the Lock the Toolbars option, then you cannot move the toolbars. To unlock the toolbars, click Lock the Toolbars again to clear the check mark.

Entering a URL in the Address Bar

Maggie explains that you can use the **Address bar** to enter URLs directly into Internet Explorer. As you learned in Session 1.1, you must enter the URL to identify a Web page's exact location. Although a complete URL includes the name of a file, entering just the IP address and the domain name will usually be enough information to find the home page of the site.

Entering a URL in the Address Bar

- Click at the end of the current text in the Address bar, and then delete any unnecessary or unwanted text from the displayed URL.
- Type the URL of the location that you want to go to.
- Press the Enter key or click the Go button on the Address bar to load the URL's Web page in the browser window.

Trinity has asked you to start your research by examining the home page for the Midland Pet Adoption Agency's Web site. She has given you the URL so that you can find it.

To load the Midland Pet Adoption Agency's Web page:

1. Click at the end of the text in the Address bar, and then delete any unnecessary or unwanted text by pressing the **Backspace** key.

   Trouble? Make sure that you delete all of the text in the Address bar so the text you type in Step 2 will be correct.

2. Type **www.midlandpet.com** in the Address bar. This is the URL for the Midland Pet Adoption Agency Web site.

3. Press the **Enter** key. The home page of the Midland Pet Adoption Agency Web site loads, as shown in Figure 1-16. When the entire page has loaded, the graphical transfer progress indicator in the status bar will stop moving and the transfer progress report panel will display the text "Done."

| Figure 1-16 | Midland Pet Adoption Agency Web page |

The URL listed in the Address bar has changed from the address you typed to one hosted at the domain *course.com*. This is because, as noted at the bottom of the Web page, the Midland Pet Adoption Agency Web site is an online demo. The URL you typed, www.midlandpet.com, is a valid URL, but it is not an independent Web site. If Midland Pet were an actual agency that owned an independent Web site, the URL in the Address bar would have changed to append the exact address of the home page, such as http://www.midlandpet.com/index.html.

Hyperlink Navigation Using the Mouse

The easiest way to move from one Web page to another is to use the mouse to click hyperlinks that the authors of Web pages embed in their HTML documents. You can also right-click the mouse on the background of a Web page to open a shortcut menu that includes navigation options.

Reference Window

Navigating Between Web Pages Using Hyperlinks and the Mouse

- Click the hyperlink.
- After the new Web page has loaded, right-click on the Web page's background.
- Click Back on the shortcut menu.

To follow a hyperlink to a Web page and return using the mouse:

1. With the Midland Pet Adoption Agency home page open in your browser, move the mouse pointer to position it over the **Training Programs** hyperlink, as shown in Figure 1-17. Note that your pointer changes to the shape of a hand with a pointing index finger.

Midland Pet Adoption Agency home page ◀ **Figure 1-17**

pointer shape changes when hovering over a hyperlink

Take me home today!

Midland Pet Adoption Agency

Home · Pets · Training Programs · Emergency Clinic · Directions & Contact

Welcome to the Web site of the Midland Pet Adoption Agency, a not-for-profit organization dedicated to improving the lives of pets and pet owners in the Midland area. The dedicated volunteers who support the Midland Pet Adoption Agency hope that you find this site to be a useful resource. Be sure to visit our Pets page and help us find a home for our little friends!

The Midland Pet Adoption Agency site is an online demo, and does not represent a real animal shelter.
Copyright © 2004 Thomson Course Technology

2. Click the **Training Programs** hyperlink. Watch the first panel in the status bar—when it displays the text "Done," you know that Internet Explorer has loaded the full page.

3. Right-click anywhere in the Web page area that is not a hyperlink to display the shortcut menu, as shown in Figure 1-18.

Figure 1-18 | Using the shortcut menu to go back to the previous page

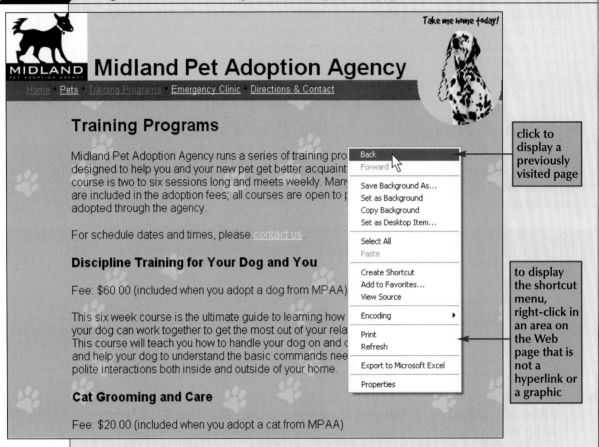

Trouble? If you right-click a hyperlink or a graphic Web page element, your shortcut menu will display a list that differs from the one shown in Figure 1-18; therefore the Back item might not appear in the same position on the menu or not appear at all. If you do not see the shortcut menu shown in Figure 1-18, click anywhere outside of the shortcut menu to close it, and then repeat Step 3.

4. Click **Back** on the shortcut menu to return to the Midland Pet Adoption Agency home page.

Returning to Previously Viewed Web Pages

You like the format of the Midland Pet Adoption Agency's home page, so you want to make sure that you can go back to that page later if you need to review its contents. Maggie explains that you can write down the URL so you can refer to it later, but an easier way is to store the URL in the Favorites list for future use. You can also use the History list and Back button to return to the pages you have previously visited, and the Home button to return to your browser's start page.

Using the Favorites List

Internet Explorer's Favorites feature lets you store and organize a list of Web pages that you have visited so you can return to them easily. The Favorites button on the Standard Buttons toolbar opens the Favorites bar shown in Figure 1-19. You can use the Favorites bar to open URLs you have stored as favorites.

Favorites bar in Internet Explorer ◄ **Figure 1-19**

Figure 1-19 shows the hierarchical structure of the Favorites feature. For example, the figure shows five links to Web sites stored in a folder named "Handy Stuff." You can organize your favorites in the way that best suits your needs and working style.

Creating a New Favorites Folder

Reference Window

- Open the Web page in Internet Explorer.
- Click the Favorites button on the Standard Buttons toolbar to open the Favorites bar.
- Click the Add button in the Favorites bar (or click Favorites on the menu bar, and then click Add to Favorites).
- If necessary, click the Create in button.
- Click the Favorites folder, and then click the New Folder button.
- Type the name of the new folder in the Folder name text box, and then click the OK button.
- Click the OK button.

You will save the URL for the Midland Pet Adoption Agency Web page as a favorite in a Pet Adoption Agencies folder, which you must first create.

To create a new Favorites folder:

▶ 1. With the Midland Pet Adoption Agency's home page open, click the **Favorites** button on the Standard Buttons toolbar to open the Favorites bar.

▶ 2. Click the **Add** button at the top of the Favorites bar. The Add Favorite dialog box opens.

▶ 3. If the text in the Name field is not "Midland Pet Adoption Agency" (without the quotation marks), delete the text, and then type **Midland Pet Adoption Agency**.

If the symbols on the Create in button appear as >>, you will need to expand the dialog box so you can select the Favorites folder in which you will create a new folder.

▶ 4. If necessary, click the **Create in** button. Note that the dialog box expands to display a list of Favorites folders and that the symbols now appear as <<.

5. Click **Favorites** in the Create in box to select that folder, and then click the **New Folder** button. The new folder will be stored as a subfolder within the Favorites folder.

6. Type **Pet Adoption Agencies** in the Folder name text box, and then click the **OK** button. See Figure 1-20. The Web page's name appears automatically in the Name text box in the Add Favorite dialog box. You can edit the suggested page name.

| **Figure 1-20** | **Creating a new Favorites folder** |

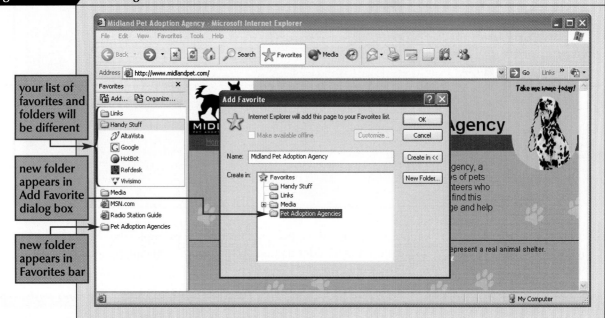

your list of
favorites and
folders will
be different

new folder
appears in
Add Favorite
dialog box

new folder
appears in
Favorites bar

7. Click the **OK** button to close the Add Favorite dialog box. Now, the favorite is saved in Internet Explorer. You can test the favorite by opening it from the Favorites bar.

8. Click the **Back** button on the Standard Buttons toolbar to return to the previous page, click the **Pet Adoption Agencies** folder in the Favorites bar to open the folder, and then click **Midland Pet Adoption Agency**. The Midland Pet Adoption Agency page opens in the browser.

   Trouble? If the Midland Pet Adoption Agency page does not open, click Favorites on the menu bar, point to the Pet Adoption Agencies folder, right-click the Midland Pet Adoption Agency favorite, and then click Properties. Click the Web Document tab, and make sure that a URL appears in the Target URL text box; if there is no URL, click the OK button to close the dialog box, click Favorites on the menu bar, click the Pet Adoption Agencies folder, right-click the Midland Pet Adoption Agency icon, and then click Delete. Repeat the steps to recreate the favorite, and then try again. If you still have trouble, ask your instructor or technical support person for help.

As you use the Web to find information about pet adoption agencies and other sites of interest, you might find yourself creating many favorites so you can return to sites of interest. When you start accumulating favorites, it is important to keep them organized. Internet Explorer helps you keep your favorites organized.

Organizing Favorites

Internet Explorer offers an easy way to organize your folders in a hierarchical structure—even after you have stored them. To rearrange URLs or even folders within folders, you use the Organize Favorites command on the Favorites menu.

Moving an Existing Favorite into a New Folder

- Click Favorites on the menu bar, and then click Organize Favorites, or click Organize button in the Favorites bar.
- Click the folder under which you want to add the new folder.
- Click the Create Folder button.
- Type the name of the new folder, and then press the Enter key.
- Drag the favorite that you want to move into the new folder.
- Click the Close button.

You explain to Maggie that you have created a new folder for Pet Adoption Agencies in the Internet Explorer Favorites bar and stored the Midland Pet Adoption Agency's URL in that folder. Maggie suggests that you might not want to keep all of the information you gather in one folder. She notes that you are just beginning your work for Trinity and that you might be collecting information about adoption agencies in different states as you conduct your research. Maggie suggests that you organize the information about adoption agencies by state. The Midland Pet Adoption Agency is located in Minnesota, so you decide to put information about the Midland Pet Adoption Agency in a separate folder named MN (which is the two-letter abbreviation for "Minnesota") under the Pet Adoption Agencies folder. As you collect information about other agencies, you will add folders for the states in which they are located, too.

To move an existing favorite into a new folder:

1. Click the **Organize** button near the top of the Favorites bar on the left side of the browser window.

2. Click the **Pet Adoption Agencies** folder in the Organize Favorites dialog box.

3. Click the **Create Folder** button. The default "New Folder" text is automatically selected.

4. Type **MN** to replace the text, and then press the **Enter** key to rename the folder.

5. Click and drag the **Midland Pet Adoption Agency** favorite to the new MN folder, and then release the mouse button. Now, the MN folder contains the favorite, as shown in Figure 1-21.

Figure 1-21	Reorganizing Favorites in folders

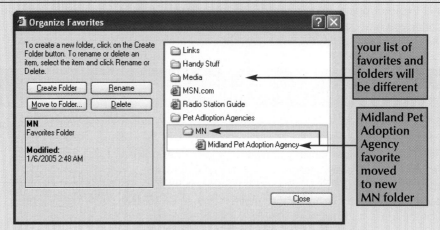

Trouble? If the Midland Pet Adoption Agency favorite is not visible in the dialog box folder list, click the MN folder to open that folder and display its contents.

6. Click the **Close** button. The Favorites bar is updated automatically to reflect your changes.

Trouble? If the Midland Pet Adoption Agency favorite is not visible in the Favorites bar, click the MN folder to open that folder and display its contents.

7. Click the **Favorites** button on the Standard Buttons toolbar to close the Favorites bar.

Using the History List

The Back and Forward buttons on the Standard Buttons toolbar and the Back and Forward options on the shortcut menu enable you to move to and from previously visited pages. As you move back and forth between pages, Internet Explorer records these visited sites in the history list. To see where you have been during a session, you also can open the history list by clicking the History button on the Standard Buttons toolbar.

To view the history list for this session:

1. Click the **History** button on the Standard Buttons toolbar. The history list opens in a hierarchical structure in a separate window on the left side of the screen. The history list stores each URL you visited during the past week or during a specified time period. It also maintains the hierarchy of each Web site; that is, pages you visit at a particular Web site are stored in a separate folder for that site. To return to a particular page, click that page's entry in the list. You can see the full URL of any item in the History bar by moving the mouse pointer over the history list item.

2. Click the **Close** button on the History bar title bar to close it.

You can right-click any entry in the history list and then copy the URL or delete it from the list. Internet Explorer stores each history entry as a shortcut in a History folder, which is in the Windows folder.

Refreshing a Web Page

The Refresh button on the Standard Buttons toolbar loads a new copy of the current Web page that currently appears in the browser window. Internet Explorer stores a copy of every Web page it displays on your computer's hard drive in a **Temporary Internet Files folder** in the Windows folder. Storing this information increases the speed at which Internet Explorer can display pages as you move back and forth through the history list because the browser can load the pages from a local disk drive instead of reloading the page from the remote Web server. When you click the Refresh button, Internet Explorer contacts the Web server to see if the Web page has changed since it was stored in the cache folder. If it has changed, Internet Explorer gets the new page from the Web server; otherwise, it loads the cache folder copy. To be certain that the browser is loading the most current version of the page from the Web server, hold down the Shift key while you click the Refresh button.

Returning to the Home Page

The Home button on the Standard Buttons toolbar displays the home (or start) page for your copy of Internet Explorer. You can change the setting for the Home toolbar button to display the page you want to use as the default home page.

Changing the Default Home Page in Internet Explorer

Reference Window

- Click Tools on the menu bar, and then click Internet Options.
- Click the General tab.
- Select whether you want Internet Explorer to open with the current page, its default page, or a blank page by clicking the corresponding button in the Home page section of the Internet Options dialog box.
- To specify a home page, type the URL of that Web page in the Address text box.
- Click the OK button.

To view the settings for the home page:

1. Click **Tools** on the menu bar, and then click **Internet Options**. The Internet Options dialog box opens, as shown in Figure 1-22. To use the currently loaded Web page as your home page, you would click the Use Current button. To use the default home page that was installed with your copy of Internet Explorer, you would click the Use Default button. If you don't want a page to open when you start your browser, you would click the Use Blank button. If you want to specify a home page other than the current, default, or blank page, you would type the URL for that page in the Address box.

| Figure 1-22 | Changing the default home page for Internet Explorer |

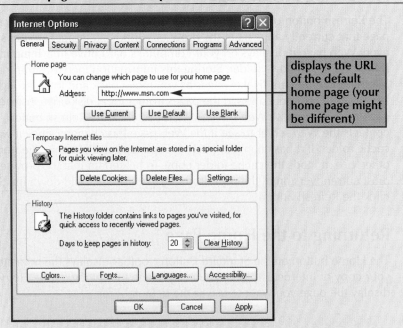

Trouble? If you are working on a computer in a school computer lab or at your employer's place of business, do not change any settings unless you are given permission to do so by your instructor or lab supervisor. Many schools and businesses set the home page defaults on all of their computers and then lock those settings.

2. Click the **Cancel** button to close the dialog box without making any changes.

Printing a Web Page

The Print button on the Standard Buttons toolbar and the Print option on the File menu let you print the current Web frame or page. You can use the Print command to make a printed copy of most Web pages (some Web pages disable the Print command).

| Reference Window | **Printing the Current Web Page** |

- Click the Print button on the Standard Buttons toolbar to print the current Web page with the default print settings.
or
- Click File on the menu bar, and then click Print.
- Select the printer you want to use, and then indicate the pages you want to print and the number of copies you want to make of each page.
- To print a range of pages, click the Pages option button, and then type the first page of the range, type a hyphen, and then type the last page of the range.
- Click the OK button.

To print a Web page:

▶ 1. Click **File** on the menu bar, and then click **Print** to open the Print dialog box.

▶ 2. Make sure that the printer selected (highlighted) in the Select Printer list box is the printer you want to use; if not, click the icon of the printer you want to use to change the selection.

▶ 3. Click the **Pages** option button in the Print range section of the Print dialog box, and then type **1** in the text box to specify that you only want to print the first page. (If the text box already contains a "1" you do not need to change it.)

▶ 4. Make sure that the Number of copies text box displays **1**.

▶ 5. Click the **Print** button to print the Web page and close the Print dialog box.

Changing the Settings for the Page Setup

You have seen how to print a Web page using the basic options available in the Print dialog box. Usually, the default settings in the Print dialog box are fine for printing a Web page, but you can use the Page Setup dialog box to change the way a Web page prints. Figure 1-23 shows the Page Setup dialog box, and Figure 1-24 describes its settings.

Page Setup dialog box | **Figure 1-23**

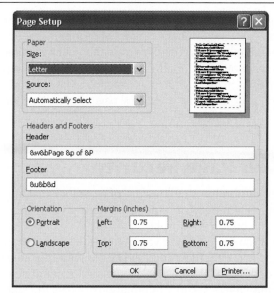

Figure 1-24 ▶ **Page Setup dialog box options**

Option	Description	Use
Paper Size	Changes the size of the printed page.	Use the Letter size default unless you are printing to different paper stock, such as Legal.
Paper Source	Changes the printer's paper source.	Use the default Auto Select unless you want to specify a different tray or manual feed for printing on heavy paper.
Header	Prints information about the Web page at the top of each page.	To obtain details on how to specify exact header printing options, click the Header text box to select it, and then press the F1 key.
Footer	Prints information about the Web page at the bottom of each page.	To obtain details on how to specify exact footer printing options, click the Footer text box to select it, and then press the F1 key.
Orientation	Selects the orientation of the printed output.	Portrait works best for most Web pages, but you can use landscape orientation to print the wide tables of numbers included on some Web pages.
Margins	Changes the margin of the printed page.	Normally, you should leave the default settings, but you can change the right, left, top, or bottom margins as needed.

When printing long Web pages, a print option that is extremely useful for saving paper is to reduce the font size of the Web pages before you print them. To do this, you would click View on the menu bar, point to Text Size, and then click Smaller or Smallest on the menu. However, this will not work for all Web pages because some pages are designed to display and print at specific sizes so that their exact page layouts are maintained.

Internet Explorer also allows users to preview pages before they print them. You can select Print Preview from the File menu item to open the Print Preview window.

Checking Web Page Security

The **Security indicator button** is a small picture of a padlock that appears at the right edge of the status bar at the bottom of the Internet Explorer browser window when a secure Web page is loaded. The button will display when the Web page is encrypted during transmission from the Web server. When you double-click this button, or when you click File on the menu bar, click Properties, and then click the Certificates button, the Certificate dialog box opens to let you check some of the security elements of the Web page. An example of this type of security information appears in Figure 1-25.

Internet Explorer Help window

Figure 1-25

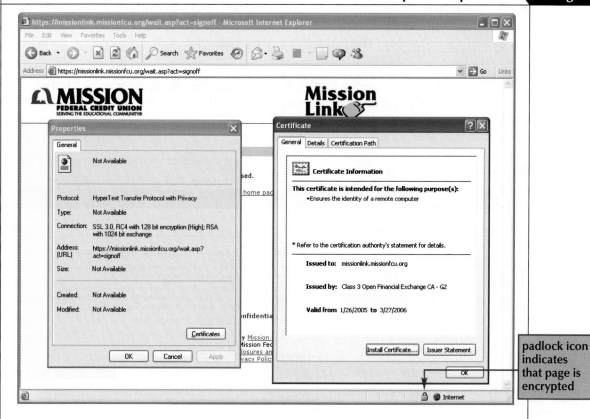

padlock icon indicates that page is encrypted

Encryption is a way of scrambling and encoding data transmissions that reduces the risk that a person who intercepts the Web page as it travels across the Internet will be able to decode and read the page's contents. Web sites use encrypted transmission to send and receive information, such as credit card numbers, to ensure privacy. When Internet Explorer loads an encrypted Web page, a padlock symbol appears in the fourth pane (second from the right) of the status bar at the bottom of the Internet Explorer window.

Getting Help in Internet Explorer

Internet Explorer includes a comprehensive online Help system. You can open the Help Contents window to learn more about the Help options that are available.

Opening Internet Explorer Help

Reference Window

- Click Help on the menu bar, and then click Contents and Index; or press the F1 key.
- Click the Contents tab.
- Click a category to open a list of topic-related hyperlinks.
- Click a hyperlink to open a specific Help topic, or click the Index tab and enter a search term.
- Click the Close button.

To open the Internet Explorer Help:

1. Click **Help** on the menu bar, and then click **Contents and Index** to open the Internet Explorer Help window.

2. If necessary, click the **Maximize** button on the Internet Explorer Help window so it fills the desktop.

3. Click the **Contents** tab, click **Finding the Web Pages You Want**, and then click **Listing your favorite pages for quick viewing** to open that help topic in the Help window. Notice that the page that opens in a Help window contains links to related or supplemental topics that you can explore, as shown in Figure 1-26.

Figure 1-26 | **Internet Explorer Help window**

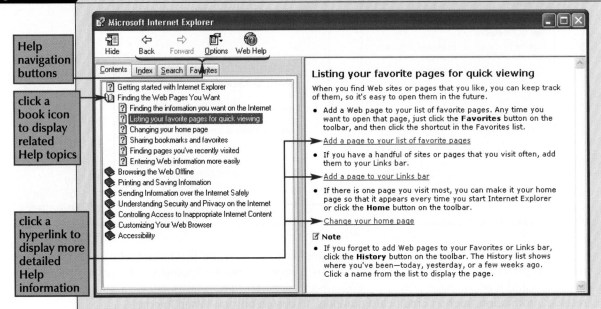

4. Click the **Close** button to close Help.

You feel confident that you have the tools you need to successfully find information on the Web. You know that Trinity will be interested in seeing the Midland Pet Adoption Agency Web page, but the page might change and you would like to have a copy of the page as it now exists. Maggie says that you can save the Web page on disk so that Trinity could open the page as it currently exists in her Web browser using the files you save on that disk.

Using Internet Explorer to Save a Web Page

There will be times when you will want to refer to the information that you have found on a Web page without having to return to the site. In Internet Explorer you can store entire Web pages, selected portions of Web page text, or particular graphics from a Web page to a disk.

Saving a Web Page

You like the Midland Pet Adoption Agency's Web site and want to save a copy of the page to a disk so you can show the Web page to Trinity. To save a Web page, you must have the page open in Internet Explorer.

Saving a Web Page to a Disk

- Open the Web page in Internet Explorer.
- Click File on the menu bar, and then click Save As.
- Click the Save in list arrow, and then select the drive that contains your disk.
- Accept the default filename, or change the filename, but retain the file extension .htm or .html.
- Click the Save button.

You will save the Midland Pet Adoption Agency home page to a disk so you can send it to Trinity for her review.

To save the Web page to a disk:

1. Use your Favorites list to return to the Midland Pet Adoption Agency home page if it is not already displayed in your browser.

2. Click **File** on the menu bar, and then click **Save As**. The Save As dialog box opens.

3. If necessary, click the **Save in** list arrow, select the drive that contains your disk, select the **Tutorial.01\Tutorial** folder, and then type **MidlandHomePageMSIE.htm** in the File name box. *Note*: you can select the Web Page option in the Save as type list and type the name of the file without typing the file extension; with the Web Page option selected the program will automatically add the correct file extension.

4. Click the **Save** button. Now the HTML document for the Midland Pet Adoption Agency's home page is saved on your disk. When you send it to Trinity, she can open her Web browser and then use the Open command on the File menu to open the Web page.

If the Web page contains graphics, such as photos, drawings, or icons, they might not be saved with the HTML document. To save a graphic, right-click it in the browser window, click Save Picture As on the shortcut menu, and then save the graphic to the same location as the Web's HTML document. The graphics file will appear on the HTML document as a hyperlink; therefore, you might have to change the HTML code in the Web page to identify the location of the graphic. Copying the graphics files to the same disk as the HTML document will *usually* work. In Internet Explorer, you can make sure that a graphic is stored with the text file by selecting Web Page as the Save as type field. With this setting, Internet Explorer will create a separate folder for all of the graphic page elements and will rewrite the HTML of the Web page to ensure that its links to the graphics files are rewritten if necessary. If the page has many graphics elements, however, it is possible that the files containing those elements will not all fit on a standard 3½-inch disk.

Saving Web Page Text to a File

You can save portions of Web page's text to a file, so that you can use the text in other programs. You will use WordPad to save text that you will copy from a Web page; however, any word processor or text editor will work.

Reference Window	**Copying Text from a Web Page to a WordPad Document**

- Open the Web page in Internet Explorer.
- Use the mouse pointer to select the text you want to copy.
- Click Edit on the menu bar, and then click Copy.
- Open WordPad (or another word processor or text editor if WordPad is not available).
- Click Edit on the WordPad menu bar, and then click Paste (or click the Paste button).
- Click the Save button, select the folder where you want to store the file, and then enter a new filename, if necessary.
- Click the Save button.

Trinity just called to let you know that she will be traveling in Minnesota next week and she would like to visit the Midland Pet Adoption Agency while she is in the area. She will meet with the director there and see if she can learn more about how the agency developed its Web site. You will visit the Midland Pet Adoption Agency's Web site and get the agency's address and telephone number so Trinity can contact the director and schedule a meeting.

To copy text from a Web page and save it as a WordPad document:

1. Return to the Midland Pet Adoption Agency home page if it is not already displayed in your browser.

2. Click the **Directions & Contact** hyperlink to open the Web page that has the address and phone number you want to copy.

3. Drag the mouse pointer over the address and telephone number to select it, as shown in Figure 1-27.

Figure 1-27	Selecting text on a Web page

4. Click **Edit** on the menu bar, and then click **Copy** to copy the selected text to the Clipboard.

   Now, you will start WordPad and then paste the copied text into a new document.

5. Click the **Start** button on the taskbar, point to **All Programs**, point to **Accessories**, and then click **WordPad** to start that program and open a new document.

6. Click the **Paste** button on the WordPad toolbar to paste the text into the WordPad document, as shown in Figure 1-28.

Pasting text from a Web page into a WordPad document ◀ Figure 1-28

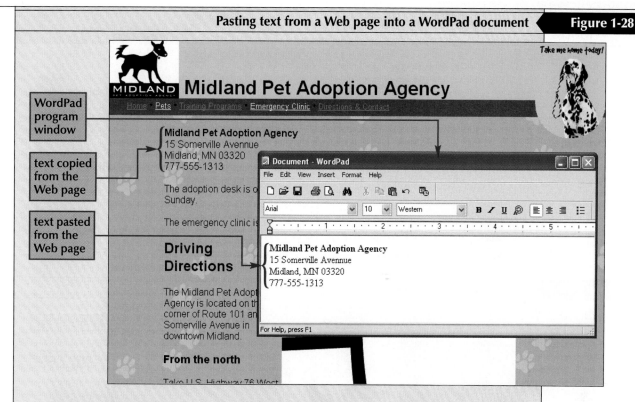

Trouble? If the WordPad toolbar does not appear, click View on the menu bar, click Toolbar, and then repeat Step 6. Your WordPad program window might be a different size from the one shown in Figure 1-28, which does not affect the steps.

▶ 7. Click the **Save** button on the WordPad toolbar to open the Save As dialog box.

▶ 8. Click the **Save in** list arrow, select the drive that contains your disk, and then select the **Tutorial.01\Tutorial** folder.

▶ 9. Delete the text in the File name text box, type **MidlandAddressPhoneMSIE.txt**, and then click the **Save** button. Now, the address and phone number of the agency are saved in a file on your disk for future reference.

▶ 10. Click the **Close** button on the WordPad title bar to close it.

You can print this information from WordPad and give it to Trinity the next time you see her. As you examine the Web page, you notice a street map that shows the location of the Midland Pet Adoption Agency. You decide that Trinity might like to have a copy of that map.

Saving a Web Page Graphic to a Disk

You consider printing the entire Web page, but you know that Trinity might like to have just the map image. You decide to save the map graphic to your disk so you can give it to Trinity.

Reference Window | **Saving an Image from a Web Page to a Disk**

- Open the Web page in Internet Explorer.
- Right-click the image you want to copy, and then click Save Picture As.
- Select the drive and the folder in which you want to save the image, and change the default filename, if necessary.
- Click the Save button.

Now you will save the image of the street map to your disk, which you will give to Trinity when you see her.

To save the street map image to a disk:

▶ **1.** Right-click the map image to open its shortcut menu, as shown in Figure 1-29.

Figure 1-29 | Saving the map image to a disk

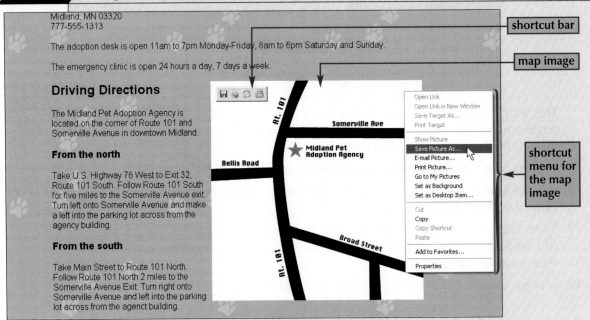

▶ **2.** Click **Save Picture As** on the shortcut menu to open the Save Picture dialog box. Internet Explorer also opens a shortcut bar whenever you move the mouse pointer over a download-able graphic on a Web page. This shortcut bar includes three buttons that you can click to save the image to a disk, print the image, or e-mail the image. A fourth button opens the My Pictures folder on your computer.

▶ **3.** Click the **Save in** list arrow, select the drive that contains your disk, and then select the **Tutorial.01\Tutorial** folder.

▶ **4.** Delete the text in the File name text box, type **MidlandMapMSIE.gif**, and then click the **Save** button to save the file.

▶ **5.** Close your Web browser.

Now, you have a disk for Trinity that has a copy of the Midland Pet Adoption Agency Web home page and map that will show her how to get there during her trip to Minnesota. She will be able to use her Web browser to open the files and print them.

Session 1.2 Quick Check

1. Describe two ways to increase the Web page area in Internet Explorer.
2. You can use the _____ button in Internet Explorer to visit previously visited sites during your Web session.
3. Clicking the _____ button on the Standard Buttons toolbar opens a search frame that contains a number of different searching options.
4. List the names of two Favorites folders (in addition to your Pet Adoption Agencies folder) that you might want to add as you continue to gather information for Trinity.
5. To ensure that Internet Explorer loads a Web page from the server rather than from its cache, you can hold down the _____ key as you click the Refresh button.
6. True or False: You can identify encrypted Web pages when viewing them in Internet Explorer.
7. Describe two ways to obtain help on a specific topic in Internet Explorer.

If your instructor assigned Session 1.3, continue reading. Otherwise complete the Review Assignments at the end of this tutorial.

Session 1.3

Starting Mozilla Firefox

You could decide to do your research on the Web for Trinity and the Danville Animal Shelter with another major Web browser, Mozilla Firefox. This introduction assumes that you have Firefox installed on your computer. You should have your computer turned on so the Windows desktop is displayed.

To start Firefox:

▶ 1. Click the **Start** button on the taskbar, point to **All Programs**, point to **Mozilla**, and then click **Firefox**. After a moment, Firefox opens.

   Trouble? If you cannot find Firefox on the All Programs menu, check to see if a Mozilla or Firefox shortcut icon appears on the desktop, and then double-click it. If you do not see the shortcut icon, ask your instructor or technical support person for help. The program might be installed in a different folder on the computer you are using.

▶ 2. If the program does not fill the screen entirely, click the **Maximize** button on the Firefox program's title bar. Your screen should look like Figure 1-30.

Figure 1-30	**Firefox main program window**

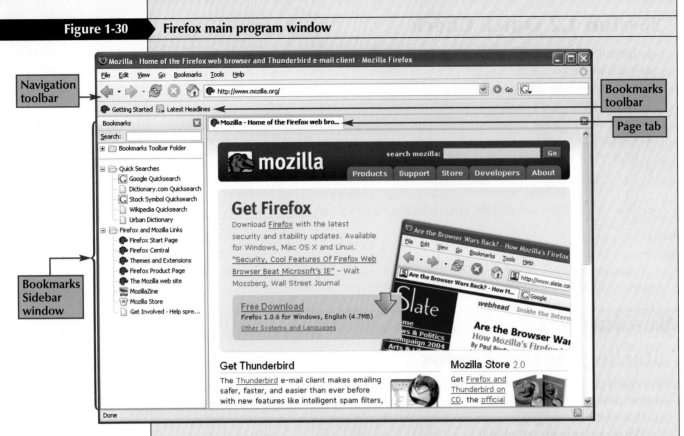

Trouble? Figure 1-30 shows the Mozilla Firefox welcome page, which is the page that Firefox opens the first time it starts. Your computer might be configured to open to a different Web page, or no page at all.

Trouble? If you don't see a page tab on your screen, then your browser is set to hide page tabs when only one Web site is open. Click Tools on the menu bar, click Options, click Advanced in the Options dialog box, and then click the Hide the tab bar when only one web site is open check box to deselect it. Click OK to close the dialog box.

Trouble? If the Bookmarks toolbar is not displayed on your screen, click View on the menu bar, point to Toolbars, and then click Bookmarks Toolbar to display the toolbar as shown in Figure 1-30.

Trouble? If the Bookmarks Sidebar window shown in Figure 1-30 is not visible in your browser window, skip Step 3.

3. Click **View** on the menu bar, point to **Sidebar**, and then click the **Bookmarks Sidebar** (or drag the right edge of the Bookmarks Sidebar frame to the left side of the browser window) to close the Bookmarks Sidebar. This will give you more room to view Web pages when using the Firefox browser. You can reopen the Bookmarks Sidebar by selecting View, Sidebar, Bookmarks from the menu bar or by clicking and dragging the left edge of the browser window to the right. The click-and-drag method for restoring the Bookmarks Sidebar works only if you closed it using that method.

Now that you understand how to start Firefox, you want to learn more about the components of the Firefox program window.

Using the Navigation Toolbar

The **Navigation toolbar** includes buttons that execute frequently used commands for browsing the Web. Figure 1-31 shows the Navigation toolbar. This toolbar contains buttons that perform basic Web browsing functions, a Location bar, and a Search bar.

Firefox Navigation Toolbar ◄ **Figure 1-31**

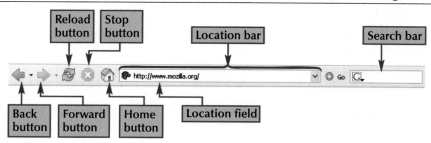

The Location bar includes a location field that allows users to type the URL of the site they wish to visit. The Navigation toolbar also has a search bar that allows users to type a search term that Firefox sends to the user's choice of search engines and Web directories.

You can use the View menu to hide or show the Firefox toolbars. The View menu commands are toggles. A **toggle** is like a push button switch on a television set; you press the button once to turn on the television and press it a second time to turn it off.

To hide the Bookmarks toolbar using the View menu:

1. Click **View** on the menu bar, point to **Toolbars**, and then click **Bookmarks Toolbar**. To redisplay the Bookmarks toolbar, you will repeat the same steps.

   Trouble? If the Bookmarks Toolbar does not have a check mark next to it, then the Bookmarks toolbar already is hidden.

2. Click **View** on the menu bar, point to **Toolbars**, and then click **Bookmarks Toolbar**. The toolbar and its tab are displayed again.

Using the Location Bar

You can use the **Location Bar** to enter URLs directly into Firefox. As you learned in Session 1.1, you must enter the URL to identify a Web page's exact location. Although a complete URL includes the name of a file, entering just the IP address or the domain name will usually be sufficient to take you to the home page of the site.

Entering a URL in the Location Bar

Reference Window

- Click at the end of the current text in the location field, and then delete any unnecessary or unwanted text from the displayed URL.
- Type the URL to which you want to go.
- Press the Enter key to load the URL's Web page in the browser window.

Trinity has asked you to start your research by examining the home page for the Midland Pet Adoption Agency's Web site. She has given you the URL so that you can find it.

To load the Midland Pet Adoption Agency's Web page:

1. Click at the end of the text in the location field, and then delete any text that is in the location field by pressing the **Backspace** key repeatedly.

   Trouble? Make sure that you delete all of the text in the location field so the text you type in Step 2 will be correct.

2. Type **www.midlandpet.com** in the location field. This is the URL of the Midland Pet Adoption Agency Web site.

3. Press the **Enter** key. The home page of the Midland Pet Adoption Agency Web site loads, as shown in Figure 1-32.

Figure 1-32	Midland Pet Adoption Agency Web page

Hyperlink Navigation Using the Mouse

The easiest way to move from one Web page to another is to use the mouse to click hyperlinks that the authors of Web pages embed in their HTML documents. You can also right-click the mouse on the background of a Web page to open a shortcut menu that includes navigation options.

Reference Window

Navigating Between Web Pages Using Hyperlinks and the Mouse

- Click the hyperlink.
- After the new Web page has loaded, right-click on the Web page's background.
- Click Back on the shortcut menu.

To follow a hyperlink to a Web page and return using the mouse:

1. Point to the **Training Programs** hyperlink shown in Figure 1-33 so your pointer changes to an icon of a hand with a pointing index finger.

Midland Pet Adoption Agency ◄ **Figure 1-33**

pointer changes shape when hovering over a hyperlink

2. Click the **Training Programs** link to load the page. Watch the second panel in the status bar. When the shadow disappears, you know that Firefox has loaded the full page.

3. Right-click anywhere in the Web page area (other than on a graphic or a hyperlink) to open the shortcut menu, as shown in Figure 1-34.

Figure 1-34 **Midland Pet Adoption Agency**

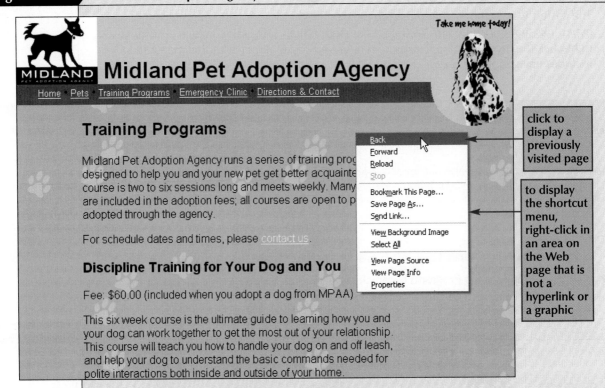

Trouble? If you right-click a hyperlink, your shortcut menu will display a list that differs from the one shown in Figure 1-34; therefore, the Back option might not appear in the same position on the menu. If you don't see the shortcut menu shown in Figure 1-34, click anywhere outside of the shortcut menu to close it, and then repeat Step 3.

4. Click **Back** on the shortcut menu to go back to the Midland Pet Adoption Agency home page.

Returning to Web Pages Previously Visited

You like the format of the Midland Pet Adoption Agency's home page, so you want to make sure that you can go back to that page later if you need to review its contents. Maggie explains that you can write down the URL so you can refer to it later, but an easier way is to store the URL as a bookmark for future use. You can also use the History list and the Back and Forward buttons to return to Web pages you have already visited, and the Home button to return to your browser's start page.

Creating a Bookmark for a Web Site

You use the bookmark feature to store and organize a list of Web pages that you have visited so you can return to them easily. Figure 1-35 shows an open Bookmarks Manager window, which contains bookmarks sorted into hierarchical categories.

Bookmarks sorted into categories ◀ **Figure 1-35**

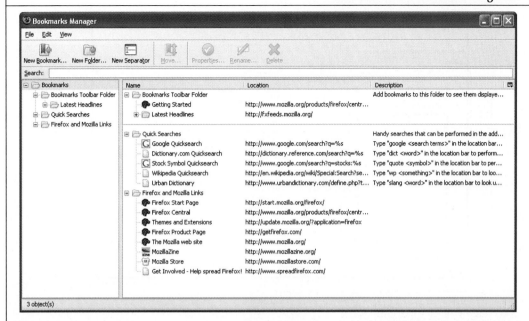

Creating a New Bookmarks Folder

Reference Window

- Click Bookmarks on the menu bar, and then click Manage Bookmarks.
- If the Bookmarks entry in the left pane of the Bookmarks Manager window is not highlighted, click it, then click the New Folder button.
- Delete the default text in the Name text box, and then type a new folder name.
- Click the OK button.

You will create a bookmark for the Midland Pet Adoption Agency Web page, but first, you need to create a folder in which to store your bookmarks. You will then save your bookmark in that folder. You might not work on the same computer again, so you will also save a copy of the bookmark file to a floppy disk for future use.

To create a new Bookmarks folder:

▶ **1.** Click **Bookmarks** on the menu bar, and then click **Manage Bookmarks**. The Bookmarks Manager window opens.

▶ **2.** If the Bookmarks entry in the left pane of the Bookmarks Manager window is not highlighted, click it, then click the **New Folder** button. The Properties for "New Folder" dialog box opens with the default text "New Folder" in its text box. In the Bookmarks Manager window, a new folder is created in the left pane.

▶ **3.** Delete the default text, type **Pet Adoption Agencies**, and then click the **OK** button. The Pet Adoption Agencies folder appears in the Bookmarks Manager window, as shown in Figure 1-36.

| Figure 1-36 | Pet Adoption Agencies folder |

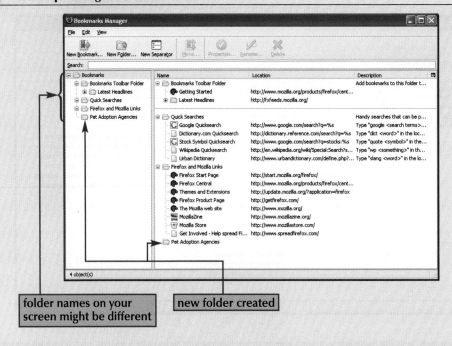

folder names on your screen might be different

new folder created

4. Click the **Close** button on the title bar to close the Bookmark Manager window.

Now that you have created a folder, you can save your bookmark for the Midland Pet Adoption Agency Web page in the new folder.

| Reference Window | **Saving a Bookmark in a Bookmarks Folder** |

- Open the page that you want to bookmark in Firefox.
- Click Bookmarks on the menu bar, and then click Bookmark This Page.
- Type a descriptive name in the box (or leave the default name for the page as is).
- Select the folder in which you want to save the bookmark.
- Click the OK button.

Before you save the bookmark, first you must return to the Web page that you want to bookmark.

To save a bookmark for the Midland Pet Adoption Agency Web page in the Bookmarks folder:

1. With the Midland Pet Adoption Agency Web page open, click **Bookmarks** on the menu bar, and then click **Bookmark This Page**. The File Bookmark dialog box opens.

2. Type **Midland Pet Adoption Agency** in the Name text box, if it does not already appear.

Trouble? If necessary, delete any unnecessary text that appears in the Name text box before you begin typing the name for the bookmark.

3. Scroll down in the Create in box to find the Pet Adoption Agencies folder, click that folder, and then click the **OK** button. The bookmark is saved in that folder. You can test your bookmark by using the bookmark to visit the site.

4. Click the **Back** button on the Navigation toolbar to go to the previous Web page.

5. Click **Bookmarks** on the menu bar, point to **Pet Adoption Agencies**, and then click **Midland Pet Adoption Agency**. The Midland Pet Adoption Agency page opens in the browser.

   Trouble? If the Midland Pet Adoption Agency page does not open, open the Bookmarks Manager window, make sure that you have the correct URL for the page, and then repeat Step 5. If you still have trouble, ask your instructor or technical support person for help.

Because you might need to visit a Web page that you have bookmarked when you are working at another computer, Firefox lets you save your bookmark file on a disk.

Reference Window

Saving a Bookmark File to a Disk

- Click Bookmarks on the menu bar, and then click Manage Bookmarks.
- Click File on the menu bar, and then click Export.
- Select the drive and folder into which you want to save the bookmark file.
- Type a name for the bookmark file.
- Click the Save button.

Because you might need to visit the Midland Pet Adoption Agency page when you are working at another computer, you will save your bookmark file on a disk.

To store the Midland Pet Adoption Agency bookmark file to a disk:

1. Click **Bookmarks** on the menu bar, and then click **Manage Bookmarks**. When you save a bookmark, you save all of the bookmarks, not just the one that you need.

2. Click **File** on the menu bar in the Bookmarks Manager window, and then click **Export**. The Export bookmark file dialog box opens.

   Trouble? If prompted to, insert a disk in the appropriate drive on your computer.

3. Select the drive that contains your disk, and then select the **Tutorial.01\Tutorial** folder.

   Trouble? If you were prompted to insert a disk in Step 2, then the correct drive and disk should automatically appear in the Save in list box.

   The file name that you give the bookmark file should indicate the Web page you have marked. The file extension must be .htm or .html so the browser into which you load this file will recognize it as an HTML file. Most browsers will recognize either file extension; however, some do not.

4. Type **MyNNBookmarks.html** in the File name text box. *Note:* You can select the Web Page option in the Save as type list and type the name of the file without typing the file extension; with the Web Page option selected, the program will automatically add the correct file extension.

5. Click the **Save** button, and then close the Bookmarks Manager window.

When you use another computer, you can open the bookmark file from your disk by starting Firefox, clicking Bookmarks on the menu bar, clicking Manage Bookmarks, clicking File on the menu bar, and then clicking Import. Change to the drive that contains your disk, and then open the bookmarks file. Your bookmark file will open in Firefox's Bookmarks Manager window on that computer.

Using the History List

The Back and Forward buttons on the Navigation toolbar and the Back and Forward options on the shortcut menu enable you to move to and from recently visited pages. These buttons duplicate the functions of the commands on the Go menu. The options on the Go menu enable you to move back and forward through a portion of the history list and allow you to choose a specific Web page from that list. To see where you have been during a session, you also can open the history list for your current session.

To view the history list for this session:

1. Click **Go** on the menu bar and then click **History** to open the history list in the sidebar.

2. Click the plus sign icon next to the **Today** folder to open the list of Web sites visited. (If the icon is a minus sign, you do not need to click it because the list of Web sites is already open.) You can click the file icon next to any entry to return to that specific Web page. If you are using a computer in a computer lab or an Internet cafe, the History list will include sites visited by anyone who has used the computer, not just you.

3. Click the **Close** button (the small "x" in a red square near the top right corner of the sidebar) on the History sidebar to close it.

You can change the way that pages are listed in the History window by using the View button near the top of the sidebar; for example, you can list the pages by Web page title or in the order in which you visited them.

Reloading a Web Page

The Reload button on the Firefox toolbar loads again the Web page that currently appears in the browser window. You can force Firefox to load the page from the Web server instead of your computer's temporary storage cache by pressing the Shift key when you click the Reload button.

Returning to the Home Page

The Home button on the Navigation toolbar displays the home (or start) page for your copy of Firefox. You can change the default URL that opens when you click the Home button by using the Options dialog box.

Changing the Default Home Page in Firefox

- Click Tools on the menu bar, and then click Options.
- Click the General icon on the left, if necessary.
- In the Home page section of the dialog box, type the URL or file name of the page you want to use as your default home page in the Location box.
- Click the OK button.

To view the settings for the default home page:

▶ **1.** Click **Tools** on the menu bar, and then click **Options**. The Options dialog box opens, as shown in Figure 1-37.

Options dialog box ◀ **Figure 1-37**

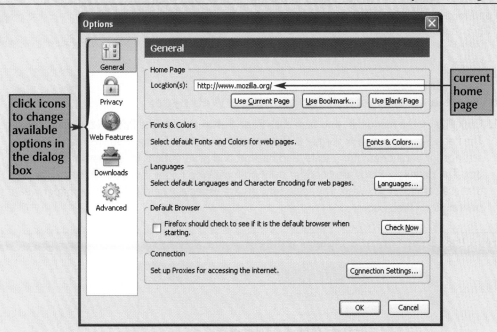

▶ **2.** To open with the current page or a home page you specify, you would click the corresponding option button in the Home Page section of the Options dialog box. You can also choose to use one of your bookmarks as your home page by clicking the Use Bookmark button. A third option is to have the browser open with a blank page by clicking the Use Blank Page button.

Trouble? If you are using a computer in a school computer lab or at your employer's place of business, do not change any settings unless you are given permission by your instructor or lab supervisor. Many organizations set the home page defaults on all of their computers and lock those settings.

To specify a home page, you would select the text in the Location box and then enter the URL of the Web page you want to use. If you load the Web page that you want as your new home page before beginning these steps, you can click the Use Current Page button to place the page's URL in the Location text box.

▶ **3.** Click the **Cancel** button to close the dialog box without making any changes.

Printing a Web Page

The Print command on the File menu lets you print the current Web frame or page. You can use this button to make a printed copy of most Web pages (some Web pages disable the Print command). Firefox provides a number of useful print options that allow you to customize the printed format of Web pages. You can use the Page Setup dialog box to create custom formats for printing Web pages in Firefox.

Reference Window | **Using Page Setup to Create a Custom Format for Printing a Web Page**

- Click File on the menu bar, and then click Page Setup.
- Select the orientation, scaling, and print background options you want to use.
- Click the Margins & Header/Footer tab.
- Type the margin settings you want to use.
- Choose elements you want to print in the left, center, and right areas of the page header and footer.
- Click the OK button.

To create a custom format for printing a Web page:

1. Click **File** on the menu bar, and then click **Page Setup** to open the Page Setup dialog box. The Page Setup dialog box Format & Options tab appears in Figure 1-38. You can change settings for page orientation, scale, and background print options in this part of the dialog box. The default settings are good for printing most Web pages, but you can customize any of these settings if you wish. The scale settings are especially helpful for saving paper when printing long Web pages.

Figure 1-38 | **Firefox Page Setup Format & Options settings**

2. Click the **Margins & Header/Footer** tab in the Page Setup dialog box to open that part of the Page Setup dialog box. You can change the page margins and specify elements of the header and footer that will print with each page in this part of the dialog box. The default settings are good for printing most Web pages, but you can customize any of these settings if you wish.

3. After you make any changes you wish to the page layout, click the **OK** button to close the dialog box.

You can also set these page print options in the Print Preview window. You would click File and then click Print Preview to open this window. Some of the page print options are available at the top of the window and they are all available by clicking the Page Setup button. Once you have set the formatting options you want for printing a Web page, you can use the Print button to print the page.

Reference Window

Printing the Current Web Page

- Click File on the menu bar, and then click Print.
- Select the printer you want to use and indicate the pages you want to print and the number of copies you want to make of each page.
- Click the OK button.

To print a Web page:

1. Click **File** on the menu bar, and then click **Print**.

2. Make sure that the printer in the Name list box displays the printer you want to use; if not, click the Name list arrow to change the selection.

3. Click the **Pages** option button in the Print range section of the Print dialog box, type **1** in the from text box, press the **Tab** key, and then type **1** in the to text box to specify that you want to print only the first page.

4. Make sure that the Number of copies text box displays **1**.

5. Click the **OK** button to print the Web page and close the Print dialog box.

Checking Web Page Security

The **Security indicator button** is a small picture of a padlock that appears at the right edge of the status bar at the bottom of the Firefox browser window when a secure Web page is loaded. The button will display when the Web page was encrypted during transmission from the Web server. When you double-click this button or when you click Tools on the menu bar, click Page Info, and then click the Security tab, you can check some of the security elements of the Web page.

Encryption is a way of scrambling and encoding data transmissions that reduces the risk that a person who intercepts the Web page as it travels across the Internet will be able to decode and read the page's contents. Web sites use encrypted transmission to send and receive information, such as credit card numbers, to ensure privacy. You can obtain more information about the details of the encryption used on a Web page by examining the Security tab of the Page Info dialog box that opens when you double-click the security indicator button. Figure 1-39 shows the Page Info dialog box for an encrypted Web page after the user double-clicked the security indicator button.

Figure 1-39	Page Info dialog box for an encrypted Web page

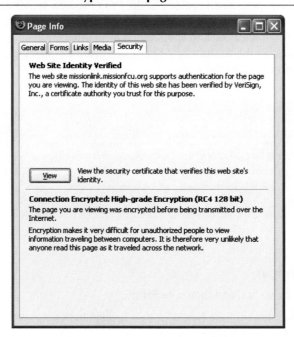

Managing Cookies

Many Web users are concerned about cookies, the small files you learned about in Session 1.1 that some Web servers write to the disk drives of client computers. Firefox stores all cookies in one file and gives users a way to manage the content of that file.

Reference Window	**Managing Cookies in Firefox**

- Click Tools on the menu bar, and then click Options to open the Options dialog box.
- Click the plus sign icon next to Cookies to open its options. (If the icon displayed is a minus sign, the Cookies options are already open.)
- Click the View Cookies button to open the Stored Cookies dialog box, and then read the information about the cookies that have been stored on your computer. To read information about a particular cookie, click the cookie name in the window at the top of the dialog box. The information about that cookie is displayed in the bottom half of the dialog box.
- Select the cookie that you want to delete, and then click the Remove Cookie button.
- Click the OK button.

You will delete a cookie stored on your computer using the Firefox cookie management tool.

To manage cookies in Firefox:

▶ **1.** Click **Tools** on the menu bar, click **Options**, click the **Privacy** icon in the left window of the Options dialog box, and then click the plus sign icon next to Cookies, if necessary.

▶ **2.** Click the **View Cookies** button to open the Stored Cookies dialog box, and then examine the cookies in the list that appears in the Stored Cookies dialog box. If your computer has many cookies stored on it, you can use the scroll bar to move up and down in the list.

▶ **3.** Click the name of one of the displayed cookies. An example of a Stored Cookies dialog box with several cookies appears in Figure 1-40. Your list of cookies will be different. Information about the selected cookie appears in the dialog box below the list of cookies.

Stored Cookies dialog box ◀ Figure 1-40

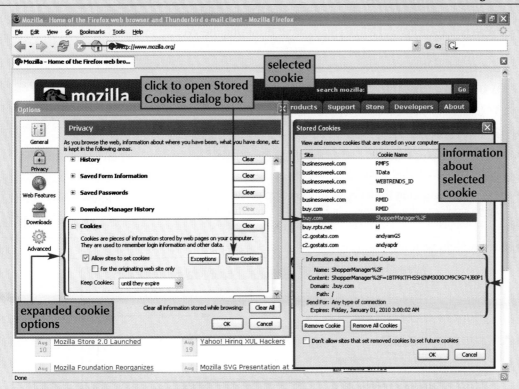

▶ **4.** Click any cookie in the list to select it. Note the Remove Cookie button near the bottom of the dialog box becomes available.

▶ **5.** Find a cookie that you want to delete, click to select it, and then click the **Remove Cookie** button. You might notice that many of the cookies on your computer are placed there by companies that sell banner advertising on Web pages (such as doubleclick.net). These companies use cookies to record which ads have appeared on pages you have viewed so that they can present different ads the next time you open a Web page.

Trouble? You might be instructed to delete specific cookies or no cookies at all. Ask your instructor or technical support person for assistance if you are unsure which cookies can be deleted.

▶ **6.** When you are finished exploring and deleting cookies, click the **Close** button to close the Stored Cookies dialog box.

To delete all the cookies that have been stored on your computer, click the Remove All Cookies button. You can also indicate whether or not you want cookies that you have removed to be stored again.

Getting Help in Firefox

Firefox includes a comprehensive Help facility. You can open the Help Contents window to learn more about the Help options that are available.

Reference Window	**Opening Firefox Help**

- Click Help on the menu bar, and then click Help Contents.
- Click the Contents tab in the left pane of the Mozilla Firefox Help window.
- Click the icon next to the general topic for which you want help.
- Click the name of the specific help topic in which you are interested.

You will use Firefox Help to read about browsing the Web.

To use Firefox Help:

1. Click **Help** on the menu bar, and then click **Help Contents**.

2. If necessary, click the **Contents** tab to display the Contents window.

3. Click the plus sign icon next to the Using Mozilla Firefox category to open a list of specific help topics in that category.

4. Click **Navigating Web Pages** to view help on that subject. Examine the page, which should be similar to the one shown in Figure 1-41, scrolling as needed.

Figure 1-41	Firefox Help window

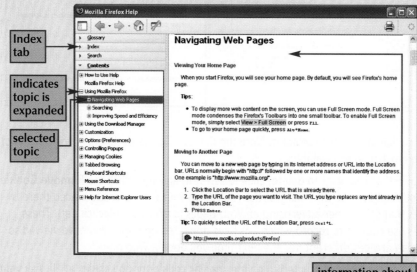

You can click any of the topic titles to obtain help on the specific topics listed. You can also click the Index tab to obtain an alphabetized list of hyperlinks to specific terms used in the Help pages.

   5. Click the **Close** button to close Help.

You feel confident that you have the tools you need to successfully find information on the Web. Trinity probably will be interested in seeing the Midland Pet Adoption Agency Web page, but you are concerned that the Web site might change before she has a chance to visit it on the Web. Maggie suggests that you save the Web page to a disk, so Trinity can view the page in its current form whenever she wishes by using the files you saved on that disk.

Using Firefox to Save a Web Page

There will be times when you will want to refer to the information that you have found on a Web page without having to revisit the site. In Firefox, you can store entire Web pages, selected portions of Web page text, or particular graphics from a Web page to a disk.

Saving a Web Page

You like the Midland Pet Adoption Agency's Web site and want to save a copy of the page to a disk so you can show the Web page to Trinity. That way, she can review it as it currently appears whenever she wishes. To save a Web page, you must have the page open in Firefox.

Reference Window

Saving a Web Page to a Disk

- Open the Web page in Firefox.
- Click File on the menu bar, and then click Save Page As.
- Select the drive or folder into which you want to save the Web page file.
- Accept the default file name, or change the file name, but retain the file extension .htm or .html.
- Click the Save button.

You will save the Midland Pet Adoption Agency page to a disk so you can send it to Trinity for her review.

To save the Web page to a disk:

   1. Use your bookmark to return to the Midland Pet Adoption Agency page, if necessary.
   2. Click **File** on the menu bar, and then click **Save Page As**. The Save As dialog box opens.
   3. Select the drive that contains your disk, select the **Tutorial.01\Tutorial** folder, and then type the name **MidlandHomePageMF.htm** in the File name box.
   4. Click the **Save** button. Now the HTML document for the Midland Pet Adoption Agency's home page is saved on your disk. When you send it to Trinity, she can start her Web browser and then use the Open command on the File menu to open the Web page.
      Trouble? If a dialog box is open on your screen telling you that 100% of MidlandHomePageMF.htm is saved, click the Close button. If the Download Manager dialog box remains open on your screen with "Finished" listed in the Progress column, click the Close button in the title bar.

If the Web page contains graphics, such as photos, drawings, or icons, they are saved in a separate folder with the same name as the HTML document if the Save as type text box is set to Web Page, complete. If you use the Web Page, HTML only setting, the graphic page elements are not saved. To save a graphic, right-click it in the browser window, click Save Image on the shortcut menu, and then save the graphic to the same location as the Web's HTML document. The graphics file will appear on the HTML document as a hyperlink; therefore, you might have to change the HTML code in the Web page to identify the location of the graphic. Copying the graphics files to the same disk as the HTML document will *usually* work.

Saving Web Page Text to a File

You can save portions of Web page text to a file, so that you can use the file in other programs. You will use WordPad to save text that you will copy from a Web page; however, any word processor or text editor will work.

Reference Window

Copying Text from a Web Page to a WordPad Document

- Open the Web page in Firefox.
- Use the mouse pointer to select the text you want to copy.
- Click Edit on the menu bar, and then click Copy.
- Start WordPad (or another word processor or text editor if WordPad is not available).
- Click Edit on the WordPad menu bar, and then click Paste (or click the Paste button).
- Click the Save button, select the folder where you want to store the file, and then enter a new file name, if necessary.
- Click the Save button.

Trinity just called to let you know that she will be traveling in Minnesota next week and she would like to visit the Midland Pet Adoption Agency while she is in the area. She will meet with the director there and see if she can learn more about how they developed their Web site. You will visit Midland Pet Adoption Agency's Web site and get the agency's address and telephone number so Trinity can contact the director and schedule a meeting.

To copy text from a Web page and save the text as a WordPad document:

1. Make sure the Midland Pet Adoption Agency home page is open in the browser window.

2. Click the **Directions & Contact** hyperlink to open the page with information about Midland's location.

3. Find the address and telephone information just under the links to other pages, and then drag the mouse pointer over the address and telephone number to select it, as shown in Figure 1-42.

Selecting text on a Web page | **Figure 1-42**

selected
text is
highlighted

4. Click **Edit** on the menu bar, and then click **Copy** to copy the selected text to the
Clipboard.

Now, you will start WordPad and then paste the copied text into a new document.

5. Click the **Start** button on the taskbar, point to **All Programs**, point to **Accessories**, and
then click **WordPad** to start the program and open a new document.

6. Click the **Paste** button on the WordPad toolbar to paste the text into the WordPad document,
as shown in Figure 1-43. (The bold formatting shown in the figure might not copy when you
paste the text into WordPad on your computer.)

Pasting text from a Web page into a WordPad document | **Figure 1-43**

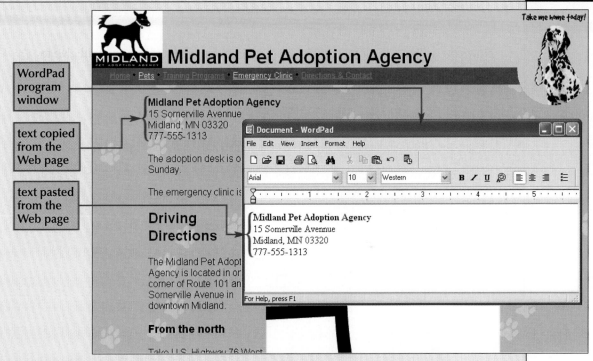

WordPad
program
window

text copied
from the
Web page

text pasted
from the
Web page

Trouble? If the WordPad toolbar does not appear, click View on the menu bar, click Toolbar, and then repeat Step 6. Your WordPad program window might be a different size from the one shown in Figure 1-43, which does not affect the steps.

7. Click the **Save** button on the WordPad toolbar to open the Save As dialog box.

8. Click the **Save in** list arrow, select the drive that contains your disk, and then select the **Tutorial.01\Tutorial** folder.

9. Delete the text in the File name text box, type **MidlandAddressPhoneMF.txt**, and then click the **Save** button to save the file. Now, the address and phone number of the agency is saved in a file on your disk for future reference.

10. Click the **Close** button on the WordPad title bar to close it.

You can print this information from WordPad and give it to Trinity the next time you see her. As you examine the Web page, you notice a street map that shows the location of the Midland Pet Adoption Agency. You decide that Trinity might like to have a copy of that map.

Saving a Web Page Graphic to a Disk

You consider printing the entire Web page, but you know that Trinity might like to have just the map image. You decide to save the map graphic to your disk so you can give it to Trinity.

Reference Window	**Saving an Image from a Web Page to a Disk**

- Open the Web page in Firefox.
- Right-click the image you want to copy, and then click Save Image As.
- Select the drive and the folder in which you want to save the image, and change the default file name, if necessary.
- Click the Save button.

Now you will save the image of the street map to your disk, which you will give to Trinity when you see her.

To save the street map image to a disk:

1. Right-click the map image to open its shortcut menu, as shown in Figure 1-44.

Saving the map image to a disk   **Figure 1-44**

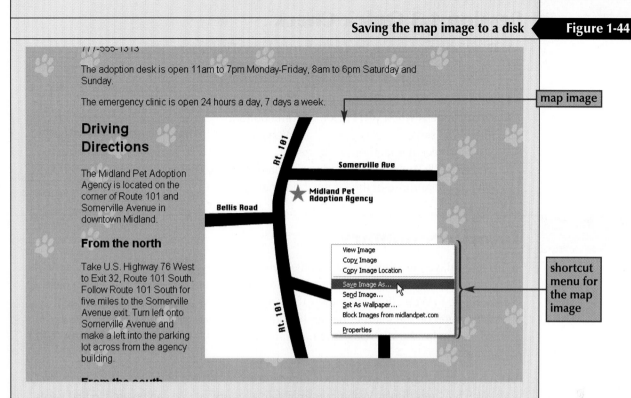

2. Click **Save Image As** on the shortcut menu to open the Save As dialog box.

3. Click the **Save in** list arrow, select the drive that contains your disk, and then select the **Tutorial.01\Tutorial** folder.

4. Delete the text in the File name text box, type **MidlandMapMF.gif**, and then click the **Save** button to save the file.

   Trouble? If a dialog box is open on your screen telling you that 100% of MidlandHomePageMF.htm is saved, click the Close button. If the Download Manager dialog box remains open on your screen with "Finished" listed in the Progress column, click the Close button in the title bar.

5. Close your Web browser.

Now, you have a disk for Trinity that has a copy of the Midland Pet Adoption Agency Web home page and a map that will show her how to get there during her trip to Minnesota. She will be able to use her Web browser to open the files and print them.

Session 1.3 Quick Check

1. Describe three ways to load a Web page in the Firefox browser.
2. You can use the _____ in Firefox to visit sites previously visited during your Web session.
3. When would you hold down the Shift key as you clicked the Reload button?
4. What happens when you click the Home button?
5. Some Web servers _____ Web page files before returning them to the client to prevent unauthorized access.
6. True or False: You can identify an encrypted Web page when viewing it in Firefox.
7. What is the purpose of the Firefox bookmark feature?

Tutorial Summary

In this tutorial, you learned how Web pages and Web sites make up the World Wide Web. The Web uses a client/server structure in which Web server computers make Web page files available to Web client computers that are running Web browser software. Each server computer on the Internet has an IP address that is mapped to a domain name. The domain name plus the Web page file name make up the Uniform Resource Locator (URL) of that file.

All Web browsers have the same basic elements and can be used to explore the Web in similar ways. Web browsers display Web pages, maintain a history list that can be used to find pages previously visited, and allow users to print and save Web pages and elements of Web pages. You learned about several Web browsers that are currently available at no or low cost.

Internet Explorer and Firefox are the two most widely used Web browsers. You learned how to navigate the Web by visiting several Web sites and to print and save Web page elements using these two browsers.

Key Terms

Common Terms

Back button	Home button	Internet Explorer
browser rendering engine	home page	IP (Internet Protocol) address
cache	HTML anchor tag	iRider
Close button	HTML document	local area network (LAN)
cookie	hyperlinks	links
copyright	hypermedia links	Maximize button
DNS (domain name system) software	hypertext links	menu bar
domain name	Hypertext Markup Language (HTML)	Microsoft Internet Explorer
domain name server	hypertext transfer protocol (HTTP)	Minimize button
encryption		Mosaic
fair use	index.html	Mozilla Firefox
file transfer protocol (FTP)	interconneted network	Mozilla Suite
Firefox	internet	Netscape Navigator
Forward button	Internet	network
frame	Internet Corporation for Assigned Names and Numbers (ICANN)	Opera
Gecko engine		Opera for Mobile
history list		page tab
		Restore button

scroll bar	Web page	Refresh button
start page	Web page area	Security indicator button
status bar	Web search engine	security zone
tag	Web server	Standard Buttons toolbar
Telnet protocol	Web site	Temporary Internet Files
title bar	Webmaster	folder
toggle	wide area network (WAN)	transfer progress report
top-level domain (TLD)	World Wide Web (Web)	*Firefox*
transfer protocol	*Internet Explorer*	bookmark
Uniform Resource	Address bar	Location Bar
Locator (URL)	favorite	Navigation toolbar
Web browser	Full Screen	Reload button
Web client	graphical transfer progress	Security indicator button
Web directory	indicator	

Practice

Get hands-on practice of the skills you learned in the tutorial using the same case scenario.

Review Assignments

Trinity is pleased with the information you gathered thus far about the Midland Pet Adoption Agency's Web pages. In fact, she is thinking about having you chair a committee that will supervise the design of a Web site for the Danville Animal Shelter. Because Trinity would like you to be well prepared to direct the committee, she has asked you to compile some information about the Web pages that other animal welfare groups have created. You will examine Web sites for additional background information by completing the following steps.

1. Start your Web browser, open the Student Online Companion page at www.course.com/newperspectives/internet6, click the Tutorial 1 link, and then click the Review Assignments link.
2. Click the hyperlinks listed under the heading Animal Welfare Organizations to explore the Web pages for organizations that have goals and activities similar to those of the Danville Animal Shelter. The list includes a large number of links; however, Web sites change their URLs and even close from time to time. If a link does not lead you to an active site or to a site that you believe is relevant to this assignment, simply choose another link.
3. Choose three interesting home pages, print the first page of each, and then create a bookmark or favorite for each of these sites. Answer the following questions for these three sites:
   a. Which sites include a photograph of the organization's building or any of its physical facilities?
   b. Which sites have photographs of pets available for adoption on the home page?
   c. Which sites provide information about the people who work for the organization (as paid employees or as volunteers)?
   d. Which sites include information about donors who have made contributions to support the organization?
   e. Which sites provide information about their charitable purpose or tax-exempt status?
4. Choose your favorite pet photograph and save it to a file.
5. Do any of the three sites you have chosen provide contact information or directions (with or without a map) to their facilities? If so, which ones? Is this information on the home page, or did you click a hyperlink to find it? Copy the contact information and save it to a text file.

6. Which site made finding specific information (about the organization or about pets available for adoption) the easiest? What did that site do differently from the other sites that made this true?
7. Write a two-page report that summarizes your findings in a form suitable for distribution at your committee's first meeting. Include a recommendation regarding specific elements the Danville Animal Shelter should consider including in its Web site.
8. Close your Web browser.

Case Problem 1

Value City Central Business Web sites range from very simple informational sites to comprehensive sites that offer information about the firm's products or services, history, current employment openings, and financial information. An increasing number of business sites offer products or services for sale using their Web sites. You just started a position on the public relations staff of Value City Central, a large retail chain of television and appliance stores. Your first assignment is to research and report on the types of information that other large firms offer on their Web sites, which you will do by completing the following steps.

1. Start your Web browser, open the Student Online Companion page at www.course.com/newperspectives/internet6, click the Tutorial 1 link, and then click the Case Problem 1 link.
2. Use the Value City Central hyperlinks to open each business site.
3. Choose three of those business sites that you believe would be most relevant to your assignment.
4. Print the home page for each Web site that you have chosen.
5. Select one site that you feel does the best job in each of the following five categories:
   a. overall presentation of the company's brand or image
   b. description of products or services offered
   c. presentation of the firm's history
   d. description of employment opportunities with the company
   e. presentation of financial statements or other financial information about the company
6. Prepare a report that includes one paragraph describing why you believe each of the sites you identified in the preceding step did the best job.
7. Close your Web browser.

Case Problem 2

Northwest Community College Your employer, Northwest Community College, is a medium-sized school that prepares students for direct entry into the workforce and for future academic studies. The school has increased its use of computers in all of its office operations. Many of Northwest's computers currently run either Microsoft Internet Explorer or Firefox; however, the administrative vice-president (AVP) has decided that the school should support only one browser to save money on user training and computer support personnel costs. The AVP has heard some good things about two other browsers: iRider and Opera. The AVP is wondering whether one of those browsers might be the right product for the school. As the AVP's special assistant, you have been asked to recommend which of these four Web browsers the school should choose to support. You will research the browsers for your report by completing the following steps.

1. Start your Web browser, open the Student Online Companion page at www.course.com/newperspectives/internet6, click the Tutorial 1 link, and then click the Case Problem 2 link.

2. Use the Northwest Community College hyperlinks to learn more about these four Web browsers.
3. Write a two-page memo to the AVP (to submit to your instructor) that outlines the strengths and weaknesses of each product. Recommend one Web browser program and support your decision using the information you collected.
4. Prepare a list of features that you would like to see in a new Web browser software package that would overcome important limitations in Firefox, Internet Explorer, iRider, or Opera. Do you think it would be feasible for a firm to develop and use such a product? Why or why not?
5. Close your Web browser.

Case Problem 3

Research

Read Web pages to learn more about cookies, identify the risks posed by cookies to a financial institution, and compare those risks to the benefits obtained by accepting cookies.

Citizens Central Bank You are a new staff auditor at the Citizens Central Bank. You have had more recent computer training than other audit staff members at Citizens, so Sally DeYoung, the audit manager, asks you to review the bank's policy on Web browser cookie settings. Some of the bank's board members expressed concerns to Sally about the security of the bank's computers. They understand that the bank has PCs on its networks that are connected to the Internet. One of the board members learned about browser cookies and was afraid that a naive bank employee might open a Web site that would write a dangerous cookie file on the bank's computer network. Not all Web servers write cookies, but those that do can read the cookie file the next time the Web browser on that computer connects to the Web server. The Web server can then retrieve information about the Web browser's last connection to the server. None of the bank's board members knows very much about computers, but all of them became concerned that a virus-laden cookie could significantly damage the bank's computer system. Sally asks you to help inform the board of directors about cookies and to establish a policy on using them. You will accomplish these tasks by completing the following steps.

1. Start your Web browser, open the Student Online Companion page at www.course.com/newperspectives/internet6, click the Tutorial 1 link, and then click the Case Problem 3 link.
2. Use the Citizens Fidelity Bank hyperlinks to learn more about cookie files.
3. Prepare a brief outline of the content on each Web page you visit.
4. List the risks that Citizens Fidelity Bank might face by allowing cookie files to be written to their computers.
5. List the benefits that individual users obtain by allowing Web servers to write cookies to the computers that they are using at the bank to access the Web.
6. Close your Web browser.

Case Problem 4

Create

Select a model charitable organization Web site and prepare a presentation in which you explain why the site would be a good example to use for your organization.

Columbus Suburban Area Council The Columbus Suburban Area Council is a charitable organization devoted to maintaining and improving the general welfare of people living in Columbus suburbs. As the director of the council, you are interested in encouraging donations and other support from area citizens and would like to stay informed of grant opportunities that might benefit the council. You are especially interested in developing an informative and attractive presence on the Web and will pursue that goal by completing the following steps.

1. Start your Web browser, open the Student Online Companion page at www.course.com/newperspectives/internet6, click the Tutorial 1 link, and then click the Case Problem 4 link.

2. Follow the Columbus Suburban Area Council hyperlinks to charitable organizations to find out more about what other organizations are doing with their Web sites.
3. Select three of the Web sites you visited and, for each, prepare a list of the site's contents. Note whether each site included financial information and whether the site disclosed how much the organization spent on administrative or nonprogram-related activities.
4. Identify which site you believe would be a good model for the council's new Web site. Prepare a presentation in which you explain to the council why you think your chosen site would be the best example to follow.
5. Close your Web browser.

Create

Examine the structure of several Web directory pages and use the information gathered to design a personal start page.

Case Problem 5

Emma Inkster Your neighbor, Emma Inkster, was an elementary school teacher for many years. She is now retired and has just purchased her first personal computer. Emma is excited about getting on the Web and exploring its resources. She has asked for your help. After you introduce her to what you have learned in this tutorial about Web browsers, she is eager to spend more time gathering information on the Web. Although she is retired, Emma has continued to be very active. She is an avid bridge player, enjoys golf, and is one of the neighborhood's best gardeners. Although she is somewhat limited by her schoolteacher's pension, Emma loves to travel to foreign countries and especially likes to learn the languages of her destinations. She would like to have a start page for her computer that would include hyperlinks that would help her easily visit and regularly return to Web pages related to her interests. Her nephew knows HTML and can create the page, but Emma would like you to help her design the layout of her start page. You know that Web directory sites are designed to help people find interesting Web sites, so you begin your search with them by completing the following steps.

1. Start your Web browser, open the Student Online Companion page at www.course.com/newperspectives/internet6, click the Tutorial 1 link, and then click the Case Problem 5 link.
2. Use the Emma Inkster hyperlinks to Web directories to learn what kind of organization they use for their hyperlinks.
3. You note that many of the Web directories use a similar organization structure for their hyperlinks and categories; however, you are not sure if that organization structure would be ideal for Emma. You decide to create categories that suit Emma's specific interests. List five general categories around which you would organize Emma's start page. For each of those five general categories, list three subcategories that would help Emma find and return to Web sites she would find interesting.
4. Write a report of 100 words in which you explain why the start page you designed for Emma would be more useful to her than a publicly available Web directory.
5. Close your Web browser.

Reinforce

Reinforce the concepts and skills you learned in this tutorial by completing this online interactive lab.

Lab Assignments

The interactive Student Edition Lab on **Getting the Most Out of the Internet** is designed to help you master some of the key concepts and skills presented in this tutorial, including:

- using a browser to view Web pages
- saving Web pages as favorites
- deleting the files in the Temporary Internet Files folder

This lab and lab assignment are available online and can be accessed from the Tutorial 1 Web page on the Student Online Companion at *www.course.com/newperspectives/internet6*.

Review

Quick Check Answers

Session 1.1

1. False
2. True
3. home page; start page
4. hypermedia links
5. Any three of these: Candidate's name and party affiliation; list of qualifications; biography; position statements on campaign issues; list of endorsements with hyperlinks to the Web pages of individuals and organizations that support her candidacy; audio or video clips of speeches and interviews; address and telephone number of the campaign office
6. A computer's IP address is a unique identifying number; its domain name is a unique name associated with the IP address on the Internet host computer responsible for that computer's domain.
7. "http://" indicates use of the hypertext transfer protocol; "www.savethetrees.org" is the domain name and suggests a charitable or not-for-profit organization that is probably devoted to forest ecology; "main.html" is the name of the HTML file on the Web server
8. A Web directory contains a hierarchical list of Web page categories; each category contains hyperlinks to individual Web pages. A Web search engine is a Web site that accepts words or expressions you enter and finds Web pages that include those words or expressions.

Session 1.2

1. You can hide its toolbars or click the Full Screen command on the View menu.
2. History
3. Search
4. Animal Shelters, Humane Societies, Animal Welfare Organizations
5. Shift
6. True
7. press F1, click Help on the menu bar

Session 1.3

1. Any three of these: Type the URL in the location field; click a hyperlink on a Web page; click the Back button; click the Forward button; click the Bookmarks button and select a page; click Go on the menu bar, click History, and then click the entry for the site you want to visit
2. history list (or the Back or Forward button)
3. When you want the browser to reload the page from the Web server instead of from the local cache on your computer.
4. Firefox loads the page that is specified in the Home page section of the Preferences dialog box (which you can open from the Edit menu).
5. encrypt
6. True
7. a Firefox feature that enables you to store and organize a list of Web pages that you have visited

Objectives

Session 2.1
- Learn about e-mail and how it works
- Learn about the Thunderbird and Opera e-mail clients
- Explore Web-based e-mail services

Session 2.2
- Configure and use Outlook Express to send, receive, and print e-mail messages
- Create and maintain an address book in Outlook Express

Session 2.3
- Configure and use Hotmail to send, receive, and print e-mail messages
- Create and maintain an address book in Hotmail

Lab

E-Mail

Student Edition Labs

Student Data Files

Basic Communication on the Internet: E-Mail

Evaluating an E-Mail Program and a Web-Based E-Mail Service

Case

Kikukawa Air

Since 1994, Sharon and Don Kikukawa have operated an air charter service in Maui, Hawaii. At first, Kikukawa Air employed only Sharon, who managed the office, reservations, and the company's financial records; and her husband Don, who flew their twin-engine, six-passenger plane between Maui and Oahu. After many successful years in business, Sharon and Don expanded their business to include scenic tours and charter service to all of the Hawaiian Islands. As a result of their expansion, Kikukawa Air now has six twin-engine planes, two turboprop planes, and a growing staff of more than 30 people.

Because Kikukawa Air has a ticket counter at airports on all of the Hawaiian Islands, many miles now separate the company's employees. Originally employees used the telephone and conference calling to coordinate the business's day-to-day operations, such as schedule and reservation changes, new airport procedures, and maintenance requests. Sharon soon realized that the long-distance rates and fees associated with conference calling services made these forms of communication too expensive to continue using. In addition to these expenses, Sharon was overwhelmed by the effort required to manage the busy schedules of many ground-service agents and pilots and to find convenient times to meet. Sharon believes that Kikukawa Air could benefit from an alternate form of communication. Sharon has hired you to investigate the use of e-mail for the different Kikukawa Air offices and ticket counter facilities. Your job includes evaluating available e-mail systems and overseeing the software's installation. Eventually you will train the staff members so they can use the new e-mail system efficiently and effectively.

▼ **Tutorial.02**

▽ **Tutorial folder**	▽ **Review folder**	▽ **Cases folder**
Physicals.doc	KAir.gif	Recycle.doc

Session 2.1

What Is E-Mail and How Does It Work?

Electronic mail, or **e-mail**, is a form of communication in which electronic messages are created and transferred between two or more computers connected to a network. E-mail is one of the most popular forms of business communication, and for many people it is their primary use of the Internet. In fact, many people view the Internet as an electronic highway that transports e-mail messages, without realizing that the Internet provides access to a wide variety of services. E-mail travels across the Internet to its destination and is deposited in the recipient's electronic mailbox. Although similar to other forms of correspondence, including letters and memos, e-mail has the added advantage of being fast and inexpensive. Instead of traveling through a complicated, expensive, and often slow mail delivery service, such as a postal system, e-mail travels quickly, efficiently, and inexpensively to its destination down the hall or around the world. You can send a message any time you want, without worrying about when the mail is collected and delivered or adding any postage. For many personal and business reasons, people rely on e-mail as an indispensable form of communication.

E-mail travels across the Internet like other forms of information—that is, in small packets that are reassembled at the destination and delivered to the recipient, whose address you specify in the message. When you send an e-mail message, the message is sent to a **mail server**, which is a hardware and software system that determines from the recipient's address one of several electronic routes on which to send the message. The message is routed from one computer to another and is passed through several mail servers. Each mail server determines the next leg of the message's journey until it finally arrives at the recipient's electronic mailbox.

Sending e-mail uses one of many Internet technologies. Special **protocols**, or rules that determine how the Internet handles message packets flowing on it, are used to interpret and transmit e-mail. **SMTP (Simple Mail Transfer Protocol)** decides which paths an e-mail message takes on the Internet. SMTP handles outgoing messages; another protocol called **POP (Post Office Protocol)** handles incoming messages. POP is a standard, extensively used protocol that is part of the Internet suite of recognized protocols. Other protocols used to deliver mail include IMAP and MIME. **IMAP (Internet Message Access Protocol)** is a protocol for retrieving mail messages from a server. The **MIME (Multipurpose Internet Mail Extensions)** protocol specifies how to encode nontext data, such as graphics and sound, so it can travel over the Internet.

When an e-mail message arrives at its destination mail server, the mail server's software handles the details of distributing the message locally, in the same way that a mailroom worker opens a mailbag and places letters and packages into individual mail slots. When the server receives a new message, it is not saved on the recipient's computer, but rather, the message is held on the mail server. When you check for new e-mail messages, you use a program stored on your personal computer (PC) to request the mail server to deliver any stored mail to your PC. The software that requests mail delivery from the mail server to your PC is known as **mail client software**, or an **e-mail program**.

An **e-mail address** uniquely identifies an individual or organization that is connected to the Internet. It is like a telephone number—when you want to call a friend or business, you dial a series of numbers that route your call through a series of switchboards until your call reaches its destination. For example, calling a friend in San Diego from another country requires you to dial the country code for the United States (the country code varies according to the country from which you are calling). Next, you must dial the three-digit area code for the part of San Diego in which your friend lives. Finally, you must dial your friend's seven-digit local number. To route an e-mail message to an individual, you must identify that person by his or her account name, or **user name**, and also by the computer on which mail for that user is stored—the **host computer** (or **host name**). The two parts of an e-mail address—the user name and the host name—are separated by an "at" sign (@). Sharon Kikukawa, for example, established the user name *sharonkikukawa* for her e-mail account. Kikukawa Air purchased the domain name kikukawaair.com to use as both its Internet address (URL) and in the e-mail addresses for its employees. Therefore, Sharon's e-mail address is sharonkikukawa@kikukawaair.com.

A user name usually identifies a person within an organization, but a user name can also represent two or more e-mail addresses of people that belong to a group, such as the members of a specific department. In some instances you can create your own user name, but usually an organization through which you obtain an e-mail account has rules about acceptable user names. Some organizations set standards so user names consist of a person's first initial followed by up to seven characters of the person's last name. Other organizations prefer that user names contain a person's first and last names separated by an underscore character (for example, Sharon_Kikukawa). Occasionally, you can pick a nickname such as "skimaniac" as your user name.

The host name is the second part of an e-mail address. The host name specifies the computer to which the mail is to be delivered on the Internet. Host names contain periods, which are usually pronounced "dot," to divide the host name. The most specific part of the host name appears first in the host address, followed by more general destination names. Sharon's host name, kikukawaair.com (and pronounced "kikukawa air dot com"), contains only two names separated by a period. The *com* in the address indicates that this company falls into the large, general class of commercial locations.

Most e-mail addresses aren't case-sensitive; in other words, the addresses sharonkikukawa@kikukawaair.com and SharonKikukawa@KikukawaAir.com are the same. It is important for you to type a recipient's address carefully; if you omit or mistype even one character, your message could be undeliverable or sent to the wrong recipient. When mail cannot be delivered, the electronic postmaster sends the mail back to you and indicates the addressee is unknown—just like conventional mail.

Most people have more than one e-mail address to manage their correspondence. It is very common for people to have a primary e-mail address that they use for personal or business correspondence, and a secondary e-mail address that they use for online subscriptions, online purchases, and mailing lists. If you are careful about how you distribute your primary e-mail address, you might reduce the amount of unsolicited mail that you receive. When your secondary e-mail address starts getting a lot of unwanted messages, you can discard it and create a new one.

Common Features of an E-Mail Message

An e-mail message consists of three parts: the message header, the message body, and the signature. The **message header** contains all the information about the message, and the **message body** contains the actual message. An optional **signature** might appear at the bottom of your e-mail messages and contain standard information about yourself that the recipient can use to contact you in a variety of ways.

Figure 2-1 shows a message that Sharon Kikukawa wrote to Bob Merrell, Jenny Mahala, Richard Forrester, the Maintenance department at Kikuakawa Air, and Don Kikukawa. The message contains an attached file named MaintenanceSchedule.xls. Sharon created this file using a spreadsheet program, saved it, and then attached it to the message. Each of the message parts is described in the next sections.

Figure 2-1 **Common features of an e-mail message**

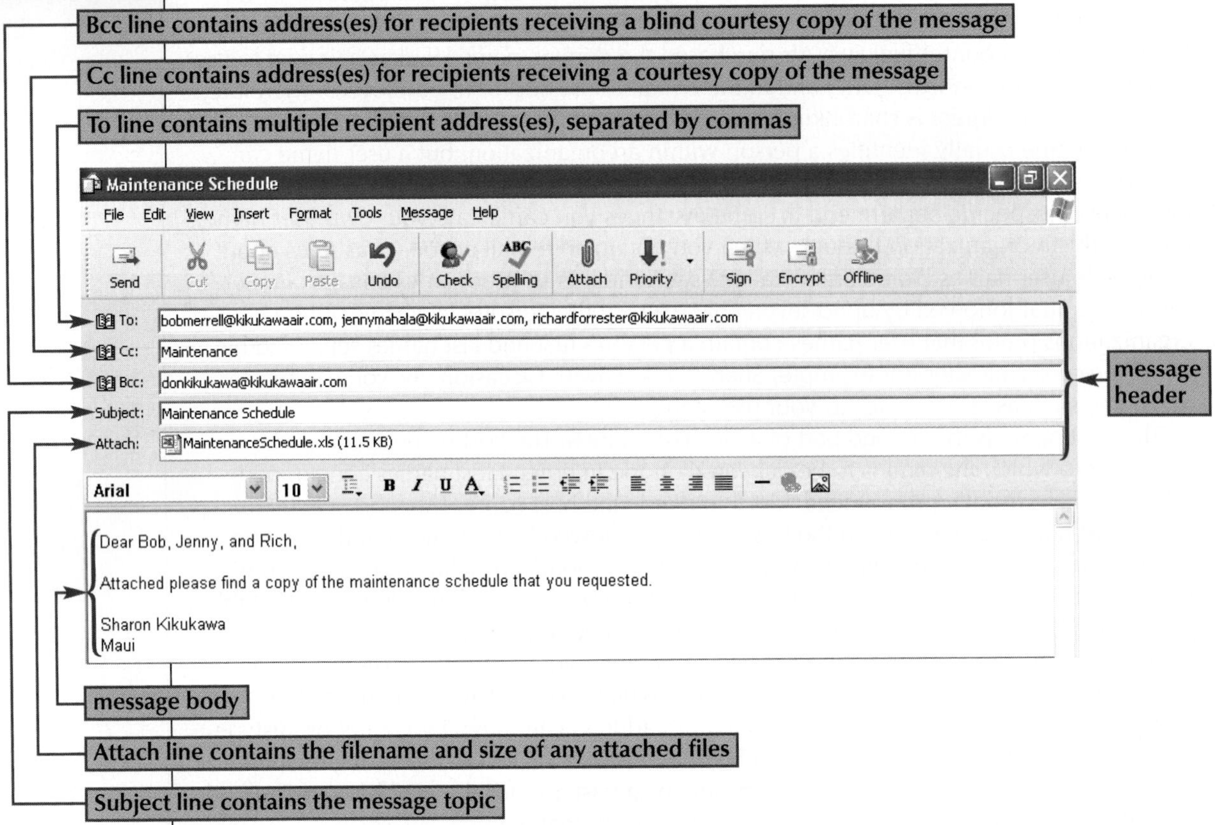

Bcc line contains address(es) for recipients receiving a blind courtesy copy of the message

Cc line contains address(es) for recipients receiving a courtesy copy of the message

To line contains multiple recipient address(es), separated by commas

message header

message body

Attach line contains the filename and size of any attached files

Subject line contains the message topic

To, Cc, and Bcc

You type the recipient's full e-mail address in the **To line** of a message header. You can send the same message to multiple recipients by typing a comma or semicolon between the recipients' e-mail addresses in the To line. There is no real limit on the number of addresses you can type in the To line or in the other parts of the message header that require an address, but some mail servers will reject messages with too many recipients (usually 50 or more). In Figure 2-1, Sharon used the To line to address her message to three recipients and separated their e-mail addresses with commas.

You can use the optional **courtesy copy (Cc)** and the **blind courtesy copy (Bcc)** lines to send mail to people who should be aware of the e-mail message, but are not the message's main recipients. When an e-mail message is delivered, every recipient can see the addresses of other recipients, except for those recipients who receive a blind courtesy copy. Because Bcc addresses are excluded from messages sent to addresses in the To and Cc lines, neither the primary recipient (in the To line) nor the Cc recipients can view the list of Bcc recipients. Bcc recipients are unaware of other Bcc recipients, as well. For example, if you send a thank-you message to a salesperson for performing a task especially well, you might consider sending a blind courtesy copy to that person's supervisor. That way, the supervisor knows a customer is happy and that the praise was unsolicited. In Figure 2-1, Sharon sent a blind courtesy copy of her e-mail message to Don Kikukawa so he could monitor the maintenance schedule without Bob, Jenny, Rich, or members of the Maintenance department being aware of his involvement.

Sometimes a physical mailing address is not one person's address, but rather, a special address called a **group**. In a group, a single e-mail address can represent several or many individual e-mail addresses. In Figure 2-1, the "Maintenance" address in the Cc line represents the three e-mail addresses of people in the Maintenance department at Kikukawa Air; there is no "Maintenance" user name.

From

The **From line** of an e-mail message includes the sender's name, the sender's e-mail address, or both. Most e-mail programs automatically insert the sender's name and e-mail address in the From line of all outgoing messages.

Subject

The content of the **Subject line** is very important. Often the recipient will scan an abbreviated display of incoming messages, looking for the most interesting or important message based on the content in the Subject line. If the Subject line is blank, then the recipient might not read the associated message immediately or at all. Including an appropriate subject in your messages helps the reader determine the message's content and importance. For example, a Subject line such as "Just checking" is less informative and less interesting than "Urgent: new staff meeting time." The e-mail message shown in Figure 2-1, for example, contains the subject "Maintenance Schedule" and thus indicates that the message concerns maintenance.

Attachments

Because of the way the messaging system is set up, you can send only text messages using SMTP, the protocol that handles outgoing e-mail. When you need to send a more complex document, such as a Word document or an Excel workbook, you send it along as an attachment. An e-mail **attachment** provides a simple and convenient way of transmitting electronic documents to one or more people. An attachment is encoded so that it can be carried safely over the Internet, to "tag along" with the message. Frequently, the attached file is the most important part of the e-mail message, and the message body contains only a brief statement, such as "Here's the file that you requested." Sharon's e-mail message (see Figure 2-1) contains an attached file, whose filename and size in kilobytes appear in the Attach line in the message header. (A **kilobyte [KB]** is approximately 1,000 characters.) You can attach more than one file to an e-mail message; if you include multiple recipients in the To, Cc, and Bcc lines of the message header, each recipient will receive the message and the attached file(s). However, keep in mind that an e-mail message with many attachments quickly becomes very large in size, and it might take some recipients with slower Internet connections a lot of time to receive your message. In addition, some Internet service providers (ISPs) place limits on the size of messages that they will accept; in some cases, an e-mail message with file attachments over one or two megabytes in size might be rejected and returned to the sender. If you need to send a large attachment to a recipient, ask for the recipient's preferences in how to send it.

When you receive an e-mail message with an attached file, you should proceed carefully before opening or viewing it. E-mail attachments, just like any other computer files, can contain malicious programs called **viruses** that can harm your computer and its files. Some users send attachments containing viruses without realizing that they are doing so; other users send viruses on purpose to infect as many computers as possible. If you receive an e-mail message from a sender that you don't recognize and the message contains an attached file, you should avoid opening that file until you are sure that it doesn't contain a virus. You can install a virus detection software program on your computer to protect it from downloading any files that contain viruses, and some Internet service providers have built-in virus detection software to accomplish the same goal. The Virus Protection section of the Student Online Companion page for Tutorial 2 contains links that you can follow to learn more about virus detection software and viruses. (The Student Online Companion is located at www.course.com/newperspectives/internet6. Click the Tutorial 2 link to access the information and links for this tutorial.)

E-mail programs differ in how they handle and display attachments. Some e-mail programs identify an attached file with an icon that represents a program associated with the attachment's file type. In addition to an icon, some programs also display an attached file's size and filename. Other e-mail programs display an attached file in a preview window when they recognize the attached file's format and can start a program on the user's computer to open the file. Double-clicking an attached file usually opens the file using a program on the user's computer that is associated with the file type of the attachment. For example, if a workbook is attached to an e-mail message, double-clicking the icon for the workbook attachment might start a spreadsheet program on your computer and open the workbook. Similarly, a Word document opens in the Word program window when you double-click the icon representing the Word document attached to the e-mail message.

Viewing an attachment by double-clicking it as previously described lets you open a read-only copy of the file, but it does not save the file on your computer. To save an attached file on your computer, you need to perform a series of steps to save the file in a specific location, such as on your computer's hard drive. Some programs refer to the process of saving an e-mail attachment as **detaching** the file. When you detach a file, you must indicate the disk and folder in which to save it. You won't always need to save an e-mail attachment; sometimes you can view it and then delete it. You will learn how to attach and detach files for your e-mail program later in this tutorial.

Message Body and Signature Files

Most often, people use e-mail to write short, quick messages. However, e-mail messages can be many pages in length, although the term "pages" has little meaning in the e-mail world. Few people using e-mail think of a message in terms of page-sized chunks; e-mail is more like an unbroken scroll with no physical page boundaries. An e-mail message is often less formal than a business letter that you might write, but it's still important to follow the rules of formal letter writing when composing an e-mail message. You should begin your messages with a salutation, such as "Dear Sharon," use proper spelling and grammar, and close your correspondence with a signature. After typing the content of your message—even a short message—you should check your spelling and grammar. You can sign a message by typing your name and other information at the end of each message you send, or you can create a signature file.

If you are using e-mail for business communication, a signature usually contains your name, title, and your company's name. Signature files can also contain a complete non-electronic address, facsimile telephone number, a voice phone number, and the company's Web site address. Some signature files might also include graphics, such as a company logo. If you are using e-mail for personal communication, signatures can be more informal. Informal signatures can include nicknames and graphics or quotations that express a more casual style found in correspondence between friends and acquaintances.

You can set your e-mail program to insert a signature automatically into every message you send so you don't have to repeatedly type its contents. You can modify your signature easily or choose not to include it in selected messages. Most e-mail programs allow you to create multiple signature files so you can choose which one to include when sending a message.

When you create a signature, don't overdo it—it is best to keep a signature to a few lines that identify ways to contact you. Figure 2-2 shows two examples of signatures. The first signature, which Sharon uses in her business correspondence to Kikukawa Air employees, is informal. Sharon uses the second, more formal signature for all other business correspondence to identify her name, title, and contact information.

Sample signatures — **Figure 2-2**

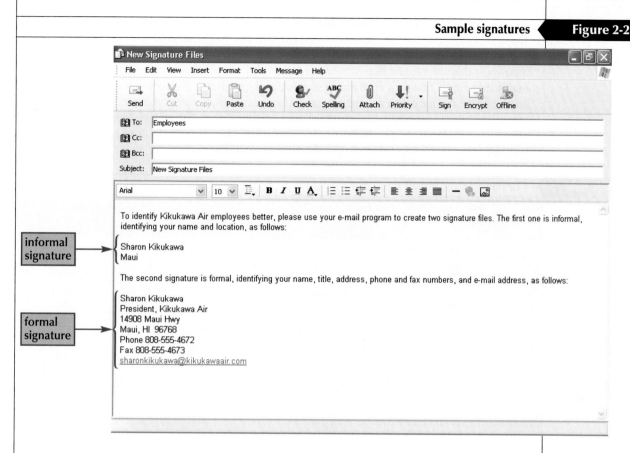

Most mail servers do not allow you to retract mail after you send it, so you should examine your messages carefully before sending them, and always exercise politeness and courtesy in your messages.

Internet Etiquette (Netiquette)

Netiquette, a term coined from the phrase "Internet etiquette," is the set of commonly accepted rules that represent proper behavior on the network known as the Internet. Just as there are rules of proper conduct on business networks, the Internet has its own set of acceptable rules. Unlike business networks where administrators and webmasters set guidelines for acceptable use and moderators are authorized to restrict usage of that network by users who don't follow those rules, the Internet is self-policing. E-mail has its own set of rules, which have evolved over time and will continue to evolve as it gains new users. The generally accepted rules for e-mail messages are:

- Avoid writing your messages in ALL CAPITAL LETTERS BECAUSE IT LOOKS LIKE YOU ARE SHOUTING.
- Keep your messages simple, short, and focused on their topics.
- Include a descriptive subject in the Subject line and a signature, so the recipient knows the content of your message and how to get in touch with you.
- Avoid sending unsolicited messages, especially those with attachments.
- Use a spell checker and read your message and correct any spelling or grammatical errors before sending it.
- Use common courtesy, politeness, and respect in all of your written correspondence.

Because it sometimes takes so little time and effort to compose an e-mail message, you might be tempted to take some shortcuts in your writing, such as omitting the salutation and using acronyms for commonly used phrases, such as the ones shown in Figure 2-3. These shortcuts are fine for informal messages that you might send to your friends and family members but they are not acceptable in business communication. An e-mail message is a business document, just like a memo or letter, and you should treat it with the same formality. Sending a message containing spelling and grammatical errors to a colleague or to an employer at which you are seeking a job is a poor reflection on you and your work. When you send a message, keep in mind that its recipient might receive tens or hundreds of messages a day. If your message contains spelling errors, acronyms, and grammatical mistakes, the recipient might not take the time to read it.

Figure 2-3 ▶ **Commonly used e-mail acronyms**

Acronym	Meaning
atm	At the moment
b/c	Because
btw	By the way
iac	In any case
iae	In any event
imho	In my humble opinion
imo	In my opinion
iow	In other words
jk	Just kidding
thx	Thanks

E-mail can be an impersonal form of communication, and as a result some writers use emoticons to express emotion. An **emoticon** is a group of keyboard characters that when viewed together represent a human expression. For example, a smiley :-) looks like a smiling face when you turn your head to the left. Other emoticons are a frown :-(a smiley with a wink ;-) and fear or surprise :-o . Some writers use emoticons to show their readers a form of electronic body language. Just like acronyms, emoticons are appropriate in informal correspondence but not in business correspondence.

You can learn more about Netiquette by following the links in the Netiquette section of the Student Online Companion page for Tutorial 2.

Common Features of E-Mail Programs

Even though there are many different ways to send and receive e-mail messages, most e-mail programs have common features for managing mail. Fortunately, once you learn the process for sending, receiving, and managing e-mail with one program, it's easy to use another program to accomplish the same tasks.

Sending Messages

After you create a message and initiate the process to send it to its recipients, your message might not be sent to the mail server immediately, depending on how the e-mail program or service is configured. A message can be **queued**, or temporarily held with other messages, and then sent when you either exit the program or check to see if you have received any new e-mail. In some cases, you might need to connect to your ISP or log into a Web site to send the message. Most e-mail programs and services, however, include a "Drafts" folder in which you can store e-mail messages that you are composing but that you aren't ready to send yet. These messages are saved until you finish and send them.

Receiving and Storing Messages

The mail server is always ready to process mail; in theory, the mail server never sleeps. When you receive e-mail, it is held on the mail server until you use your e-mail program to ask the server to retrieve your mail. Most e-mail programs allow you to save delivered mail in any of several standard or custom mailboxes or folders on your PC. However, the mail server is a completely different story. Once the mail is delivered to your PC, one of two things can happen to it on the server: either the server's copy of your mail is deleted, or it is preserved and marked as delivered or read. Marking mail as delivered or read is the server's way of distinguishing new mail from mail that you have read. For example, when Sharon receives mail on the Kikukawa Air mail server, she might decide to save her accumulated mail on the server—even after she reads it—so she can access her e-mail messages again from another computer. On the other hand, Sharon might want to delete old mail to save space on the mail server. Both methods have advantages. Saving old mail on the server lets you access your mail from any PC that can connect to your mail server. However, if you automatically delete mail after reading it, you don't have to worry about storing and organizing messages that you don't need, which requires less effort. Some ISPs and e-mail providers impose limits on the amount of material you can store so that you must occasionally delete mail from your mailbox to avoid interruption of service. In some cases, once you exceed your storage space limit, you cannot receive any additional messages until you delete existing messages from the server, or the service deletes your messages without warning to free up space in your mailbox. Regularly clearing your mailbox of unwanted and old messages is a good idea regardless of the e-mail program you use because it frees up space on your mail server, in your mailbox, or on your computer's hard drive.

Printing a Message

Reading mail on the computer is fine, but there are times when you will need to print some of your messages. Most e-mail programs let you print a message you are composing or that you have received. The Print command usually appears on the File menu, or as a Print button on the toolbar.

Filing a Message

Most e-mail programs let you create folders in which to store related messages in your mailbox. You can create new folders when needed, rename existing folders, or delete folders and their contents when you no longer need them. You can move mail from the incoming folder to any other folder to file it. Some programs let you define and use a **filter** to move incoming mail into one or several folders automatically based on the content of the message. Filters are especially useful for moving messages from certain senders into designated folders, and for moving **junk mail** (or **spam**), which is unsolicited mail usually advertising or selling an item or service, to a trash folder. If your e-mail program does not provide filters, you can filter the messages manually by reading them and filing them in the appropriate folders.

Forwarding a Message

You can forward any message that you receive to one or more recipients. When you **forward** a message to another recipient, a copy of the original message is sent to the new recipient you specify without the original sender's knowledge. You might forward a misdirected message to another recipient or to someone who was not included in the original message routing list.

For example, suppose you receive a message intended for someone else, or the message requests information that only a colleague can provide. In either case, you can forward the message you received to the person who can best deal with the request. When you forward a message, your e-mail address and name appear automatically in the From line; most e-mail programs amend the Subject line with the text "Fw," "Fwd," or something similar to indicate that the message has been forwarded. You simply add the recipient's address to the To line and send the message. Sometimes a forwarded message is sent as an attached file; sometimes it is sent as quoted text. A **quoted message** is a copy of the sender's original message with your inserted comments. A special mark (a > symbol or a solid vertical line), sometimes precedes each line of the quoted message. Figure 2-4 shows a quoted message; notice the > symbol to the left of each line of the original message and the "FW:" text in the Subject line, indicating a forwarded message.

Figure 2-4  **Sample forwarded message**

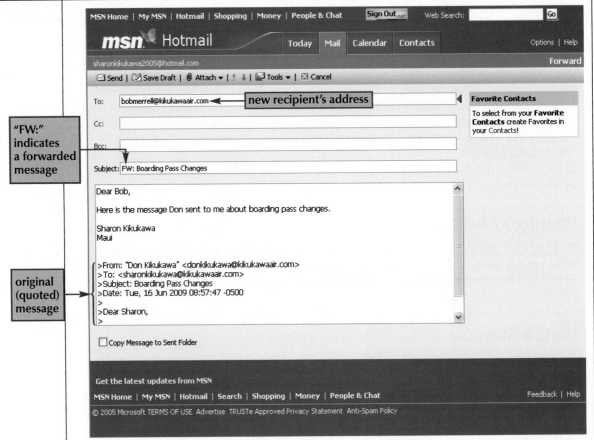

When forwarding a message to a new recipient, and especially when forwarding a message that was forwarded originally to you, keep in mind that a forwarded message includes the e-mail addresses of all the message's previous recipients and senders. Some people might not want to have their addresses sent to other users, who might in turn send them unwanted e-mail messages. If you need to send something you received to a new recipient, and it's not important that the new recipient know who sent you the original message, you should use the Copy and Paste commands in your e-mail program to paste the content of the forwarded message into a new message, thus protecting the privacy of the message's original recipients and making the message easier to read for its new recipients.

Replying to a Message

Most e-mail programs provide two options for replying to a message that you have received. You can reply to just the original sender using the Reply option, or you can reply to the original sender and all other To and Cc recipients of the original message using the Reply All option. When you **reply** to a message that you received, the e-mail program creates a new message and automatically addresses it to the original sender (when you choose the Reply option) or to the original sender and all of the original To and Cc recipients of the message (when you choose the Reply All option). Replying to a message is a quick way of sending a response to someone who sent a message to you. Most e-mail programs will copy the contents of the original message and place it in the message body of the reply. Like forwarded messages, a special mark might appear at the beginning of each line to indicate the text of the original message. When you are responding to more than one question, you might type your responses below the original questions. That way, the recipient can better understand the context of your responses. When you respond to a message that was sent to several people, make sure that you choose the correct option when replying.

Deleting a Message

In most e-mail programs, deleting a message is a two-step process to prevent you from accidentally deleting important messages. First, you temporarily delete a message by placing it in a "trash" folder or by marking it for deletion. Then you permanently delete the trash or marked messages by emptying the trash or indicating to the e-mail program to delete the messages. It is a good idea to delete mail you no longer need because it takes up a lot of space on the drive or server on which your e-mail messages are stored.

Maintaining an Address Book

E-mail addresses are sometimes difficult to remember and type. You use an **address book** to save e-mail addresses and to associate those addresses with **nicknames**, which are special names that are easy to remember. You can use a nickname to represent a person, such as "Mom," or a group, such as all employees working in the Maintenance department at Kikukawa Air.

The features of an e-mail address book vary by e-mail program. Usually, you can organize information about individuals and groups. Each entry in the address book can contain an individual's full e-mail address (or a group e-mail address that represents several individual addresses), full name, and complete contact information. In addition, some e-mail programs allow you to include notes for each contact. You can assign a unique nickname to each entry so it is easier to address your e-mail messages.

After saving entries in your address book, you can refer to them at any point while you are composing, replying to, or forwarding a message. You can review your address book and sort the entries in alphabetical order by nickname, or you can view them in last name order.

E-Mail Programs

When you install a browser on your computer, default mail client software might be installed with it. For example, when you install Microsoft Internet Explorer, Outlook Express is installed to manage your incoming and outgoing e-mail messages and any newsgroups to which you have subscribed. You can use any e-mail program to manage your POP e-mail messages. If you have multiple browsers installed on your computer, then you might also have multiple e-mail programs.

You aren't required to use the e-mail program that was installed with your browser, but you must configure the e-mail program that you want to use to send and receive your e-mail messages. Before you decide which e-mail program to use, you should be familiar with the different ones available. In Session 2.2, you will learn how to configure and use Outlook Express; in Session 2.3, you will learn how to configure and use Hotmail. Because you might end up using different e-mail programs in the future, it is important to know about two other popular e-mail programs, Mozilla Thunderbird and Opera's M2 e-mail client, which have been receiving very favorable reviews by technical publications and experts.

Mozilla Thunderbird

Mozilla Thunderbird is part of the Mozilla open source project. Although Thunderbird complements the Mozilla Firefox Web browser, Thunderbird is available only as a separate download from the Mozilla Web site. A link to Thunderbird's Web site is provided on the Student Online Companion for Tutorial 2.

When you start Thunderbird for the first time, you have the option of importing items from other e-mail programs on your computer. If you choose this option, the address book entries and other settings from the e-mail program on your computer that you select will be imported into Thunderbird. You'll also see the Account Wizard, which lets you set up a mail, RSS news/blogs, or newsgroup account. Figure 2-5 shows the Account Wizard dialog box.

| Figure 2-5 | Thunderbird Account Wizard dialog box |

The first thing you need to set up is your e-mail account so you can send and receive e-mail messages through your Internet service provider. You need to enter your name and e-mail address, your incoming and outgoing mail server information and user name, and the account name you'd like to use to identify your e-mail account. After setting up your e-mail account, you can use Thunderbird to send and receive e-mail messages. Figure 2-6 shows the Thunderbird Inbox window.

Thunderbird Inbox window   Figure 2-6

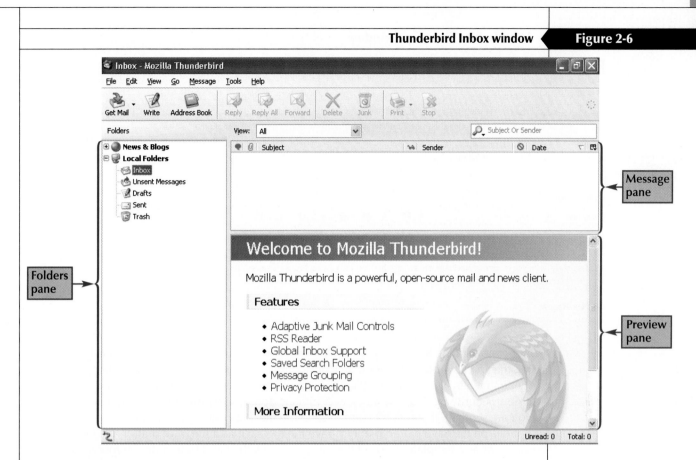

Thunderbird uses a Folders pane, a Message pane, and a Preview pane to organize your e-mail messages. To write a message, click the Write button on the toolbar. The Compose window opens, in which you enter the e-mail address of the message's recipient in the To box. You can send the message to multiple recipients by separating their e-mail addresses with commas. To send Cc or Bcc messages to additional recipients, press the Enter key to move to the next line in the message header, click the To button, select the message recipient type, and then type the recipient's e-mail address. You can also click the Contacts button to open the Contacts pane and view the e-mail addresses saved in your Thunderbird address book. You can use the Attach button to attach files, Web pages, or personal cards to your message. Figure 2-7 shows the Compose window after writing a message to Sharon Kikukawa and attaching a file named Physicals.doc. A carbon copy of the message is addressed to Don Kikukawa.

| Figure 2-7 | **Thunderbird Compose window** |

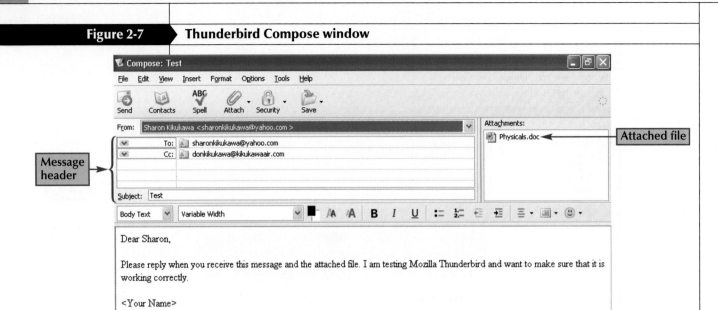

Before sending the message, you can check the document for spelling errors by clicking the Spell button on the toolbar. Clicking the Security button on the toolbar opens a menu that lets you encrypt or digitally sign the message. In addition, you can choose the "View Security Info" option to view certificate and security information about the message you are sending. If you don't want to send the message right away, you can use the options on the Save button menu to save the message as a file, as a draft in the Drafts folder, or as a template. To send the message, click the Send button on the toolbar. By default, messages are sent immediately when you click the Send button, and copies of your sent messages are saved in the Sent folder in the Folders pane.

When you receive a message, the message header appears in the Message pane. Clicking the message opens it in the Preview pane, as shown in Figure 2-8.

Receiving a message in Thunderbird | **Figure 2-8**

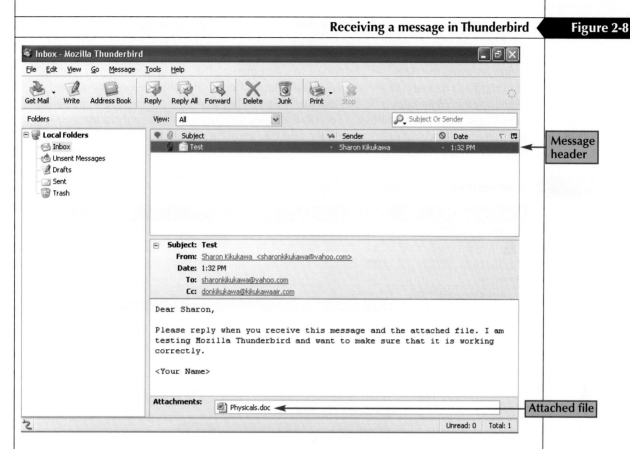

To view an attached file, right-click the filename in the Attachments box, and then click Open on the shortcut menu. An Opening dialog box opens and gives you the choice of opening the file using a program on your computer, or saving the file to disk.

After receiving a message, you can reply to the sender or to all message recipients by clicking the message in the Message pane, and then clicking the Reply or Reply All button on the toolbar. To forward the message to another recipient, click the Forward button on the toolbar. By default, messages are forwarded as attachments. If you prefer to forward inline messages, you can change this setting by clicking Tools on the menu bar, and then clicking Options to open the Options dialog box. After clicking the Composition button, click the Forward messages list arrow, and then click Inline. To print a message, click the Print button on the toolbar, and then select the printer and other options for printing the message.

Just like in other e-mail programs, Thunderbird lets you create folders to manage your messages. To create a new folder in the Folders pane, right-click Local Folders (or your mailbox account name) at the top of the Folders pane to open the shortcut menu, and then click New Folder. In the New Folder dialog box, type the name of the folder, specify where to create it (if necessary), and then click the OK button. To file a message in a folder, drag it from the Message pane to the folder in which you want to save it. To delete a message, select the message in the Message pane, and then click the Delete button on the toolbar. Messages are not permanently deleted until you empty the trash by right-clicking the Trash folder in the Folders pane, and then clicking Empty Trash on the shortcut menu.

To manage your contacts in Thunderbird, click the Address Book button on the toolbar. The Address Book window shown in Figure 2-9 opens and displays the contacts in your personal address book and in the collected addresses book. You can add new e-mail addresses using the New Card button or manage mailing lists using the New List button. To compose a message to someone in your address book, click the person's name, and then click the Write button on the toolbar. Thunderbird lets you store more than just a person's name and e-mail address; if you double-click the contact name in the address book, you can enter a person's phone number, address, and other information, such as a screen name for instant messages.

| Figure 2-9 | **Thunderbird Address Book window** |

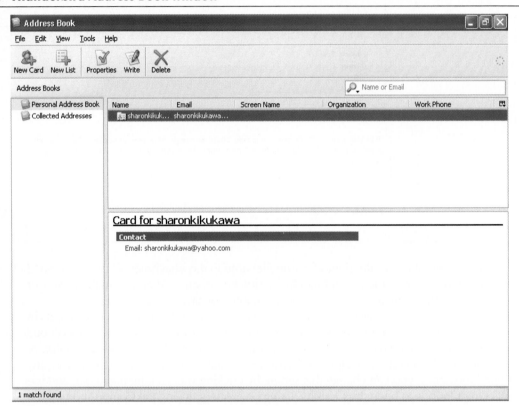

A powerful feature of Thunderbird is its adaptive spam and junk mail filters. When you receive junk mail, clicking the Junk button on the toolbar changes the message and its sender to junk mail and displays a junk mail icon and notice as shown in Figure 2-10.

Using the Thunderbird junk mail feature | Figure 2-10

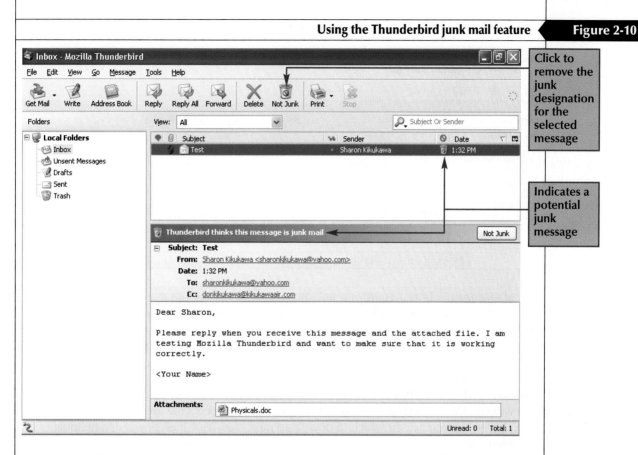

You can set Thunderbird to move messages into a junk folder so it's easy for you to identify and delete unwanted messages later. If Thunderbird thinks that mail is junk but it is not, clicking the Not Junk button on the toolbar changes the sender back to a permitted sender. You can use the Junk Mail Controls option on the Tools menu to set up the junk mail filter so it learns how to identify your incoming mail. After using Thunderbird for a couple of weeks, it will "learn" how to recognize junk mail so you see less of it in your Inbox.

To make it easy to find messages based on criteria that you specify, Thunderbird lets you create Saved Search folders. A **Saved Search folder** looks like a regular mail folder, but when you click it, it searches every folder and message for matches using criteria that you specify. To create a Saved Search folder, click File on the menu bar, point to New, and then click Saved Search. The New Saved Search Folder dialog box opens, in which you must specify a Saved Search folder name, location, and the criteria that define the search. For example, you might create a Saved Search folder that finds all messages sent by a specific person, or messages that are older than 60 days. When you run the search, matching messages will appear in the Message pane. Figure 2-11 shows a Saved Search folder named Sharon in the Folders pane. Double-clicking the Sharon Saved Search folder finds all messages in which Sharon Kikukawa is the sender.

| **Figure 2-11** | **Using a Saved Search folder in Thunderbird** |

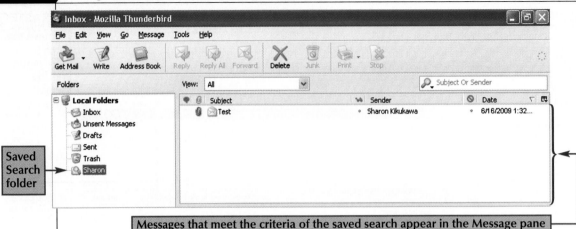

Messages that meet the criteria of the saved search appear in the Message pane

A new feature in Thunderbird is the ability to subscribe to and receive newsfeeds automatically using Really Simple Syndication. **Really Simple Syndication (RSS)** is an XML file format that makes it possible to share updates such as headlines and other Web site content via a newsfeed, which is simply a file containing summaries of stories and news from a Web log (blog) or Web site. Most RSS newsfeeds must be read through a program called an **aggregator** that lets you receive newsfeed content. However, some new e-mail programs, including Thunderbird and Opera, make it possible to use an e-mail client to receive RSS newsfeeds. When you subscribe to a newsfeed, you can accept the default update schedule or choose a frequency on which to download messages. Most newsfeeds update their content throughout the day. If you choose the option to download stories on a short frequency, such as hourly, you'll receive notices of new stories being posted throughout the day without having to check the source. To create a newsfeed account in Thunderbird, click File on the menu bar, point to New, and then click Account. The Account Wizard dialog box opens. Select the RSS News & Blogs option button, click the Next button, and then enter an account name (the default name is "News & Blogs"). After creating a newsfeed account, it appears in the Folders pane. Double-click the newsfeed account to view the options for working with RSS newsfeeds and blogs. Figure 2-12 shows the options for working with RSS newsfeeds.

Creating a News & Blogs account in Thunderbird ◄ **Figure 2-12**

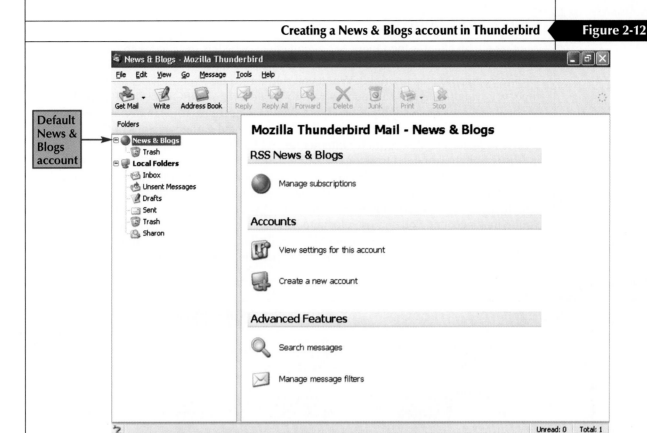

To add an RSS newsfeed to your account, click Manage subscriptions. The RSS Subscriptions dialog box opens. Click the Add button to open the News Feed Properties dialog box, in which you enter the URL of the RSS newsfeed and the location in which to store messages. You can also choose to display message summaries instead of the full articles. After clicking the OK button, Thunderbird will verify the newsfeed address and begin downloading messages. To view the messages, click the newsfeed name in the newsfeed account. Messages will appear in the Message pane and the message contents will appear in the Preview pane, similar to how you view and manage e-mail messages. To change the default download frequency for a newsfeed, click Tools on the menu bar, click Account Settings, and then click the newsfeed account. If necessary, add a check mark to the Check for new articles every check box, and then type a value in minutes in the text box.

You can also use Thunderbird to manage your Usenet newsgroup subscriptions by clicking File on the menu bar, pointing to New, and then clicking Account. Select the option to create a Newsgroup account, enter your name and e-mail address, enter your news server name, and then enter an account name. After creating a newsgroup account, click it in the Folders pane to display the options for managing subscriptions. Click Manage newsgroup subscriptions to open the Subscribe dialog box, enter the first few characters of the newsgroup to which you want to subscribe in the Show items that contain text box, select the newsgroup, and then click the Subscribe button. To view messages from the newsgroup you selected, click the newsgroup name in the Folders pane.

Opera M2 Client

Another e-mail client is the **Opera M2** e-mail client, which is installed with the Opera Web browser. You can download the Opera browser by following the link on the Student Online Companion for Tutorial 2. When you start the Opera Web browser for the first time, you can use the New account wizard to create a regular (POP) or IMAP e-mail account, newsreader account, or an Opera Web mail account. You can also import information from Outlook Express, Netscape Mail, Eudora, and earlier versions of Opera into Opera or create a chat account for Internet Relay Chat (IRC).

The first thing you need to set up is your e-mail account so you can send and receive e-mail messages through your Internet service provider. You need to enter your name and e-mail address, your incoming and outgoing mail server information and user name, and the account name you'd like to use to identify your e-mail account. After setting up your e-mail account, you can use Opera to send and receive e-mail messages. To send and receive messages using the Opera M2 e-mail client, start the Opera browser, and then click the Mail button on the Panels toolbar to open the Mail panel shown in Figure 2-13.

Figure 2-13	Opera Mail panel

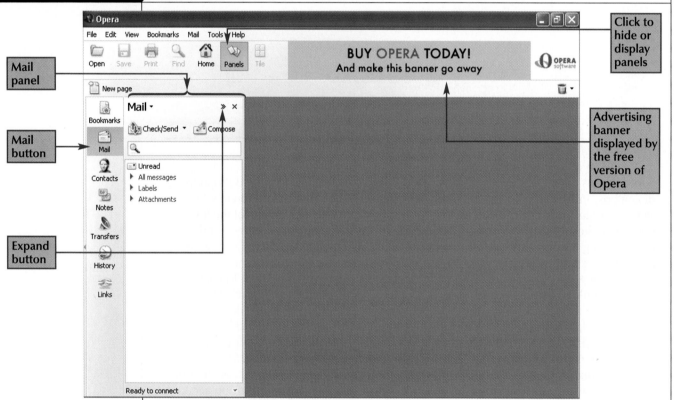

The Mail panel includes buttons to check (receive) and send e-mail, and a Compose button to create new messages. If you click the Expand button shown in Figure 2-13, a Mail tab opens and displays more information than is shown in the Mail panel. Figure 2-14 shows the expanded Mail tab after closing the Mail panel (by clicking the Panels button on the toolbar). You can use whichever format you prefer; most people use the Mail panel to check for new messages quickly without closing the current page being displayed by the browser. When composing new mail messages, you might want to use the Mail tab to see more of the message and your Inbox on the screen.

Opera Mail tab   **Figure 2-14**

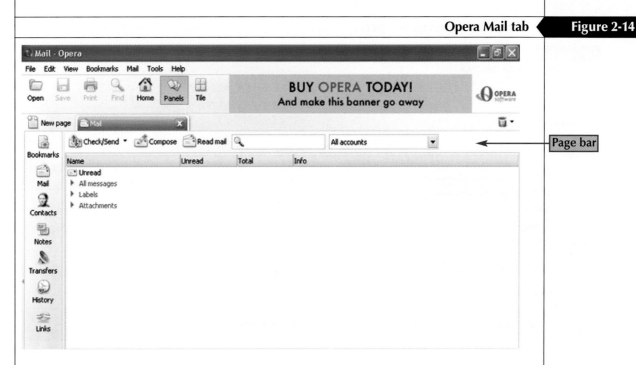

To write a message, click the Compose button. A new tab named Compose message appears on the Page bar. You can type e-mail addresses in the To, CC, and Bcc boxes to add them to your message. To view contacts saved in your address book, click the Contacts button on the Panels toolbar, which opens the Contacts panel to the left of the Compose message tab. To attach a file to your message, click the Attach button on the Mail bar, and then browse to and select the file. After attaching the file, it appears in the Attachment window. Figure 2-15 shows the Compose message tab after writing a message to Sharon Kikukawa and attaching a file named Physicals.doc. A carbon copy of the message is addressed to Don Kikukawa. Notice the promotional message that appears at the bottom of all outgoing messages sent from Opera. If you don't want to include this message in your outgoing e-mail messages, you can select and delete it from the Compose message window before sending your message.

Figure 2-15 Composing a message in Opera

Before sending a message, you can click the Check spelling button on the Mail bar to check the document for spelling errors. Clicking the View button on the Mail bar lets you configure the Compose message tab to show and hide the different parts of the message header, such as the e-mail account name, priority field, and the CC and Bcc boxes. To send the message, click the Send button on the Mail bar. A ScreenTip opens in the lower-left corner of the browser window to indicate that your message is being sent. By default, messages are sent immediately when you click the Send button on the Mail bar, and copies of your sent messages are saved in the Sent folder.

To download new messages, click the Check/Send button on the Mail bar. When you receive a new message, a ScreenTip opens in the lower-left corner of the browser window. To view your mailboxes, click All messages on the Mail tab. Figure 2-16 shows that one message was received.

Figure 2-16 Receiving a message in Opera

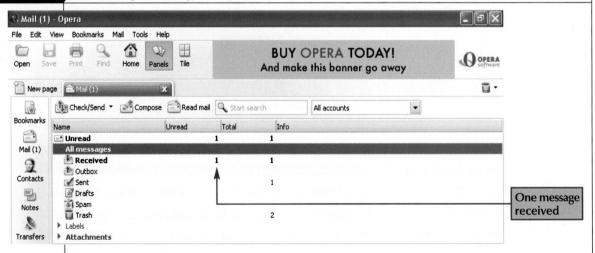

To view the Received tab, double-click it; Figure 2-17 shows one new message. By default, Opera downloads only the headers for e-mail messages that you receive. When you open the Received tab and select the message you received, Opera downloads the message body. This method of downloading message headers and then downloading the message body requires you to be online to read messages after downloading the message headers.

Viewing a new message in Opera ◄ **Figure 2-17**

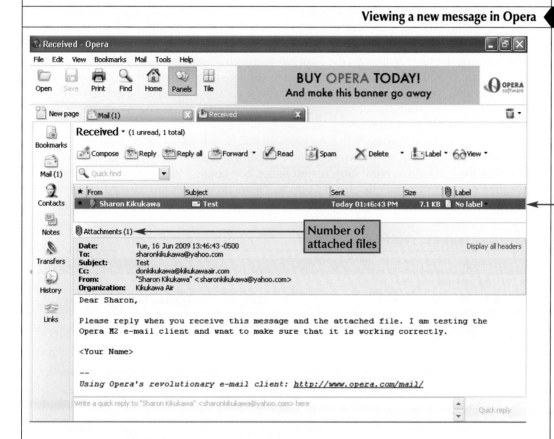

To view an attached file, scroll to the bottom of the new message (if necessary), and then click the attachment. The Download file dialog box opens and gives you the choice of opening the attachment using a program on your computer or saving the file to a disk or network location. To find all messages that have attached files, you can click Attachments on the Mail tab to view all messages with attached files, separated by file type (documents, images, music, video, and compressed file archives).

After receiving a message, you can reply to the sender or to all recipients by clicking the Reply or Reply all button on the Mail bar. To forward a message to another recipient, click the Forward button on the Mail bar. By default, Opera sends forwarded messages as inline text. To redirect a message to a new recipient, click and hold the list arrow on the Forward button on the Mail bar, and then click Redirect. This option makes it easy to send a message to a new recipient without adding the "Fwd:" prefix to the Subject line. To print a message, click the Print button on the Main bar.

After reading a message, you can mark it as read by clicking the Read button on the Mail bar. Clicking the Spam button on the Mail bar flags the sender of the selected message so that future messages sent to you by this sender are automatically saved in the Spam folder. Clicking the Delete button on the Mail bar deletes the message and moves it to the Trash folder. To permanently delete the message, right-click the Trash folder on the Mail tab, and then click Empty trash on the shortcut menu. Clicking the list arrow on the Label button on the Mail bar lets you assign a category to received messages so that you can quickly identify and easily search for important messages, messages that require action, and messages that are funny or valuable. Clicking Labels on the Mail tab lists messages that you have assigned to categories so you can identify and sort them easily. The View button on the Mail bar contains options for displaying relevant information about all of your messages, such as only the message headers, messages received during predefined time periods (such as "last week" or "yesterday"), and threaded replies.

A unique feature of Opera's M2 e-mail client is how it stores its messages. In other e-mail programs, messages are stored in folders in a mailbox. Opera's messages are stored in a single database so that messages are easy to search for and retrieve. You can sort messages by using the View button on the Mail bar to assign messages to categories as you receive them, or you can create custom filters to sort messages based on their content or sender. Because messages are not saved into folders, viewing messages based on their content or category results in all messages matching your search criteria being selected, regardless of the folder in which they are stored.

When you display a Web page that includes an RSS newsfeed, an "RSS" icon appears in the browser's address bar, as shown in Figure 2-18. If you want to subscribe to the newsfeed, click the RSS icon. A New subscription dialog box opens and asks you to confirm your subscription. After you click the Yes button, Opera downloads the messages from the newsfeed and displays them on a new tab. To read a message, click the message header.

Figure 2-18 ▶ **Subscribing to an RSS newsfeed in Opera**

To view the newsfeeds to which you have subscribed, click Feeds on the menu bar, and then click Manage feeds. You can use the New, Add, Delete, and Edit buttons in the Subscribe to RSS newsfeeds dialog box to manage your subscriptions, including the frequency at which messages are downloaded. To view the individual messages sent by the newsfeed, double-click the newsfeed's name. The Mail bar opens so you can reply to, forward, and read the messages sent by the newsfeed using the same skills you would use to manage regular e-mail messages.

Web-Based E-Mail Services

Many Internet Web sites provide free e-mail addresses and accounts for registered users along with the capability to use any Web browser with Internet access to send and receive e-mail messages. Many people rely on Web-based e-mail as their primary e-mail address; others use Web-based e-mail accounts to set up a separate, personal address when their employer or other owner of their primary e-mail address restricts the use of personal e-mail. Some popular choices for free Web-based e-mail services are Yahoo! Mail, ExciteMail, and Hotmail. You can follow the links in the Free E-mail Services section of the Student Online Companion page for Tutorial 2 to learn more about these free e-mail services. Figure 2-19 shows a message composed using Hotmail.

Web-based e-mail message | Figure 2-19

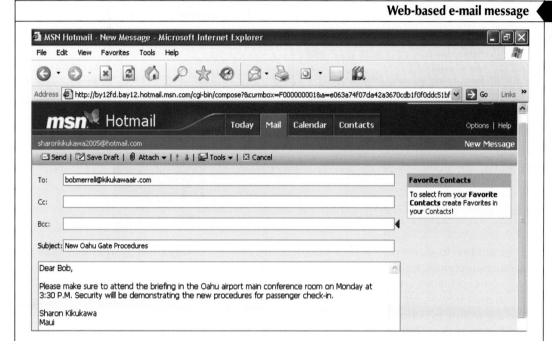

To get your free e-mail address, use your Web browser to visit the sponsor's Web site. After locating the link to the site's e-mail service, you will need to provide some basic information about yourself, such as your name, address, and phone number. Then you choose a user name and password. If the e-mail service verifies that your user name is available, it activates your account immediately. If the user name you selected is in use, the service will ask you to submit a new user name or change the one you chose slightly by adding additional characters to it. Web-based e-mail provides a way for people who do not have an account with an ISP to use e-mail in public libraries, businesses, and other places that provide connections to the Internet. You can use your Web-based e-mail service from anywhere in the world where there is an Internet connection. None of the messages that you send and receive are stored on the computer that you use; everything happens on the Web-based mail server. The e-mail messages you send and receive are protected by your password and function just like e-mail messages sent from an e-mail program running on a PC.

You might wonder how these companies can provide free e-mail—after all, nothing is free. The answer is advertising. When you use a Web-based mail service, you will see advertising, such as the links in the page shown in Figure 2-20. You will also see links to other services offered by the Web-based mail service. Figure 2-20 also includes links to sites that sell airline tickets and provide information on topics such as music, money, and the stock market.

Figure 2-20 ▷ **Ads shown in Hotmail**

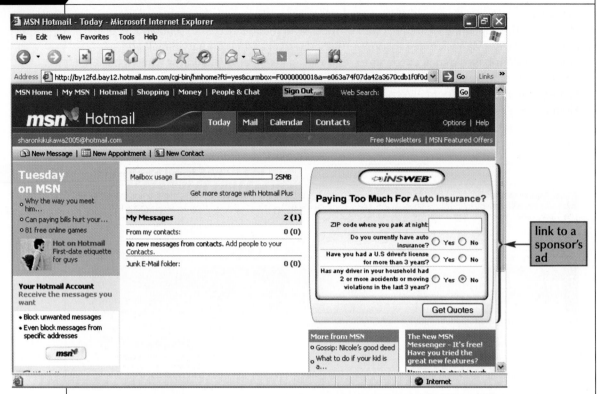

In addition to showing its account holders advertising messages and providing links to additional services, e-mail messages sent from Web-based mail accounts might also contain some sort of advertisement, such as a promotional message or a link to the Web-based mail service. Advertising revenues pay for free e-mail, so you must decide whether you are willing to endure some advertising in exchange for using the free e-mail service. Most users of these free services agree that seeing some ads is a small price to pay for the great convenience the free e-mail provides.

The only real drawback of Web-based e-mail services, other than having to view the advertising messages that pay for the free e-mail service, is that your mailbox size might be limited to a specified amount of file space in which to store your messages. Some Web-based e-mail services offer an option to purchase additional space for a small fee. Fortunately, most e-mail messages are small in file size. As long as you delete old messages and messages with large file attachments, you should be able to manage your free mailbox effectively.

Gmail from Google

When Google launched the test program for its new e-mail service, called **Gmail**, it received a lot of publicity from the media. At the time, Web-based e-mail providers such as Yahoo! and Hotmail had been gradually reducing the free storage space allotted to individual subscribers for e-mail messages from 50 megabytes to two to four megabytes in favor of "premium" services that included additional features and storage capacity for a monthly fee. After Gmail began testing its free e-mail system, which promises more than two gigabytes of storage space for every user, other online Web-based e-mail services had to change their offerings quickly to avoid losing their subscribers. Figure 2-21 shows the Gmail Inbox.

Google Gmail Inbox window ◄ | Figure 2-21

One of the initial concerns about Gmail was how Google planned to support it. The service is paid for by adding advertisements to e-mail messages based on searches of those messages. Ads are added to the user's messages based on predefined keywords included in the messages. Although there is no human intervention to produce the advertisements, some users have concerns about the privacy of the e-mail messages they receive because they are scanned and read by computers. Some people do not like the idea of seeing advertisements based on the content of the messages they send and receive because they see it as an invasion of privacy.

Another issue that concerns many users is how their messages are stored. With more than two gigabytes of storage space, you can save virtually every message you receive—in fact, Google actually encourages you to do so. Because Google performs routine maintenance on its servers, such as backups and archives, your messages might be stored forever in these files. Even if you delete your messages, they still might exist in these files, making your private messages part of a permanent archive. This same scenario applies to most free Web-based e-mail accounts, regardless of the provider.

As Google works to increase the number of participants in Gmail, other free Web-based e-mail services are expanding their current offerings. In addition, new services are popping up, such as ICQmail from ICQ. You can find links to Gmail and ICQmail on the Student Online Companion for Tutorial 2.

Regardless of which type of e-mail program you use, most e-mail programs have similar features and capabilities.

Web Logs

Web logs, or **blogs** for short, have been around for awhile but were catapulted into the mainstream media when political candidates for president started using them as a way to organize their supporters and provide a forum in which candidates could freely discuss campaign issues in an unfiltered way. Democratic presidential candidate Howard Dean was the first person to use a blog to organize a grassroots campaign that included public forums, candidate interviews, and ways to contribute to the campaign. Although Dean eventually lost the presidential nomination, his use of blogs and blog technology gained momentum for the remaining candidates. Both Democratic challenger Senator John Kerry and President George W. Bush used blogs to communicate with their core supporters and respond to stories in the media. Some blogs were not officially sponsored by the candidates themselves but were used as ways to support the candidates. Eventually, there were blogs of all kinds that were used as forums to advance or challenge much of what was being said about the candidates and their policies during the campaign.

Although blogs are a very popular and easy way to disseminate information, it is important to keep in mind that blogs are not subject to the same ethical guidelines of professional reporters, and that the information contained in any blog should always be regarded as personal opinion and not as "hard" news. After the fiasco of the 2000 presidential election, in which major television networks proclaimed victory for Vice President Al Gore in the state of Florida before all of the polls were closed in that state, the television networks were careful during election night for the 2004 presidential election to avoid "calling" a state or the election for one candidate until they were certain of the result. Networks were slower to call states for candidates because they were being careful not to make the same mistake of the 2000 presidential election. However, many bloggers were criticized after the 2004 presidential election for posting exit polls throughout the day and potentially swaying the outcome for the candidate that they supported. Around noon on Election Day, 2004, many of the most popular and widely read blogs were forecasting victory for Senator Kerry, but as the actual election results were reported by individual states later that evening, much of the information put forth by the blogs was proved to be inaccurate. Bloggers based their forecasts on exit polls that provided incorrect results because their samples were not representative of all voters. Mainstream media was concerned because the incorrect data provided and widely disseminated by the bloggers hurt the credibility of the media as a whole. Many people read the messages posted on the blogs, believed the information was true, and were unaware of the potential for error as a result of sampling errors. In addition, many of the blogs were slanted to represent a particular candidate, and they reported stories with that bias.

Although some blogs are blamed for the incorrect polling results during the 2004 presidential election, blogs are an important way of gathering public opinion. Prior to the election, CBS News reported a story questioning the legitimacy of President Bush's service in the Texas Air National Guard in the 1970s. The story was based on documents that many people believed to be forged. Bloggers responded to the story immediately—some even while the story was airing on CBS—to question the validity of the documents on which the story was based. In this case, the bloggers kept public pressure on the network to prove the validity of the documents, something that CBS News was ultimately unable to do. Although the blogs were extremely active in reporting the story, mainstream media outlets, which were subject to ethical guidelines for professional reporters and were more careful to report only verified facts, eventually picked up the stories being circulated in the blogs and reported them. Eventually, CBS News recanted its allegations. It was widely speculated in the media that blogs led the charge for the withdrawal of the story.

"You've Got Spam!"

Spam, also known as **unsolicited commercial e-mail (UCE)** or **bulk mail**, includes unwanted solicitations, advertisements, or e-mail chain letters sent to an e-mail address. For most Internet users, spam represents waste in terms of the time it takes to download, manage, and delete. Besides wasting people's time and their computers' disk space, spam can consume large amounts of Internet capacity. If one person sends a useless e-mail message to 100,000 people, that unsolicited message consumes Internet resources for a few moments that would otherwise be available to users with legitimate communication needs. Although spam has always been an annoyance, companies are increasingly finding it to be a major problem. In addition to consuming bandwidth on company networks and space on e-mail servers, spam distracts employees who are trying to do their jobs and requires them to spend time deleting unwanted messages. In addition, a considerable number of spam messages include content that is offensive to its recipients. Researchers estimate that the amount of spam received by the average company increased from approximately 1% in 1995 to a whopping 80% in the year 2005.

Many grassroots and corporate organizations have decided to fight spam aggressively. America Online, for example, has taken an active role in limiting spam through legal channels. Many companies now offer software that organizations can run on their e-mail servers to limit the amount of spam that is delivered to the organization's e-mail addresses. Although individual users can install client-based spam-filtering programs on their computers or set filters that might be available within their e-mail client software, most companies find it more effective and less costly to eliminate spam before it reaches users.

As spam has grown to become a serious problem for all e-mail users and providers, an increasing number of approaches have been devised or proposed to combat it. Some of these approaches require the passing of laws, and some require technical changes in the mail handling systems of the Internet. Other approaches can be implemented under existing laws and with current technologies, but only with the cooperation of many organizations and businesses.

Individuals can attempt to limit the amount of spam they receive by reducing the likelihood that a spammer can automatically generate their e-mail addresses. Many organizations create e-mail addresses for their employees by combining elements of each employee's first and last names. For example, small companies often combine the first letter of an employee's first name with the entire last name to generate e-mail addresses for all employees. Any spam sender able to obtain an employee list can generate long lists of potential e-mail addresses using the names on the list. If no employee list is available, the spammer can simply generate logical combinations of first initials and common names. The cost of sending e-mail messages is so low that a spammer can afford to send thousands of messages to randomly generated addresses in the hope that a few of them are valid.

A second way for individuals to reduce spam is to control the exposure of their e-mail addresses. Spammers use software robots to search the Internet for character strings that include the "@" character that appears in every e-mail address. These robots search Web pages, discussion boards, chat rooms, and other online sources that might contain e-mail addresses. Again, the spammer can afford to send thousands of messages to e-mail addresses gathered in this way. Even if only one or two people respond, the spammer can earn a profit because the cost of sending e-mail messages is so low.

Some individuals use multiple e-mail addresses to thwart spam. They use one address for display on a Web site, another to register for access to Web sites, another for shopping accounts, and so on. If a spammer starts using one of these addresses, the individual can stop using it and switch to another. Many Web hosting services include a large number (often 100–200) of e-mail addresses as part of their service, so this is a good tactic for people or small businesses with their own Web sites.

These three strategies focus on limiting spammer's access to, or use of, an e-mail address. Other approaches use one or more techniques that filter e-mail messages based on their contents. Many U.S. jurisdictions have passed laws that provide penalties for sending spam. In January, 2004, the U.S. CAN-SPAM law (the law's name is an acronym for "Controlling the Assault of Non-Solicited Pornography and Marketing") went into effect. Researchers who track the amount of spam noted a drop in the percentage of spam messages in February and March, 2004. A MessageLabs study tracked the drop from 62% in January to 59% in February and 53% in March. However, by April, the rate was back up to a new high, 68%. It appears that spammers slowed down their activities immediately after the effective date of CAN-SPAM to see if a broad federal prosecution effort would occur. When the threat did not materialize, the spammers went right back to work.

The CAN-SPAM law is the first U.S. federal government effort to legislate controls on spam. It regulates all e-mail messages sent for the primary purpose of advertising or promoting a commercial product or service, including messages that promote the content displayed at a Web site. The law's main provisions are that unsolicited e-mail messages must identify the sender, contain an accurate message subject and a notice that the message is an advertisement or solicitation, make it possible for the recipient to "opt out" of future mailings within 10 days of receipt of the request, include the sender's physical postal address, and prohibit the sender from selling or transferring an e-mail address with an opt out request to any other entity. Each violation of a provision of the law is subject to a fine of up to $11,000. Additional fines are assessed for those who violate one of these provisions and also harvest e-mail addresses from Web sites, send messages to randomly generated addresses, use automated tools to register for e-mail accounts that are subsequently used to send spam, and relay e-mail messages through a computer or network without the permission of the computer's or network's owner.

Few industry experts expect CAN-SPAM or similar laws to be effective in preventing spam on the Internet. After all, spammers have been violating existing deceptive advertising laws for years. Many spammers use e-mail servers located in countries that do not have (and that are unlikely to adopt) anti-spam laws. Enforcement is a problem, too. Spammers can move their operations from one server to another in minutes.

Some critics argue that any legal solution to the spam problem is likely to fail until the prosecution of spammers becomes cost-effective for governments. To become cost-effective, prosecutors must be able to identify spammers easily (to reduce the cost of bringing an action against them) and must have a greater likelihood of winning the cases they file (or must see a greater social benefit to winning). The best way to make spammers easier to find is to make changes in the e-mail transport mechanism in the Internet's infrastructure. To learn more about legislation geared to prevent spam, follow the links on the Student Online Companion page for Tutorial 2.

Now that you understand some basic information about e-mail and e-mail software, you are ready to start using your e-mail program. If you are using Microsoft Outlook Express, your instructor will assign Session 2.2; if you are using Hotmail, your instructor will assign Session 2.3.

Review

Session 2.1 Quick Check

1. The special rules governing how information is handled on the Internet are collectively called _____.
2. What are the three parts of an e-mail message?
3. True or False: On receipt, Bcc recipients of an e-mail message are aware of other Bcc recipients who received the same e-mail message.
4. Can you send a Word document over the Internet? If so, how?
5. What are the two parts of an e-mail address and what information do they provide?
6. Why is it important to delete e-mail messages that you no longer need?
7. What is a Saved Search folder and in which program is this feature available?
8. How do you identify that an RSS newsfeed is available when using Opera?

Session 2.2

Microsoft Outlook Express

Microsoft Outlook Express, or simply **Outlook Express**, is an e-mail program that you use to send and receive e-mail. Outlook Express is installed with Internet Explorer. (Microsoft Outlook, another e-mail program, is part of the Microsoft Office suite of programs. It lets you send and receive e-mail and do other tasks, such as manage a calendar.)

You are eager to begin your evaluation of e-mail software for Sharon. You start Outlook Express by using the Start menu. Figure 2-22 shows the Outlook Express Inbox window. You can customize Outlook Express in many ways by resizing, hiding, and displaying different windows and their individual elements, so your screen might look different from Figure 2-22.

Outlook Express Inbox window | Figure 2-22

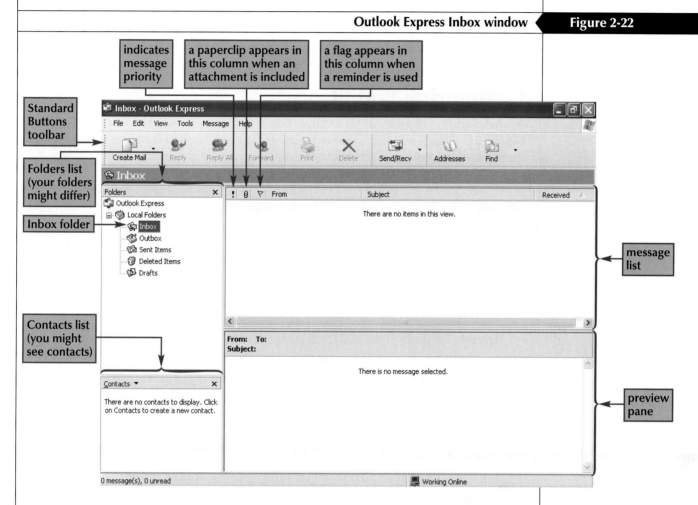

The Inbox window contains four panes: the Folders list, the Contacts list, the message list, and the preview pane. The **Folders list** displays a list of folders for receiving, saving, and deleting mail messages. You might see more folders than those shown in Figure 2-22, but you should see the five default folders. The **Inbox folder** stores messages you have received, the **Outbox folder** stores outgoing messages that have not been sent, the **Sent Items folder** stores copies of messages you have sent, the **Deleted Items folder** stores messages you have deleted, and the **Drafts folder** stores messages that you have written but have not sent. Your copy of Outlook Express might also contain folders you have created, such as a folder in which you store all messages from a certain recipient.

The **Contacts list**, which might be hidden, contains information about the addresses stored in your address book. You can click a contact in the Contacts list to address a new message quickly to an individual or group.

The **message list** contains summary information for each message that you receive. The first three columns on the left might display icons indicating information about the e-mail message. The first column indicates the message's priority; you might see an exclamation point to indicate a message with high priority; a blue arrow icon to indicate a message with low priority; or nothing, which indicates normal priority. The sender indicates a message's priority before sending it; most messages have no specified priority, in which case no icon will appear in the column. The second column displays a paperclip icon when a message includes an attachment. Finally, if you click the third column for a message you have received, a red flag will appear. You can use a flag to remind yourself to follow up on the message later.

The message list also displays the sender's name in the From column, the message's subject in the Subject column, and the date and time the message was received in the Received column. You can sort messages by clicking any column in the message list.

The message that is selected in the message list appears in the preview pane. The **preview pane** appears below the message list and displays the content of the selected message in the message list. You can use the horizontal scroll bar to scroll the message.

Configuring E-Mail

You are ready to get started using Outlook Express. These steps assume that Outlook Express 6 is already installed on your computer. First, you need to configure Outlook Express so it will retrieve your mail from your ISP.

To configure Outlook Express to manage your e-mail:

1. Click the **Start** button on the Windows taskbar, point to **All Programs**, and then click **Outlook Express** to start the program. Normally, you do not need to be connected to the Internet to configure Outlook Express; however, your system might be configured differently. If necessary, connect to the Internet.

   Trouble? If you cannot find the Outlook Express program on your computer, ask your instructor or technical support person for assistance.

   Trouble? If the Internet Connection Wizard starts, click the Cancel button.

   Trouble? If an Outlook Express dialog box opens and asks to make Outlook Express your default mail client, click the No button.

   Trouble? If an Outlook Express dialog box opens and asks to import information from another e-mail program installed on your computer, click the Cancel button.

2. If necessary, click the **Inbox** folder in the Folders list to select it.

3. Click **Tools** on the menu bar, click **Accounts**, and then if necessary, click the **Mail** tab in the Internet Accounts dialog box so you can set up your mail account settings.

   Trouble? If you have already set up your mail account (or if someone has set up an account for you), click the Close button in the Internet Accounts dialog box and skip this set of steps. If you are unsure about any existing account, ask your instructor or technical support person for help.

4. Click the **Add** button in the Internet Accounts dialog box, and then click **Mail**. The Internet Connection Wizard starts. You use this wizard to identify yourself, your user name, and the settings for your mail server. See Figure 2-23.

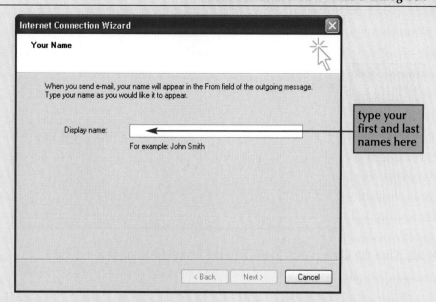

5. Type your first and last names in the Display name text box, and then click the **Next** button to open the next dialog box, in which you specify your e-mail address.

6. Type your full e-mail address (such as student@university.edu) in the E-mail address text box, and then click the **Next** button. The next dialog box asks you for your incoming and outgoing mail server names.

7. Type the names of your incoming and outgoing mail servers in the text boxes where indicated. Your instructor, technical support person, or ISP will provide this information to you. Usually, an incoming mail server name is POP, POP3, or IMAP followed by a host name. An outgoing mail server name usually is SMTP or MAIL followed by a host name. When you are finished, click the **Next** button to continue.

8. In the Account name text box, type your Internet mail user name, as supplied by your instructor, technical support person, or ISP. Make sure that you type only your user name and not your host name.

9. Press the **Tab** key to move the insertion point to the Password text box. To protect your password's identity, Outlook Express displays dots or asterisks in this text box instead of the characters you type. To prevent other users from being able to access your mail account, you will clear the Remember password check box. When you access your mail account, Outlook Express will prompt you for your password. If you are working on a computer to which you have sole access, you might want to set Outlook Express to remember your password, so you don't need to type it every time you access your e-mail.

10. If necessary, click the **Remember password** check box to clear it, and then click the **Next button**.

11. Click the **Finish** button to save the mail account information and close the Internet Connection Wizard. The Internet Accounts dialog box reappears, and your account is listed on the Mail tab. Figure 2-24 shows Sharon Kikukawa's information.

Figure 2-24	Mail account created for Sharon Kikukawa

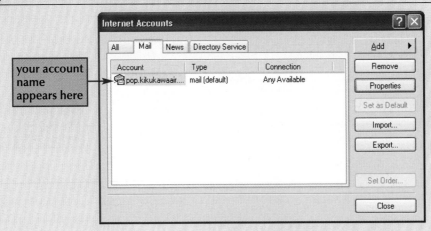

12. Click the **Close** button in the Internet Accounts dialog box to close it.

Now Outlook Express is configured to send and receive messages, so you are ready to send a message to Sharon. *Note:* In this tutorial, you will send messages to a real mailbox with the address sharonkikukawa@yahoo.com. Follow the instructions carefully and use the correct address. Messages sent to this mailbox are deleted without being opened or read.

Sending a Message Using Outlook Express

You are ready to use Outlook Express to send a message with an attached file to Sharon. Send a courtesy copy of the message to your own e-mail address to simulate receiving a message.

Sending a Message Using Outlook Express

- Click the Create Mail button on the toolbar to open the New Message window.
- In the To box, type the recipient's e-mail address. To send the message to more than one recipient, separate additional e-mail addresses with commas. If necessary, click View on the menu bar, and then click All Headers to display the Bcc box.
- Type the e-mail address of any Cc or Bcc recipients in the appropriate boxes. Separate multiple recipients' e-mail addresses with commas.
- If necessary, click the Attach button on the toolbar, in the Insert Attachment dialog box, browse to and select a file to attach to the message, and then click the Attach button.
- In the message body, type your message.
- Check your message for spelling and grammatical errors.
- Click the Send button on the toolbar.

To send a message with an attachment:

1. Make sure that the **Inbox** folder is selected in the Folders list, and then click the **Create Mail** button on the toolbar to open the New Message window. If necessary, click the **Maximize** button on the New Message window. See Figure 2-25. The New Message window contains its own menu bar, toolbar, message display area, and boxes in which you enter address and subject information. The insertion point is positioned in the To box when you open a new message.

New Message window ◀ **Figure 2-25**

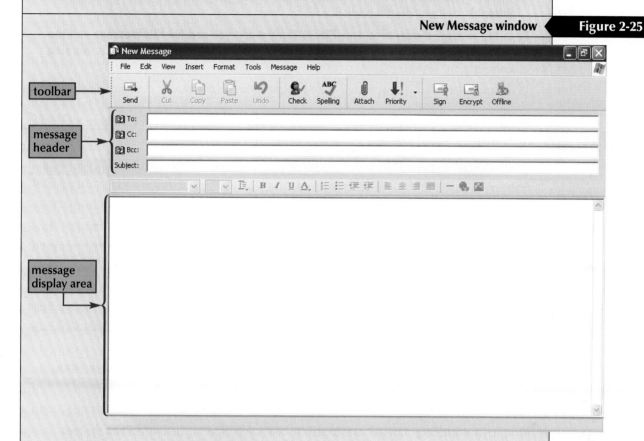

Trouble? If you do not see the Bcc box in the message header, click View on the menu bar, and then click All Headers.

2. In the To box, type **sharonkikukawa@yahoo.com**, and then press the **Tab** key to move to the Cc box.

    Trouble? Make sure that you use the address sharonkikukawa@yahoo.com. If you type Sharon's e-mail address incorrectly, your message will be returned as undeliverable.

3. Type your full e-mail address in the Cc box. When you send this message, you and Sharon will both receive it.

    Trouble? If you make a typing mistake on a previous line, use the arrow keys or click the insertion point to return to a previous line so you can correct your mistake. If the arrow keys do not move the insertion point backward or forward in the message header, press Shift + Tab or the Tab key to move backward or forward, respectively.

4. Press the **Tab** key twice to move the insertion point to the Subject box, and then type **Test**. Notice that the title bar now displays "Test" as the window title.

5. Click the **Attach** button on the toolbar. The Insert Attachment dialog box opens.

6. Click the **Look in** list arrow, and then navigate to the drive and folder that contains your Data Files.

7. Double-click the **Tutorial.02** folder, double-click the **Tutorial** folder, and then double-click **Physicals**. The Insert Attachment dialog box closes, and the attached file's icon, filename, and file size appear in the Attach box.

8. Click the insertion point in the message display area, type **Dear Sharon,** and then press the **Enter** key twice to insert a blank line.

9. In the message display area, type **Please reply when you receive this message and the attached file. I am testing Outlook Express and want to make sure that it is working correctly.**

10. Press the **Enter** key twice, and then type your first and last names to sign your message. See Figure 2-26.

Figure 2-26	Composing an e-mail message

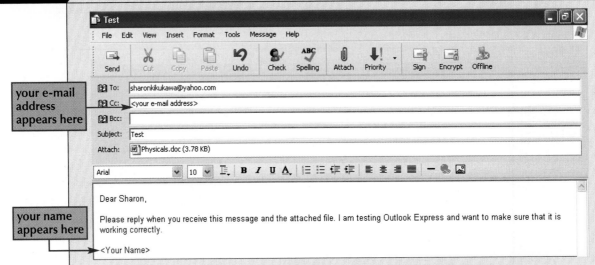

11. Click the **Spelling** button on the toolbar to check your spelling before sending the message. If necessary, correct any typing errors. When you are finished, click the **OK** button to close the Spelling dialog box.

12. Click the **Send** button on the toolbar to mail the message. The Test window closes and the message is stored in the Outbox folder, as indicated by the "(1)" in the Outbox folder.

    Trouble? If a Send Mail dialog box opens and tells you that the message will be sent the next time you click the Send/Recv button, click the OK button to continue.

    Trouble? If Outlook Express is configured to send messages when you click the Send button, you won't see the "(1)" in the Outbox folder. This difference causes no problems.

Depending on your system configuration, Outlook Express might not send your messages immediately. It might queue (hold) messages until you connect to your ISP or click the Send/Recv button on the toolbar. If you want to examine the setting and change it, click Tools on the menu bar, click Options, and then click the Send tab in the Options dialog box. If the Send messages immediately check box contains a check mark, then Outlook Express sends messages when you click the Send button on the toolbar. Otherwise, Outlook Express holds messages until you click the Send/Recv button.

Receiving and Reading a Message

When you receive new mail, messages that you haven't opened yet are displayed with a closed envelope icon next to them in the message list; messages that you have opened are displayed with an open envelope icon next to them. You check for new mail next.

Reference Window

Using Outlook Express to Send and Receive Messages

- If necessary, connect to your ISP.
- Click the Send/Recv button on the toolbar.

To check for incoming mail:

▶ 1. Click the **Send/Recv** button on the toolbar, type your password in the Password text box of the Logon dialog box (if necessary), and then click the **OK** button. Depending on your system configuration, you might not need to connect to your ISP and type your password to retrieve your messages. Within a few moments, your mail server transfers all new mail to your Inbox. The Test message was sent to Sharon and also to your e-mail address, which you typed in the Cc box. Notice that the Inbox folder in the Folders list is bold, but other folders are not. A bold folder indicates that it contains unread mail; the number in parentheses next to the Inbox folder indicates the number of messages you received.

Trouble? If an Outlook Express message box opens and indicates that it could not find your host, click the Hide button to close the message box, click Tools on the menu bar, click Accounts, and then click the Properties button. Verify that your incoming and outgoing server names are correct, and then repeat Step 1. If you still have problems, ask your instructor or technical support person for help.

Trouble? If you do not see any messages in your Inbox, then you either did not receive any new mail or you might be looking in the wrong folder. If necessary, click the Inbox folder in the Folders list. If you still don't have any mail messages, wait a few moments, and then repeat Step 1 until you receive a message.

▶ 2. If necessary, click the **Test** message in the message list to open the message in the preview pane. See Figure 2-27.

Figure 2-27	Receiving an e-mail message

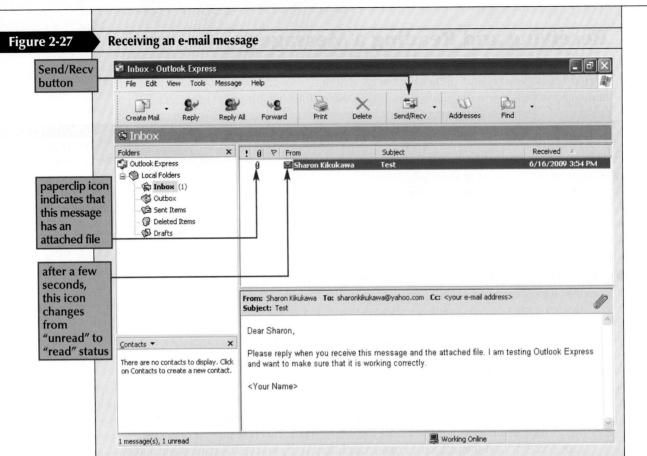

You received your copy of the message that you sent to Sharon. The paperclip icon indicates the message has an attachment. When you receive a message with one or more attachments, you can open the attachment or save it.

Viewing and Saving an Attached File

You want to make sure that your attached file was sent properly, so you decide to open it. Then you will save the file.

Reference Window	**Viewing and Saving an Attached File in Outlook Express**

- Click the message that contains the attached file in the message list to display its contents in the preview pane.
- Click the paperclip icon in the preview pane to open the shortcut menu, and then click the attached file's name. Close the program window that opens after viewing the file.
- Click the paperclip icon in the preview pane to open the shortcut menu, and then click Save Attachments.
- Click the file to save or click the Select All button to save all attached files, click the Browse button, and then change to the drive and folder in which to save the attached file(s).
- Click the Save button.

To view and save the attached file:

1. Make sure that the **Test** message is selected in the message list.
2. Click the **paperclip icon** in the upper-right corner of the preview pane to open the shortcut menu. See Figure 2-28.

Viewing an attached file | Figure 2-28

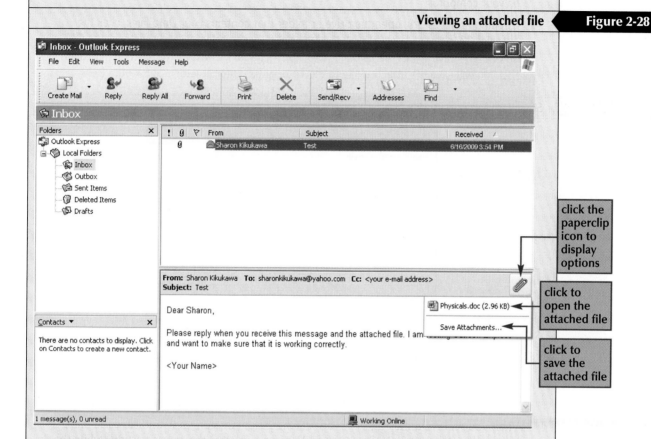

click the paperclip icon to display options

click to open the attached file

click to save the attached file

Trouble? If the options on the shortcut menu are dimmed, then Outlook Express is configured to remove all potentially unsafe attachments from messages. Click the paperclip icon to close the menu. If you are working in a public computer lab, ask your instructor or technical support person for help. If you are working on a private computer, click Tools on the menu bar, click Options, click the Security tab, and then clear the "Do not allow attachments to be saved or opened that could potentially be a virus." check box. Click the OK button to close the Options dialog box, and then recompose, send, and receive the Test message. It is strongly suggested that you install and configure antivirus software when disabling this option to protect your computer from viruses.

The shortcut menu shows that a file named Physicals.doc, with a file size of approximately 3 KB, is attached to the message. If this message contained other attachments, they would also appear on the shortcut menu. Clicking Physicals.doc starts a program on your computer that can open the file. Clicking Save Attachments lets you save the file to the drive and folder that you specify.

3. Click **Physicals.doc** on the shortcut menu. Microsoft Word or another word-processing program on your computer starts and opens the attached file. If necessary, maximize the program window that opens.

Trouble? If an Open Attachment Warning dialog box opens warning you that the file might contain viruses, click the Open it option button, and then click the OK button.

4. Click the **Close** button on the program window. Now that you have viewed the attachment, you can save it.

5. Click the **paperclip icon** in the preview pane, and then click **Save Attachments** on the shortcut menu. The Save Attachments dialog box opens. The Physicals.doc file is already selected for you.

6. Click the **Browse** button. The Browse for Folder dialog box opens and lists all of the drives on your computer.

7. Scrolling as necessary, open the drive or folder that contains your Data Files, click the **Tutorial.02** folder to open it, click the **Tutorial** folder to select it, and then click the **OK** button. The Save Attachments dialog box appears again. The Save To location indicates that you will save the attached file to the Tutorial.02\Tutorial folder. See Figure 2-29.

| Figure 2-29 | Save Attachments dialog box |

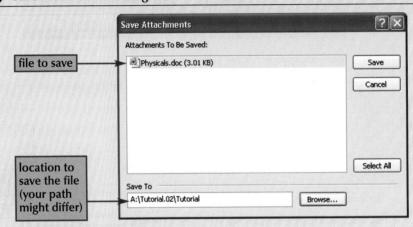

8. Click the **Save** button to save the attached file, and then click the **Yes** button to overwrite the file with the same name on your Data Disk.

When you receive a message with an attached file, you can view and save the attachment for as long as you store the message. When you delete the message, you delete the file attached to the message. When you detach a file from an e-mail message and save it on a disk or drive, it is just like any other file that you save.

Replying to and Forwarding Messages

You can forward any message you receive to one or more e-mail addresses. Similarly, you can respond to the sender of a message quickly and efficiently by replying to a message.

Replying to an E-Mail Message

To reply to a message, select the message in the message list, and then click the Reply button on the toolbar to reply only to the sender, or click the Reply All button to reply to the sender and other people who received the original message (those e-mail addresses listed in the To and Cc boxes). Outlook Express will open a new "Re:" message window and place the original sender's address in the To box; if you clicked the Reply All button, then other e-mail addresses that received the original message will appear in the To and Cc boxes as appropriate. You can leave the Subject box as is or modify it. Most e-mail programs, including Outlook Express, will copy the original message and place it in the message body. Usually, a special mark to the left of the response indicates a quote from the text of the original message. Figure 2-30 shows a reply to the Test message.

Replying to a message ◀ **Figure 2-30**

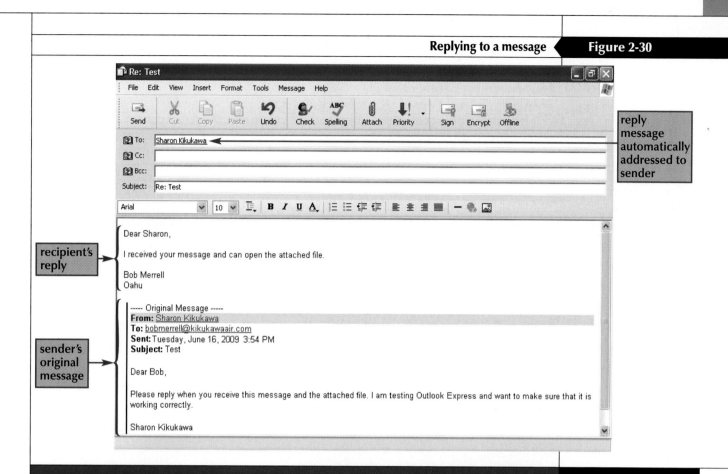

recipient's reply

sender's original message

reply message automatically addressed to sender

Replying to a Message Using Outlook Express

Reference Window

- Click the message in the message list to which you want to reply.
- Click the Reply button on the toolbar to reply only to the sender, or click the Reply All button on the toolbar to reply to the sender and other "To" and "Cc" recipients of the original message.
- Type other recipients' e-mail addresses in the message header as needed.
- Change the text in the Subject box as necessary.
- Edit the message body as necessary.
- Click the Send button on the toolbar.

Forwarding an E-Mail Message

When you forward a message, you are sending a copy of your message, including any attachments, to one or more recipients who were not included in the original message. (If you do not want to forward the original sender's attached file to the new recipients, select the attachment filename in the Attach line, and then press the Delete key.) To forward an existing mail message to another user, open the folder containing the message you want to forward, select it in the message list, and then click the Forward button on the toolbar. The "Fw:" window opens, where you can type the address of the recipient in the To box. If you want to forward the message to several people, type their addresses, separated by commas (or semicolons), in the To box (or Cc or Bcc boxes). Outlook Express inserts a copy of the original message in the message display area (as it does when you reply to a message). However, no special mark appears in the left margin to indicate the original message. Figure 2-31 shows a forwarded copy of the Test message.

Figure 2-31 ▷ **Fowarding a message**

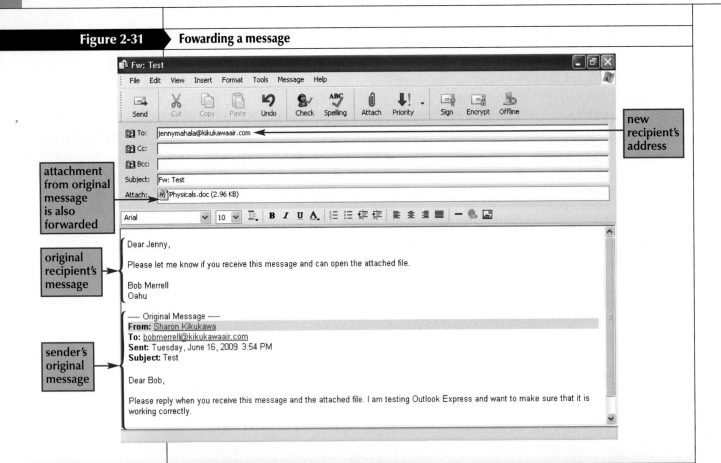

Reference Window

Forwarding an E-Mail Message Using Outlook Express

- Click the message in the message list that you want to forward.
- Click the Forward button on the toolbar to open the "Fw:" window, which contains a copy of the original message.
- Click the To box, and then type one or more e-mail addresses, separated by commas.
- Click the blank line above the quoted message, and then type an optional message to add a context for the recipient(s).
- Click the Send button on the toolbar.

Occasionally, you receive important messages, so you want to make sure that you can file and print them as needed.

Filing and Printing an E-Mail Message

You can use the Outlook Express mail folders to file your e-mail messages by topic or category. When you file a message, you move it from the Inbox to another folder. You can also make a *copy* of a message in the Inbox and save it in another folder by right-clicking the message in the message list, clicking Copy to Folder on the shortcut menu, and then selecting the folder in which to store the copy. You file Sharon's message in a new folder named "FAA" for safekeeping. Later, you can create other folders to suit your style and working situation.

To create a new folder:

1. Right-click the **Inbox** folder in the Folders list to open the shortcut menu, and then click **New Folder**. The Create Folder dialog box opens. When you create a new folder, first you must select the folder at the level above which to create the new folder. Because the Inbox folder is selected, the new folder that you create is a subfolder of the Inbox folder.

2. Type **FAA** in the Folder name text box. See Figure 2-32.

Creating a new folder | **Figure 2-32**

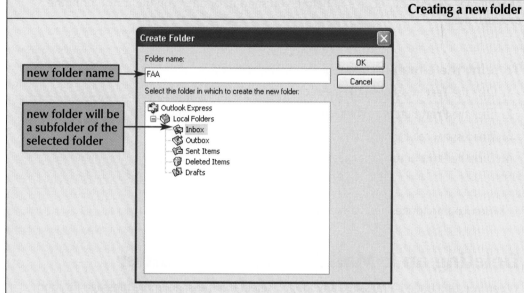

3. Click the **OK** button to create the new folder and close the Create Folder dialog box. The FAA folder appears in the Folders list as a subfolder of the Inbox folder.

After you create the FAA folder, you can transfer messages to it. Besides copying or transferring mail from the Inbox folder, you can select messages in any other folder and then transfer them to another folder.

To file the Test message:

1. Click the **Test** message in the message list to select it.

2. Drag the **Test** message from the message list to the FAA folder in the Folders list. See Figure 2-33.

Filing a message | **Figure 2-33**

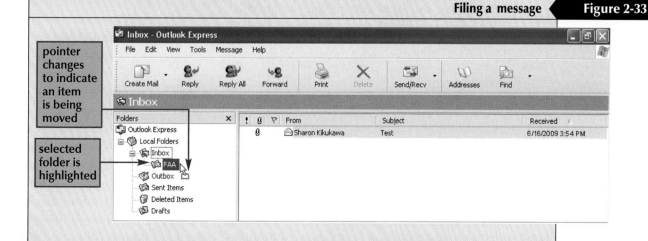

3. When the FAA folder is selected, release the mouse button. The Test message is now stored in the FAA folder.

4. Click the **FAA** folder in the Folders list to display its contents. The Test message appears in the FAA folder.

You might want to print certain messages for future reference. You can print a message at any time—when you receive it, before you send it, or after you file it. You print the message next.

To print the e-mail message:

1. Click the **Test** message in the message list to select it.

2. Click the **Print** button on the toolbar. The Print dialog box opens.

3. If necessary, select your printer in the list of printers.

4. Click the **Print** button. The message is printed.

When you no longer need a message, you can delete it.

Deleting an E-Mail Message and Folder

When you don't need a message any longer, select the message in the message list, and then click the Delete button on the toolbar. You can select multiple messages by pressing and holding the Ctrl key, clicking each message in the message list, and then releasing the Ctrl key. When you click the Delete button on the toolbar, each selected message is deleted. You can select folders and delete them using the same process. When you delete a message or a folder, you are really moving it to the Deleted Items folder. To remove items permanently, use the same process to delete the items from the Deleted Items folder. If you are using a public PC in a university computer lab, it is always a good idea to delete all of your messages from the Inbox and then to delete them again from the Deleted Items folder when you finish your session. Otherwise, the next person who uses Outlook Express will be able to access and read your messages.

Reference Window	**Deleting an E-Mail Message or a Folder in Outlook Express**

- Click the message you want to delete in the message list. If you are deleting a folder, click the folder in the Folders list that you want to delete.
- Click the Delete button on the toolbar.
- To delete items permanently, click the Deleted Items folder to open it, select the message(s) or folder(s) that you want to delete permanently, click the Delete button on the toolbar, and then click the Yes button.

or

- Right-click the Deleted Items folder to open the shortcut menu, click Empty 'Deleted Items' Folder, and then click the Yes button.

To delete the message:

▶ 1. If necessary, select the **Test** message in the message list.

▶ 2. Click the **Delete** button on the toolbar. The message is deleted from the FAA folder and is moved to the Deleted Items folder.

▶ 3. Click the **Deleted Items** folder in the Folder list to display its contents.

▶ 4. Click the **Test** message to select it, and then click the **Delete** button on the toolbar. A dialog box opens and asks you to confirm the deletion. See Figure 2-34.

Deleting a message ◀ **Figure 2-34**

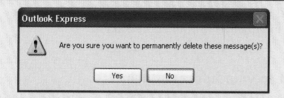

▶ 5. Click the **Yes** button. The Test message is deleted from the Deleted Items folder.

To delete the FAA folder, you follow the same process.

To delete the FAA folder:

▶ 1. Click the **FAA** folder in the Folders list to select it. Because this folder doesn't contain any messages, the message list is empty.

▶ 2. Click the **Delete** button on the toolbar. A dialog box opens and asks you to confirm moving the folder to the Deleted Items folder.

▶ 3. Click the **Yes** button. The FAA folder moves to the Deleted Items folder. The Deleted Items folder has a plus box to its left, indicating that this folder contains another folder.

▶ 4. Click the **plus box** to the left of the Deleted Items folder, and then click the **FAA** folder to select it.

▶ 5. Click the **Delete** button on the toolbar, and then click the **Yes** button in the message box to delete the FAA folder permanently.

▶ 6. Click the **Inbox** folder in the Folders list to return to the Inbox.

Maintaining an Address Book

As you use e-mail to communicate with business associates and friends, you might want to save their addresses in an address book to make it easier to enter addresses into the header of your e-mail messages.

Adding a Contact to the Address Book

You can open the Outlook Express address book by clicking the Addresses button on the toolbar. To create a new address, open the address book, click the New button on the toolbar, click New Contact from the drop-down list, and then enter information into the Properties dialog box for that contact. On the Name tab, you can enter a contact's name and e-mail address; use the other tabs to enter optional address, business, personal, and other information about that contact. If you enter a short name in the Nickname text box, then you can type the nickname instead of a person's full name when you address a new message.

Reference Window

Adding a Contact to the Outlook Express Address Book

- Click the Addresses button on the toolbar.
- In the Address Book window, click the New button on the toolbar, and then click New Contact.
- On the Name tab of the Properties dialog box, enter the contact's name and e-mail address. Use the other tabs in the Properties dialog box as necessary to enter other information about the contact.
- Click the OK button to add the contact to the address book.
- Click the Close button.

Now you can add information to your address book. You begin by adding Sharon Kikukawa's contact information to your address book.

To add a contact to your address book:

1. Click the **Addresses** button on the toolbar. The Address Book window opens. If necessary, maximize the Address Book window.

2. Click the **New** button on the toolbar, and then click **New Contact**. The Properties dialog box opens with the insertion point positioned in the First text box on the Name tab.

3. Type **Sharon** in the First text box. As you type the contact's first name (and eventually the last name), the name of the Properties dialog box changes to indicate that the properties set in this dialog box belong to the specified contact.

4. Press the **Tab** key twice to move the insertion point to the Last text box, type **Kikukawa** in the Last text box, and then press the **Tab** key three times to move the insertion point to the Nickname text box.

5. Type **Sharon** in the Nickname text box, and then press the **Tab** key to move the insertion point to the E-mail Addresses text box.

6. Type **sharonkikukawa@yahoo.com** in the E-mail Addresses text box, and then click the **Add** button. Sharon's contact is complete. See Figure 2-35.

Figure 2-35 | Adding a contact to the address book

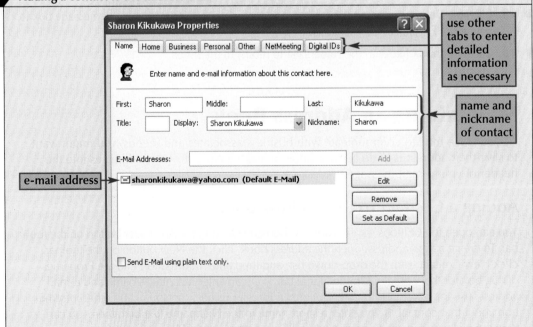

7. Click the **OK** button. The Properties dialog box closes and you return to the Address Book window. Sharon's contact now appears in the Address Book window.

8. Repeat Steps 2 through 7 to create new contacts for the following Kikukawa Air employees:

First	Last	Nickname	E-mail Address
Zane	**Norcia**	**Zane**	**zanenorcia@kikukawaair.com**
Jenny	**Mahala**	**Jen**	**jennymahala@kikukawaair.com**
Richard	**Forrester**	**Rich**	**richardforrester@kikukawaair.com**

9. When you are finished entering the contacts, click the **Close** button on the Address Book window title bar to close it. Now the Contacts list shows the entries you just added to your address book.

Now that these e-mail addresses are stored in the address book, when you start typing the first few letters of a nickname or first name, Outlook Express will complete the entry for you. Clicking the Check button on the toolbar in the New Message window changes the names you typed to their matching entries in the address book. If you need to change an address, click to select it and then press the Delete key.

When you receive mail from someone who is not in your address book, double-click the message to open it, right-click the "From" name to open the shortcut menu, and then click Add to Address Book. This process adds the sender's name and e-mail address to your address book, where you can open his or her information as a contact and edit and add information as necessary.

Adding a Group of Contacts to the Address Book

You can use Outlook Express to create a group. Usually you create a group of contacts when you regularly send messages to a group of people.

For example, Sharon frequently sends messages to Zane, Jen, and Rich as a group because they have the same positions at the Kikukawa Air ticket counters. She asks you to create a group of contacts in her address book so she can type one nickname for the group of e-mail addresses, instead of having to type each address separately.

Adding a Group of Contacts to the Address Book	Reference Window

- Click the Addresses button on the toolbar.
- In the Address Book window, click the New button on the toolbar, and then click New Group.
- In the Properties dialog box, type a nickname for the group in the Group Name text box.
- Click the Select Members button to open the Select Group Members dialog box.
- Click a name in the left list box to add to the group, and then click the Select button. Continue adding names to the group until you have selected all group members.
- Click the OK button twice.

To add a group of contacts to your address book:

1. Click the **Addresses** button on the toolbar, and then, if necessary, maximize the Address Book window.

2. Click the **New** button on the toolbar, and then click **New Group**. The Properties dialog box opens and displays tabs related to group settings.

3. With the insertion point positioned in the Group Name text box, type **Ticket Agents**. This nickname will represent the individual e-mail addresses for employees working in this position.

4. Click the **Select Members** button. The Select Group Members window opens, with existing contacts appearing in a list box on the left side of the window.

5. Click **Jenny Mahala** in the left list box, and then click the **Select** button. A copy of Jenny's contact is added to the Members list box.

6. Repeat Step 5 to add the contacts for **Richard Forrester** and **Zane Norcia** to the group. Figure 2-36 shows the completed group.

Figure 2-36	Creating a group of contacts

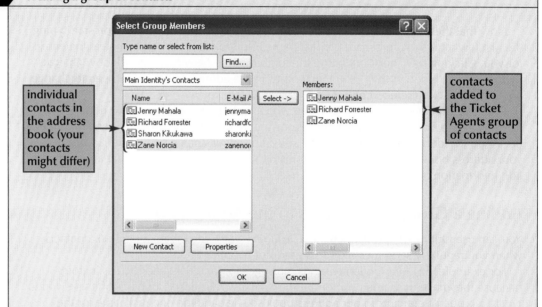

7. Click the **OK** button to close the Select Group Members dialog box. The Properties dialog box for the Ticket Agents group contains three group members.

8. Click the **OK** button to close the Ticket Agents Properties dialog box. The nickname of the new group, Ticket Agents, appears in the address book in the left pane of the window and the members of the group are listed in the right pane.

9. Close the Address Book window by clicking the **Close** button on its title bar. The Ticket Agents group appears in the Contacts list.

Now, test the new group of contacts by creating a new message.

To address a message to a group of contacts and close Outlook Express:

1. Click the **Create Mail** button on the toolbar. The New Message window opens.

2. Type **Ticket Agents** in the To box. As you type the first two or three letters, Outlook Express might complete your entry for you by selecting the Ticket Agents group.

3. Press the **Tab** key.

4. Click the **Check** button on the toolbar, right-click **Ticket Agents** in the To box to open the shortcut menu, and then click **Properties**. The Properties dialog box shows the three group members who will receive messages sent to the Ticket Agents group. Now, when Sharon sends mail to the ticket agents, she can type the group name "Ticket Agents" in any of a message's boxes (To, Cc, or Bcc) instead of typing each address individually.

5. Click the **OK** button to close the Ticket Agent Properties dialog box, click the **Close** button on the New Message window title bar, and then click the **No** button to close the message without saving it.

6. Click **File** on the menu bar, and then click **Exit**. Outlook Express closes.

When you need to modify a group's members, you can delete one or more members from the group by opening the address book, double-clicking the group name, and then deleting a selected member's name by clicking the Remove button. Similarly, you can add members using the group's Properties dialog box.

In this session, you have learned how to use Outlook Express to create, send, receive, and manage e-mail messages. You have also learned how to create and use an address book to manage e-mail addresses.

Session 2.2 Quick Check

Review

1. The folder that stores messages you have written but have not yet sent is the _____ folder.
2. True or False: You can set Outlook Express so it remembers your Internet account password.
3. What happens when Outlook Express queues a message?
4. When you receive a message with an attachment, what two options are available for the attached file?
5. When you delete a message from the Inbox folder, can you recover that message? Why or why not?
6. What information can you store about a person you have added as a contact?

If your instructor assigned Session 2.3, continue reading. Otherwise, complete the Review Assignments at the end of this tutorial.

Session 2.3

Hotmail

Hotmail is a Web-based e-mail service powered by MSN.com that you use to send and receive e-mail. To use Hotmail, you must use a Web browser to connect to the Hotmail Web site, where you create and sign in to an account to retrieve and send e-mail messages.

Most people who use Hotmail and other Web-based e-mail services have Internet access from their employer, school, public library, or friend. The Hotmail service is free, but you must have a way to access it using a Web browser and an existing Internet connection, which someone else might supply for you. Many public and school libraries provide free Internet access where you can access your Hotmail account. No matter where you are in the world, if you can connect to the Internet, you can access your Hotmail account. This portability makes Web-based e-mail a valuable resource for people who travel or do not have a computer or other device on which to use e-mail.

You are eager to begin your evaluation of e-mail services for Sharon. To begin using Hotmail, you need to use your Web browser to connect to the Hotmail Web site. Then create a user account and send and receive messages.

Creating a Hotmail Account

The steps in this session assume that you have a Web browser and can make an Internet connection. Before you can use Hotmail, you need to establish a user account. A user account establishes your name and Hotmail e-mail address so that you can use Hotmail to send and receive e-mail messages.

To begin setting up a Hotmail user account:

1. Start your Web browser, open the Student Online Companion page at **www.course.com/newperspectives/internet6**, click the **Tutorial 2** link, click the **Session 2.3** link, and then click the **Hotmail** link. The sign-in page for Hotmail opens in your browser. See Figure 2-37.

| Figure 2-37 | Hotmail Sign In page |

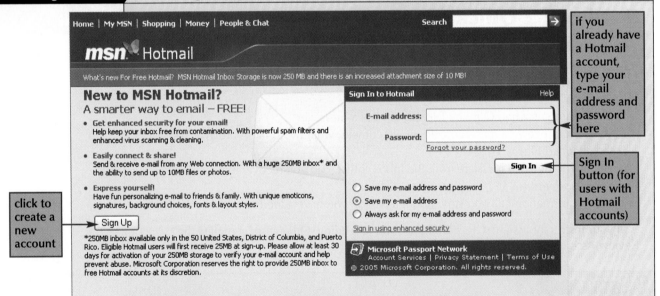

Trouble? The Hotmail sign-in page and other Hotmail pages might change over time. Check the Student Online Companion page for Tutorial 2 for notes about any differences you might encounter.

Trouble? You must have an Internet connection to set up a Hotmail user account. If you cannot connect to the Internet, ask your instructor or technical support person for help.

Trouble? If you already have a Hotmail account, use the Sign In page to log on to your account, and then skip this set of steps.

2. Click the **Sign Up** button. (If you do not see a Sign Up button, Hotmail may have redesigned the Web site. Examine the page carefully until you find the button or tab that lets you create a Hotmail account.)

The MSN Hotmail Plans page shown in Figure 2-38 opens (this page will change over time). Currently, Hotmail offers three types of accounts: free, Hotmail Plus, and Outlook Live. You will create a free account.

MSN Hotmail Plans page ◄ **Figure 2-38**

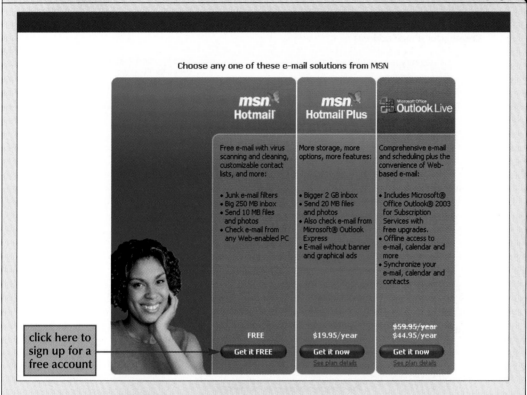

3. Click the **Get it FREE** button (or the button that lets you create a free Hotmail account). The Hotmail Sign Up page shown in Figure 2-39 opens.

   Trouble? If Hotmail discontinues its free e-mail service, use the links in the E-Mail Services section of the Student Online Companion page for Tutorial 2 to activate an e-mail account with another provider.

   Trouble? If a Security Alert dialog box opens, click the OK button to close it.

Figure 2-39	Hotmail Sign Up page

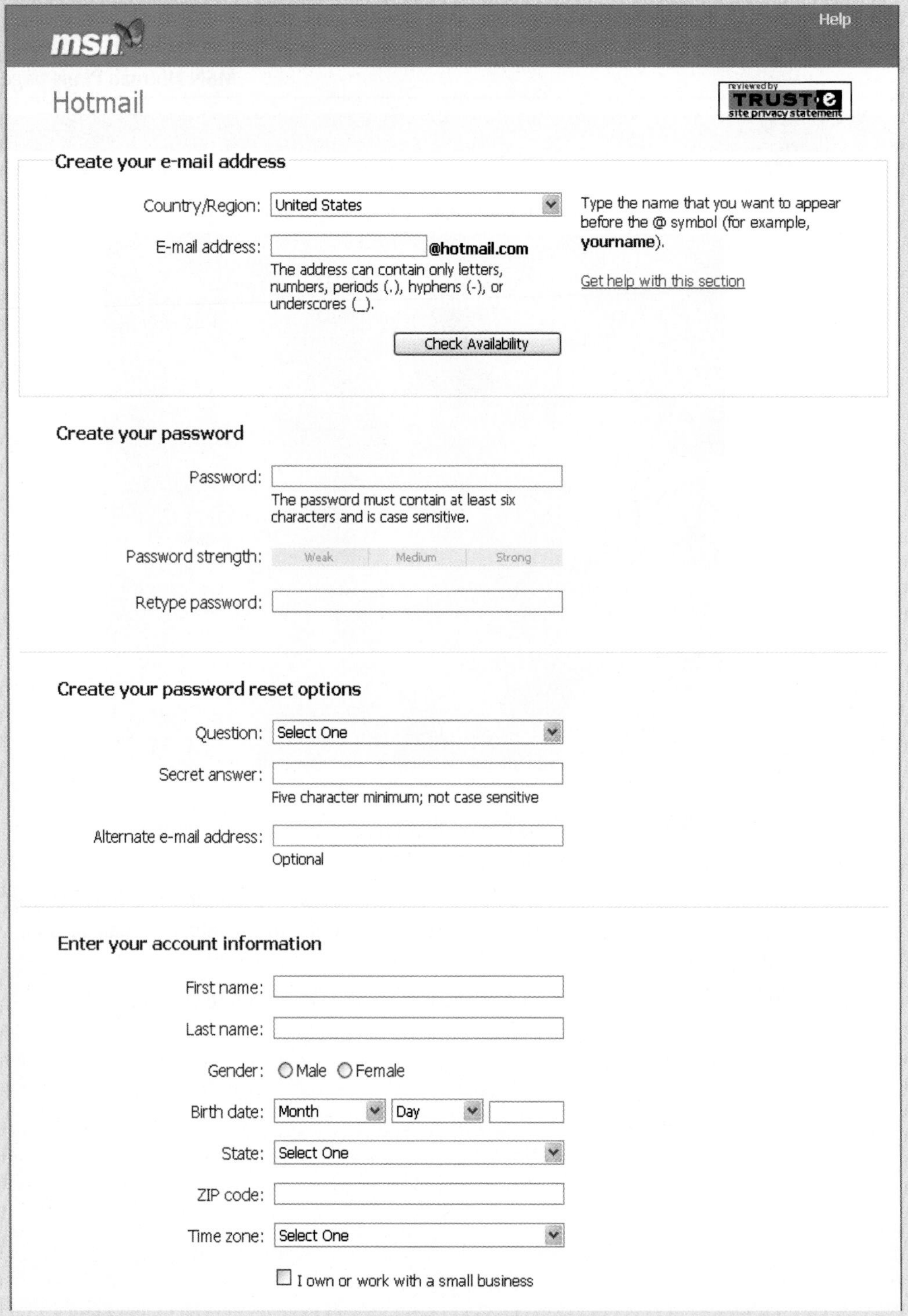

Trouble? The Hotmail Sign Up page might change over time. If your page looks different, follow the on-screen instructions to create a Hotmail account.

4. In the Create your e-mail address section, use the **Country/Region** list arrow to select the country in which you live. The default setting is United States.

Now that you have provided some information to Hotmail, you need to create your user name (Hotmail also calls this a sign-in name, an e-mail address, or a Passport), which will be your Hotmail e-mail address. Your user name must begin with a letter. A user name can contain letters, numbers, or underscore characters (_), but it cannot contain any spaces. After creating a user name, you must create a password containing letters and/or numbers, but no spaces. You type your password twice to ensure that you entered it correctly. Finally, to help remember your password in the event that you forget it, you enter a secret question and its answer so Hotmail can verify your identity in the future, as necessary.

To create a Hotmail e-mail address:

1. Click the **E-mail address** text box, and then type a user name. You can use any name you like, but it must be unique. You can try your first and last name, separated by an underscore character, followed optionally by your birth date or year of birth, such as sharon_kikukawa0922. Hotmail addresses can contain only letters, numbers, periods, hyphens, and underscores.

   Trouble? If you need help creating a user name, click the link on the page to get help.

2. Click the **Check Availability** button to see if the user name you selected is available. A message appears that tells you whether the e-mail address you selected is available. If it is not, try a different address until you find one.

   Trouble? Do not continue to Step 3 until you find an available Hotmail e-mail address.

3. Scroll down the page and type a password with at least six characters in the Password text box. The most effective passwords are ones that are not easily guessed and that contain letters and numbers. As you type your password, dots or asterisks appear in the Password text box to protect your password from being seen by other users. In addition, the Password strength indicator analyzes the password you typed to identify its strength. A weak password is one that contains only letters, such as "pencil." A stronger password includes letters and numbers, such as "pencil87." The strongest password is one that does not form a word and that includes mixed-case letters, numbers, and special characters, such as "p2nc1L%."

4. Press the **Tab** key to move to the Retype password text box, and then type your password again. Make sure to type the exact same password.

5. Click the **Question** list arrow, and then select a secret question.

6. Press the **Tab** key, and then type the answer to your question. Your answer must contain at least five characters.

7. Press the **Tab** key, and then type an alternate e-mail address if you have one. This is the e-mail address that Hotmail will send your password to in case you forget it. (If you do not have an alternate e-mail address, you can skip this step.)

Now that you have created a Hotmail e-mail address and a password, you need to enter your account information.

To enter your account information:

1. Click in the **First name** text box, type your first name, press the **Tab** key to move to the Last name text box, and then type your last name. Your first and last names will appear in all Hotmail e-mail messages that you send.

2. Click the **option** button in the Gender section to indicate your gender.

3. Use the **Month** and **Day** list arrows to indicate the month and date of your birth, click the **text box** to the right of the Day list box, and then type the four-digit year of your birth.

4. If you live in the United States, click the **State** list arrow, and then click the state in which you live.

5. Click the **ZIP code** text box, and then type your zip code. Hotmail will use this information to provide you with additional services, such as local weather forecasts, that you might request in the future.

6. If necessary, click the **Time zone** list arrow, and then click the time zone in which you live. Hotmail will use this setting to provide accurate date and time information in your e-mail messages.

The last part of creating a Hotmail e-mail address is to prove to Hotmail that you are a person and not an automated program, and also to read and accept the agreements that govern the use of a Hotmail account.

To finish creating a Hotmail e-mail address:

1. Scroll down the page so that you see the characters in the picture. See Figure 2-40.

Figure 2-40 | **Registration check**

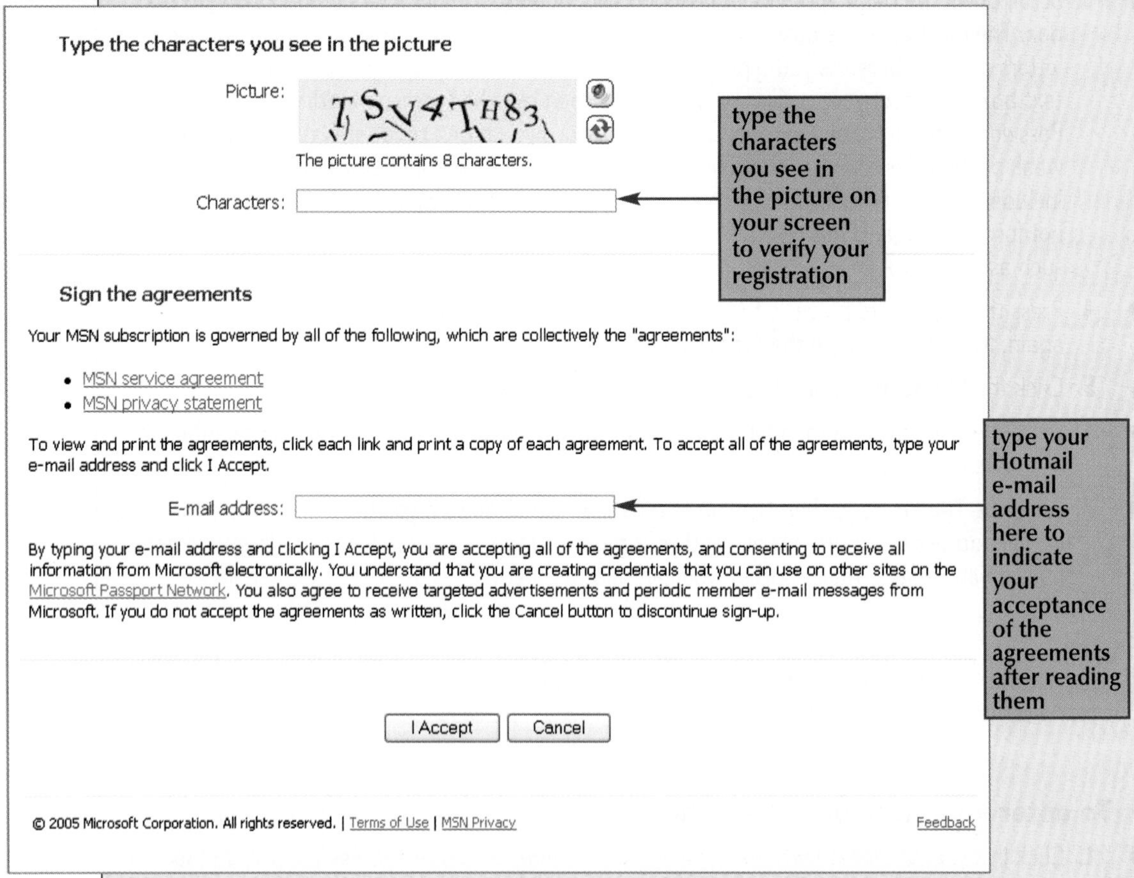

Type the characters you see in the picture

Picture: *J S V 4 T H 8 3*

The picture contains 8 characters.

Characters: [ ]

type the characters you see in the picture on your screen to verify your registration

Sign the agreements

Your MSN subscription is governed by all of the following, which are collectively the "agreements":

- MSN service agreement
- MSN privacy statement

To view and print the agreements, click each link and print a copy of each agreement. To accept all of the agreements, type your e-mail address and click I Accept.

E-mail address: [ ]

type your Hotmail e-mail address here to indicate your acceptance of the agreements after reading them

By typing your e-mail address and clicking I Accept, you are accepting all of the agreements, and consenting to receive all information from Microsoft electronically. You understand that you are creating credentials that you can use on other sites on the Microsoft Passport Network. You also agree to receive targeted advertisements and periodic member e-mail messages from Microsoft. If you do not accept the agreements as written, click the Cancel button to discontinue sign-up.

[I Accept]   [Cancel]

© 2005 Microsoft Corporation. All rights reserved. | Terms of Use | MSN Privacy   Feedback

2. Click in the **Characters** text box, and then type the characters you see in the picture. Make sure to type letters in the same case as the ones shown in the picture. (Do not type the characters you see in Figure 2-40.) This process ensures that a person is creating a Hotmail e-mail address, instead of an automated program. The registration check protects Hotmail users from service delays and from receiving junk e-mail messages.

3. Read the agreements, which appear as hyperlinks in the "Sign the agreements" section. After reading these agreements, type your Hotmail e-mail address in the text box, and scroll down and click the **I Accept** button. Your registration is complete when the page shown in Figure 2-41 opens.

Confirmation of Hotmail e-mail account | Figure 2-41

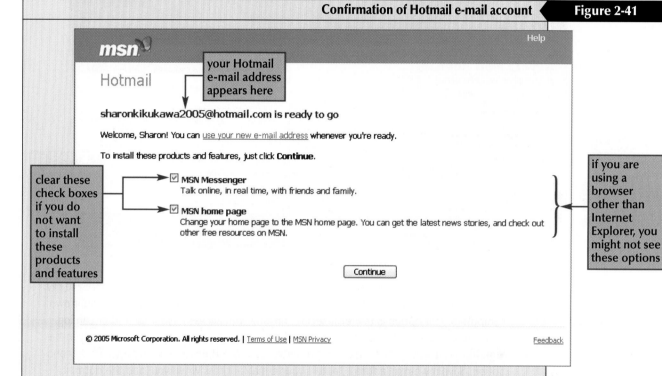

Trouble? Hotmail might redesign its Web site, in which case your screen might not match the one shown in Figure 2-41. If you do not see a page like the one shown in Figure 2-41, or if your page indicates that you did not successfully create a Hotmail account, follow the on-screen instructions to correct any identified problems. If the Sign In page appears again, complete the steps to create your account to continue.

Now that you have created a Hotmail e-mail address, you can sign into your Hotmail account by clicking the Continue button on the Sign Up page.

To sign into your Hotmail account and begin using Hotmail:

1. If desired, click the **MSN Messenger** and **MSN home page** check boxes to clear them so you will not enable MSN Messenger (an online chat service) and change your browser's home page to MSN.com. If you would like to keep these products and features, leave one or both check boxes selected.

2. Click the **Continue** button. A page offering a selection of free newsletters and offers opens.

3. Click the check box next to any newsletters you wish to receive on a regular basis or any of the categories of offers for sale items that you wish to receive in your e-mail Inbox, and then scroll down to the bottom of the page and click the **Continue** button. (Note that you may leave all of the check boxes unchecked.) The Hotmail Sign In page opens.

4. Type your Hotmail e-mail address in the E-mail address text box, press the **Tab** key, and then type your password. See Figure 2-42.

| Figure 2-42 | Hotmail Sign In page |

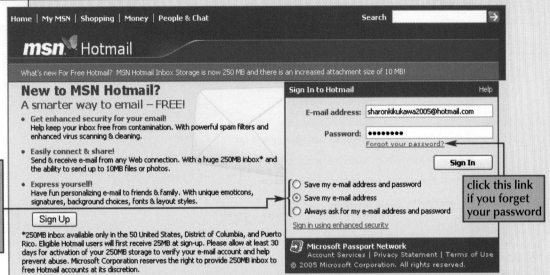

options for securing your Hotmail e-mail address and password

click this link if you forget your password

There are three security options for signing into a Hotmail account. The first one, Save my e-mail address and password, is for users who access their Hotmail accounts on their own computers. This option is the least secure; anyone with access to your computer can log into your account, because your e-mail address and password appear automatically in the Sign In to Hotmail section when your browser loads the Hotmail Sign In page. The second option, Save my e-mail address, enters your e-mail address when you load the Hotmail home page, but not your password. This option is more secure than the first one, because you must type your password to access your Hotmail account. The third option, Always ask for my e-mail address and password, is for users who access their Hotmail account from different computers. Because you must enter your Hotmail e-mail address and your password, it is the most secure way to access your account.

5. Click the option button for the security that best suits your situation, and then click the **Sign In** button.

The Activate Your Account page opens and reminds you to sign into your account once within the next 10 days, and at least once every 30 days, for your account to remain active. See Figure 2-43.

Activate Your Account page ◄ **Figure 2-43**

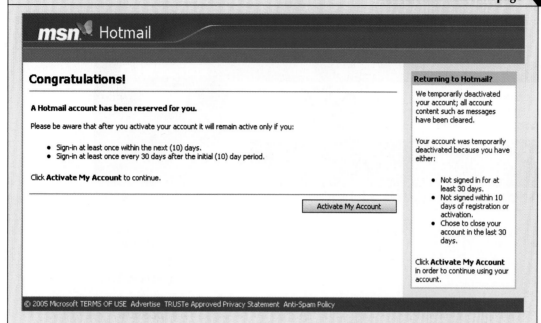

Trouble? Your Activate Your Account page might look different from the one shown in Figure 2-43. This difference causes no problems.

Trouble? If you receive a message that your e-mail address or password is not found, clear the E-mail address and Password text boxes, and then re-enter your information. If you are still having problems, you may have entered your password incorrectly. Click the Forgot your password? link and follow the on-screen directions to retrieve your password, and then try logging into your Hotmail account again. If you are still having problems, ask your instructor or technical support person for help.

6. Click the **Activate My Account** button. The TERMS OF USE page opens.

7. Read the agreement, and then click the **I Accept** button to continue. The FREE Newsletters & Offers page opens. You can use this page to have newsletters and offers sent to your Hotmail account.

8. Without making any selections, scroll down the page, and then click the **Continue** button. The MSN Hotmail Today page opens.

9. Click the **Mail** tab. The MSN Hotmail – Inbox page opens. See Figure 2-44.

Figure 2-44 ▷ MSN Hotmail – Inbox page

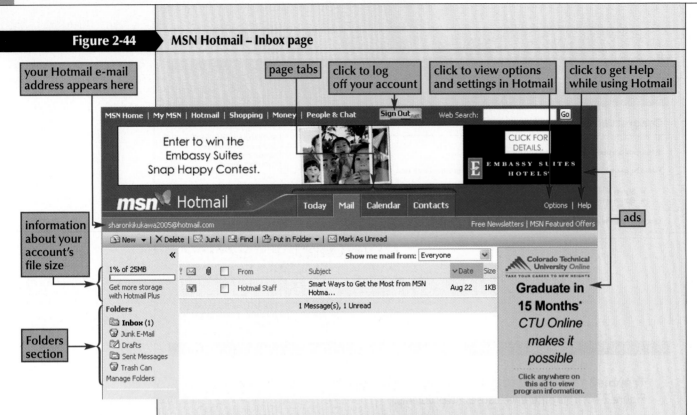

your Hotmail e-mail address appears here

page tabs

click to log off your account

click to view options and settings in Hotmail

click to get Help while using Hotmail

information about your account's file size

ads

Folders section

Trouble? Your MSN Hotmail – Inbox page might look different from the one shown in Figure 2-44. This difference causes no problems.

Trouble? Your computer might be configured to hide the display of ads such as the ones shown in Figure 2-44, in which case you might not see them. Hotmail is a free service; the money that advertisers pay to include their ads makes the Hotmail service possible.

The MSN Hotmail – Inbox page shown in Figure 2-44 displays the Today, Mail, Calendar, and Contacts tabs. The Today tab is the page that first opens when you log on to your Hotmail account. It includes the latest information about the day's current events, your mailbox, and appointments that you have scheduled using your calendar. You can also use the hyperlinks near the bottom of the page to open other pages in the MSN site with information about shopping, finances, and other topics.

The **Mail tab** displays a list of messages that you have received and provides options for working with e-mail messages. "Hotmail Staff" will send a message to you with the subject "Smart Ways to Get the Most from MSN Hotmail" or a similarly worded subject when you first access your Hotmail account. The Folders section on the left shows you how many messages are stored in each of the specified folders. Clicking a folder name in the Folders section opens that folder and displays its contents. The meter above the Folders section indicates how much of your free storage space is available. You can use this meter to determine when you need to delete some of your stored messages to free up space.

The **Calendar tab** contains options for organizing your scheduled appointments and daily calendar. The **Contacts tab** contains options for managing your address book. You can click the Options and Help links near the top of the page to open pages containing program options and help for Hotmail users, respectively.

Now that you have created a Hotmail account, you are ready to send a message to Sharon. *Note*: In this tutorial, you will send messages to a real mailbox with the address sharonkikukawa@yahoo.com. Follow the instructions carefully and use the correct address. Messages sent to this mailbox are deleted without being opened or read.

Sending a Message Using Hotmail

You are ready to use Hotmail to send a message with an attached file to Sharon. Send a courtesy copy of the message to your own e-mail address to simulate receiving a message.

Reference Window

Sending a Message Using Hotmail

- Open the MSN Hotmail home page, log on to your account, click the Mail tab, click the list arrow for the New button, and then click Mail Message.
- In the To text box, type the recipient's e-mail address. To send the message to more than one recipient, separate additional e-mail addresses with commas.
- Type the e-mail address of any Cc or Bcc recipients in the appropriate text boxes. Separate multiple recipients' e-mail addresses with commas.
- If necessary, click the Attach button, click File, click the Browse button to locate and select the file to attach, click the Open button, and then click the OK button near the top of the page to finish attaching files or click the OK and Attach Another button to attach additional files.
- In the message body, type your message.
- Check your message for spelling and grammatical errors.
- Click the Send button.

To send a message with an attachment:

1. Click the **list arrow** for the New button, and then click **Mail Message**. The New Message page opens. See Figure 2-45.

Figure 2-45 | **Hotmail New Message page**

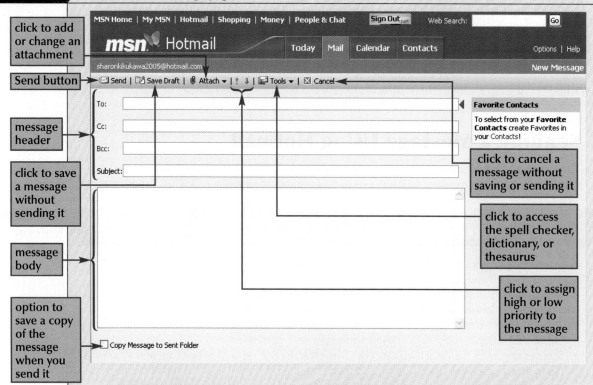

click to add or change an attachment

Send button

message header

click to save a message without sending it

message body

option to save a copy of the message when you send it

Trouble? Depending on the speed of your Internet connection, it might take a few seconds to load new pages. Check your browser's status bar to make sure that pages have fully loaded before using them.

2. In the To text box, type **sharonkikukawa@yahoo.com**, and then press the **Tab** key to move to the Cc text box.

   Trouble? Make sure that you use the address sharonkikukawa@yahoo.com, instead of sharonkikukawa@kikukawaair.com. If you type Sharon's e-mail address incorrectly, your message will be returned as undeliverable.

3. Type your full e-mail address in the Cc text box. When you send this message, you and Sharon will both receive it.

   Trouble? If you make a typing mistake on a previous line, use the arrow keys or click the insertion point to return to a previous line so you can correct your mistake. If the arrow keys do not move the insertion point backward or forward in the message header, press Shift + Tab or the Tab key to move backward or forward, respectively.

4. Press the **Tab** key twice to move the insertion point to the Subject text box, and then type **Test**.

5. Click the **Attach** button, and then click **File**. The Attach File page opens. You can use Hotmail to send file attachments of up to 10 megabytes in size.

6. Click the **Browse** button, and then use the **Look in** list arrow in the Choose file (or File Upload) dialog box and select the drive or folder that contains your Data Files.

7. Double-click the **Tutorial.02** folder, double-click the **Tutorial** folder, double-click **Physicals**, and then click the **OK** button. The New Message page now shows the attached file's name and size in the Attachments section.

8. Click the insertion point in the message display area, type **Dear Sharon,** and then press the **Enter** key twice to insert a blank line.

9. In the message display area, type **Please reply when you receive this message and the attached file. I am testing Hotmail and want to make sure that it is working correctly.**

10. Press the **Enter** key twice, and then type your first and last names to sign your message. See Figure 2-46.

Completed message | **Figure 2-46**

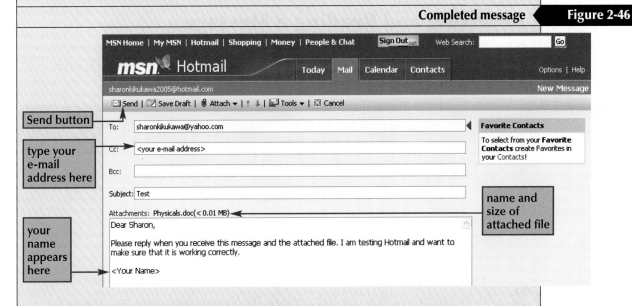

11. Click the **Tools** button, and then click **Spell Check**. If necessary, correct any errors. If your message is free of spelling errors, no dialog box opens and a "No Spelling Errors Detected" message appears above the To text box.

12. Click the **Send** button to mail the message. The Sent Message Confirmation page opens and shows that your message has been sent. See Figure 2-47.

Sent Message Confirmation page | **Figure 2-47**

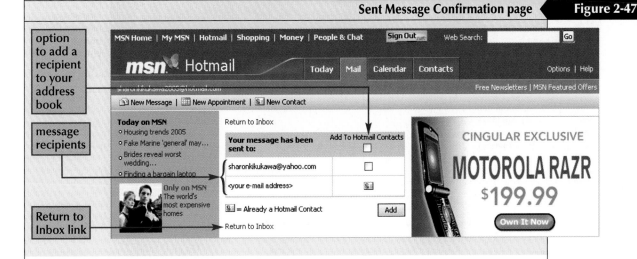

Because Sharon's e-mail address does not appear in your Hotmail address book, Hotmail provides an option for you to add this address by selecting the check box in the Save Address column. You will add addresses to the address book later, so no action is necessary now.

Receiving and Reading a Message

When you receive new mail, messages that you have not opened are displayed with closed envelope icons, and messages that you have opened are displayed with open envelope icons. You check for new mail next.

Reference Window | **Using Hotmail to Receive Messages**

- Open the MSN Hotmail home page and log on to your Hotmail account.
- Click the Mail tab.

To check for incoming mail:

▶ 1. Click the **Mail** tab. The Test message appears in the Inbox. The sender's name is formatted as a hyperlink. To read the message, you click the hyperlink.

▶ 2. Click the sender's name for the Test message. The Message page opens and displays the Test message. See Figure 2-48.

Figure 2-48 ▶ Message page

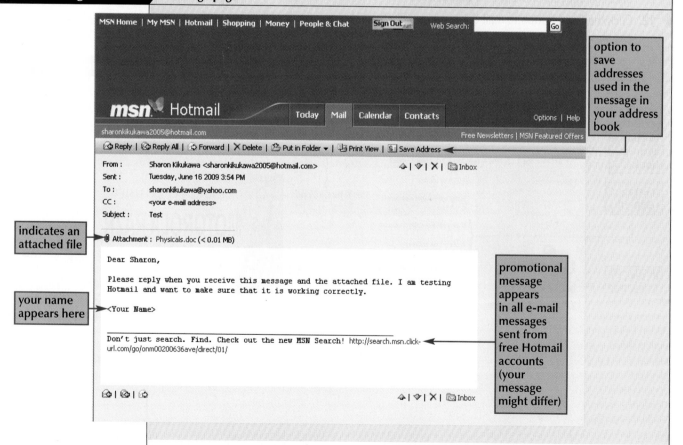

You received your copy of the Test message that you sent to Sharon. The filename in the Attachment section indicates that you received an attached file with the message. When you receive a message with one or more attachments, you can open the attachment or save it.

Viewing and Saving an Attached File

You want to make sure that your attached file was sent properly, so you decide to open it. You then save the file.

Reference Window

Viewing and Saving an Attached File in Hotmail

- Click the sender's name for the message that contains the attachment.
- To open the file using a program on your computer, click the attached file's name in the Attachment section to scan the file for viruses, click the Download File button, and then click the option to open the file (if necessary, choose a program to open the file). Close the program window that opens.
- To save the file to a disk or drive, click the attached file's name in the Attachment section to scan the file for viruses, click the Download File button, and then click the option to save the file. Use the Save in list arrow to change to the drive and folder in which to save the attached file, click the Save button, and then click the Close button.
- Click the Cancel button.

To view and save the attached file:

1. Click the **Physicals.doc** link in the Attachment section. Hotmail automatically scans the file for viruses to protect your computer. A message appears indicating that no virus was found in the file.

   Trouble? If Hotmail finds a virus in the file, follow the on-screen instructions to continue.

2. Click the **Download File** button. The File Download dialog box opens. You can open the file using a program on your computer, save the file to a disk, cancel the download, or click the More Info button to open a Help window for your browser.

   Trouble? If you are using Firefox, the dialog box that opens is named Opening Physicals.doc. This difference causes no problems.

3. Click the **Open** button. Word or another word-processing program on your computer starts and opens the attached file. If necessary, maximize the program window that opens.

   Trouble? If you are using Firefox as your browser, click the **Open it with the default application option** button in the Opening Physicals.doc dialog box, and then click the **OK** button.

4. Click the **Close** button on the program window's title bar. Now that you have viewed the attachment, you can save it.

   Trouble? If a Downloads window opens, click the Close button on its title bar.

5. Click the **Download File** button, click the **Save** button or the **Save to disk** option button, and then, if necessary, click the **OK** button. If you are using Internet Explorer, the Save As dialog box opens.

   Trouble? If you are using Firefox, the file is saved on the desktop unless you specified a different folder in which to download files. Move the downloaded Physicals.doc file into the Tutorial.02\Tutorial folder, click the Yes button to overwrite the existing file with the same name, and then skip Steps 6 and 7.

6. If necessary, browse to the drive or folder containing your Data Files, open the **Tutorial.02** folder, open the **Tutorial** folder, click the **Save** button, and then click the **Yes** button to overwrite the existing file with the same name. The Download complete dialog box opens when the file has been transferred.

7. If you are using Internet Explorer, click the **Close** button. You return to the Message page.

When you receive a message with an attached file, you can view and save the attachment for as long as you store the message. When you delete the message, you delete the file attached to the message. When you detach a file from an e-mail message and save it on a disk or drive, it is just like any other file that you save.

Replying to and Forwarding Messages

You can forward any message you receive to one or more e-mail addresses. Similarly, you can respond to the sender of a message quickly and efficiently by replying to a message. Replying to and forwarding messages are common tasks for e-mail users.

Replying to an E-Mail Message

To reply to a message, click the Reply button to reply only to the sender, or click the Reply All button to reply to the sender and other people who received the original message (those e-mail addresses listed in the To and Cc text boxes). Hotmail will open the Reply page and place the original sender's address in the To text box; other e-mail addresses that received the original message will appear in the To and Cc text boxes as appropriate. You can leave the Subject text box as is or modify it. Most programs, including Hotmail, will copy the original message and place it in the response window. The > symbol appears to the left of the response to indicate the text of the original message. Figure 2-49 shows a reply to the Test message.

| Figure 2-49 | Replying to a message |

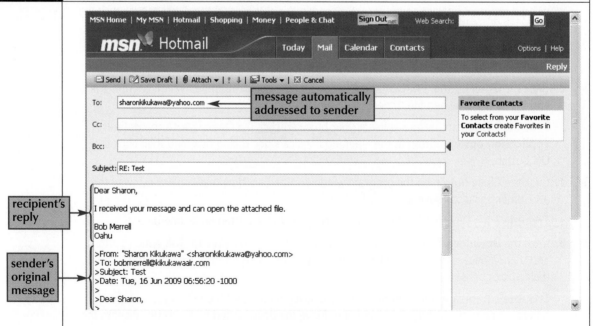

Replying to a Message Using Hotmail

- Open the message to which you want to reply.
- Click the Reply button to reply only to the sender, or click the Reply All button to reply to the sender and other "To" and "Cc" recipients of the original message.
- Type other recipients' e-mail addresses in the message header as needed.
- Change the text in the Subject box if necessary.
- Edit the message body as necessary.
- Click the Send button.

Forwarding an E-Mail Message

When you forward a message, you are sending a copy of your message, including any attachments, to one or more recipients who were not included in the original message. (If you do not want to forward the original sender's attached file to the new recipients, click the Attach button, click Remove Attachments, and then click the Delete column for each attachment you want to remove. Click the OK button to return to the Forward page.) To forward an existing mail message to another user, open the message you want to forward, and then click the Forward button. The Forward page opens, where you can type the address of the recipient in the To text box. If you want to forward the message to several people, type their addresses, separated by commas, in the To text box (or Cc or Bcc text boxes). Hotmail inserts a copy of the original message in the message display area (as it does when you reply to a message) with a > symbol to its left. Figure 2-50 shows a forwarded copy of the Test message.

Fowarding a message ◄ **Figure 2-50**

message showing that the attached file will be forwarded and does not contain any viruses

original recipient's message

sender's original message

new recipient's address

Reference Window | **Forwarding an E-Mail Message Using Hotmail**

- Open the message that you want to forward.
- Click the Forward button.
- Click the To text box, and then type one or more e-mail addresses, separated by commas. Add Cc and Bcc e-mail addresses as necessary.
- Click the blank line above the quoted message, and then type an optional message to add a context for the recipient(s).
- Click the Send button.

Occasionally, you receive important messages, so you want to make sure that you can file and print them as needed.

Filing and Printing an E-Mail Message

You can use the Hotmail folders to file your e-mail messages by category. When you file a message, you move it to another folder. You file Sharon's message in a new folder named "FAA" for safekeeping. Later, you can create other folders to suit your style and working situation.

To create the new folder:

1. Click the **Mail** tab, and then click the **Manage Folders** link in the Folders section. The Manage Folders page opens. See Figure 2-51.

Figure 2-51 | **Manage Folders page**

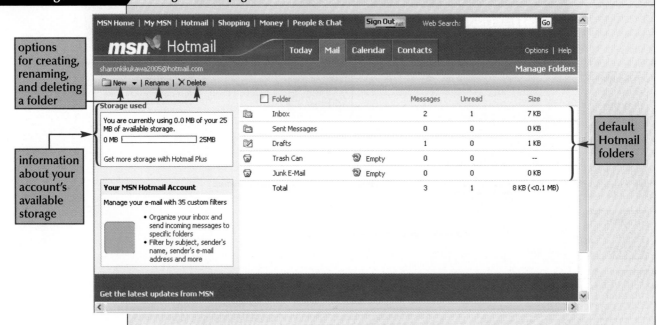

By default, Hotmail includes five folders: **Inbox** stores your new messages, **Sent Messages** stores messages that you have sent when you set it to do so, **Drafts** stores messages that you have written and saved but have not yet sent, **Trash Can** stores messages that you have deleted, and **Junk Mail** stores e-mail messages from senders that you specify as bulk mailers, advertisers, or any address from which you don't want to receive mail.

2. Click the **list arrow** for the New button, and then click **Folder**. The New Folder page opens.

3. With the insertion point in the Folder Name text box, type **FAA**, and then click the **OK** button. The FAA folder appears in the list of folders.

4. Click the **Inbox** folder link on the Manage Folders page.

After you create the FAA folder, you can transfer messages to it. Besides transferring mail from the Inbox folder, you can select messages in any other folder and then transfer them to another folder.

To file the Test message:

1. Click the check box for the **Test** message to add a check mark to it.

2. Click the **Put in Folder** button, and then click **FAA**. After a moment, the message is transferred to the FAA folder.

3. Click the **FAA** folder in the Folders section. The Test message appears in the FAA folder.

You can print a message at any time—when you receive it, before you send it, or after you file it. You print the message next.

To print the e-mail message:

1. Click the sender's name for the **Test** message to open it.

2. Click the **Print View** button. A new window opens and displays a "printer-friendly" version of the message.

3. Click the **Print** button on your browser's toolbar. The message is printed.

   Trouble? Depending on how your printer is configured, a Print dialog box might open. If so, click the OK or Print button to print the message.

4. Close the window with the printer-friendly version of the message, and then click the **Mail** tab.

When you no longer need a message, you can delete it.

Deleting an E-Mail Message and Folder

When you don't need a message any longer, you can delete it by opening the message and clicking the Delete button. You can delete a folder by selecting its check box on the Manage Folders page and then clicking the Delete button. When you delete a message or folder, you are simply moving it to the Trash Can folder. The default setting for Hotmail accounts is for the system to delete all messages in the Trash Can folder every day. However, if you want to remove items permanently and right away, you can delete them from the Trash Can folder.

Deleting an E-Mail Message Using Hotmail　　　　　　　　　　Reference Window

- Open the folder that contains the message you want to delete, click the check box for the message to add a check mark to it, and then click the Delete button.
- To delete items permanently, open the Trash Can folder, click the Empty button, and then click the OK button.

To delete the message:

1. Click the **FAA** folder in the Folders section.
2. Click the **check box** for the Test message. This action selects the message.
3. Click the **Delete** button. The message is deleted from the FAA folder and is moved to the Trash Can folder.
4. Click the **Trash Can** folder in the Folders section. The Test message appears in the folder.
5. Click the **Empty** button, and then click the **OK** button in the message box. All messages are deleted from the Trash Can folder.

To delete the FAA folder, you must return to the Manage Folders page.

Reference Window	**Deleting a Hotmail Folder**

- Click the Manage Folders link in the Folders section.
- Click the check box for the folder that you want to delete to add a check mark to it.
- Click the Delete button, and then click the OK button.

To delete the FAA folder:

1. Click the **Manage Folders** link in the Folders section to open the Manage Folders page. The values of zero in the Messages, Unread, and Size columns for the FAA folder all indicate that this folder is empty.
2. Click the **check box** to the left of the FAA folder to add a check mark to it, click the **Delete** button, and then click the **OK** button. The FAA folder is deleted.

Maintaining an Address Book

As you use e-mail to communicate with business associates and friends, you might want to save their addresses in an address book to make it easier to address your messages.

Adding a Contact to the Address Book

You can open the Hotmail address book by clicking the Contacts tab. To create a new address, click the list arrow for the New button, click Contact, and then use the text boxes to enter a person's information. Each individual address must have a quickname (nickname), a first and last name, and an e-mail address; the rest of the information is optional.

Reference Window	**Adding a Contact to the Hotmail Address Book**

- Click the Contacts tab to open the List View - ALL page.
- Click the list arrow for the New button, and then click Contact to open the New Contact page.
- Enter the person's quickname, first name, last name, and e-mail address in the appropriate text boxes. Use the other text boxes as necessary to enter other information about the person.
- Click the Save button.

Now you can add information to your address book. You begin by adding Sharon Kikukawa's contact information to your address book.

To add a contact to your address book:

▶ 1. Click the **Contacts** tab. The List View - ALL page opens.

▶ 2. Click the **list arrow** for the New button, and then click **Contact**. The New Contact page opens. At a minimum, you need to enter a quickname for the person, as well as the person's first and last names and e-mail address. Other information on this page is optional.

▶ 3. With the insertion point in the Quickname text box, type **Sharon**.

▶ 4. Click the **First Name** text box, type **Sharon**, press the **Tab** key to move the insertion point to the Last Name text box, and then type **Kikukawa**.

▶ 5. Click the **Primary E-mail** list arrow, and then click **Work**. You can specify different e-mail addresses for an individual based upon their use, such as work or personal.

▶ 6. Click the **Work** text box in the Online Addresses section, and then type **sharonkikukawa@yahoo.com**. Sharon's contact is complete. See Figure 2-52.

Information for Sharon Kikukawa   **Figure 2-52**

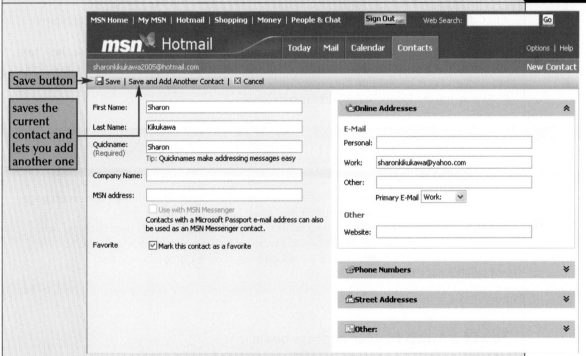

7. Notice the optional information that you can store about an individual, and then click the **Save** button. Sharon's contact now appears in the address book.

Trouble? If a Confirm dialog box opens, click the No button.

8. Repeat Steps 2 through 7 to create new contacts for the following Kikukawa Air employees:

Quickname	First Name	Last Name	Work e-mail address
Zane	**Zane**	**Norcia**	**zanenorcia@kikukawaair.com**
Jen	**Jenny**	**Mahala**	**jennymahala@kikukawaair.com**
Rich	**Richard**	**Forrester**	**richardforrester@kikukawaair.com**

9. When you are finished entering the contacts, click the **list arrow** for the New button, and then click **Mail Message**. The contacts you stored in the address book appear in the Favorite Contacts box.

Now that these e-mail addresses are stored in the address book, you can click the To, Cc, or Bcc text box, and then click a name in the Favorite Contacts box to enter that person's e-mail address in the message header.

When you send mail to someone who is not in your address book, the Sent Message Confirmation page includes a Save Address check box for that address. Clicking the check box for a new contact and then clicking the Save button opens the Save Address page, where you can add the person's quickname and first and last names to the address book.

Adding a Group to the Address Book

You can use Hotmail to create a group. Usually you create a group when you regularly send messages to a specific group of people.

Sharon frequently sends messages to Zane, Jen, and Rich as a group, because they have the same positions at the Kikukawa Air ticket counters. She asks you to create a group in her address book so she can type one quickname for the group of e-mail addresses, instead of having to type each address separately.

Reference Window

Adding a Group to the Hotmail Address Book

- Click the Contacts tab.
- Click the list arrow for the New button, and then click Group to open the New Group page.
- Type a group name for the group in the Group Name text box.
- Select the first group member's name in the My Contacts box, and then click the Add button to add the person to the Group Members box. Continue adding names to the group until you have entered the e-mail addresses for all group members.
- Click the Save button.

To add a group to your address book:

1. Click the **Contacts** tab, click the **list arrow** for the New button, and then click **Group**. The New Group page opens. On this page, you enter the group name and the individual e-mail addresses for members of the group.

2. With the insertion point in the Group Name text box, type **Ticket Agents**. This quickname will represent the individual e-mail addresses of the individual ticket agents.

3. In the My Contacts box, click **Jenny Mahala** to select it, and then click the **Add** button. Jenny's name is added as the first member of the group.

4. In the My Contacts box, click **Richard Forrester**, and then click the **Add** button.

5. Repeat Step 4 to add **Zane Norcia** to the Group Members box. The group now contains three e-mail addresses.

▶ **6.** Click the **Save** button. The Groups list now shows the Ticket Agents group. See Figure 2-53.

New group added to the address book ◀ **Figure 2-53**

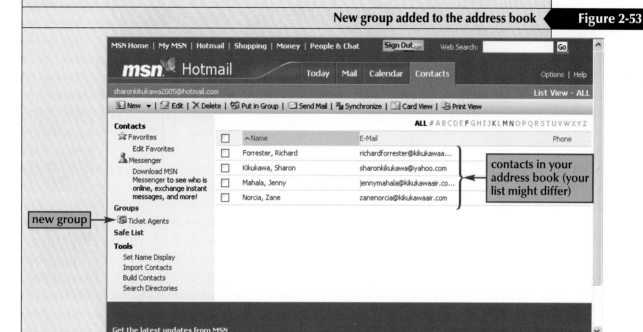

▶ **7.** Click the **list arrow** for the New button, and then click **Mail Message**.

Now, test the new group by creating a new message.

To address a message to a group:

▶ **1.** With the insertion point in the To text box, click **Ticket Agents** in the Favorite Contacts box. The Ticket Agents quickname is added to the To text box. You will also send a copy of this message to Sharon, so you need to select her address.

▶ **2.** Click the **Cc** text box, and then click Sharon's e-mail address in the Favorite Contacts box. Sharon's e-mail address is added to the Cc text box. See Figure 2-54.

Figure 2-54	Using the Favorite Contacts list

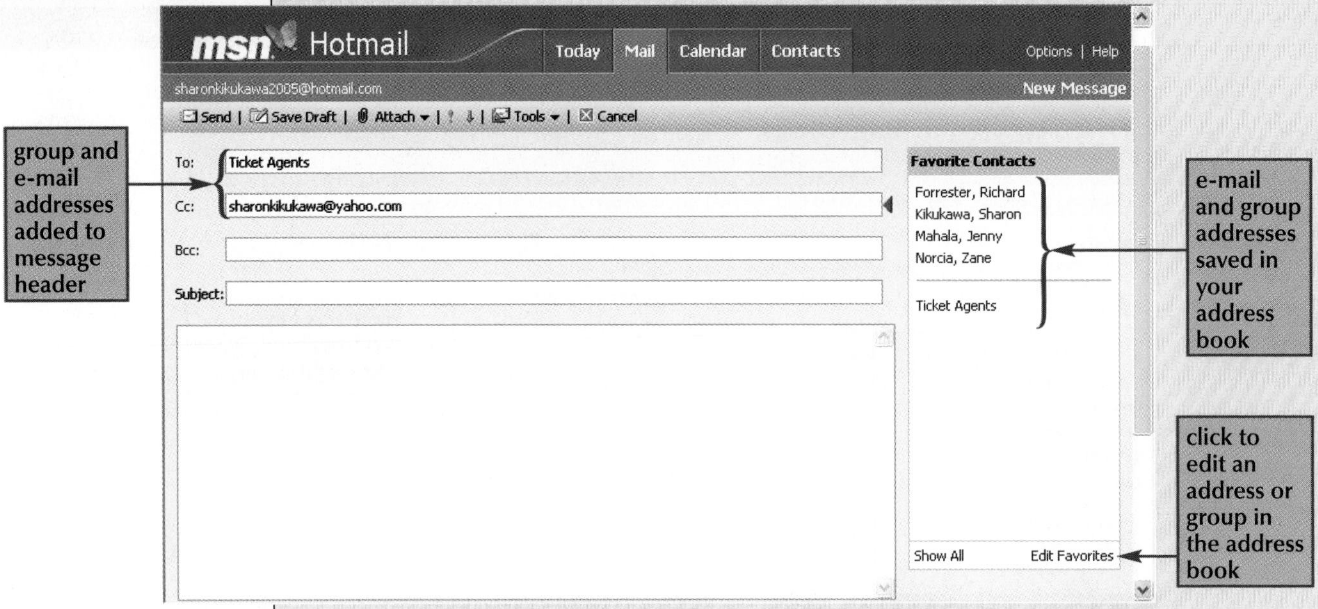

group and e-mail addresses added to message header

e-mail and group addresses saved in your address book

click to edit an address or group in the address book

3. Click the **Cancel** button. You return to the Mail tab.

When you need to modify a group's members, you can do so by clicking the Contacts tab, clicking the group's quickname in the Groups list, and selecting members to add or remove from the My Contacts and Group Members boxes as necessary.

You are finished evaluating Hotmail, so you need to log off your Hotmail account and close your browser. It is important that you log off before closing the browser to ensure the security of your e-mail and to prevent unauthorized access. Your Hotmail account is active if you use it. If you do not sign into your Hotmail account within 10 days after creating it, or for 30 days at any point after that, your account will become inactive. If you do not sign in to your Hotmail account for more than 90 days, it is permanently deleted.

To log off Hotmail and close your browser:

1. Click the **Sign Out** button at the top of the page. The MSN.com home page opens.

2. Click the **Close** button on your browser's title bar to close the browser.

In this session, you learned how to use Hotmail to create, send, receive, and manage e-mail messages. You also learned how to create and use an address book to manage e-mail addresses.

Review

Session 2.3 Quick Check

1. To set up a Hotmail account, what information must you provide to MSN.com?
2. True or False: If you are using a computer in a public library to access your Hotmail account, you should log off your account when you are finished viewing your messages to protect your privacy.
3. Does Hotmail queue a message or send it right away?
4. When you receive a message with an attachment in Hotmail, what two options are available for the attached file?
5. When you delete a message from the Inbox, can you recover that message? Why or why not?
6. What information can you store about a person using the Hotmail address book?

Review

Tutorial Summary

In this tutorial, you learned how to send and receive e-mail messages. You also learned how to print, file, save, delete, respond to, and forward e-mail messages. You created an address book into which you stored the name, e-mail address, and other important details about a person or a group of people. Now that you have learned these important skills, you can use the e-mail program of your choice to send and receive your own e-mail messages. As you use your e-mail program, expand your skills by using its Help system to explore the many other features that it includes but that are not covered here.

Key Terms

Common Terms

address book	host computer	protocol
aggregator	host name	queued
attachment	IMAP (Internet Message	quoted message
blind courtesy copy (Bcc)	Access Protocol)	Really Simple Syndication
blog	junk mail	(RSS)
bulk mail	kilobyte (KB)	reply
courtesy copy (Cc)	mail client software	Saved Search folder
detaching	mail server	signature
electronic mail	message body	SMTP (Simple Mail Transfer
e-mail	message header	Protocol)
e-mail address	MIME (Multipurpose	spam
e-mail program	Internet Mail	Subject line
emoticon	Extensions)	To line
filter	Mozilla Thunderbird	unsolicited commercial
forward	netiquette	e-mail (UCE)
From line	nickname	user name
Gmail	Opera M2	virus
group	POP (Post Office Protocol)	Web log

Outlook Express

Contacts list	Inbox folder	Outlook Express
Deleted Items folder	message list	preview pane
Drafts folder	Microsoft Outlook Express	Sent Items folder
Folders list	Outbox folder	

Hotmail

Calendar tab	Inbox folder	Today tab
Contacts tab	Junk Mail folder	Trash Can folder
Drafts folder	Mail tab	
Hotmail	Sent Messages folder	

Practice

Practice the skills you learned in the tutorial using the same case scenario.

Review Assignments

Data File needed for the Review Assignments: KAir.gif

Now that you have learned about different types of e-mail programs, Sharon asks you to submit a recommendation about which program to use for Kikukawa Air. Sharon also wants to see how graphics are sent over the Internet, so she asks you to send her the Kikukawa Air logo to simulate how it will appear when sent by Kikukawa employees. To evaluate e-mail alternatives for Sharon, complete the following steps.

1. Start your e-mail program or log on to your Web-based e-mail account.
2. Add your instructor's full name and e-mail address to the address book. Create an appropriate nickname that will be easy for you to remember.
3. Add a group contact to the address book using the full names and e-mail addresses of three of your classmates. Create appropriate nicknames for each person.
4. Create a new message. Use nicknames to send the message to Sharon and to your instructor. Send a courtesy copy of the message to yourself, and use the group contact you created to send a blind courtesy copy of the message to your classmates. Use the subject "E-mail Recommendation" for the message.
5. In the message body, type three or more sentences describing your overall impressions about the different e-mail alternatives you have explored. Recommend the program that Kikukawa Air should use based on the program's features, ease of use, and other important considerations that you determine.
6. In the message body, press the Enter key twice, and then type your full name and e-mail address on separate lines.
7. Attach the file named **KAir.gif** from the Tutorial.02\Review folder included with your Data Files to the message.
8. Check your spelling before you send the message and correct any mistakes. Proofread your message and verify that you have created it correctly, and then send the message.
9. Wait about 30 seconds, check for new mail (enter your password, if necessary), and then open the message you sent to Sharon and your instructor. Print the message.
10. In a new message addressed only to your instructor, describe the appearance of the file you attached to the message. Use the subject "Attached Graphics File" and in the message body, explain your findings in terms of attaching a graphic to an e-mail message. Send the message.
11. Permanently delete the messages you received and *sent* from your e-mail program. (*Hint:* Delete messages from the folder where you receive messages and also from the folder that stores a copy of all sent messages. Make sure to delete messages from the folder that stores your deleted messages, as well.)
12. Exit your e-mail program or log off your Web-based e-mail account.

Apply

Apply the skills you learned to save an e-mail message to a file.

Case Problem 1

There are no Data Files needed for this Case Problem.

Worldwide Golf Resorts Worldwide Golf Resorts is a corporation based in Kansas City, Missouri, that owns and operates golf resorts in 22 countries worldwide. These resorts are popular destinations for people on vacation, and two of them host annual professional golf tournaments. You work for the regional vice president, Michael Pedersen, and handle all of his business correspondence. The Information Technology department just installed Michael's new Windows XP computer and now you need to send a test message to make sure that Michael's e-mail account is working correctly. You will create and send the message by completing the following steps.

1. Start your e-mail program or log on to your Web-based e-mail account.
2. Add to your address book the full name, nickname, and e-mail address of your instructor and two classmates.
3. Create a group contact for the two classmates you added to the address book in Step 2 using the nickname "managers."
4. Create a new message addressed to your instructor. On the Cc line, enter the group nickname you added to the address book in Step 3. On the Bcc line, enter your e-mail address. Use the subject "Worldwide Golf Resorts test message."
5. In the message display area, type a short note telling the recipients that you are sending a message for Michael and ask them to respond to you when they receive your message. Sign your message with your first and last names.
6. Send the message, wait a few seconds, and then retrieve your messages from the server. Print the message you sent to your instructor.

Explore

7. If you are using Outlook Express, save the message in the Tutorial.02\Cases folder included with your Data Files, using the message's subject as the filename. Choose the option to save the file in HTML format.
8. Create a mail folder or mailbox named Golf, and then file the message you received in the Golf folder.

Explore

9. Permanently delete the messages you received and *sent* from your e-mail program and the Golf folder. (*Hint:* Delete the folder and message, delete the message you sent from the folder that stores sent messages, and then empty the folder that stores deleted items.)
10. Exit your e-mail program or log off your Web-based e-mail account.

Research

Use the Help system for your e-mail program to learn how to create a signature for your outgoing e-mail messages.

Case Problem 2

There are no Data Files needed for this Case Problem.

Grand American Appraisal Company You are the office manager for Grand American Appraisal Company, a national real-estate appraisal company with its corporate headquarters in Los Angeles. Grand American handles real-estate appraisal requests from all over the United States and maintains a large list of approved real-estate appraisers located throughout the country. When an appraisal request is phoned into any regional office, an office staff member phones or faxes the national office to start the appraisal process. The appraisal order desk in Los Angeles receives the request and is responsible for locating a real-estate appraiser in the community in which the property to be appraised is located. After the Los Angeles office identifies and contacts an appraiser by phone, the appraiser has two days to perform the appraisal and either phone or fax the regional office with a preliminary estimate of value for the property. The entire process of phoning the regional office and then phoning or faxing the national office is both cumbersome and expensive.

Your supervisor asks you to use your e-mail program to set up an account for yourself so you can use e-mail for the appraisal requests instead of the current fax system. You will create a signature file to attach to your messages to identify your name, city, e-mail address, and appraiser license number by completing the following steps.

1. Start your e-mail program or log on to your Web-based e-mail account.
2. Obtain the e-mail address of a classmate, who will assume the role of the Los Angeles order desk. Add your classmate's full name, nickname, and e-mail address to the address book.
3. Add your instructor's full name, nickname, and e-mail address to the address book.
4. Use your classmate's nickname to address a new message to him or her. Type your e-mail address and your instructor's nickname on the Cc line, and then type "Request for appraisal" on the Subject line.
5. Type a short message that requests the assignment of an appraiser. Include your street address and the request date in the message.

Explore

6. Use the Help system to learn how to create a signature file with your first and last names on the first line, your city and state on the second line, your e-mail address on the third line, and "License number" plus any six-digit number on the fourth line. (*Hint:* If you are using Outlook Express, search Help using the Index tab for "signatures, personal" and then follow the directions. Do not select the option to attach your signature to all outgoing messages. If you are using Hotmail, click the Options link, click the Mail link on the left side of the page, and then click the Personal Signature link to create a signature.)

Explore

7. Include your signature in the new message. (*Hint:* In Outlook Express, click Insert on the menu bar, and then click Signature. Hotmail will attach your signature file automatically.)
8. Send the message, wait a few seconds, and then retrieve your messages from the server. Print the message you sent to your classmate.

Explore

9. Permanently delete the messages you received and *sent* from your e-mail program. (*Hint:* Delete the message from the folder where you receive messages and also from the folder that stores a copy of all sent messages. Make sure to delete messages from the folder that stores your deleted messages, as well.)

Explore

10. If you are using Outlook Express, delete your signature. (*Hint:* Select your signature on the Signatures tab in the Options dialog box, and then click the Remove button.)
11. Exit your e-mail program or log off your Web-based e-mail account.

Research

Use the Help system for your e-mail program to learn how to create a signature for your outgoing e-mail messages.

Case Problem 3

Data File needed for this Case Problem: Recycle.doc

Recycling Awareness Campaign You are an assistant in the Mayor's office in Cleveland, Ohio. The mayor has asked you to help with the recycling awareness campaign. Your job is to use e-mail to increase awareness of the recycling centers throughout the city and to encourage Cleveland's citizens and businesses to participate in the program. You will send an e-mail message to members of the city's chamber of commerce with an invitation to help increase awareness of the program by forwarding your message and its attached file to their employees and colleagues by completing the following steps.

1. Start your e-mail program or log on to your Web-based e-mail account.
2. Add the full names, e-mail addresses, and nicknames of five classmates to your address book to act as chamber of commerce members. After creating individual entries in the address book for your classmates, add them to a group contact named "Chamber" in your address book. Then add the full name, e-mail address, and nickname of your instructor to your address book.
3. Create a new message and address it to the Chamber group. Add your instructor's nickname to the Cc line and your e-mail address to the Bcc line. Use the subject "Recycling campaign for businesses—please get the word out!"

Explore

4. Write a two- or three-line message urging the chamber members to promote the city's new business recycling campaign by forwarding your message and the attached file to local businesses. Make sure to thank them for their efforts on behalf of the Mayor's office.
5. Attach the file named **Recycle.doc** located in the Tutorial.02\Cases folder included with your Data Files to the message.

Explore

6. Use the Help system in your e-mail program to learn how to create and use a signature file. Your signature should include your full name on the first line, the title "Assistant to the Mayor" on the second line, and your e-mail address on the third line. (*Hint:* If you are using Outlook Express, search Help using the Index tab for "signatures, personal" and then follow the directions. Do not select the option to attach your signature to all outgoing messages. If you are using Hotmail, click the Options link, click the Mail link on the left side of the page, and then click the Personal Signature link to create a signature.)

Explore

7. Include your signature file in the new message. (*Hint:* In Outlook Express, click Insert on the menu bar, and then click Signature. Hotmail will attach your signature file automatically.)
8. Proofread and spell check your message, and then send your message. After a few moments, retrieve your e-mail message from the server and print it.
9. Forward the message to one of the classmates in your address book. Add a short message to the forwarded message that asks the recipient to forward the message to appropriate business leaders per your program objectives.

Explore

10. Save a *copy* of your message in a new subfolder of the Inbox named Recycling, and then delete the message from the Inbox.

Explore

11. Permanently delete the messages you received and *sent* from your e-mail program and the Recycling folder. (*Hint:* Delete the folder and message, delete the message you sent from the folder that stores sent messages, and then empty the folder that stores deleted items.)
12. If you are using Outlook Express, delete your signature file. (*Hint:* Select your signature on the Signatures tab in the Options dialog box, and then click the Remove button.)
13. Exit your e-mail program or log off your Web-based e-mail account.

Practice

Apply the skills you learned in this tutorial to create a group contact for a group of students.

Case Problem 4

There are no Data Files needed for this Case Problem.

Student Study Group In two weeks, you have a final exam, and you want to organize a study group with your classmates. Everyone in your class has an e-mail account provided by your school. You want to contact some classmates to find out when they might be available to get together in the next week to study for the exam. To create a study group, you will complete the following steps.

1. Start your e-mail program or log on to your Web-based e-mail account.
2. Obtain the e-mail addresses of at least four classmates, and then enter them on the To line of a new message. On the Cc line, enter your e-mail address, and then on the Bcc line, enter your instructor's e-mail address. Do *not* add these names to your address book.
3. Use the subject "Study Group" for the message. In the message body, tell your class-mates about the study group by providing possible meeting times and locations. Ask recipients to respond to you through e-mail by a specified date if they are interested. Sign the message with your full name and e-mail address.
4. Proofread and spell check your message, and then send your message. After a few moments, retrieve your e-mail message from the server and open it.
5. Add each address on the To and Cc lines to your address book.
6. Create a new group contact named "study group" using the addresses you added to your address book in Step 5. Then forward a copy of your message to the study group.
7. Send your message. After a few moments, retrieve your e-mail message from the server and print it.
8. Permanently delete the messages you received and *sent* from your e-mail program. (*Hint:* Delete the messages from the Inbox, delete the message you sent from the folder that stores sent messages, and then empty the folder that stores deleted items.)
9. Exit your e-mail program or log off your Web-based e-mail account.

Create

Expand the skills you learned in this tutorial to create a document that you can send to a group of recipients as an e-mail attachment.

Case Problem 5

There are no Data Files needed for this Case Problem.

Murphy's Market Research Services You work part-time for Murphy's Market Research Services, a company that surveys students about various topics of interest to college students. A local music store, CD Rocks, wants you to send a short survey via e-mail to students at your university to learn more about student-buying habits for music CDs. You need to find out the names of three of their favorite music CDs, where they prefer to shop for music CDs, and how much time they spend each day listening to music. You will create the survey using any word-processing program, such as Microsoft Word, WordPad, or WordPerfect, and then you will attach the survey to your e-mail message. You need to receive the survey results within three weeks, so you will ask the respondents to return the survey via e-mail within that time period. You will create and send the survey by completing the following steps.

1. Using any word-processing program, create a new document named **Survey** and save it with the program's default filename extension in the Tutorial.02\Cases folder included with your Data Files.
2. Create the survey by typing the following questions (separate each question with two blank lines) in the new document:
   a. What are the titles of your three favorite music CDs?
   b. Where is the best place (online or retail) to shop for music CDs?
   c. Approximately how much time per day do you spend listening to music?
3. At the bottom of the document, type a sentence that thanks respondents for their time, and then on a new line, type your first and last names. Save the document, and then close your word-processing program.
4. Start your e-mail program or log on to your Web-based e-mail account.
5. Obtain the e-mail addresses of three classmates, and then enter them on the To line of a new message. On the Cc line, enter your e-mail address, and then on the Bcc line, enter your instructor's e-mail address. Do *not* add these names to your address book.
6. Use the subject "Music Survey" for the message. In the message body, ask recipients to open the attached file and to complete the survey by typing their responses into the document. Make sure that recipients understand that you need them to return the survey within three weeks. As an incentive for completing the survey, ask recipients to return the survey via e-mail but to print their completed survey and bring it to their local CD Rocks outlet for a $2 discount on any purchase. Sign the message with your full name, the company name (Murphy's Market Research Services), and your e-mail address.
7. Attach the survey to your e-mail message, and then send the message. After a few moments, retrieve your e-mail message from the server.

Explore

8. Open the attached file, and then complete the survey. Before saving the file, use your word-processing program's Print command to print the document.

Explore

9. In your word-processing program, click File on the menu bar, and then click Save As. Navigate to the Tutorial.02\Cases folder included with your Data Files and then save the file as **Completed Survey**, using the program's default filename extension. Close your word-processing program.

10. Forward the message to your instructor, attach the **Completed Survey** file to the message, make sure that the original message text appears in the message body, type a short introduction (such as "Here is my completed survey."), sign your message with your full name and e-mail address, and then send the message.

Explore

11. Permanently delete the messages you received and *sent* from your e-mail program. (*Hint:* Delete the messages from the Inbox, delete the message you sent from the folder that stores sent messages, and then empty the folder that stores deleted items.)

12. Exit your e-mail program or log off your Web-based e-mail account.

Reinforce

Student Edition Labs

Lab Assignments

The interactive Student Edition Lab **E-Mail** is designed to help you master some of the key concepts and skills presented in this tutorial, including:

- sending and receiving e-mail messages
- replying to e-mail messages
- storing and deleting e-mail messages

This lab and lab assignment are available online and can be accessed from the Tutorial 2 Web page on the Student Online Companion at www.course.com/newperspectives/internet6.

Review

Quick Check Answers

Session 2.1

1. protocols
2. message header, message body, signature
3. False
4. Yes; you can attach the Word document file to an e-mail message.
5. The user name identifies a specific individual and the host name identifies the computer on which that individual's account is stored.
6. By deleting unnecessary messages, you clear space on the drive or server on which your e-mail messages are stored.
7. A folder that contains a saved search; clicking the folder runs the search and finds all messages that match the search criteria. This feature is available in Thunderbird.
8. An RSS icon appears in the browser's address bar for pages that have RSS newsfeeds.

Session 2.2

1. Drafts
2. True
3. Outlook Express holds messages that are queued until you connect to your ISP and click the Send/Recv button on the toolbar.
4. You can view the attached file if your computer has a program that can open it, or you can save the attached file on your computer.
5. Yes, you can recover the message because it is stored in the Deleted Items folder.
6. name, e-mail address, nickname, address, business information, personal information, and so on

Session 2.3

1. Your name, preferred language, country, state, zip code, time zone, gender, birth date, and occupation; you must also submit a unique sign-in name, a password, and a secret question and answer.
2. True
3. Hotmail sends messages right away because all work is completed with a live Internet connection.
4. You can view the attached file if your computer has a program that can open it, or you can save the attached file on your computer.
5. Yes, you can recover the message because it is stored in the Trash Can folder.
6. name, e-mail address, quickname, address, business information, personal information, and so on

New Perspectives on
The Internet

Tutorial 3   WEB 155
Searching the Web
Using Search Engines and Directories Effectively

Tutorial 4   WEB 201
Information Resources on the Web
Finding, Evaluating, and Using Online Information Resources

Tutorial 5   WEB 245
Downloading and Storing Data
Using FTP and Other Services to Transfer and Store Data

Read This Before You Begin: Tutorials 3–5

To the Student

Data Files

To complete the Level II Internet Tutorials (Tutorials 3 through 5), you will need the starting student Data Files. Your instructor will either provide you with these Data Files or ask you to obtain them yourself.

The Level II Internet tutorials require the folders shown in the next column to complete the Tutorials, Review Assignments, and Case Problems. You will need to copy these folders from a file server, a standalone computer, or the Web to a drive and folder where you will be storing your Data Files. You instructor will tell you which computer, drive letter, and folder(s) contain the files you need. You can also download the files by going to *www.course.com*; see inside the back cover for more information on downloading files, or ask your instructor or technical support person for assistance.

If you are storing your Data Files on floppy disks, you will need **one** blank, formatted, high-density disk for these

tutorials. Label your disk as shown, and copy the folders indicated on to it.

▼**Internet Data Disk 2**

Tutorial.05

When you begin a tutorial, refer to the Student Data Files section at the bottom of the tutorial opener page, which indicates the folders and files you need for the tutorial. Each end-of-chapter exercise also indicates the files you need to complete that exercise.

Student Edition Labs

The Level II Internet tutorials feature two online Student Edition Labs (in Tutorials 4 and 5) to help you understand the following concepts: Computer Ethics and Keeping Your Computer Virus Free. You can access the labs by going to the Student Online Companion page for the tutorial in which each one appears, and then clicking the Student Edition Labs link.

To the Instructor

The Data Files are available on the Instructor's Resource CD for this title. Follow the instructions in the Help file on the CD-ROM to install the files to your network or standalone computer.

See the "To the Student" section above for information on how to set up the Data Files that accompany this

text. To complete the tutorials in this book, students must have a Web browser, an e-mail account, and an Internet connection.

You are granted a license to copy the Data Files to any computer or computer network used by students who have purchased this book.

System Requirements

If you are going to work through this book using your own computer, you need:

- **Computer System** Microsoft Internet Explorer 6.0 or higher, or Firefox 1.07 or higher, and Windows 2000 or higher must be installed on your computer. Note that the figures and steps in this edition were written using Windows XP, so Windows 2000 users may notice minor differences in the figures and the steps. This book assumes a complete installation of the Web browser software and its components, and that you

have an existing e-mail account and an Internet connection. Because your Web browser might be different from the ones used in the figures in the book, your screens might differ slightly at times.

- **Data Files** You will not be able to complete the tutorials or exercises in this book using your own computer until you have the Data Files.

- **Student Edition Labs** The Student Edition Labs are available through the Student Online Companion for this book.

www.course.com/NewPerspectives

Objectives

Session 3.1
- Determine whether a research question is specific or exploratory
- Learn how to formulate an effective Web search strategy to answer research questions
- Learn how to use Web search engines, Web directories, and Web metasearch engines effectively

Session 3.2
- Use Boolean logic and filtering techniques to improve your Web searches
- Use advanced search options in Web search engines
- Assess the validity and quality of Web research resources
- Learn about the future of Web search tools

Searching the Web

Using Search Engines and Directories Effectively

Case

International Executive Reports

International Executive Reports (IER) is a company that publishes a variety of weekly newsletters, monthly reports, and annual reviews of major trends in economic conditions and management developments for top-level managers and other people who serve on the governing boards of large companies and not-for-profit organizations. IER publications are mailed or e-mailed to subscribers. The subscription rates range from $300 to $900 per year.

The IER writing staff provides content for all of its publications. In some cases, content that is developed for one publication is edited and used in other publications. Anne Hill, the managing director for content at IER, has recruited an excellent staff of editors, writers, and researchers who work together to create a wide variety of content. Anne has hired you to fill an intern position on the research staff. Your job will involve online research and fact-checking for two of the staff writers, Dave Burton and Ranjit Singh. Dave is an international business specialist and Ranjit is an economist who writes about current economic trends.

You tell Anne that you are just learning to use the Web yourself, but she explains that this will be your full-time job during your internship and that she is counting on you to become skilled in conducting Web searches. Anne also tells you that she has been working with the Web for many years and that she is happy to help you with questions you might have as you find your way around the Web.

Student Data Files

There are no student data files needed for this tutorial.

Types of Search Questions

Anne is present at your first meeting with Dave and Ranjit. She explains that Dave uses the Internet to obtain information about every country in the world and do background research on most major businesses and industries. Dave tells you that his reports can always use more facts and that he is looking forward to having you help him with Internet research. Anne agrees and adds that one of the most valuable skills that an intern can have is an ability to "get the facts."

Ranjit says that his writing does not rely as much on current events and facts; rather, he writes longer, more thought-provoking pieces about broad economic and business issues. Quick access to facts is not nearly as important to him as it is to Dave. Ranjit hopes that you can provide him with new ideas that he could explore in his columns. He knows that the Web is a good place to find unusual and interesting views on the economy and general business practices, and he explains that he wants you to help him by using the Web as a source of interesting concepts and ideas rather than as a place to find fast answers to specific questions. Ranjit is always looking for new angles on old ideas, so he is optimistic that you can find many useful Web resources for him.

As they leave the meeting, both writers comment that they are happy to have an eager assistant "working the Web" for them. Anne then emphasizes that the writers will need different kinds of help because of their different writing goals. Dave will need quick answers to specific questions. For example, he might need to know the population of Bolivia or the languages spoken in Thailand. Ranjit will be looking for help finding new perspectives and a wide range of information on broad topics. For example, he might need you to find Web sites that contain collections of research papers that discuss the causes of the Great Depression.

You can use the Web to obtain answers to both of these question types—specific and exploratory—but each requires a different search strategy. A **specific question** is a question that you can phrase easily and one for which you will recognize the answer when you find it. In other words, you will know when to end your search. The search process for a specific question is one of narrowing the field down to the answer you seek. In contrast, an **exploratory question** is an open-ended question that can be harder to phrase; it also is difficult to determine when you find a good answer. The search process for an exploratory question requires you to fan out in a number of directions to find relevant information.

Specific questions require you to start with broad categories of information and gradually narrow the search until you find the answer to your question. Figure 3-1 shows this process of sequential, increasingly focused questions.

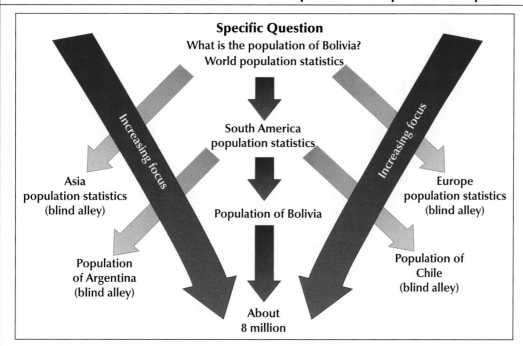

As you narrow your search, you might find that you are heading in the wrong direction or down a blind alley. In that case, you need to move back up the funnel shown in Figure 3-1 and try another path.

Exploratory questions start with general questions that lead to other, less general questions. The answers to the questions at each level should lead you to more information about the topic in which you are interested. This information then leads you to more questions. Figure 3-2 shows how this questioning process leads to a broadening scope as you gather information pertinent to the exploratory question.

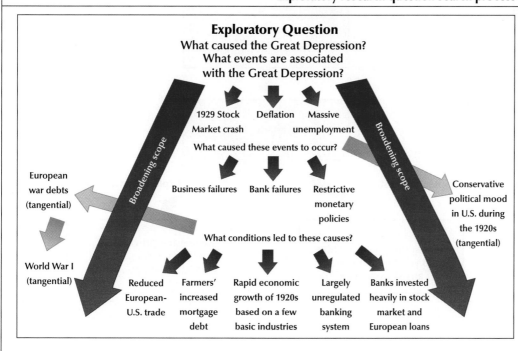

As your exploratory search expands, you might find yourself collecting tangential information that is somewhat related to your topic but does not help answer your exploratory question. The boundary between useful and tangential information is often difficult to identify precisely.

Web Search Strategy

Now that you understand the different types of questions that Ranjit and Dave will ask as you begin to work for them, Anne suggests that you learn something about searching the Web. You tell her that you know the Web is a collection of interconnected HTML documents and that you know how to use Web browser software to navigate the hyperlinks that connect these documents. Anne explains that the search tools available on the Web are an integral part of these linked HTML documents, or Web pages. She adds that there is a standard strategy for effectively searching the Web.

Before you begin any Web search, you must decide whether your question is specific or exploratory. Then you can begin the actual Web search process, which includes four steps. The first step is to carefully formulate and state your question. Next, you select the appropriate tool or tools to use in your search. After obtaining your results from a Web search tool, you need to evaluate these results to determine if they answer your question. If they do not, you continue the search by refining or redefining your question and then selecting a different search tool to see if you get a different result. The first three steps are the same for both types of question, but the determination of when your search process is completed is different for the two types of questions. Figure 3-3 illustrates the search process.

Figure 3-3	Web search process

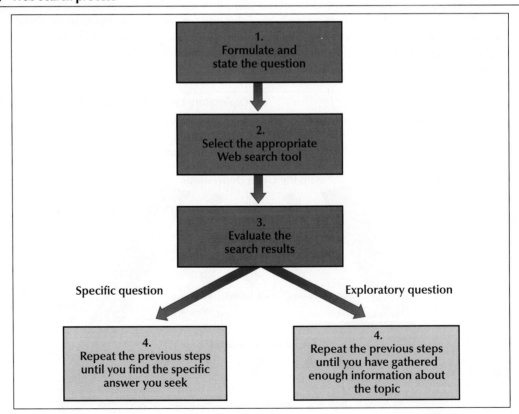

You can repeat this process as many times as necessary until you obtain the specific answer you seek or the range of information regarding your exploratory topic that you find satisfactory. Sometimes, you might find that the nature of your original question is different than you had originally thought. You also might find that you need to reformulate, or more clearly state, your question. As you restate your question, you should try to think of synonyms for each word. Unfortunately, many words in the English language have multiple meanings. If you use a word in your search that is common and has many meanings, you can be buried in irrelevant information or be led down many blind alleys. Identifying unique phrases that relate to your topic or question is a helpful way to avoid some of these problems.

An important part of any search is evaluating the search results you obtain. You will learn how to assess the validity and reliability of Web pages you find during your searches in the next tutorial.

Using Search Engines

To implement any Web search strategy, you will use one or more Web search tools. The four broad categories of Web search tools include search engines, directories, metasearch engines, and other Web resources such as Web bibliographies. The Additional Information section of the Student Online Companion page for Tutorial 3 includes links to many of these Web search tools. (The Student Online Companion page is located at www.course.com/ newperspectives/internet6.)

In this section, you will learn the basics of using each type of search tool. Remember that searching the Web is a challenging task for any of these tools. No one knows exactly how many pages exist on the Web, but the number is now in the billions. Each of these pages might have thousands of words, images, or links to downloadable files. Thus, the content of the Web is far greater than any library. Unlike the content of a library, however, the content of the Web is not indexed in any standardized way. Fortunately, the tools you have to search the Web are powerful.

Understanding Search Engines

A Web **search engine** is a Web site (or part of a Web site) that finds other Web pages that match a word or phrase you enter. That word or phrase is called a **search expression** or a **query**. A search expression or query might also include instructions that tell the search engine how to search; you will learn how to formulate search expressions that include additional search instructions later in this tutorial. The basic search page for AltaVista, an early but still popular search engine site, is shown in Figure 3-4.

AltaVista basic search page ◄ **Figure 3-4**

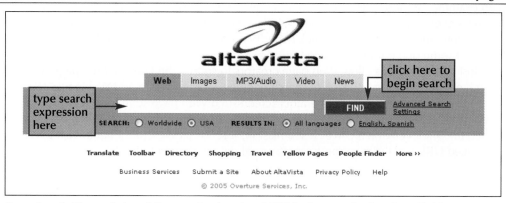

A basic search page includes a text box for entering a search expression and a command button to begin the search. The basic search page for Google, one of the most popular search engines, appears in Figure 3-5.

Figure 3-5	**Google basic search page**

A search engine does not search the Web to find a match; it searches only its *own* database of information about Web pages that it has collected, indexed, and stored. This information includes the URL of the Web page (recall from Tutorial 1 that a Web page's URL, or uniform resource locator, is its address). If you enter the same search expression into different search engines, you will often get different results because each search engine has collected a different set of information in its database and each search engine uses different procedures to search its database.

Most search engines report the number of hits they find. A **hit** is a Web page that is indexed in the search engine's database and that contains text that matches your search expression. All search engines provide a series of **results pages**, which are Web pages that contain hyperlinks to the Web pages that contain text that matches your search expression.

Each search engine uses a Web robot to build its database. A **Web robot**, also called a **bot** or a **spider**, is a program that automatically searches the Web to find new Web sites and update information about old Web sites that already are in the database. One of a Web robot's more important tasks is to delete information in the database when a Web site no longer exists. The main advantage of using an automated searching tool is that it can examine far more Web sites than an army of people ever could. However, the Web changes every day, and even the best search engine sites cannot keep their databases completely updated. When you click hyperlinks on a search engine results page, you will find that some of the Web pages no longer exist.

Most search engines allow Web page creators to submit the URLs of their pages to search engine databases. This gives search engines another way to add Web pages to their databases. Most search engine operators screen such Web page submissions to prevent a Web page creator from submitting a large number of duplicate or similar Web pages. When the search engine receives a submission, it sends its Web robot out to visit the submitted URL and the robot performs its usual data-gathering tasks.

The organizations that operate search engines often sell advertising space on the search engine Web page and on the results pages. An increasing number of search engine operators also sell paid placement rights on results pages. For example, Toyota might want to purchase rights to the search term "car." When you enter a search expression that includes the word "car," the search engine creates a results page that will have a link to Toyota's Web site at or near the top of the results page. Most, but not all, search engines label these paid placement links as "sponsored," and they are usually called **sponsored links**. If the advertising appears in a box on the page (usually at the top, but sometimes along the side or at the bottom of the page), it is usually called a **banner ad**.

Search engines use the revenue from sponsored links and banner ads to generate profit after covering the costs of maintaining the computer hardware and software required to search the Web and to create and search the database. The only price you pay for access to these excellent search tools is that you will see banner ads on many of the pages, and you might have to scroll through a few sponsored links at the top of results pages; otherwise, your usage is free.

An example of a search results page (for a search on the word "car") from the Google search engine appears in Figure 3-6. You can see the sponsored links to advertisers that have paid for the placement on this page.

Google search results for the search term "car" ◀ **Figure 3-6**

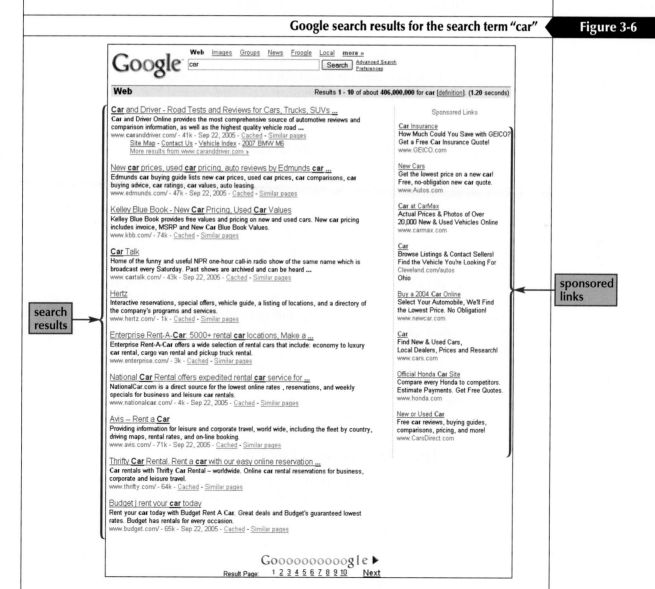

You just received an e-mail message from Dave with your first research assignment. He wants to mention the amount of average rainfall in Belize to make a point in a piece that he is writing. This search question is a specific question, not an exploratory question, because you are looking for a fact and you will know when you have found that fact. You can use the four steps from Figure 3-3 as follows:

1. Formulate and state the question. You have identified key search terms in the question that you can use in your search expression: *Belize*, *rainfall*, and *annual*. You use these terms because they all should appear on any Web page that includes the answer to Dave's question. None of these terms are articles, prepositions, or other common words, and none have multiple meanings. The term *Belize* should be especially useful in narrowing the search to relevant Web pages.
2. Because the question is very specific, you decide that a basic search using a search engine would be a good tool to use.
3. When you obtain the results, you need to review and evaluate them and then decide whether they provide an acceptable answer to your question.
4. If the results do not answer the question to your satisfaction, you need to redefine or reformulate the question so it is more specific and then conduct a second search using a different tool, question, or search expression.

To find the average annual rainfall in Belize:

1. Start your Web browser, open the Student Online Companion page at **www.course.com/newperspectives/internet6**, click the **Tutorial 3** link, and then click the **Session 3.1** link.

2. Select any one of the search engines below the Basic Search Engines heading, click the link to that search engine, and then wait while the browser opens that search engine's Web page.

3. Type **Belize annual rainfall** in the search expression text box.

4. Click the appropriate button to start the search. The search results appear on a new page. That page should state that there are hundreds, perhaps even thousands, of Web pages that might contain the answer to your question.

5. Scroll down the results page and examine your search results. Click some of the links until you find a page or several pages that provide annual rainfall information for Belize. If you do not find any useful links on the first page of search results, click the link to more search results pages (usually located at the bottom of the first results page). Click the **Back** button on your Web browser to return to the results page after going to each hyperlink. You should find that Belize has several climate zones and that the annual rainfall ranges from 50 to 170 inches, or 130 to 430 centimeters.

You bring the results of your search to Dave. After looking them over, Dave asks you to search again using a different search engine.

Using More Than One Search Engine

Dave had expected that you would find one rainfall amount that would be representative of the entire country, but that is not the case. Web searches often disclose information that helps you adjust the assumptions you made when you formulated the original research question. Dave wants you to check another source to confirm your results, so you decide to search for the same information in another search engine.

To conduct the same search to confirm your results:

▶ **1.** Return to the Student Online Companion page for Session 3.1, and then click a link to another of the search engines listed below the Basic Search Engines heading.

▶ **2.** Type **Belize annual rainfall** in the search expression text box.

▶ **3.** Click the appropriate button to start the search. You will most likely see a completely different set of links on your search results page.

▶ **4.** Scroll down the results page and examine your search results, and then click some of the links until you find a page that provides the average annual rainfall for Belize. Return to the results page after going to each hyperlink. Once again, you should find that Belize has several climate zones and that the annual rainfall ranges from 50 to 170 inches, or 130 to 430 centimeters.

Your second search returned a different set of links because each search engine includes different Web pages in its database and because different search engines use different rules to evaluate search expressions. Some search engines will return hits for pages that include *any* of the words in the search expression. Other search engines return hits only for pages that include *all* of the words in the search expression.

The best way to determine how a specific search engine interprets search expressions is to read the Help pages on the search engine Web site. As you become an experienced Web searcher, you will find that you primarily rely on two or three particular search engines. Read the Help pages on those Web sites regularly because search engines do change the way they interpret search expressions from time to time. Figure 3-7 shows the Help page for the AltaVista site's basic search function.

AltaVista Help page for basic searches | Figure 3-7

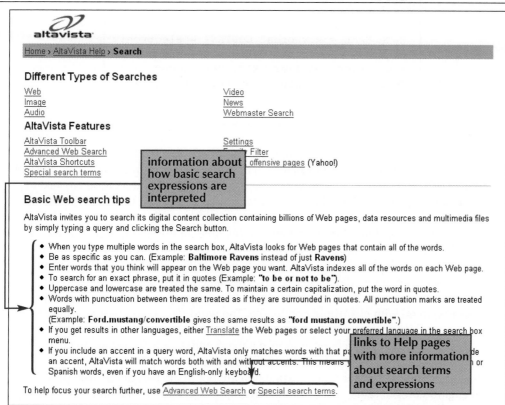

If you found the same information after running both searches, you can give Dave an answer with the second confirmation he requested. If not, you should run additional searches to determine the reason your answers are not consistent, or report to Dave that you have obtained inconsistent results for your search.

You might have noticed that many of the links on the results pages led to Web sites that have no information about Belize rainfall at all. That is why most researchers routinely use several search engines. Answers that are difficult to find using one search engine are often easy to find with another.

Understanding Search Engine Databases

Search engine databases store different collections of information about the pages that exist on the Web at any given time. Many search engine robots do not search all of the Web pages at a particular site. Further, each search engine database indexes the information it has collected from the Web differently. Some search engine robots collect information only from a Web page's title, description, keywords, or HTML tags; others read only a certain number of words from each Web page. Figure 3-8 shows the first few lines of HTML from a Web page that contains information about electronic commerce.

| Figure 3-8 | META tags in a Web page |

```
<HEAD>

<TITLE>
Current Developments in Electronic Commerce
</TITLE>

<META NAME ="description" CONTENT="Current
news and reports about electronic commerce
developments.">

<META NAME ="keywords" CONTENT ="electronic
commerce, electronic data interchange,
value added reseller, EDI, VAR, secure
socket layer, business on the internet">

</HEAD>
```

The description and keywords tags are examples of HTML meta tags. A **meta tag** is HTML code that a Web page creator places in the page header for the specific purpose of informing Web robots about the content of the page. Meta tags do not cause any text to appear on the page when a Web browser loads it; rather, they exist solely for the use of search engine robots.

The information contained in meta tags can become an important part of a search engine's database. For example, the keywords META tag shown in Figure 3-8 includes the phrase "electronic data interchange." These keywords could be a very important phrase in a search engine's database because the three individual words *electronic*, *data*, and *interchange* are common terms that often are used in search expressions that have nothing to do with electronic commerce. The word *data* is so common that many search engines are programmed to ignore it. A search engine that includes the full phrase "electronic data interchange" in its database will greatly increase the chances that a user interested in that topic will find this particular page.

If the terms you use in your search expression are not in the part of the Web page that a search engine stores in its database, the search engine will not return a hit for that page. Some search engines store the entire content of every Web page they index. This practice is called **full text indexing**. Many search engines, even those that claim to be full text indexed search engines, omit common words such as *and*, *the*, *it*, and *by* from their databases. These common words are called **stop words**. You can find out if a particular search engine omits stop words by examining the Help pages provided by the search engine Web site; many search engines include information about their search engines, robots, and databases on their Help or About pages.

Search Engine Features

One advance in search engine technology is page ranking. **Page ranking** is a way of grading Web pages by the number of other Web pages that link to them. The URLs of Web pages with high rankings are presented first on the search results page. A page that has more Web pages linking into it is given a higher ranking than a page that has fewer pages linking into it. In complex page ranking schemes, the value of each link varies with the linking page's rank.

For example, a Web page with many inbound links might have a lower ranking than another Web page that has fewer inbound links if the second page's inbound links are from Web pages that, in turn, have a large number of inbound links themselves. As you can imagine, calculating page ranks can be very complex! Google has been a leader in the use of page ranking and in the development of highly sophisticated page ranking algorithms.

Another feature that search engines are including in their pages is natural language querying. A **natural language query interface** allows users to enter a question exactly as they would ask a person that question. The search engine analyzes the question using knowledge it has been given about the grammatical structure of questions and then uses that knowledge to convert the natural language question into a search query. This procedure of converting a natural language question into a search expression is sometimes called **parsing**. One of the first search engines to offer a natural language query interface was Ask Jeeves. You decide to see how Ask Jeeves handles the Belize rainfall question.

Most search engines use **stemming** to search for variants of keywords automatically. For example, if you search using the keywords *Canada travel guide*, most search engines will return hits that include the keywords "Canadian" and "Canada," as well as pages containing the plural form of the word "guide." Unfortunately, you cannot dictate which variant of your keywords the search engine will use.

To examine the natural language query interface at Ask Jeeves:

1. Return to the Student Online Companion page for Session 3.1, and then click the **Ask Jeeves** link to open the Ask Jeeves search engine page.

2. Type **What is the annual rainfall in Belize?** in the text box, as shown in Figure 3-9.

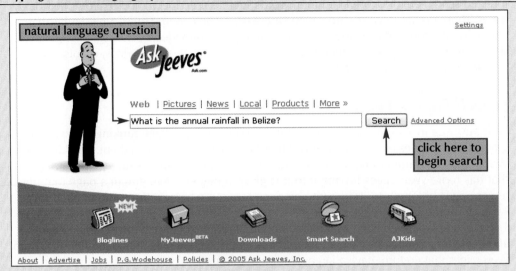

3. Click the **Search** button to run the search. The search results appear on a new page.

4. Scroll down the results page and examine your search results, and then click some of the links to determine whether Ask Jeeves' natural language query interface has provided a good list of search results. Note that the first page of search results offers suggestions for related searches that you can try if your natural language query does not help you answer your question. You can click any of these to see if a reformulated search query offers better results than your original question. Return to the results page after going to each hyperlink.

Using Directories and Hybrid Search Engine Directories

Search engines provide a powerful tool for executing keyword searches of the Web. However, most search engine URL databases are built by computers running programs that perform the search automatically, so they can miss important classification details that a human searcher would notice instantly. For example, if a search engine's robot found a Web page with the title "Test Data: Do Not Use," it would probably include content from the page in the search engine database. If a person were to read such a warning in a Web page title, that person would know not to include the page's contents. However, with billions of Web pages on the Web, the volume of data that a search engine robot obtains as it travels the Web makes it impossible to have people screen every Web page.

Web directories use a completely different approach from search engines to build useful indexes of information on the Web. A **Web directory** is a listing of hyperlinks to Web pages that is organized into hierarchical categories. The difference between a search engine and a Web directory is that the Web pages included in a Web directory are selected and organized into categories before visitors use the directory. In a search engine, the database is searched in response to a visitor's query, and results pages are created in response to each specific search. Most Web directories have human editors who decide which Web pages will be included in the directory and how they will be organized; however, some Web directories use computers to perform these tasks. Web directory editors, who are knowledgeable experts in one or more subject areas and skilled in various classification techniques, review candidate Web pages for inclusion in the directory. When these experts decide that a Web page is worth listing in the directory, they determine the appropriate category in which to store the hyperlink to that page. Most Web directories allow a Web page to be indexed in several different categories. The main weakness of a directory is that users must know which category is likely to yield the information they desire. If users begin searching in the wrong category, they might follow many hyperlinks before they realize that the information they seek is not in that category. Some directories overcome this limitation by including hyperlinks in category levels that link to lower levels in other categories.

One of the oldest and most respected directories on the Web is Yahoo!. David Filo and Jerry Yang, two Stanford doctoral students who wanted a way to keep track of interesting sites they found on the Internet, started Yahoo! in 1994. Since 1994, Yahoo! has grown to become one of the most widely used resources on the Web. Yahoo! currently lists hundreds of thousands of Web pages in its categories—a sizable collection, but only a small portion of the billions of pages on the Web. Although Yahoo! does use some automated programs for checking and classifying its entries, it relies on human experts to do most of the selection and classification work. The Yahoo! Web directory home page appears in Figure 3-10. To open the Yahoo! Directory home page, you can click the Yahoo! Web Directory link on the Yahoo! home page.

| Figure 3-10 | **Yahoo! Web directory home page** |

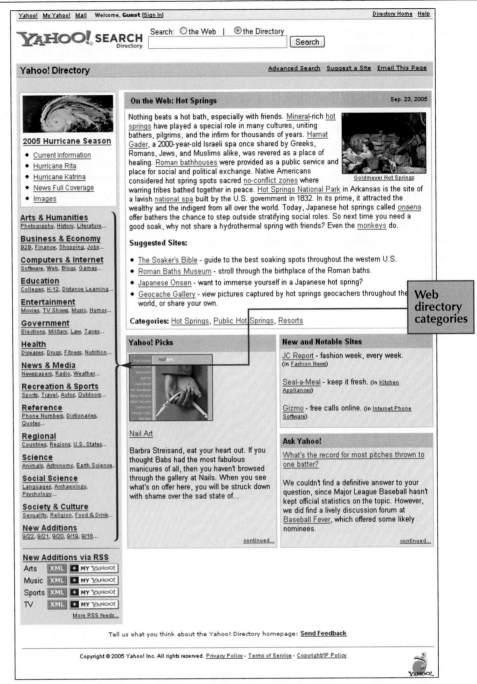

Reproduced with permission of Yahoo! Inc. © 2005 by Yahoo! Inc. YAHOO! and the YAHOO! logo are trademarks of Yahoo! Inc.

The search tool that appears near the top of the page is a search engine within the Yahoo! directory. You can enter search terms into this tool, and Yahoo! will search its listings to find a match. This combination of search engine and directory is sometimes called a **hybrid search engine directory**; however, most directories today include a search engine function, so many people simply call these sites Web directories. No matter what it is called, the combination of search engine and directory provides a powerful and effective tool for searching the Web. Using a hybrid search engine directory can help you identify which category in the directory is likely to contain the information you need. After you enter a category, the search engine is useful for narrowing a search even further; you can enter a search expression and limit the search to that category.

The Web Site Directory section of the Yahoo! home page is a list of links to the Yahoo! Web directory contents. Under each of the 14 main categories, Yahoo! lists several sub-categories. These are not the only subcategories; they are just a sample of those that are the largest or most used. You can click a main category hyperlink to see all of the subcategories under that category.

The Open Directory Project is an interesting Web directory because the editors volunteer their time to create the directory's entries. The home page for the Open Directory Project is shown in Figure 3-11.

Open Directory Project home page ◄ **Figure 3-11**

```
d|m|o|z  open directory project
                              about dmoz | suggest URL | help | link | editor login
```

Web directory categories

| Search   *advanced* |

Arts	**Business**	**Computers**
Movies, Television, Music...	Jobs, Real Estate, Investing...	Internet, Software, Hardware...
Games	**Health**	**Home**
Video Games, RPGs, Gambling...	Fitness, Medicine, Alternative...	Family, Consumers, Cooking...
Kids and Teens	**News**	**Recreation**
Arts, School Time, Teen Life...	Media, Newspapers, Weather...	Travel, Food, Outdoors, Humor...
Reference	**Regional**	**Science**
Maps, Education, Libraries...	US, Canada, UK, Europe...	Biology, Psychology, Physics...
Shopping	**Society**	**Sports**
Autos, Clothing, Gifts...	People, Religion, Issues...	Baseball, Soccer, Basketball...

World
Deutsch, Español, Français, Italiano, Japanese, Nederlands, Polska, Dansk, Svenska...

Become an Editor Help build the largest human-edited directory of the web

Copyright © 1998-2005 Netscape

5,156,479 sites - 69,719 editors - over 590,000 categories

Just as you are becoming familiar with the layout of these Web directories, Dave calls. He would like you to help him by finding some background information on The Conference Board, an organization that does research on business issues and publishes statistics about economic growth and business activity. You tell Dave that you will call him back as quickly as possible. Following the guidelines for searching on the Web that you learned earlier in this tutorial, you decide that Dave's question is about a specific fact and you:

1. Identify key search terms—*Conference Board, business*, and *organization*—that you will use in your search.
2. Use a Web directory to find the answer, so you can search in the business directory instead of searching the entire Web.
3. Examine the results and decide whether a second search using a different category or search terms is necessary.
4. Plan to repeat the first three steps until you determine whether The Conference Board provides any information about itself on the Web.

To find The Conference Board on the Web:

▶ **1.** Return to the Student Online Companion page for Session 3.1, choose one of the sites listed below the Web Directories heading, click the link for the site you chose and wait while your browser opens the site's home page.

▶ **2.** Examine the categories on the directory's home page and click a link that is likely to contain information about The Conference Board. A link that contains the word "Business" or "Economics" would be a good choice.

▶ **3.** Examine the page that loads in your browser. Search for links to subcategories that include words such as "organizations," "industry groups," "statistics," or "indicators." You might need to search several levels down in the directory to find information about The Conference Board. Some Web directories include a search function that lets you search within a category once you have found a likely candidate. If the Web directory you chose to use includes this feature, be sure to try it.

▶ **4.** If you do not find the information you seek in one category, try another. You can also try a different Web directory if you are unable to find the information in the first Web directory you chose to use. Figures 3-12 and 3-13 show the results pages for searches in two Web directories, Yahoo! and Gigablast, respectively. Your results will probably be somewhat different, even if you use the same Web directory sites.

Yahoo! Web directory search results page ◄ | **Figure 3-12**

Yahoo! My Yahoo! Mail   Welcome, **Guest** [Sign In]   Directory Home   Help

YAHOO! SEARCH
Directory

Search: ⦿ the Web | ○ the Directory | ○ this category

[   ] [Search]

Business Organizations > The Conference Board   Advanced Search   Suggest a Site   Email this page

Directory > Business and Economy > Organizations > **Conference Board, The**

SITE LISTINGS By Popularity | Alphabetical   (What's This?)

Sites 1 - 2 of 2   ┌───┐
                                  │ link to The Conference Board Web site │
                                  └───┘

- Conference Board, The - nonprofit business membership and research organization for senior executives internationally; produces the Consumer Confidence Index, and Leading Economic Indicators.

- Ron Brown Award for Corporate Leadership - presented annually by the President of the United States to honor companies for corporate citizenship.

SPONSOR RESULTS (What's this?) (Become a Sponsor)

- CEO- Corporate Training & Development - We enable world-class companies to increase productivity and performance through their people. CEO offers customized Corporate Training & Development for Businesses, Organizations, & Gov't.
www.ceoptions.com

- Bookstore Online, Amazon.com - If you love to read, Amazon is your Internet bookstore. Millions of books like "Corporate Leadership" at remarkable savings.
www.amazon.com

SPONSOR RESULTS

CEO- Corporate Training & Development
We enable world-class companies to increase productivity and ...
www.ceoptions.com

Bookstore Online, Amazon.com
If you love to read, Amazon is your Internet bookstore. Millions of ...
www.amazon.com

Turnaround & Restructuring Specialist
Turnaround & restructuring for wealth recovery. Comprehensive ...
www.alex-wolf.com

Save on Books at Overstock.com
Leadership Chronicles of a Corporate Sage-$10.99 at Overstock.com, ...
www.overstock.com

Organizational Leadership Courses
Request Complimentary Information from Colleges & Schools across the ...
www.find-education.com

See your message here...

Copyright © 2005 Yahoo! Inc. All rights reserved. Privacy Policy - Terms of Service - Copyright/IP Policy

Figure 3-13	Gigablast Web directory search results page

You should be able to find information about The Conference Board at one or more of the sites listed, so you can call Dave back after you have reviewed the sites and developed an outline of the background information that he asked you to find. Now that you have seen how to use a search engine and a hybrid search engine directory, you are ready to use an even more powerful combination of Web research tools: the metasearch engine.

Using Metasearch Engines

A **metasearch engine** is a tool that combines the power of multiple search engines. Some metasearch tools also include directories. The idea behind metasearch tools is simple. Each search engine on the Web has different strengths and weaknesses because each search engine

- uses a different Web robot to gather information about Web pages,
- stores a different amount of Web page text in its database,
- selects different Web pages to index,
- has different storage resources,
- interprets search expressions somewhat differently.

You have already seen how these differences cause different search engines to return vastly different results for the same search expression. To perform a complete search for a particular question, you might need to use several individual search engines. Using a metasearch engine lets you search several engines at the same time, so you need not conduct the same search many times. Metasearch engines do not have their own databases of Web information; instead, a metasearch engine accepts your search expression and transmits it to several search engines. These search engines run the search expression against their databases of Web page information and return results to the metasearch engine. The metasearch engine then reports consolidated results from all of the search engines it queried. A few years ago, some Web search experts believed that metasearch engines would become unnecessary as the larger search engines expanded their coverage of the Web. But the Web continues to grow so rapidly that it outpaces the abilities of any single search engine to keep up with it. Metasearch engines still make it easier to do a complete search of the Web.

Mamma.com was one of the first metasearch engines on the Web. Mamma.com forwards search queries to a number of major search engines and Web directories, including About.com, Google, MSN, Open Directory, Wisenut, and others. The specific search engines and directories that Mamma.com uses changes from time to time because newer and better search tools become available and old favorites disappear. Each entry on the search results page is labeled with the search engine or Web directory that found it. When more than one source provides the same result, that entry is labeled with all of the sources. Figure 3-14 shows the Mamma.com metasearch engine home page.

Figure 3-14 ▶ Mamma.com metasearch engine home page

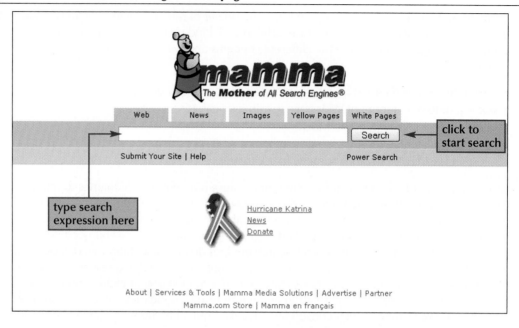

You want to learn how to use metasearch engines so that you can access information faster. You decide to test a metasearch engine using Dave's Belize rainfall question.

Reference Window | **Using a Metasearch Engine**

- Formulate your search question.
- Open the metasearch engine home page in your Web browser.
- Enter the search expression into the metasearch engine.
- Evaluate the results and decide whether to revise the question or your choice of search tools.

To use a metasearch engine:

▶ 1. Return to the Student Online Companion page for Session 3.1, choose one of the sites listed below the Metasearch Engines heading, click the link for the site you chose, and then wait while your browser opens the site's home page.

▶ 2. Type **Belize annual rainfall** in the search text box.

▶ 3. Execute the search by clicking the appropriate button.

▶ 4. Examine and evaluate your search results. If you did not find the information you were seeking, repeat your search using a different metasearch engine.

As you scroll through the search results pages, you can see that there is a wide variation in the number and quality of the results provided by each search engine and directory. You might notice a number of duplicate hits; however, most of the Web pages returned by one search tool are not returned by any other.

Figure 3-15 shows the results page from one of the more interesting metasearch engines, Kartoo. Kartoo presents results in a graphic format. Each image is a link and the images are clustered around words that appear in the results pages. When the pointer is moved over a word, the links appear as lines between the word and the images. In the figure, the pointer has been moved over the word "weather" and the clustering of links based on that term are shown as orange lines. You can refine your search by clicking one of the words to add it to your search expression.

Kartoo metasearch graphic results | Figure 3-15

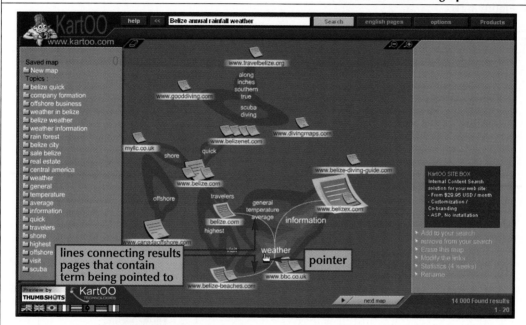

Using Other Web Resources

Various resources available for searching the Web do not fit exactly into one of the three preceding categories. These search resources are similar to bibliographies, but instead of listing books or journal articles, they contain lists of hyperlinks to Web pages. Just as some bibliographies are annotated, many of these resources include summaries or reviews of Web pages. These resources are often called **Web bibliographies**, but many other names are used for them, including **resource lists**, **subject guides**, **clearinghouses**, and **virtual libraries**. Sometimes they are called Web directories, which can be somewhat confusing. Web bibliographies are usually more focused on specific subjects than Web directories, and Web bibliographies usually do not include a tool for searching within their categories.

These other resources can be very useful when you want to obtain a broad overview or a basic understanding of a complex subject area. A search for such information using a search engine or directory is likely to turn up a narrow list of references that are too detailed and that assume a great deal of prior knowledge. For example, using a search engine or directory to find information about quantum physics will probably give you many hits to technical papers and Web pages devoted to current research issues in quantum physics. However, your search probably will yield very few Web pages that provide an introduction to the topic. In contrast, a Web bibliography page can offer hyperlinks to information regarding a particular subject that is presented at various levels. Many of these resources include annotations and reviews of the sites they list. This information can help you identify Web pages that fit your level of knowledge or interest.

Some Web bibliographies, such as the Librarian's Index to the Internet, are general references. Most are more focused, such as Martindale's The Reference Desk, which emphasizes science-related links. Some Web bibliographies, such as the Scout Report and the Argus Clearinghouse, are no longer actively updated, but they are maintained on the Web as useful information resources.

Many Web bibliographies are created by librarians at university and public libraries. You can find Web bibliographies on specific subjects by entering a search term along with the words "subject guide" into a search engine. The results of an example search on the words "Native American subject guide" conducted in the Google search engine appear in Figure 3-16.

Figure 3-16 ▶ **Results of a Google search on "Native American subject guide"**

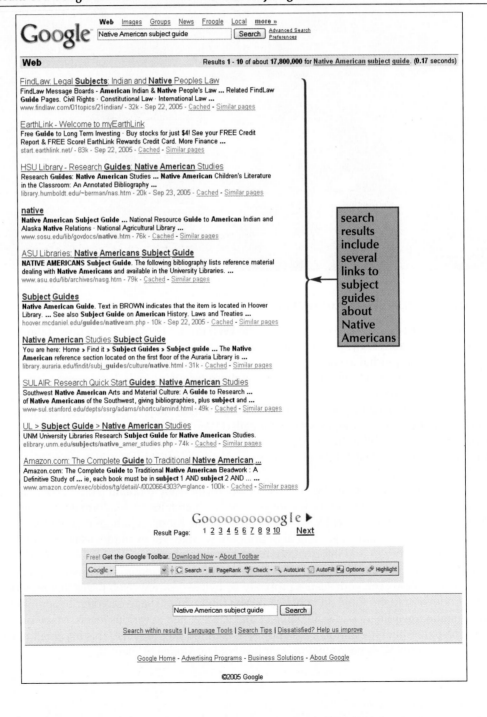

Another way to find Web bibliographies is to use a Web directory site. Many Web directories include links to subject-specific Web bibliographies within the category listings for those subjects. For example, the Yahoo! Web directory includes a link titled "Web Directories" within its Social Science category. This link leads to a list of Web bibliographies on the subject of social science. It also has similar links in many of the social science subcategories, such as Economics. Other Web directories include similar links.

Ranjit stops by your office to ask for your help. He is planning to write a series of pieces on the business and economic effects of current trends in biotechnology. The potential effects of genetic engineering research particularly intrigue him, but he admits that he does not know much about any of these topics. Ranjit wants you to find some Web sites that he can use to learn more about biotechnology trends in general and genetic engineering research in particular. You determine that Ranjit's request is an exploratory search. You decide to use a Web bibliography site for your research on the question that Ranjit has given you. You know that biotechnology is a branch of the biological sciences, so you and Ranjit identify three category terms: *biotechnology*, *genetic engineering*, and *biology* to use as your search categories.

To use a Web bibliography to conduct an exploratory search:

1. Return to the Student Online Companion page for Session 3.1, choose one of the sites listed below the Web Bibliographies heading, click its link, and wait while the browser opens the site's home page.

2. Examine the page for links that might lead to information about biotechnology, genetic engineering, or biology. Follow those links to gather information for Ranjit.

3. Examine your search results and determine whether you have gathered sufficient useful information to respond to Ranjit's request. If you have not, repeat the search using a different Web bibliography. Remember, you can often find useful subject guides by entering the search term along with the words "subject guide" into a regular search engine.

4. Close your browser.

You have completed your search for Web sites that might help Ranjit. Many of these sites contain hyperlinks to other useful sites that Ranjit might want to explore. You can deliver information from these pages to Ranjit by printing copies of the Web pages, sending the URLs by e-mail, or saving the Web pages and attaching them to an e-mail message. Because your answer to Ranjit's question involves so many pages at different sites, your best approach would be to send an e-mail message with a list of relevant URLs.

Session 3.1 Quick Check

Review

1. What are the key characteristics of an exploratory search question?
2. True or False: Many Web search engine operators use advertising revenue to cover their expenses and to earn a profit.
3. The part of a search engine site that searches the Web to collect information for the search engine's database is called a(n) _____.
4. A search engine that uses page ranking will list a Web page nearer the top of search results pages if that page has many _____.
5. True or False: Most search engines index all Web page words in their databases.

6. List one advantage and one disadvantage of using a Web directory instead of a Web search engine to locate information.
7. How does a hybrid search engine directory overcome the disadvantages of using either a search engine or a directory alone?
8. How does a metasearch engine process the search expression you enter into it?
9. What are the key features offered by Web bibliographies?

Session 3.2

Boolean Logic and Filtering Techniques

The most important factor in obtaining good results from a search engine, a metasearch engine, or a search tool within a hybrid search engine directory is careful selection of the search terms you use. When the object of your search is straightforward, you can usually choose one or two words that will work well. More complex search questions require more complex queries, which you can use along with Boolean logic, search expression operators, wildcard operators, or filtering techniques, to broaden or narrow your search expression. In the next four sections, you will learn how to use each of these techniques.

The Boolean operators and filtering techniques you will learn to use in this session can also be helpful when you are doing searches in library databases. These databases, which can be very expensive to purchase, provide much information that cannot be found on the Internet. You can check with your school library, your company library, or your local public library to find out which of these databases they have available. Each database has its own implementation of Boolean operators and filtering tools, but the principles you learn here will help you in formulating your searches of these library databases.

Boolean Operators

When you enter a single word into a Web search tool, it searches for matches to that word. When you enter a search expression that includes more than one word, the search tool makes assumptions about the words that you enter. You learned in Session 3.1 that some search engines assume that you want to match *any* of the keywords in your search expression whereas other search engines assume that you want to match *all* of the keywords. These differing assumptions can make dramatic differences in the number and quality of hits returned. Many search engines are designed to offer both options because users might want to match all of the keywords on one search and any of the keywords on a different search. One way of implementing these options is to accept Boolean operators as part of the search expression.

George Boole was a nineteenth-century British mathematician who developed **Boolean algebra**, the branch of mathematics and logic that bears his name. In Boolean algebra, all values are reduced to one of two values. In most practical applications of Boole's work, these two values are *true* and *false*. Although Boole did his work a hundred years before computers became commonplace, his algebra was useful to computer engineers and programmers. At the very lowest level of analysis, all computing is a manipulation of a single computer circuit's on and off states. Unlike the algebra you might have learned in your math classes, Boolean algebra does not use numbers or mathematical operators. Instead, Boolean algebra uses words and logical relationships.

Some parts of Boolean algebra are useful in search expressions. **Boolean operators**, also called **logical operators**, are a key part of Boolean algebra. Boolean operators specify the logical relationship between the elements they join, just as the plus sign arithmetic operator specifies the mathematical relationship between the two elements it joins. Three basic Boolean operators—AND, OR, and NOT—are recognized by most search engines. You can use these operators in many search engines by simply including them with search terms. For example, the search expression "exports AND France" returns hits for pages that contain both words, the expression "exports OR France" returns hits for pages that contain either word, and "exports NOT France" returns hits for pages that contain the word *export* but not the word *France*. Some search engines use "AND NOT" to indicate the Boolean NOT operator.

Some search engines recognize variants of the Boolean operators, such as "must include" and "must exclude" operators. For example, a search engine that uses the plus sign to indicate "must include" and the minus sign to indicate "must exclude" would respond to the expression "exports + France - Japan" with hits that included anything about exports and France, but only if those pages did not include anything about Japan.

Figure 3-17 shows several ways to use Boolean operators in more complex search expressions that contain the words *exports*, *France*, and *Japan*. The figure shows the matches that a search engine will return if it interprets the Boolean operators correctly. Figure 3-17 also describes information-gathering tasks in which you might use these expressions.

Using Boolean operators in search expressions ◄ **Figure 3-17**

Search Expression	Search Returns Pages that Include	Use to Find Information About
exports AND France AND Japan	All of the three search terms.	Exports from France to Japan or from Japan to France.
exports OR France OR Japan	Any of the three search terms.	Exports from anywhere, including France and Japan, and all kinds of information about France and Japan.
exports NOT France NOT Japan	Exports, but not if the page also includes the terms France or Japan.	Exports to and from any countries other than France or Japan.
exports AND France NOT Japan	Exports and France, but not Japan.	Exports from France to anywhere but Japan or to France from anywhere but Japan.

Other Search Expression Operators

When you join three or more search terms with Boolean operators, it is easy to become confused by the expression's complexity. To reduce the confusion, you can use precedence operators, a tool you probably learned in basic algebra, along with the Boolean operators. A **precedence operator**, also called an **inclusion operator** or a **grouping operator**, clarifies the grouping within a complex expression and is usually indicated by the parentheses symbols. Figure 3-18 shows several ways to use precedence operators with Boolean operators in search expressions.

Using Boolean and precedence operators in search expressions ◄ **Figure 3-18**

Search Expression	Search Returns Pages that Include	Use to Find Information About
Exports AND (France OR Japan)	Exports and either France or Japan.	Exports from or to either France or Japan.
Exports OR (France AND Japan)	Exports or both France and Japan.	Exports from anywhere, including France and Japan, and all kinds of other information about both France and Japan.
Exports AND (France NOT Japan)	Exports and France, but not if the page also includes Japan.	Exports to and from France, except those going to or from Japan.

Some search engines use double quotation marks to indicate precedence grouping; however, most search engines use double quotation marks to indicate search terms that must be matched exactly as they appear within the double quotation marks. Using an exact match search phrase can be particularly useful because most search engines ignore stop words by default. You can force most search engines to include a stop word (that they would, by default, ignore) in a search expression by enclosing it in double quotation marks (or by including it in an exact search phrase that is enclosed in double quotation marks).

Another useful search expression tool is the location operator. A **location operator**, or **proximity operator**, lets you search for terms that appear close to each other in the text of a Web page. The most common location operator offered in Web search engines is the NEAR operator. If you are interested in French exports, you might want to find only Web pages in which the terms *exports* and *France* are close to each other. Unfortunately, each search engine that implements this operator uses its own definition of how close "NEAR" is. One search engine might define NEAR to mean "within 10 words," whereas another search engine might define NEAR to mean "within 20 words." To use the NEAR operator effectively, you must read the search engine's Help file carefully.

Wildcard Characters

A few search engines support some use of a wildcard character in their search expressions. A **wildcard character** allows you to omit part of a search term. The search engines that include this function most commonly use the asterisk (*) as the wildcard character. For example, the search expression "export*" would return pages containing the terms *exports*, *exporter*, *exporters*, and *exporting* in many search engines. Some search engines let you use a wildcard character in the middle of a search term. For example, the expression "wom*n" would return pages containing both *woman* and *women*.

Search Filters

Many search engines allow you to restrict your search by using search filters. A **search filter** eliminates Web pages from a search. The filter criteria can include such Web page attributes as language, date, domain, host, or page component (URL, hyperlink, image tag, or title tag). For example, many search engines provide a way to search for the term *exports* in Web page titles and ignore pages in which the term appears in other parts of the page.

Complex Searches

Most search engines implement many of the operators and filtering techniques you have learned about, but search engine syntax varies. Some search engines provide separate advanced search pages for these techniques; others allow you to use advanced techniques such as Boolean operators on their simple search pages.

In this section, we describe how to conduct complex searches in several specific search engines. The steps are correct as this book is printed, but the Web is a changing medium. When you perform these steps, the screens you see might look different and you might need to modify the steps. If you encounter difficulties, ask your instructor for assistance or read the Help pages on the search engine site. If major changes occur, we will post information on the Student Online Companion Web site about how to make the searches work.

Using AltaVista Advanced Search

Ranjit is writing about the role that trade agreements play in limiting the flow of agricultural commodities between countries. His current project concerns the German economy. He wants you to find some Web page references for him that might provide useful background information for his column. Ranjit is especially interested in learning more about the German perspective on trade issues.

You recognize this as an exploratory question and decide to use the advanced query capabilities of the AltaVista search engine to conduct a complex search for Web pages that Ranjit might use for his research. AltaVista offers very good support for Boolean and precedence operators.

To create a useful search expression, you must identify search terms that might lead you to appropriate Web pages. Some terms you might use for Ranjit's search are *Germany*, *trade*, *treaty*, and *agriculture*. You want to provide Ranjit with a reasonable number of hyperlinks to Web pages, but you do not want to inundate him with thousands of URLs, so you decide to combine the search terms using Boolean and precedence operators to create a search expression that will focus only on useful sites. You also decide to use the wildcard character to allow the search to find plural and extended forms of the terms *treaty* (such as *treaties*) and *agriculture* (such as *agricultures*, *agricultural*, and *agriculturally*).

Conducting a Complex Search Using AltaVista

Reference Window

- Open the AltaVista search engine in your Web browser.
- Select the Advanced Search option.
- Formulate and enter a suitable search expression.
- Click the Find button.
- Evaluate the results and, if necessary, revise your search expression.

To perform a complex search using AltaVista:

1. Start your Web browser, open the Student Online Companion page at **www.course.com/newperspectives/internet6**, click the **Tutorial 3** link, click the **Session 3.2** link, and then click the **AltaVista** link and wait while the browser opens the AltaVista home page.

2. Click the **Advanced Search** link on the AltaVista page.

3. Click the **Search with...** option button, click in the **this boolean expression** text box, and then type **Germany AND (trade OR treat*) AND agricult*** in the text box.

4. Click the **Find** button to start the search. The results appear in Figure 3-19.

Figure 3-19 ▶ Complex search in AltaVista with Boolean and precedence operators

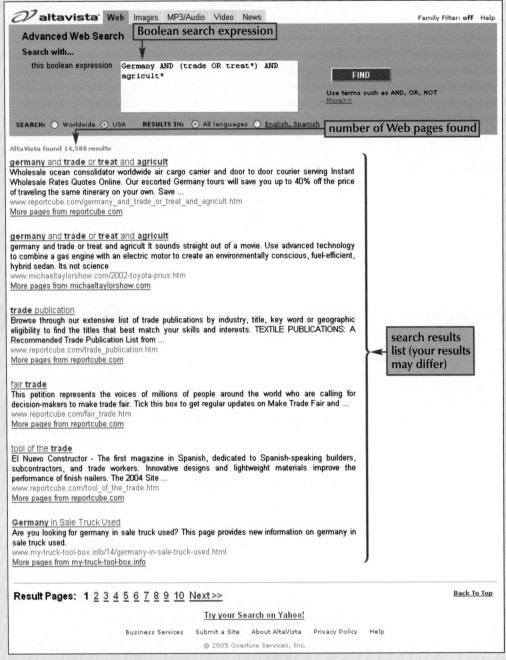

Reproduced with permission of Overture Services, Inc. ©2005 by Overture Services, Inc. AltaVista and the AltaVista logo are trademarks of Overture Services, Inc.

Filtered Search in Ask Jeeves

Some search engines provide specific filtering options in addition to or instead of Boolean operators. The Ask Jeeves search engine offers several such options on its Advanced Search Options page, including filters for date and geographic region.

Dave stops by your office to tell you he is writing about upcoming rice harvests in Vietnam and Indonesia. He wants you to check on developments that have occurred during the past six months in that part of the world. You decide to use the Ask Jeeves search engine to run a filtered search query for Dave.

Conducting a Filtered Search Using Ask Jeeves

- Open the Ask Jeeves search engine page in your Web browser.
- Select the Advanced Options link.
- Formulate and enter a suitable search expression.
- Set any filters you want to use for the search.
- Click the Ask button.
- Evaluate the results and, if necessary, revise your search expression.

To perform a filtered search using Ask Jeeves:

1. Return to the Student Online Companion page for Session 3.2, and then click the **Ask Jeeves** link and wait while the browser opens the Ask Jeeves home page.

2. Click the **Advanced Options** link to open the Ask Jeeves Advanced Search page.

3. Click in the search text box, and then type **rice harvest**.

4. Click the **Geographic Region** list arrow, and click **Southeast Asia** to set the Region filter.

5. Click the first list arrow in the **Date page was modified** area of the page, and then click **Last 6 Months** to set the Date filter. Figure 3-20 shows the Ask Jeeves Advanced Search page with the search expression entered and the filters set.

Figure 3-20 ▶ **Using search filters in Ask Jeeves**

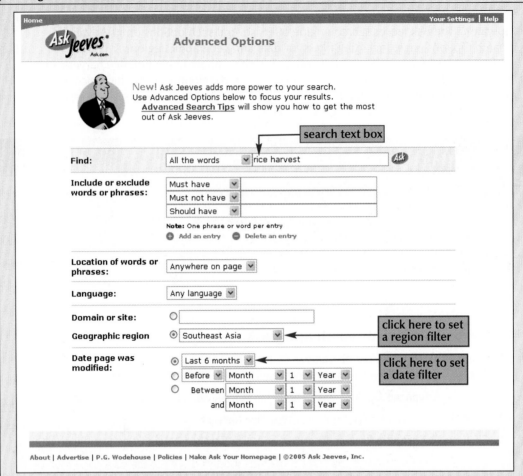

Trouble? You might see a different month and year listed in the second line of the Date filter. Because that option is not selected, the setting of that filter will not affect your search results.

6. Click the **Ask** button next to the search text box to start the search. Figure 3-21 shows the search results page, where you can see the search expression, the filter settings, and a list of hyperlinks to related Web pages. The description also includes suggestions for search terms you can use to narrow your search if you wish.

Ask Jeeves filtered search results page   **Figure 3-21**

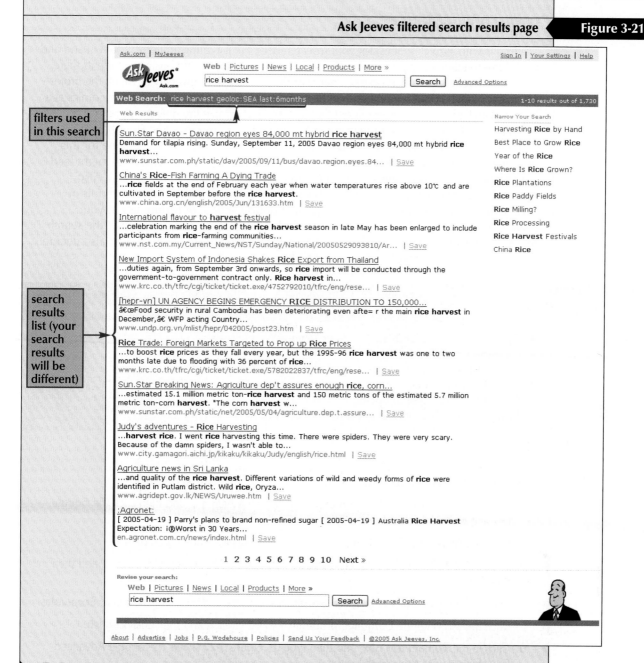

filters used in this search

search results list (your search results will be different)

7. Examine your search results and determine whether you have gathered sufficient useful information to respond to Dave's request. Since the search returned some links that contain information relevant to Dave's query, you can conclude your work by forwarding the URLs to Dave.

Filtered Search in Google

Dave calls with a quick request for your research help. He is writing an item about Finland and would like to interview a professor he once met who taught graduate business students there. He does not remember the professor's name or the name of the university at which the professor teaches, but he does remember that the professor was part of the School of Economics at a university in Finland. Dave is confident that he would recognize the university's name if he saw it again. He asks if you can search the Web to find the names of some Finnish universities.

After evaluating Dave's request, you decide to use the Google search engine for this task. To create a useful search expression, you must identify search terms that might lead you to appropriate Web pages. You decide to include *Finland* as a search term. Also, Dave told you that graduate schools of business in Europe are often called Schools of Economics, so you decide to include the exact phrase *School of Economics* in your search. You know that the country code for Finland is *.fi* so you decide to limit the search to Web pages in that top-level domain. Because Dave reads only English, you also decide to limit the search to pages that are in English.

Reference Window	**Conducting a Filtered Search Using Google Advanced Search**

- Open the Google search engine page in your Web browser.
- Click the Advanced Search link.
- Formulate and enter suitable search expression elements.
- Formulate and set appropriate search filters.
- Click the Google Search button.
- Evaluate the results and, if necessary, revise your search expression.

To perform a filtered search using Google Advanced Search:

▶ 1. Return to the Student Online Companion page for Session 3.2, and then click the **Google** link and wait while the browser opens the Google home page.

▶ 2. Click the **Advanced Search** link to open the Google Advanced Search page.

▶ 3. Click in the **Find results with all of the words** text box at the top of the page, and then type **Finland**.

▶ 4. Click in the **Find results with the exact phrase** text box, and then type **School of Economics**.

▶ 5. Click the arrow on the **Language** drop-down selection box, and then click **English**.

▶ 6. Click in the **Domain** text box, and then type **.fi**. Figure 3-22 shows the Google Advanced Search page with the search expressions entered and the filters set.

Google Advanced Search page | Figure 3-22

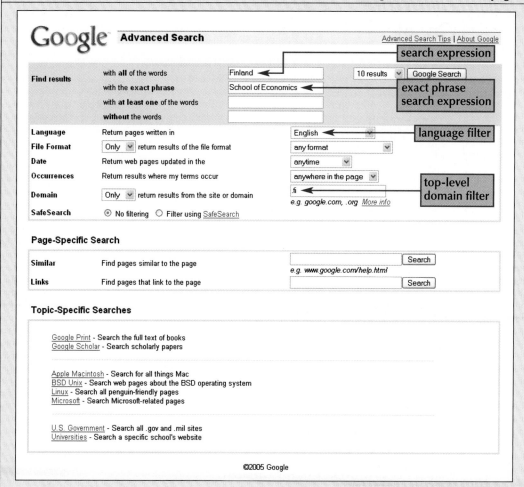

7. Click the **Google Search** button to start the search. The top portion of the search results page appears in Figure 3-23 and includes a number of links to Finnish universities that should be helpful to Dave.

Figure 3-23 | **Google Advanced Search results page**

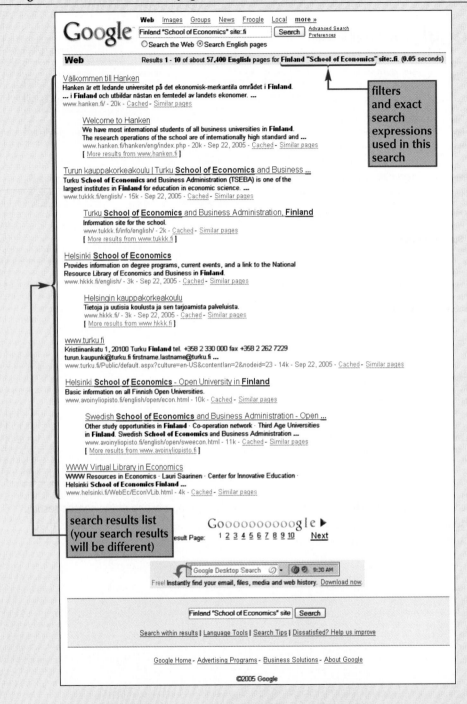

8. Examine your search results and determine which of the hyperlinks in the search results lead to Finnish universities. You can send a list of these links to Dave in an e-mail message. Remember that you might need to examine several pages of search results to find exactly what you need.

Search Engines with Clustering Features

One problem with using search engines is that they often generate thousands (or even millions) of hits. Scrolling through hundreds of results pages looking for useful links is not very efficient. Vivísimo is a search engine that uses an advanced technology to group its results into clusters. The clustering of results provides a filtering effect; however, the filtering is done automatically by the search engine after it runs the search. You would like to try this search engine to see if its results clustering feature provides results that are easier to review.

Ranjit is writing about fast-food franchises in various developing countries around the world. He would like to feature this industry's experience in Indonesia in upcoming newsletters and monthly reports and asks you for help. You decide to run this search for Ranjit using the Vivísimo search engine. To create a useful search expression, you must identify search terms that might lead you to appropriate Web pages. Some terms you might use include *fast food*, *franchise*, and *Indonesia*. You are not interested in Web pages that have the individual terms *fast* and *food*, so you will use double quotation marks to specify the phrase "*fast food*." The Vivísimo search engine does not support full Boolean logic, so you will enter a simple expression and let Vivísimo's clustering feature filter your results.

Obtaining Clustered Search Results Using Vivísimo	Reference Window

- Open the Vivísimo search engine page in your browser.
- Formulate and enter a suitable search expression.
- Click the Search button.
- Evaluate the results and, if necessary, revise your search expression.

To obtain clustered search results using Vivísimo:

▶ 1. Return to the Student Online Companion page for Session 3.2, and then click the **Vivísimo** link and wait while your browser opens the Vivísimo Search page.

▶ 2. Click in the search text box, and then type **"fast food" franchise Indonesia**. Make sure that you type the quotation marks so that you find the phrase "fast food" instead of the individual terms.

▶ 3. Click the **Cluster** button to start the search. Figure 3-24 shows the search results page, which includes a number of promising hyperlinks.

Figure 3-24 ▶ **Vivísimo search results page**

4. In the list of Clustered Results links at the left side of the page, click the category links that look promising. You can click the circles that contain plus signs to reveal links to sub-categories. Examine your search results from each cluster and determine whether you have gathered enough information about the fast-food industry in Indonesia for Ranjit.

5. When you have finished examining the results, close your Web browser.

A unique feature of Vivísimo is that it collects search results into clusters and it runs the clustering algorithms as the search results are returned. That is, instead of classifying Web pages into categories in its database, it creates the categories dynamically after it processes the search expression. Your search provides Ranjit with a number of useful links and he thanks you for a job well done.

Future of Web Search Tools

A number of different companies and organizations are working on ways to make searching the Web easier for the increasing numbers of people who use the Web. One weakness of most current search engines and Web directories is that they only search static Web pages. A **static Web page** is an HTML file that exists on a Web server computer. The robots used by search engines to build their databases can find and examine these files. An increasing number of Web sites do not store information as HTML files. Instead, they store information in a database, and when a user submits a query, the Web server searches the database and generates a Web page on the fly that includes information from the database. These generated Web pages are called **dynamic Web pages**. For example, if you visit Amazon.com and search for books about birds, the Amazon.com Web server queries a database that contains information about books and generates a dynamic Web page that includes that information. This Web page is not stored permanently on the Web server and cannot be found or examined by search engine robots. Much of this information can only be accessed by users that have a login and password. In 2001,

Michael Bergman of BrightPlanet published a paper that explored the difficulties that search engines face when trying to include this information in their search databases. He called this information the **deep Web**; other researchers use the terms **hidden Web** and **invisible Web**. You can learn more about the deep Web and current research on ways to search it by visiting the Complete Planet Web site.

Work on natural language interfaces continues as search engine sites strive to make the job of searching even easier for users. An increasing number of search engines offer natural language querying as an option for entering search expressions. Although it is unlikely that these interfaces will provide the same power as Boolean searches anytime soon, they are much easier for infrequent Internet searchers to use. You also learned earlier in this Tutorial that Kartoo uses graphic display technology to present its search results.

Using People to Enhance Web Directories

One company, About.com, hires people with expertise in specific subject areas to create and manage its Web directory entries in those areas. Although both Yahoo! and MSN Search use subject matter experts this way, About.com takes the idea one step further and identifies its experts. Each of the About.com experts, called Guides, hosts a page with hyperlinks to related Web pages, moderates discussion areas, and provides an online newsletter. This creates a community of interested persons from around the world that can participate in maintaining the Web directory. Figure 3-25 shows the top portion of the About.com page that discusses classic literature.

About.com classic literature subject page ◄ **Figure 3-25**

The Open Directory Project uses the services of more than 40,000 volunteer editors who maintain listings in their individual areas of interest. The Open Directory Project offers the information in its Web directory to other Web directories and search engines at no charge. Many of the major Web directory, search engine, and metasearch engine sites regularly download and store the Open Directory Project's information in their databases. For example, AlltheWeb, AltaVista, DogPile, and Google all include Open Directory Project information in their databases.

Evaluating the Validity and Quality of Web Research Resources

Now that you have been working for IER for a while, Anne wants to meet with you to review some of the standards and practices for information IER collects using the Internet. One of the most important issues in doing Web research is assessing the validity and quality of the information provided on the Internet. Because the Web has made publishing so easy and inexpensive, virtually anybody can create a Web page on almost any subject.

Research published in scientific or literary journals is subjected to peer review. Similarly, books and research monographs are often reviewed by peers or edited by experts in the appropriate subject area. However, information on the Web is seldom subjected to the review and editing processes that have become a standard practice in print publishing.

When you search the Web for entertainment or general information, the damage that could be caused by gathering inaccurate or unreliable information is not great. When you are searching the Web for an answer to a serious research question, however, the risks of obtaining and relying on inaccurate or unreliable information can be significant.

You can reduce your risks by carefully evaluating the quality of any Web resource on which you plan to rely for information related to an important judgment or decision. To develop an opinion about the quality of the resource, you can evaluate three major components of any Web page: the Web page's authorship, content, and appearance.

Author Identity and Objectivity

The first thing you should try to do when evaluating a Web research resource is to determine who authored the page. If you cannot easily find authorship information on a Web site, you should question the validity of the information included on that site. A Web site that does not identify its author has very little credibility as a research resource. Any Web page that presents empirical research results, logical arguments, theories, or other information that purports to be the result of a research process should identify the author *and* present the author's background information and credentials. The information on the site should be sufficient to establish the author's professional qualifications. You should also check secondary sources for corroborating information. For example, if the author of a Web page indicates that he or she is a member of a university faculty, you can find the university's Web site and see if the author is listed as a faculty member. The Web site should also provide author contact information, such as a street, e-mail address, or telephone number, so that you can contact the author or consult information directories to verify the addresses or telephone numbers.

In some cases, it can be difficult to determine who owns a specific Web server or provides the space for the Web page. You can make a rough assessment, however, by examining the domain identifier in the URL. If the site claims affiliation with an educational or research institution, the domain should be .edu for educational institution. A not-for-profit organization would most likely have the .org domain, and a government unit or agency would have the .gov domain. These are not hard-and-fast rules, however. For example, some perfectly legitimate not-for-profit organizations have URLs with a .com domain.

You also should consider whether the qualifications presented by the author pertain to the material that appears on the Web site. For example, the author of a Web site concerned with gene-splicing technology might list a Ph.D. degree as a credential. If the author's Ph.D. is in history or sociology, it would not support the credibility of the gene-splicing technology Web site. If you cannot determine the specific areas of the author's educational background, you can look for other examples of the author's work on the Web. By searching for the author's name and terms related to the subject area, you should be able to find other sites that include the author's work. The fact that a Web site author has written extensively on a subject can add some evidence—though not necessarily conclusive—that the author has expertise in the field.

In addition to identifying the author's identity and qualifications, the author information should include details about the author's affiliations—either as an employee, owner, or consultant—with organizations that might have an interest in the research results or other information included in the Web site. Information about the author's affiliations will help you determine the level of independence and objectivity that the author can bring to bear on the research questions or topics. For example, research results supporting the contention that cigarette smoke is not harmful presented in a site authored by a researcher with excellent scientific credentials might be less compelling if you learn that the researcher is the chief scientist at a major tobacco company. By reading the page content carefully, you might be able to identify potential bias in the results presented.

Content

Content is a criterion that can be more difficult to judge than the author's identity and objectivity; after all, you were searching for Web sites so you could learn more about your search topic, which implies that you probably are not an expert in that content area. However, you can look for some things in the Web site's presentation to help determine the quality of information. If the Web page has a clearly stated publication date, you can determine the timeliness of the content. You can read the content critically and evaluate whether the included topics are relevant to the research question at hand. You might be able to determine whether important topics or considerations were omitted. You also might be able to assess the depth of treatment the author gives to the subject.

Form and Appearance

The Web does contain pages full of misinformation and outright lies that are nicely laid out, include professionally produced graphics, and have grammatically correct and properly spelled text. However, many pages that contain low-quality or incorrect information are poorly designed and not well edited. For example, a Web page devoted to an analysis of Shakespeare's plays that contains spelling errors indicates a low-quality resource. Loud colors, graphics that serve no purpose, and flashing text are all Web page design elements that often suggest a low-quality resource.

Evaluating the Quality of a Web Site

Having explained how the IER research team applies these principles of assessing Web page quality, Anne asks you to evaluate a Web page. Anne has been doing research on how companies can appeal to children on the Web by promoting products while not taking advantage of the children who visit their sites. She has been gathering a list of URLs that she will take to an editorial meeting where she hopes to get the project approved. Anne would like you to evaluate the quality of a URL titled "Kids' Corner" that is on her list.

Evaluating a Web Research Resource

Reference Window

- Open the Web page in your Web browser.
- Identify the author, if possible. If you can identify the author, evaluate his or her credentials and objectivity.
- Examine the content of the Web site.
- Evaluate the site's form and appearance.
- Draw a conclusion about the site's overall quality.

To evaluate the quality of the Kids' Corner Web page:

1. Return to the Student Online Companion page for Session 3.2.
2. Click the **Kids' Corner** link and wait while the browser loads the Web page that appears in Figure 3-26. Examine the content of the Web page, read the text, examine the titles and headings, and consider the page's appearance.

Figure 3-26 ▶ **Kids' Corner Web page**

Jakob Nielsen's Alertbox, April 14, 2002:

Kids' Corner: Website Usability for Children

Summary:
Our usability study of kids found that they are as easily stumped by confusing websites as adults. Unlike adults, however, kids tend to view ads as content, and click accordingly. They also like colorful designs, but demand simple text and navigation.

Millions of children already use the Internet, and millions more are coming online each year. Many websites specifically target children with educational or entertainment content, and even mainstream websites are adding "kids' corner" sections for children -- either as a public service or to build brand loyalty from an early age.

Despite this growth in users and services, very little is known about how children actually use websites or how to design sites that will be easy for them to use. Most website designs for kids are based on **pure folklore about how kids supposedly behave** -- or, at best, by insights gleaned when designers observe their own children, who are hardly representative of average kids, typical Internet skills, or common knowledge about the Web.

Testing Children's Web Use

To find out how kids really use the Web, we conducted usability studies with 55 children who varied in age from 6 to 12 (first through fifth graders). We tested 39 kids in the United States and 16 in Israel, to broaden the international applicability of our recommendations.

We observed the children interacting with 24 sites designed for children, and three mainstream sites designed for adults (Amazon, Yahoo!, and Weather.com). For the targeted sites, we tested some sites specifically devoted to children, such as Alfy, MaMaMedia, and Sesame Street, and several kid-oriented subsites produced by mainstream companies, such as ABC News for Kids and Belmont Bank's Kids' Corner.

Even though participants in our study were very young, they often had the **greatest success using websites intended for adults**. Sites such as Amazon and Yahoo! are committed to utter simplicity and compliance with Web design conventions, and have become so easy to use that they support little kids very well. In contrast, many of the children's sites had complex and convoluted interaction designs that stumped our test users. As one first-grade boy said, *"The Internet is a lot of times BORING because you can't find anything when you go on to it."*

Usability Problems Hurt Kids

The idea that children are **masters of technology** and can defeat any computer-related difficulty is a myth. Our study found that children are **incapable of overcoming many usability problems**. Also, poor usability, combined with kids' lack of patience in the face of complexity, resulted in many simply leaving websites. A fourth-grader said, *"When I don't know what to do on a Web page, I just go look for something else."*

Also, children don't like slow downloads any more than adults do. As one first-grade girl said, *"Make it go faster! Maybe if I click it, it will go faster..."*

Young children often have **hand-me-down computers**, whether at home (where they often inherit older machines when their parents upgrade) or at school (where budget constraints mandate keeping machines in service for many years). Kids also typically have slow connections and outdated software. Given these limitations, websites must **avoid technical problems** or crashes related to access by low-end equipment. Faced with an error message, kids in our study told us that they see them a lot, and that the best thing to do is to ignore them or close the window and find something else to do.

Several types of **classic Web usability problems** caused difficulties for the kids in our study:

- **Unclear navigational confirmation** of the user's location confused users both within sites and when leaving them.
- **Inconsistent navigation** options, where the same destination was referred to in different ways, caused users to visit the same feature repeatedly, because they didn't know they had already been there.
- **Non-standard interaction techniques** caused predictable problems, such as making it impossible for users to select their preferred game using a "games machine."
- **Lack of perceived clickability** affordances, such as overly flat graphics, caused users to miss features because they overlooked the links.
- **Fancy wording** in interfaces confused users and prevented them from understanding the available choices.

Age-Appropriate Content

Extensive text was problematic for young children, who are just beginning to read. We observed severe usability problems when kids were inadvertently thrown into sections that were written above their current reading level.

Also, kids are **keenly aware of their age** and differentiate sharply between material that is appropriate for them and material for older or younger kids, however close in age they might be. At one website, a six-year-old said, *"This website is for babies, maybe four or five years old. You can tell because of the cartoons and trains."*

Source: http://www.useit.com/alertbox/20020414.html

You can see that the author of the page is Jakob Nielsen and that the page has a clear, simple design. You note that the grammar and spelling are correct and the content is neither inflammatory nor overly argumentative, although it does reflect a strong specific viewpoint on the issue. The date on which the page was published is clearly stated at the top of the page. You note that this page appears to be a part of a Web publication called "Alertbox" by looking at the page's URL and by noting the link at the top of the page.

▶ **3.** Click the **Alertbox** link near the top of the Web page to learn more about the Web publication.

You see that the full title of the publication is *Alertbox: Current Issues in Web Usability* and that it is written by Dr. Jakob Nielsen, a principal of the Nielsen Norman Group. You can also see that the site offers a free e-mail newsletter and that it has a clearly stated privacy policy that governs use of any e-mail addresses submitted. Although some sites state policies that they do not follow, the existence of a clearly stated policy is a good indicator of a high quality site.

▶ **4.** Click the links to the **Jakob Nielsen** biography page and to the **Nielsen Norman Group** information page. These links appear under the publication title near the top of the page. Review the information on these pages and use that information along with the information you gained in the previous steps to evaluate the quality of the Kid's Corner page.

▶ **5.** Close your Web browser.

The information you examined should lead you to conclude that the Kid's Corner page is of high quality. Dr. Nielsen and his organization are both well respected in the field of Web site usability research. If you would like to do an additional exploration regarding this topic, you could use your favorite search engine to conduct searches on combinations of terms such as "Nielsen" and "Web usability." The determination of Web site quality is not an exact science, but with practice, you can develop your skills in this area.

Dave and Ranjit are pleased with your research efforts. Anne is so impressed with your work that she wants you to conduct some short classes to demonstrate the use of Web search tools to other IER research staff members.

Session 3.2 Quick Check

Review

1. The three basic Boolean operators are _____, _____, and _____.

2. Write a search expression using Boolean and precedence operators that returns Web pages that contain information about wild mustang horses in Wyoming but not information about the Ford Mustang automobile.

3. True or False: The NEAR location operator always returns phrases that contain all keywords within 10 words of each other in a search expression.

4. True or False: In most search engines, the wildcard character is a * symbol.

5. Name three kinds of filters you can include in a Google search run from its Advanced Search page.

6. In an advanced or Boolean search expression, parentheses are an example of a(n) _____ operator.

7. Name one distinguishing feature of the Vivísimo search engine.

8. List three features to consider when evaluating the quality of a Web site.

Tutorial Summary

In this tutorial, you learned how to formulate specific and exploratory research questions and how to use a structured Web search process to find information on the Web. You learned how to develop search expressions, which you used in three types of Web search tools: search engines, Web directories, and metasearch engines. You learned what Boolean operators, precedence operators, and location operators are and how they work in several major search engines. You also learned how to use wildcards in search expressions and how to use several types of filtering techniques to narrow your search results. You learned how to use information about Web page author identity and objectivity along with the content, form, and appearance of the Web pages themselves to evaluate their validity and reliability.

Key Terms

banner ad
Boolean algebra
Boolean operator
bot
clearinghouse
deep Web
dynamic Web page
exploratory question
full text indexing
grouping operator
hidden Web
hit
hybrid search engine
    directory
inclusion operator

invisible Web
location operator
logical operator
meta tag
metasearch engine
natural language query
    interface
page ranking
parsing
precedence operator
proximity operator
query
resource list
results page
search engine

search expression
search filter
specific question
spider
sponsored links
static Web page
stemming
stop words
subject guide
virtual library
Web bibliography
Web directory
Web robot
wildcard character

Review Assignments

Dave and Ranjit are keeping you busy at IER. You have noticed that Dave and Ranjit frequently need information about the economy and economic forecasts. Your internship will be over soon, so you would like to leave them with links to some resources that they might find useful after you leave. To create those links, complete the following steps:

1. Start your Web browser, open the Student Online Companion page at www.course.com/newperspectives/internet6, click the Tutorial 3 link, and then click the Review Assignments link. The Review Assignments section of the Tutorial 3 page contains links organized under three headings: Search Engines, Web Directories, and Metasearch Engines.

2. Choose at least one search tool from each category and conduct searches using combinations of search terms "economy," "economics," "forecasts," "conditions," and "outlook."

3. Expand or narrow your search using each tool until you find five Web sites that you believe are comprehensive guides or directories that Anne, Dave, and Ranjit should include in their bookmarks or favorites lists to help them locate information about international business stories.

4. For each Web site, record the URL and write a paragraph that explains why you believe the site would be useful to an international business news writer. Identify each site as a guide, directory, or other resource.

5. For each Web site, conduct an evaluation of the quality of the site. In a paragraph (for each site) rate the site's quality as low, medium, or high and explain the reasons for your rating.

6. When you are finished, close your Web browser.

Apply

Apply the skills you learned in this tutorial to choose a search tool and use it to find information about a specific geographic location.

Case Problem 1

Midland University Earth Sciences Institute   You are an intern at the Midland University Earth Sciences Institute. The Institute conducts research on the primary effects of earthquakes on land stability, soil composition, and water redirection. The Institute also examines secondary effects such as changes in plant and animal life in the earthquake zone. When an earthquake strikes, the Institute sends a team of geologists, soil chemists, biologists, botanists, and civil engineers to the quake's site to examine the damage to structures, land formations, lakes, and rivers. An earthquake can occur without warning nearly anywhere in the world, so the Institute needs quick access to information about local conditions in various parts of the world, including the temperature, rainfall, money exchange rates, demographics, and local customs. It is early July when you receive a call that an earthquake has just occurred in northern Chile. To obtain information about local mid-winter conditions there so that you can help the Institute prepare its team, complete the following steps.

1. Start your Web browser, open the Student Online Companion page at www.course.com/newperspectives/internet6, click the Tutorial 3 link, and then click the Case 1 link. The Case 1 section contains links to lists of search engines, directories, and metasearch engines.

2. Choose one of the search tools you learned about in this tutorial to conduct searches for information on local conditions in northern Chile. For the weather conditions information, be sure to obtain information about those conditions during the month of July.

3. Prepare a short report that includes the daily temperature range, average rainfall, current exchange rate for U.S. dollars to Chilean pesos, and any information you can obtain about the characteristics of the local population.

4. When you are finished, close your Web browser.

Challenge

Choose a search tool and use it to find information about companies that sell a specific product.

Case Problem 2

Lightning Electrical Generators, Inc.   You work as a marketing manager for Lightning Electrical Generators, Inc., a firm that has built generators for more than 50 years. The generator business is not as profitable as it once was and John Delaney, the firm's president, has asked you to investigate new markets for the company. One market that John would like to consider is the uninterruptible power supply (UPS) business. A UPS unit supplies continuing power to a single computer or to an entire computer system if the regular source of power fails. Most UPS units provide power only long enough to allow an orderly shutdown of the computer. John wants you to study the market for UPS units in the United States. He also wants to know which firms currently make and sell UPS products. Finally, he would like some idea of the power ratings and prices of individual units. To provide John the information he needs, complete the following steps.

1. Start your Web browser, open the Student Online Companion page at www.course.com/newperspectives/internet6, click the Tutorial 3 link, and then click the Case 2 link. The Case 2 section contains links to lists of search engines, directories, and metasearch engines.
2. Use one of the search tools to conduct searches for information about specific UPS products for John. You should design your searches to find the manufacturers' names and information about the products that they offer.
3. Prepare a short report that includes the information you have gathered for at least five UPS products, including the manufacturer's name, model number, product features, and suggested price.
4. When you are finished, close your Web browser.

Case Problem 3

Challenge

Choose a search tool and use it to find Web pages that have specific information, then evaluate the quality of that information.

Eastern College English Department You are a research assistant in the Eastern University English Department. The department head, Professor Garnell, has a particular interest in Shakespeare. She has spent years researching the question of whether William Shakespeare actually wrote the plays and poems attributed to him. Some scholars, including Professor Garnell, believe that most of Shakespeare's works were written by Christopher Marlowe. Professor Garnell would like to include links on the department Web page to other researchers who agree with her, but she wants only high quality sites represented. To gather the URLs that Professor Garnell wants, complete the following steps.

1. Start your Web browser, open the Student Online Companion page at www.course.com/newperspectives/internet6, click the Tutorial 3 link, and then click the Case 3 link. The Case 3 section contains links to lists of search engines, directories, and metasearch engines.
2. Use one of the search tools to find Web sites that contain information about the Shakespeare-Marlowe controversy.
3. Use the procedures outlined in this tutorial to evaluate the quality of the sites you found in the previous step.
4. Choose at least five Web sites that Professor Garnell might want to include on her Web page. For each Web site, record the URL and write at least one paragraph in which you describe the evidence you have gathered about the site's quality. You should include at least one site that is low quality in your collection.
5. When you are finished, close your Web browser.

Case Problem 4

Research

Choose a search tool and use it to find Web pages that have specific information, then evaluate that information to determine its suitability for a specific purpose.

Glenwood Employment Agency You work as a staff assistant at the Glenwood Employment Agency. Eric Steinberg, the agency's owner, wants you to locate Web resources for finding open positions in your geographic area. Eric would like this information to gauge whether his own efforts are keeping pace with the competition. He wants to monitor a few good pages but does not want to conduct exhaustive searches of the Web every week. To help Eric find current employment information, complete the following steps.

1. Start your Web browser, open the Student Online Companion page at www.course.com/newperspectives/internet6, click the Tutorial 3 link, and then click the Case 4 link. The Case 4 section contains links to lists of search engines, directories, and metasearch engines.
2. Use one of the search tools to find Web sites containing information about job openings in your geographic area. You can use search expressions that include Boolean and precedence operators to limit your searches.
3. Prepare a list of at least five URLs of pages that you believe would be good candidates for Eric's monitoring program.
4. For each URL that you find, write a paragraph that explains why you selected it and then identify any particular strengths or weaknesses of the Web site based on Eric's intended use.
5. When you are finished, close your Web browser.

Case Problem 5

Create

Choose a search tool and use it to find Web pages that have specific information. Review the information and create a report or presentation that evaluates the effectiveness of the chosen search tool for this purpose.

Lynda's Fine Foods For many years, Lynda Rice has operated a small store that sells specialty foods, such as pickles and mustard, and related gift items. Lynda is thinking about selling her products on the Web because they are small, relatively expensive, and easy to ship. She believes that people who buy her products might appreciate the convenience of ordering via the Web. Lynda would like to find some specialty food store sites on the Web to learn about possible competitors and to obtain some ideas that she might use when she creates her own Web site. To research selling specialty food items on the Web, complete the following steps.

1. Start your Web browser, open the Student Online Companion page at www.course.com/newperspectives/internet6, click the Tutorial 3 link, and then click the Case 5 link. The Case 5 section contains links to lists of search engines, directories, and metasearch engines.
2. Use one of the search tools to find Web sites that offer gift items such as pickles or mustard. You can use search expressions that include Boolean and precedence operators to limit your searches.
3. Repeat your search using one of the Web directory tools.
4. Compare the results you obtained using a search engine and using a Web directory. Explain in a memorandum of about 100 words which search tool was more effective for this type of search. Your instructor might ask you to prepare a presentation to your class in which you summarize your conclusions.
5. When you are finished, close your Web browser.

Quick Check Answers

Session 3.1

1. open-ended, hard to phrase, difficult to determine when you have found a good answer
2. True
3. Web robot, bot, or spider
4. inbound links from other Web pages
5. False. Most search engines exclude stop words such as *and* or *the*.
6. Advantage: Experts have selected, examined, and classified the entries in a Web directory. Disadvantage: You must know which category to search to find information.
7. The power of the search engine operates on the expert-selected and classified entries in the directory.
8. It forwards the expression to a number of other search engines, and then presents and organizes the search results it receives from them.
9. They offer lists of hyperlinks to other Web pages, frequently including summaries or reviews of the Web sites, organized by subject.

Session 3.2

1. AND, OR, NOT
2. One possibility is: (mustang OR horse) AND Wyoming NOT (Ford OR automobile OR auto OR car)
3. False. The number of words will be different in different search engines.
4. True
5. Any three of these: language, file format, date, where the search terms appear on the Web page, domain, and Safe Search
6. precedence, inclusion, or grouping
7. It organizes search results into clusters of related hyperlinks; it performs this clustering dynamically after it has processed the search expression and gathered the results from its database.
8. identity and objectivity of author(s), content, form, and appearance

Objectives

Session 4.1
- Find current news and weather information on the Web
- Obtain maps and city guides
- Find businesses and people on the Web

Session 4.2
- Find library and text resources on the Web and cite them properly when you use them
- Learn how to cite Web resources
- Learn how copyrights affect your use of resources you find on the Web
- Find graphics and multimedia resources on the Web
- Learn about the future of online publishing

Information Resources on the Web

Finding, Evaluating, and Using Online Information Resources

Case

Cosby Promotions

You have just started a new position as the executive assistant to the president of Cosby Promotions, Marti Cosby. Cosby Promotions is a growing booking agency that handles promotion and concert contract negotiations for musicians and bands. Cosby Promotions works with a wide variety of music acts. Current clients include bands that play pop, Latin, heavy metal, techno, industrial, and urban. The agency does not currently handle many country music acts, but Marti wants to expand its country music business over the next few years. She explains that the music business is fast moving because the popularity of musical artists often changes rapidly. The promotion and booking strategies that will work best for a particular client one month might not work well the next month. Promotional tie-ins and sponsorships are also important revenue sources for music acts and the needs of specific sponsors change with shifts in the preferences of their customers.

Your primary job is to help Cosby Promotions' staff members stay current on news items and trends that might affect the agency's clients. Marti expects you to use your basic understanding of Web searching techniques to help the agency identify and track important information about its clients and potential sponsors. Your other duties will include updating agency executives and clients about local conditions at travel destinations and working with the agency's Web site design team to develop an effective Web presence.

In addition to working with Marti and the executive team, you will work closely with Susan Zhu, the agency's research director. Susan has worked at Cosby Promotions for six years in a variety of research jobs. The research department undertakes background investigations related to issues that arise in the agency's dealings with its clients. For example, whenever Marti starts working on a booking for a concert hall or other venue that is new for the agency, she asks Susan to provide background on the venue. Susan is looking forward to having you work with her as part of the Cosby Promotions research team.

Student Data Files

There are no student data files needed for this tutorial.

Session 4.1

Current Information on the Web

In earlier tutorials, you learned how to use search engines, directories, and other resources to find information on the Web. As you begin your new job, Marti explains that many of your assignments will involve finding recent news and information about clients, potential sponsors, performance venues, and changes in the music industry. In this session, you will learn how to use search engines and directories to find recent news stories and other current information.

To help you find current news and information, many search engines and directories include sections devoted to news items. For example, the Excite directory's home page includes a collection of hyperlinks to general news stories, sports scores, stock market reports, weather, and even horoscopes, as shown in Figure 4-1. If you are willing to register with Excite, you can follow the Personalize links (near the top of the Web page) to specify the kind of information that appears on this page when you log on.

| **Figure 4-1** | Excite home page |

links to personalization and customization features

links to stock market reports

links to current news stories

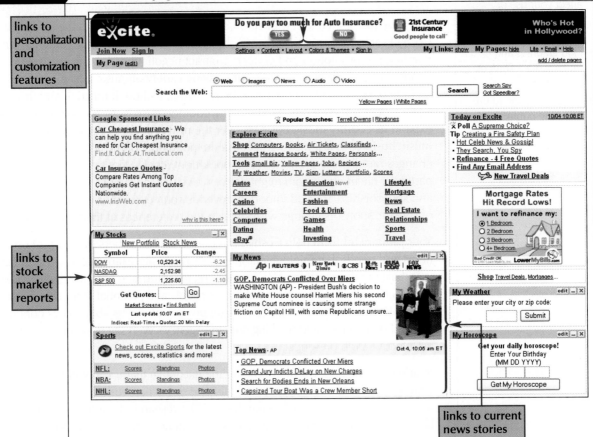

The Yahoo! directory offers similar information. It includes an "In the News" section on its home page and offers links to current finance, health, news, sports, and weather information from that page, as shown in Figure 4-2.

Yahoo! home page   **Figure 4-2**

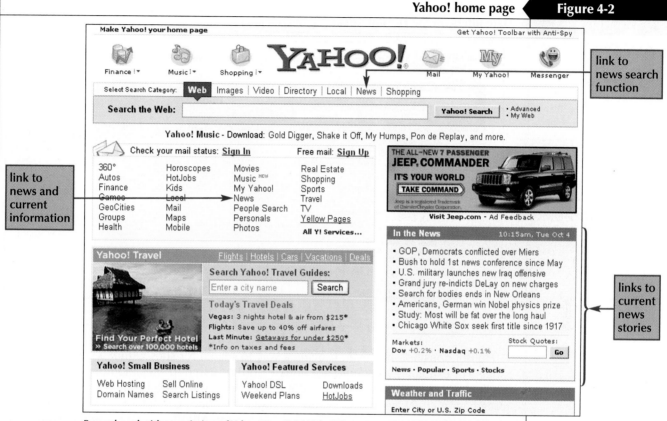

Search engines can also be useful tools for finding recent news stories. Many search engines allow you to choose a date range when you enter a search expression. HotBot is a Web site that lets you run searches on Ask Jeeves and Google using the same search page with the same options for both. HotBot's Advanced Search page, shown in Figure 4-3, provides two ways to perform date-limited searches. You can choose one of HotBot's preset time range options, such as "in the last week" or "in the last 3 months," to limit your search to sites that were last modified within your selected time period. Alternatively, you can limit searches to dates before or after a specific date. In the section of the HotBot Advanced Search page that appears in Figure 4-3 you can see the two date filter options.

| Figure 4-3 | Date filters on the HotBot Advanced Search page |

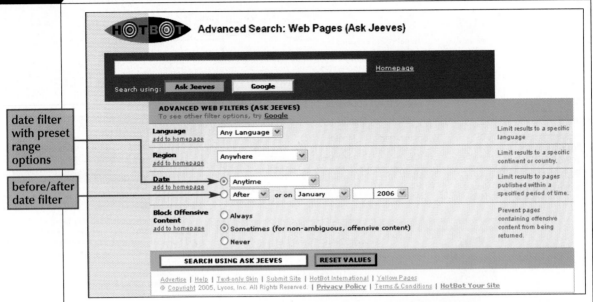

HotBot does not, however, provide a way to search for sites within a specified date range. For example, you could not limit a HotBot search to sites modified between April 24, 2006, and November 11, 2006. As you learned in Tutorial 3, a good Internet researcher will always know how to use more than one search tool. To search for sites modified between specific dates, you could use the AltaVista search engine, which allows you to set an exact "between" date range on its Advanced Search page. Figure 4-4 shows the AltaVista Advanced Search page with an exact date range set.

Date filters on the AltaVista Advanced Search page ◄ **Figure 4-4**

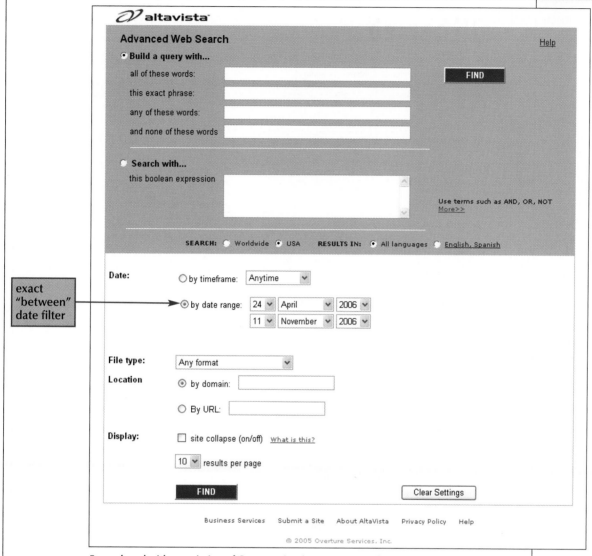

Reproduced with permission of Overture Services, Inc. ©2005 by Overture Services, Inc. AltaVista and the AltaVista logo are trademarks of Overture Services, Inc.

The AlltheWeb search engine uses a slightly different approach. It allows you to set separate "after" and "before" date filters. By setting both of these filters, you can construct an exact "between" date filter. Figure 4-5 shows these filters on the AlltheWeb Advanced Search page with an exact date range set.

Figure 4-5 ▸ Date filters on the AlltheWeb Advanced Search page

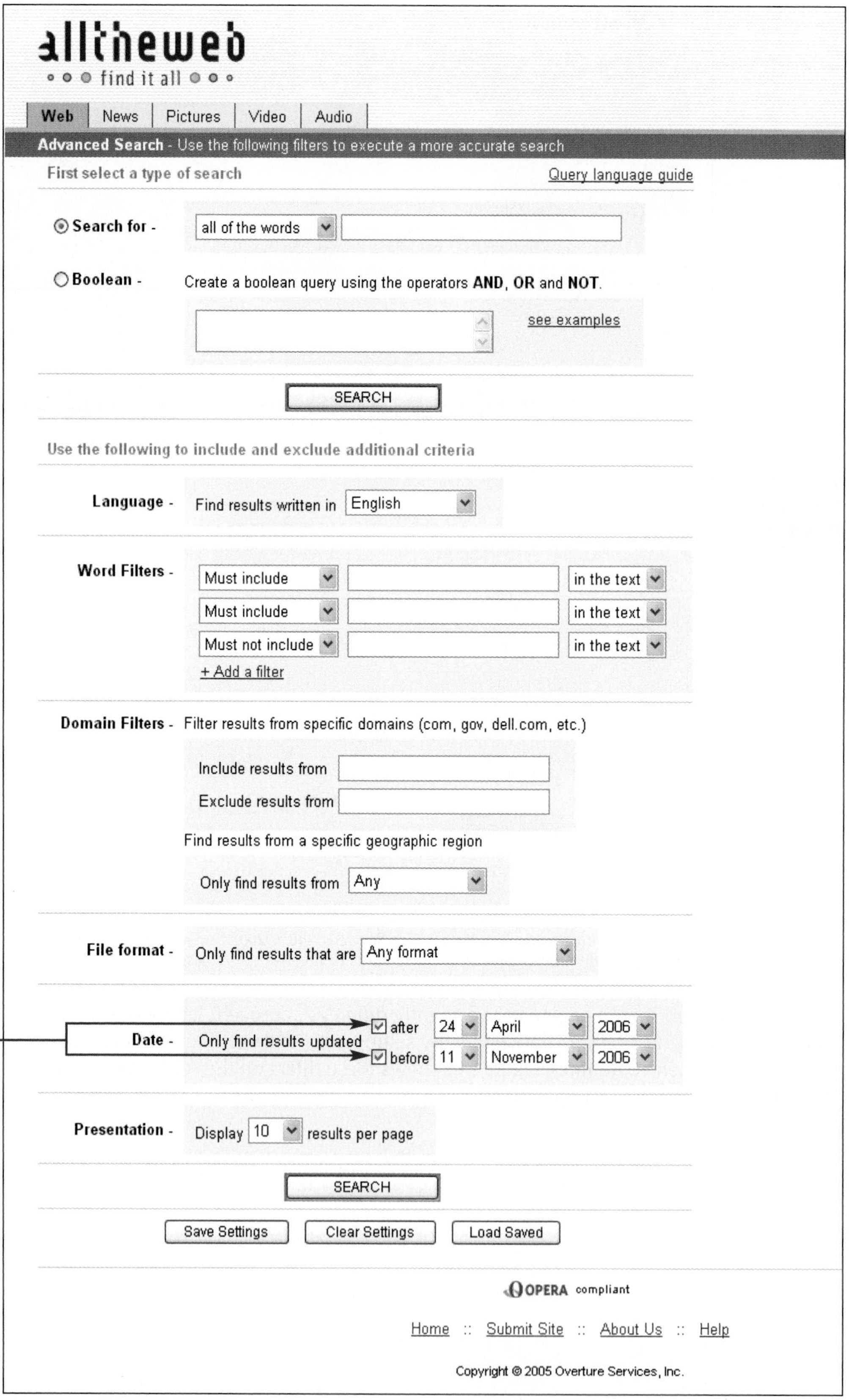

after and before date filters

Reproduced with permission of Overture Services, Inc. © 2005 by Overture Services, Inc. AllTheWeb and the AllTheWeb logo are trademarks of Overture Services, Inc.

Marti calls to tell you that she has been negotiating with Honda on behalf of one of Cosby Promotions' heavy metal bands. Honda wants to increase its appeal to younger drivers and is looking to sponsor a band that will appeal to that market. Marti knows that other agencies will be pitching bands to Honda for this sponsorship, so she wants as much background information on Honda as possible before she meets with them next week. She would like you to search the Web and collect the URLs of sites that mention Honda; she is especially interested in learning more about the kinds of promotional activities Honda is already doing. Marti needs the most recent information available, so you will search for sites that have been modified within the last few months.

Finding Web Sites that Have Been Modified Recently	Reference Window

- Go to the Web site for a search engine or directory that allows date-range restrictions.
- Formulate your search expression.
- Set the date-range restriction in the search tool.
- Run the search.
- Evaluate the search results. If you do not find useful results, select an alternative search tool, and then run the search again.

Consider the search tools available. Your search term—*Honda*—is a brand name, so it is likely that directory builders will collect many useful sites that include that term in their databases. Another option is to use a search engine for this query. Search engines might include more recent listings because the editorial review process of many Web directories takes time to complete. Remember, if you do not find what you are looking for with one search tool, you can try your search again using different tools until you are satisfied with your results.

To find specific Web pages based on last modified dates:

1. Start your Web browser, open the Student Online Companion page at **www.course.com/newperspectives/internet6**, click the **Tutorial 4** link, and then click the **Session 4.1** link.

2. Choose one of the search tools below the Search Engines and Web Directories with Date Filters heading, and then click the link to the tool you have chosen to open its search page.

3. Formulate a search expression that will locate promotions for Honda. For most of the search tools, typing the expression **Honda promotion** in the search text box should work.

4. Select a date filter to limit your search to the most recent few months (depending on the search tool you chose, you can use either a preset filter for the last three or four months or an exact date filter), and then click the appropriate tool's **Search** (or similar) button to start the search.

5. Examine your search results to determine whether you have found any information that might be useful to Marti. If not, return to the Student Online Companion page for Tutorial 4 and then repeat Steps 2 through 4 using a different search tool.

Figure 4-6 shows a part of the results page generated by the Google search engine for this query. The page includes several results that might be useful to Marti. Your results, even if you use Google, will be different.

Figure 4-6	Google date-filtered search results

search
expression

date filter
setting

search
results

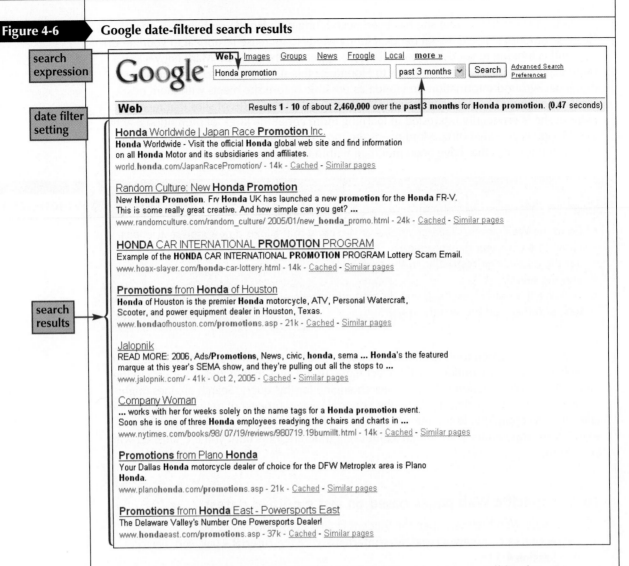

You can send the URLs to Marti in an e-mail message, or you can tell her how to obtain the same search results. For now, you decide to copy and paste the URLs that look promising and send them to her in an e-mail message.

Getting the News

Marti stops by to see you the day after you sent her the URLs she requested. She is pleased with many of the recently modified Web pages you found. Now, she asks you to find current news stories about Honda that might not appear in a search of recently modified Web pages.

Finding current news stories on the Web can be easy if you know where to look. Most search engines and Web directories include links to broadcast networks, wire services, and newspapers. A **wire service** (also called press agency or a news service) is an organization that gathers and distributes news to newspapers, magazines, broadcasters, and other organizations that pay a fee to the wire service. Although there are hundreds of wire services in the world, most news comes from the four largest wire services: United Press International (UPI) and the Associated Press (AP) in the United States, Reuters in Great Britain, and Agence France-Presse in France.

All of the major U.S. broadcasters, including ABC, CBS, CNN, Fox, MSNBC, and NPR have Web sites that carry news features. Broadcasters in other countries, such as the BBC, also provide news reports on their Web pages. The Reuters Web page includes current news stories in addition to the news services that it sells. Major newspapers, such as the *New York Times*, the *Washington Post*, and the *Los Angeles Times*, have Web sites that include current news and many other features from their print editions. Many of these broadcast news, wire service, and newspaper Web sites include search features that allow you to search the site for specific news stories. When you think about the time it will take to do a comprehensive search of the major news sites for Marti, you decide to ask Susan for advice.

Susan tells you that the Internet Public Library - Online Newspapers site includes hyperlinks to hundreds of international and domestic newspapers. There are a number of similar sites, which are often called **Web news directories**, that offer links to the Web sites of newspapers and other media outlets. You can explore them by opening the Student Online Companion page for this tutorial at www.course.com/newperspectives/internet6, clicking the Tutorial 4 link, and then following the links listed under the "Web News Directories" heading. Figure 4-7 shows the Newspapers page of the Internet Public Library Web site, which is hosted by the University of Michigan.

Figure 4-7   Internet Public Library links to newspaper Web sites

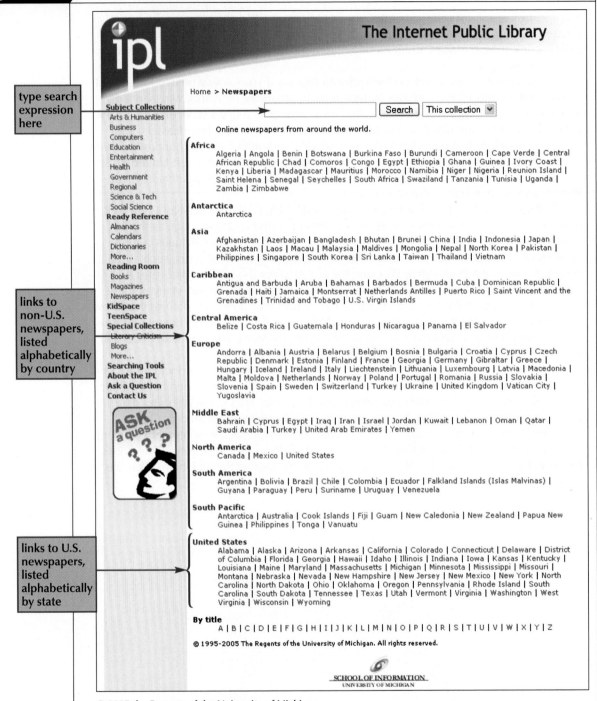

type search expression here →

links to non-U.S. newspapers, listed alphabetically by country →

links to U.S. newspapers, listed alphabetically by state →

© 2005 the Regents of the University of Michigan.

As you can see in Figure 4-7, this site has a search field, but it searches only the title and the main entry for each newspaper and does not search the newspaper sites' contents. Therefore, you could use it to identify all of the newspapers in New Jersey or all of the newspapers that had the word Tribune in their titles, but you could not use it to find news stories that include the word Honda. You need to select a newspaper, go to the newspaper site, and conduct your search there. To search a hundred newspapers, you would need to do your search a hundred times. This drawback is shared by most Web news directory sites.

Fortunately, a number of Web sites let you search the content of current news stories in multiple publications and wire services. These sites are often called **news search engines**.

Yahoo! News includes the AP and Reuters wire services along with news it purchases from other leading newspapers and magazines. Google News includes stories from more than 4,000 news sources. The NewsHub site updates its news database with information from a number of wire services every 15 minutes. Some news search engines provide ways to search **Web logs** (also called **Weblogs** or **blogs**), which are Web sites that contain commentary on current events written by individuals. To obtain both breadth and currency of coverage, experienced searchers often run the same query using more than one of these search tools.

You decide to use a news search engine to find recent news stories about Honda.

Searching Current News Stories

Reference Window

- Select a news search engine site.
- Open the site in your Web browser.
- Enter your search expression into the search text box.
- Set any date filters you want to use to limit your search.
- Run the search and evaluate your results.

To find recent news stories on the Web that mention Honda:

1. Return to the Student Online Companion page for Session 4.1, choose one of the tools below the News Search Engines heading to use in your search, and then click the link to the tool you have chosen to open its search page.

2. Type the search term **Honda** in your chosen site's search text box, and then click the site's **Search** (or similar) button to start the search.

3. Select a date filter to limit your results to the most recent few weeks (depending on the search tool you chose, you can use either a preset filter or an exact date filter).

4. Examine your search results to determine whether you have found any information that might be useful to Marti. If not, repeat Steps 1 through 3 using a different search tool.

Figure 4-8 shows a part of the results page generated by the AltaVista news search engine for this query. Your results, even if you use AltaVista, will be different.

Figure 4-8   **AltaVista News search results page**

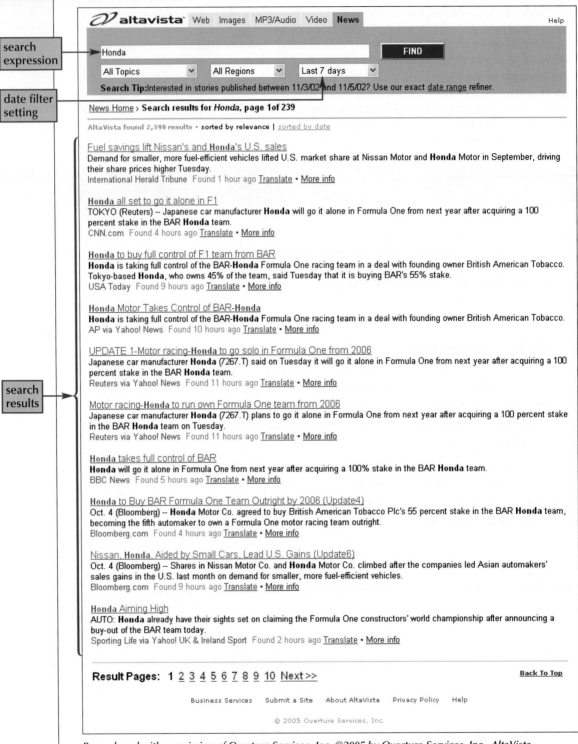

Reproduced with permission of Overture Services, Inc. ©2005 by Overture Services, Inc. AltaVista and the AltaVista logo are trademarks of Overture Services, Inc.

You have compiled a list of useful URLs about Honda's current promotional and sponsorship activities for Marti. You have also gained experience in searching for current topics by examining Web pages that have been modified recently and by using tools that search the Web specifically for news reports.

Weather Reports

Marti will travel to Nashville later in the week to meet with some new country music artists that she hopes to sign as clients for the agency. Marti already has made her travel plans, and she is interested in the weather forecast for the area. A number of Web sites offer weather information and forecasts. The two most popular—The Weather Channel and AccuWeather—provide weather forecast information to many other Web sites, such as Excite, *USA Today*, and Yahoo!. The AccuWeather home page appears in Figure 4-9.

AccuWeather home page | **Figure 4-9**

You decide to check two weather sources for Marti because you know that meteorology is not an exact science.

Finding a Weather Forecast

- Open a weather information Web site in a Web browser.
- Locate the weather report for the city or area in which you are interested.
- Repeat the steps to find other weather information in different weather information Web sites.

To find weather forecasts for the Nashville area:

1. Return to the Student Online Companion page for Session 4.1.

2. Choose one of the tools below the Weather Information Web Sites heading to use in your search, and then click the link to the site you have chosen to open its home page. Most of these sites allow you to search on either the name of the city or its zip code.

3. Type the city name and state **Nashville**, **TN** or the zip code for downtown Nashville, **37201**, in your chosen site's search text box, and then click the site's **Go** (or similar) button to find the local Nashville forecast.

4. Repeat Steps 1 through 3 using a different weather information site.

Figure 4-10 shows a part of the Nashville local forecast page on The Weather Channel site. The page you see, even if you use The Weather Channel site, will be different.

The Weather Channel local forecast page for Nashville ◄ **Figure 4-10**

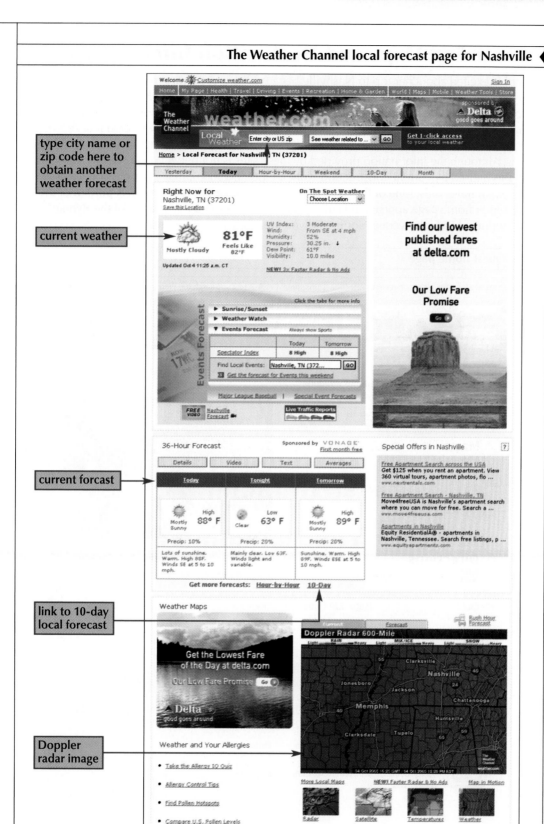

type city name or zip code here to obtain another weather forecast

current weather

current forcast

link to 10-day local forecast

Doppler radar image

Usually, weather-forecasting sites will report slightly different (and sometimes completely different) forecasts for the same time period in the same area. Many people who obtain weather forecasts from the Web regularly check two or three sites and compare the forecasts.

Obtaining Maps and Destination Information

Marti is excited about her trip to Nashville because she is a country music fan who grew up listening to broadcasts of the Grand Ole Opry on the radio. Since this will be her first trip to Nashville, Marti would like to include a stop at Ryman Auditorium, the original home of the Grand Ole Opry. You offer to find a map of Nashville on the Web that shows the location of Ryman Auditorium. A number of Web sites provide maps and driving directions. Although the information provided by these sites is not perfect (new roads and detours caused by current construction work are not included), many people find them to be helpful travel aids. One of the most popular of these sites is MapQuest. A portion of the MapQuest home page appears in Figure 4-11. Marti gives you the address of the Ryman Auditorium, 116 Fifth Avenue North, and you are ready to go to work.

Figure 4-11	MapQuest home page

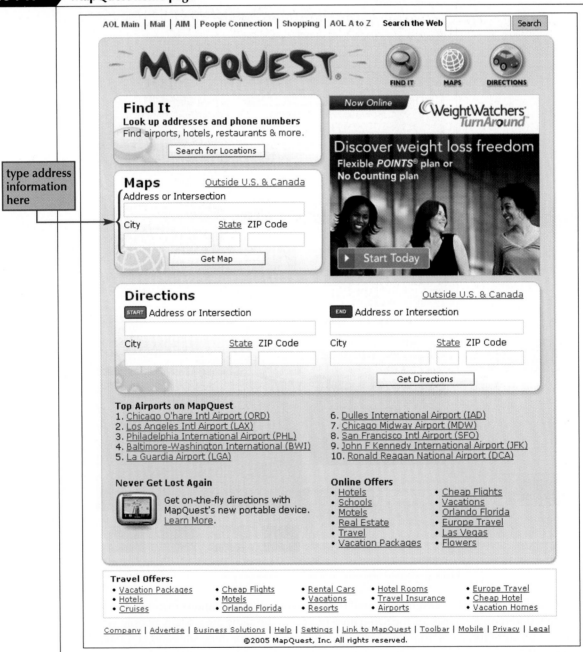

type address information here

Finding a Local Area Map on the Web

- Open a Web site that offers maps in your Web browser.
- Enter the location of the map you need to find.
- Zoom the map scale in or out to suit your requirements.
- Print or download the finished map.

To obtain a map of the Nashville area near Ryman Auditorium:

▶ **1.** Return to the Student Online Companion page for Session 4.1, choose one of the tools below the Web Sites with Maps and Directions heading to use in your search, and then click the link to the site you have chosen to open its home page.

▶ **2.** Type the address, **116 Fifth Avenue North**, the city name, **Nashville**, and the state abbreviation, **TN**, in the appropriate text boxes of your chosen site's Web page. Then click the site's **Get Map** (or similar) button to open a page that includes a map of the area near Ryman Auditorium.

▶ **3.** When the page that includes the map loads, use the controls on that page to zoom in or out until you have a map image that you think will meet Marti's needs.

Some sites allow you to e-mail the map image or download it to your computer or a handheld computing device such as a personal digital assistant (PDA). These sites usually include links to terms and conditions that govern your use of any maps you download, print, or e-mail. Be sure to review those terms and conditions for your chosen site.

Figure 4-12 shows the results of this search using two Web sites, Google Maps and MSN Maps & Directions. The map you obtain, even if you use one of these sites, might look different. Each site offers a slightly different view of the area with different features displayed. Each of these features might be more or less important in a given situation. For example, if Marti is planning to drive to the Ryman auditorium, she might find the MSN site's freeway exit numbers to be helpful. Because these differences exist, many people regularly use two or three different Web sites when they are planning a trip.

Figure 4-12 | **Ryman Auditorium area map in Google Maps and MSN Maps & Directions**

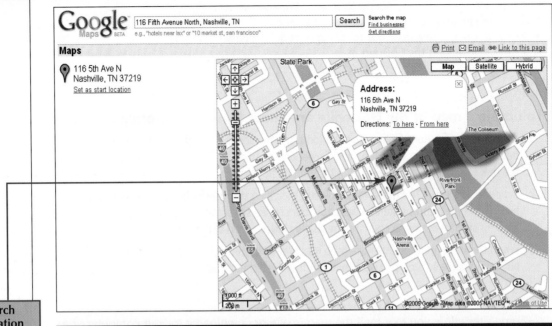

search location

You have located a map that will meet Marti's needs on the Nashville trip. To help Marti on her trip, you decide you should also find some information about restaurants and other points of interest in Nashville. The Web offers a number of sites with information about cities that are popular travel destinations.

Reference Window

Obtaining Travel Destination Information

- Go to a city guide Web site in your Web browser.
- Search the site for your destination city, region, or country.
- Explore the hyperlinks provided by the site for your destination.

To obtain information about Nashville restaurants and entertainment:

▶ **1.** Return to the Student Online Companion page for Session 4.1, choose one of the tools below the City Guides heading to use in your search, and then click the link to the site you have chosen to open its home page.

▶ **2.** Find your chosen site's page for Nashville, TN. The procedure you use will depend on which site you chose; however, most sites require you to type **Nashville** in a search text box or click a **Nashville** link. If you are unable to find an entry for Nashville on your chosen site, select a different site for your search.

▶ **3.** Examine the results page to find information about restaurants and entertainment in Nashville.

You can find a variety of useful information using city guide sites. In addition to information about entertainment and restaurants, you can often obtain useful information about specific attractions. For example, Figure 4-13 shows detailed information about the Ryman Auditorium that you might find by using the Citysearch site.

Citysearch Ryman Auditorium page ◀ Figure 4-13

Finding Businesses and People on the Web

Some Web sites include listings of businesses and people, much like the print directories that you have probably used to find telephone numbers. These sites often include search engines that specialize in finding information about people and businesses on the Web.

Finding Businesses

Over the next few years, Marti is planning to develop reciprocal relationships with local booking agencies in Nashville. She would like to make some initial contacts during this trip and asks you to search the Web to find a list of booking agencies in Nashville. Web sites that store information about businesses only are often called **yellow pages directories**. You can use a yellow pages directory to find booking agencies located in Nashville.

Reference Window | **Finding Business Listings on the Web**

- Navigate to a yellow pages directory site in your Web browser.
- Enter information about the nature and geographic location of the business that you want to find.
- Run the search.
- Examine and evaluate the results to determine whether you should revise your search or try another search engine.

To find Nashville booking agencies on the Web:

1. Return to the Student Online Companion page for Session 4.1, choose one of the tools below the Yellow Pages Directories heading to use in your search, and then click the link to the site you have chosen to open its home page.

2. The exact procedure you will use for your search will depend on which directory you chose. Most sites require you to enter a search term for the category of the business you want to find. For this search, you should try terms such as *agent*, *artist*, *recording artist*, or *booking agency*. If your first search is unsuccessful, try another search with a different search term. If none of the search terms yields satisfactory results, return to the Student Online Companion page for Session 4.1 and try using a different yellow pages directory site.

3. Examine your results pages to find information about booking agencies in Nashville.

This search can be challenging because there is no single category description that is universally used by companies that book performing musicians. Figure 4-14 shows the results page for a search using the term "agent" on the SuperPages.com yellow pages directory site. As you can see, the search returned the category "Artists Managers & Agents," which includes a number of listings for booking agencies in Nashville. Your search will probably yield a different list of booking agencies, even if you use the SuperPages.com directory.

SuperPages.com search results page ◀ **Figure 4-14**

search expression, city, and state used to obtain these results

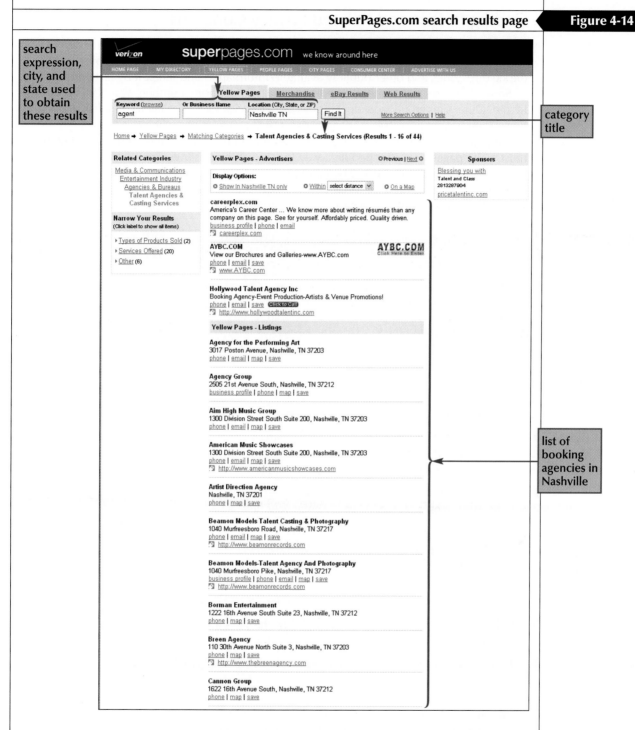

category title

list of booking agencies in Nashville

You are satisfied that you have found enough information about Nashville weather, attractions, and booking agencies to make Marti's trip to that city memorable and successful.

In addition to using the Web to find businesses, you can use it to find individuals.

Finding People and Related Privacy Concerns

Many Web sites let you search for individuals' names, addresses, and telephone numbers. These sites, often called **white pages directories**, collect information from published telephone directories and other publicly available information and index it by last name.

Some Web sites make unpublished and unlisted telephone numbers available for public use. Other sites group individual listings by categories such as religious or political affiliation. Many people expressed concerns about privacy violations when this type of information became easily accessible on the Web. In response to these privacy concerns, most white pages sites offer people a way to remove their listings. For example, Switchboard will accept a list removal request made on its Web page or sent by e-mail. You might want to determine whether white pages directories have a correct listing for you and whether or not you want your listing to appear in a white pages site.

Reference Window	**Searching for Your White Pages Listing**

- Open a white pages directory Web site in your Web browser.
- Enter your name and part of your address.
- Run the search, and then examine the search results.
- Consider repeating the search with various combinations of partial address information or variants of the correct spelling of your name.

To search for your listing on a white pages directory:

1. Return to the Student Online Companion page for Session 4.1, choose one of the tools below the White Pages Directories heading to use in your search, and then click the link to the site you have chosen to open its home page.

2. The exact procedure you will use for your search will depend on which directory you chose; however, most sites require you to enter your first name, your last name, and a part of your address such as the city and state.

   Trouble? If your telephone number is listed under another person's name, use that person's name to find your listing.

   Trouble? If you do not find your listing, try searching for a friend's listing or your parents' listing. You can also try your search in a different white pages directory.

3. Examine your listing and, if you wish, follow the site's instructions for modifying or deleting your listing.

4. Close your Web browser and, if necessary, log off your Internet connection.

You have accomplished many tasks and helped Marti quite a bit. Next, you will learn about multimedia resources on the Web and the copyright issues that arise when you use them.

Session 4.1 Quick Check

1. Reuters is an example of a(n) _____.
2. When would you use a search engine with a date filter rather than a news directory or news search engine?
3. Explain why you might want to consult two or three Web resources for weather information before leaving on an out-of-town trip.
4. List two advantages of using a Web map and directions site instead of a paper map or atlas.
5. Describe three types of information that you might obtain from a city guide Web page.
6. True or False: City guide Web sites are usually created by an agency of the city government.
7. A Web site that helps people find businesses by name or category is often called a(n) _____.
8. A Web site that helps people find the telephone numbers or e-mail addresses of other individuals is often called a(n) _____.

Session 4.2

Online Library, Text, and Multimedia Resources

Because the Web has made publishing so easy and inexpensive, virtually anybody can create a Web page on almost any subject. These pages contain many useful items of information and form an online library of sorts. The resources of this vast online library include text, graphics, and multimedia files. In this session you will learn how to find these resources, use them in compliance with copyright laws, and properly cite their sources.

Library Resources

Susan meets with you and explains that she would like you to do more work for the research department. You ask Susan about the future of traditional libraries, given that so much information is available on the Web. She admits that she might be biased, having worked in a library for several years, but she believes that libraries will likely be around for a long time. In fact, the Web has made existing libraries more accessible to more people. Traditional libraries and online collections of works that have serious research value have begun to recognize each other as complementary rather than as competing, and library users have started to see many new and interesting research resources. One example of this is the LibrarySpot Web site, which is a collection of hyperlinks organized in the same general way that a physical library might arrange its collections.

To explore the LibrarySpot Web site:

► **1.** Return to the Student Online Companion page for Session 4.2, click the **LibrarySpot** hyperlink, and then wait while your Web browser loads the Web page shown in Figure 4-15.

| Figure 4-15 | LibrarySpot home page |

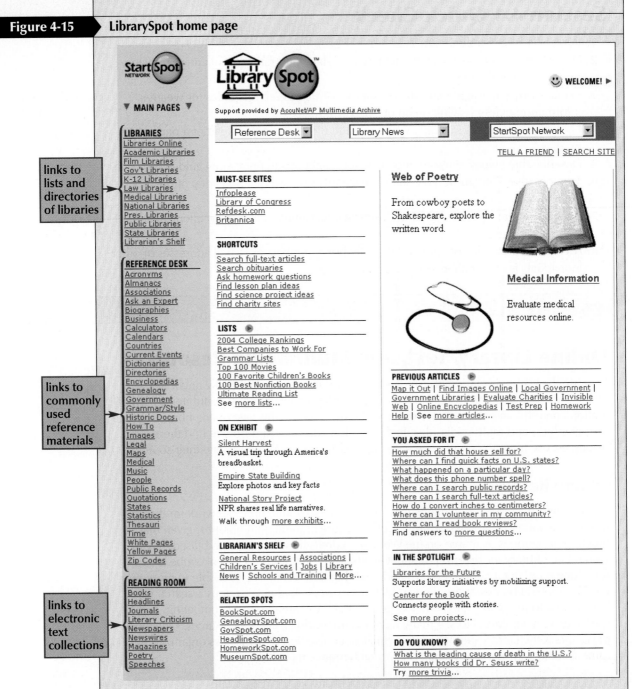

As you can see in Figure 4-15, the LibrarySpot site includes many of the same things you would expect to find in a public or school library. It lets you access reference materials, electronic texts, and other library Web sites from one central Web page. This library is, however, open 24 hours a day and seven days a week.

Marti had asked you to find the name of the river that runs through Nashville.

2. Using the links listed under the heading "Reference Desk" on the LibrarySpot home page, search for information about Nashville to find the river's name. A good place to start would be the **Encyclopedias** link. Note the river's name so that you can include it in your report to Marti about Nashville.

Another useful resource is the U.S. Library of Congress Web site, which includes links to a huge array of research resources, ranging from the Thomas Legislative Information site to the Library of Congress archives. The home page of the Library of Congress Web site is shown in Figure 4-16.

U.S. Library of Congress home page | **Figure 4-16**

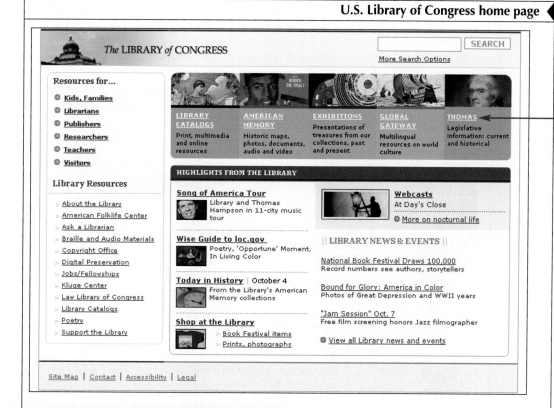

The Thomas Legislative Information Web site provides you with search access to the full text of bills that are before Congress, the *Congressional Record*, and Congressional Committee Reports. The American Memory link leads you to archived photographs, sound and video recordings, maps, and collections of everything from 17th century dance instruction manuals to baseball cards. The Exhibitions link leads you to information about current and past displays sponsored by the Library of Congress.

The Student Online Companion page for Tutorial 4 contains many other hyperlinks to useful library and library-related Web sites in the Additional Information section under the "Library Information Sites" heading. Feel free to explore the libraries of the Web the next time you need to complete a research assignment for school or your job.

Text and Other Archives on the Web

The Web contains a number of text resources, including dictionaries, thesauri, encyclopedias, glossaries, and other reference works. Many people find reference works easier to use when they have a computerized search interface. For example, when you open a dictionary to find the definition of a specific word, the structure of the bound book actually interferes with your ability to find the answer you seek. A computer interface allows you to enter a search term—in this case, the word to be defined—and saves you the trouble of scanning several pages of text to find the correct entry.

Of course, publishers sell dictionaries and encyclopedias on CDs, but the Web provides many alternatives. These alternatives range in quality from very low to very high. Many of the best resources offered on the Web require you to pay a subscription fee. The free reference works on the Web are worth investigating, however; they are good enough to provide acceptable service for many users. In addition to dictionaries and encyclopedias, the Web includes grammar checkers, rhyming dictionaries, and language-translation pages. The Student Online Companion page for this tutorial includes a collection of links to a number of these reference resources in the Additional Information section under the heading "Reference Resources."

The Web also offers a number of full-text copies of works that are no longer protected by copyright. Two of the most well-known Web sites for full-text storage are the Project Gutenberg and Bartleby.com Web sites. These volunteer efforts have collected the contributions of many people throughout the world who have spent enormous amounts of time entering or converting printed text into electronic form. The Project Gutenberg site is supported by donations. The Bartleby.com site was converted into a privately held corporate site in 1999. Since then, it has used advertising to generate revenue to support its operations. The Bartleby.com home page appears in Figure 4-17.

Figure 4-17 ▶ **Bartleby.com home page**

The Web itself has become the subject of archivists' attention. The Internet Archive's Wayback Machine provides researchers a series of snapshots of Web pages as they were at various points in the history of the Web. The Internet Archive site also stores text, moving image, audio, and other files that have been contributed to the site. The wide array of information at the Internet Archive site makes it a valuable resource for a variety of research projects. The Internet Archive home page is shown in Figure 4-18.

Internet Archive home page ◄ | **Figure 4-18**

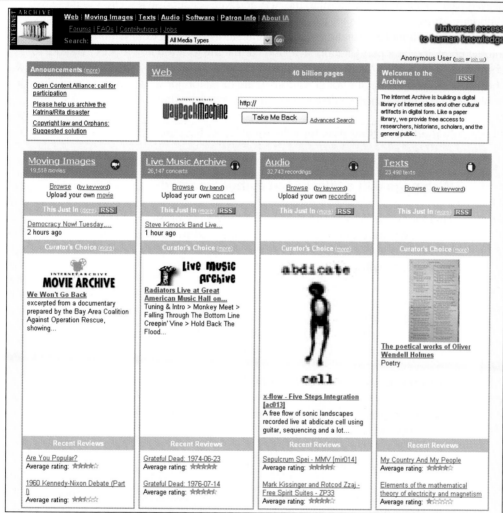

The Student Online Companion page for Tutorial 4 includes links to Web sites that offer electronic texts and archives in the Additional Information section under the heading "Electronic Texts and Archives."

Citing Web Research Resources

As you search the Web for research resources, you should collect information about the sites you visit so you can include a proper reference to your sources in any research report you write based on your work. You should record the URL and name of any Web site that you use, either in a word-processor document, as a Navigator bookmark, or as an Internet Explorer favorite. Citation formats are very well-defined for print publications, but formats for electronic resources are still emerging. For academic research, the two most widely followed standards for print citations are those of the American Psychological Association (APA) and the Modern Language Association (MLA). The APA and MLA formats for Web page citations are similar to each other and both include: name of the author or Web page creator (if known), title of the Web site in italics (if the page is untitled, provide a description of the page but do not italicize the description), name of the site's sponsoring organization (if any), date the page was retrieved, and the URL enclosed in chevron symbols (< >). If you do not enclose the URL in chevron (or other) symbols, do not add a period at the end of the URL. This prevents readers from thinking that the period is a part of the URL. Figure 4-19 shows examples of Web page citations that conform to the APA and MLA citation styles. Links to these two Web sites, and to additional sites that contain citation style and formatting resources, are listed in the Additional Information section of the Student Online Companion page for this tutorial under the heading "Citation Style and Formatting for Web References." Be sure to check the APA and MLA Web sites for updates to these styles before using them. Also, always check to see if your instructor (for classroom work) or editor (for work you are submitting for publication) has established guidelines that are different from these.

| Figure 4-19 | **Commonly used formatting style for references to Web pages** |

Web page with a title and an author, undated

Hinman, L.M. *Ethics Updates.* (n.d.). University of San Diego. Retrieved March 12, 2006, from http://ethics.sandiego.edu

Web page with a title and an author, dated

Loveland, T. (2004, Fall). Technology education standards implementation in Florida. *Journal of Technology Education* 16(1). Retrieved April 19, 2006, from http://scholar.lib.vt.edu/ejournals/JTE/v16n1/loveland.html

Web page with a title but no author, undated

The Linux Home Page. (n.d.). Linux Online, Inc. Retrieved May 15, 2006, from http://www.linux.org/

Web page with no title and no author, undated

United States Postal Service home page. (n.d.). Retrieved June 18, 2006, from http://www.usps.com

The APA and MLA formats for citations to books, journal articles, and other research resources that were published in print form but are also accessible on the Web are more complex than the formats for Web pages. You should consult the APA and MLA Web sites for the latest rules.

One of the problems that both the APA and MLA face when setting standards is the difficulty of typesetting long URLs in print documents. No clear standards specifying where or how to break long URLs at the end of a print line have emerged. Most authorities currently agree that the URL should be broken at a slash that appears in the URL and that a hyphen should not be added at the end of the line that occurs in the middle of the URL (as shown in the second example in Figure 4-19).

Any method of citing Web pages faces one serious and yet unsolved problem—moving and disappearing URLs. The Web is a dynamic medium that changes constantly. The citation systems that academics and librarians use for published books and journals work well because the printed page has a physical existence. A Web page exists only in an HTML document on a Web server computer. If that file's name or location changes, or if the Web server is disconnected from the Internet, the page is no longer accessible. Perhaps future innovations in Internet addressing technologies will solve this problem.

Copyright Issues

Marti would like to create a Web page for each musical artist that the agency represents. Many of the agency's artists have their own Web sites, but Marti would like to have a page for each artist on the Cosby Promotions Web site with a standard set of information (including a link to the artist's own Web site, if one exists). She would like you to undertake a long-term assignment for her by paying close attention to the multimedia elements of the Web pages you view as you undertake searches for the agency's staff members. She asks you to note any particularly effective uses of Web page design elements and forward any relevant URLs to her. So that you will understand how these elements work and be better able to gather this information, Marti has asked Susan to give you a tour of multimedia elements in Web pages. The first issue Susan wants to discuss with you is how copyright law governs the use of the text and multimedia elements you obtain online.

Many Web page elements and other items you can find online are a form of **intellectual property**. Intellectual property is a general term that includes all products of the human mind. These products can be tangible or intangible. Intellectual property rights include the protections afforded to individuals and companies by governments through governments' granting of copyrights and patents, and through registration of trademarks and service marks.

A **copyright** is a right granted by a government to the author or creator of a literary or artistic work; in other words, the tangible expression of an idea. The right is for the specific length of time provided in the copyright law and gives the author or creator the sole and exclusive right to print, publish, or sell the work. Creations that can be copyrighted include virtually all forms of artistic or intellectual expression, including books, music, artworks, recordings (audio and video), architectural drawings, choreographic works, product packaging, and computer software. In the United States, works created after 1977 are protected for the life of the author plus 70 years. Works copyrighted by corporations or not-for-profit organizations are protected for 95 years from the date of publication or 120 years from the date of creation, whichever is earlier.

In the past, many countries (including the United States) required the creator of a work to register that work to obtain copyright protection. U.S. law still allows registration, but registration is no longer required. A work that does not include the words "copyright" or "copyrighted," or the copyright symbol (©), and that was created after 1977, is copyrighted automatically by virtue of the copyright law unless the creator makes a specific statement on the work that it is not copyrighted.

Once the term of the copyright has expired, the work is in the **public domain**, which means that you are free to copy the files without requesting permission from the source. Older literary works, such as Dickens' *A Tale of Two Cities*, are in the public domain and may be copied and reprinted freely. An author or creator can intentionally place work into the public domain at any time. For example, some Web sites provide graphics files that you can use free of charge. Even though you can freely use public domain information, you should check the site carefully for requirements about whether and how you should acknowledge the source of the material when it is used.

Copyrights and Ideas

Susan explains that the idea contained in a product is not copyrightable. The particular form of expression of an idea is what creates a work that can be copyrighted. For example, you cannot copyright the idea to write a song about love, you can copyright only the song you end up writing. If an idea cannot be separated from its expression in a work, that work cannot be copyrighted. For example, mathematical calculations cannot be copyrighted.

A collection of facts can be copyrighted, but only if the collection is arranged, coordinated, or selected in a way that causes the resulting work to rise to the level of an original work. For example, the Yahoo! Web Directory is a collection of links to URLs. These facts existed before Yahoo! selected and arranged them into the form of its directory. However, most intellectual property lawyers would argue that the selection and arrangement of the links into categories probably makes the directory copyrightable.

Copyright Protection and Internet Technologies

Susan explains that when you use your Web browser to read text on a Web page, view a graphic image, listen to a sound, or watch a video clip, your Web browser downloads the multimedia element from the Web server and stores it in a temporary file on your computer's hard drive. This technological process creates a new, intermediate level of ownership that did not exist before the emergence of the Web. For example, when you go to an art gallery and view a picture, you do not take possession of the picture in any way; in fact, if you went around touching all of the pictures in the gallery, a security guard would probably ask you to leave. When you visit an online art gallery, however, your Web browser takes temporary possession of a copy of the file containing the image. As you have learned in earlier tutorials, it is easy to make a permanent copy of Web page images—even though your copy might violate the image owner's rights.

The potential for Web copyright violations is much greater than other types of copyright violations, such as photocopying pages from a book, because of the technology that underlies the operation of the Internet. Some Web site owners disclaim liability by storing only hyperlinks to other Web pages that contain copyright-violating multimedia elements; whether this is an effective shield against liability is not yet clear.

For example, in most cases, scanning a copy of a popular cartoon from a newspaper or magazine and placing it on a Web page is a violation of the owner's copyright. Some cartoonists regularly search the Web, looking for unauthorized copies of their work. They threaten or take legal action when they find Web sites that appear to violate their copyrights.

Ethical Issues: Fair Use and Plagiarism

The U.S. copyright law includes an exemption from infringement actions for fair use of copyrighted works. The **fair use** of a copyrighted work includes copying it for use in criticism, comment, news reporting, teaching, scholarship, or research. The law's definition of fair use is intentionally broad and can be difficult to interpret.

There have been many court cases on the fair use issue. These cases usually turn on two considerations: how the copyrighted material was used and the amount of the copyrighted material that was used. Uses that might generate revenue or deprive the copyright owner of revenue are least likely to be held as fair use. Uses of published works are more likely to be held fair use than uses of unpublished works because the copyright owner through publication has had a chance to benefit from the work. The smaller the amount of the work that is used, the more likely the use will be considered fair use. However, even a small amount of the work can be a violation if it is the heart of the work. This is especially true with musical compositions. The use of even a small portion of a song can be a violation. Again, there is no hard-and-fast rule that determines fair use. If a copyright holder disputes your use, the matter will be settled by the subjective assessment of a judge or jury.

When you make fair use of a copyrighted work in your school assignments or research, you should always be careful to provide a citation to the original work. If you are unsure whether your use is indeed fair use, the safest course of action is to contact the copyright owner and ask for permission to use the work. Acknowledging a source can be especially important when you use public domain material in papers, reports, or other school projects. Failure to cite the source of material that you use (whether it is in the public domain or it is protected by copyright) is called **plagiarism** and can be a serious violation of your school's academic honesty policy. The Internet makes it easy to copy someone else's work and commit plagiarism. A number of companies have created sites that teachers can use to identify plagiarism in papers that students submit. One of these sites, Turnitin.com, offers tips for students who want to avoid committing plagiarism unintentionally. The Turnitin.com Research Resources page, which includes information for both students and teachers about plagiarism, appears in Figure 4-20.

Turnitin.com Research Resources page   **Figure 4-20**

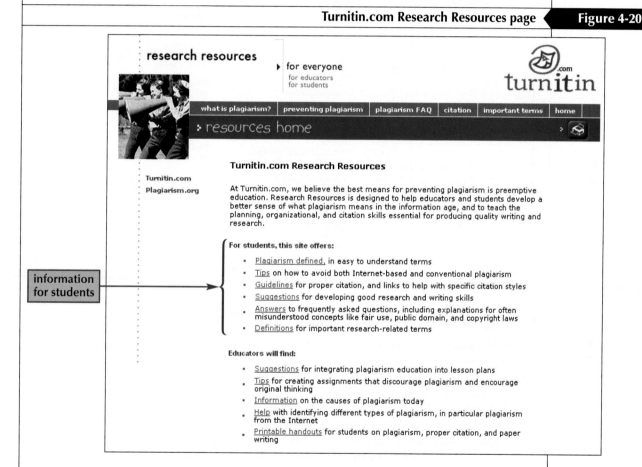

Some Web sites offer text and other types of files free as samples and offer other files for sale. The free files often carry a restriction against selling or redistributing them, even though you may be able to use them without cost on your own personal Web page. You must carefully examine any site from which you download text or other files to determine what usage limitations apply. If you cannot find a clear statement of copyright terms or a statement that the files are in the public domain, you should not use them on your Web page or anywhere else. The Student Online Companion page for Tutorial 4 contains a number of links to Web sites with further information about respecting copyrights online in the Additional Information section under the "Copyright Information Resources" heading. One of the most useful of these sites is the Stanford University Copyright & Fair Use site shown in Figure 4-21.

Figure 4-21 Stanford University Copyright & Fair Use home page

Images and Graphics on the Web

The Additional Information section of the Student Online Companion page for this tutorial contains links to Web pages that offer photographs and images under the heading "Photographs and Images." Several sites permit downloading of at least some of the files for personal or commercial use. You can also find links under that heading to search engines and Web directories that can help you find image and graphics files on the Web.

Most images on the Web are in one of two file formats, GIF or JPEG. **GIF**, an acronym for **Graphics Interchange Format**, is an older format that does a very good job of compressing small- or medium-sized files. Most GIF files you find on the Web have a .gif extension. This file format can store only up to 256 different colors. The GIF format is widely used on the Internet for images that have only a few distinct colors, such as line drawings, cartoons, simple icons, and screen objects. Some of the more interesting screen objects on the Web are animated GIF files. An **animated GIF file** combines several images into a single GIF file. When a Web browser that recognizes the animated GIF file type loads this type of file, it cycles through the images in the file and gives the appearance of cartoon-like animation. The size and color-depth limitations of the GIF file format prevent animated GIFs from delivering high-quality video, however.

JPEG, an acronym for **Joint Photographic Experts Group**, is a newer file format that stores many more colors than the GIF format—more than 16 million more, in fact—and more colors yields a higher-quality image. The JPEG format is particularly useful for photographs and continuous-tone art (images that do not have sharp edges). Most JPEG files that you find on the Web have a .jpg file extension.

Both of these formats offer file compression, which is important on the Web. Uncompressed graphics files containing images of significant size or complexity are too large to transmit efficiently. JPEG file compression is "lossy." A **lossy compression** procedure erases some elements of the graphic so that when it is displayed, it will not be as clear as the original image. The greater the level of compression, the more graphic detail is lost.

Although most graphic images on the Web are in either the JPEG or GIF formats, you might encounter images that use other file formats, including Windows bitmap file format (.bmp), Tagged Image File Format (or TIFF) format (.tif), PC Paintbrush format (.pcx), and the Portable Network Graphics (or PNG) format (.png). The Windows bitmap, TIFF, and PC Paintbrush formats are all uncompressed graphics formats. Web page designers usually avoid these formats because a Web browser takes too long to download them. The PNG format is a new format that the World Wide Web Consortium has approved as a standard. Although its promoters hope that it will become the prevailing Web standard, it is not yet widely used.

One of the best Web resources for the fine arts is the WebMuseum site, which occasionally features special exhibitions. The WebMuseum's mainstay is its Famous Paintings collection, which includes images of artwork from around the world. Susan wants you to see the museum's portrait of Vincent van Gogh so you can gain experience using and searching for graphics files at a museum Web site.

To view Vincent van Gogh's self-portraits at the WebMuseum site:

1. Return to the Student Online Companion page for Session 4.2, click the **WebMuseum** link, and then wait while your Web browser loads the Web page.

2. Click the **Famous Artworks** collections hyperlink.

3. Click the **Artist Index** hyperlink.

4. Scroll down the list of artists to find the **Gogh, Vincent van** hyperlink, and then click it.

5. Click the **Self-Portraits** hyperlink to open the page shown in Figure 4-22.

Figure 4-22 | **WebMuseum Vincent van Gogh page**

WebMuseum, Paris

Gogh, Vincent van: Self-Portraits

In the most limited definition of the term, Impressionism as the objective study of light did not encourage so essentially a subjective study as the self-portrait but in the later expansion of the movement this self-representation was given renewed force by Cézanne and van Gogh. The latter has often been compared with Rembrandt in the number and expressiveness of his self-portraits but while Rembrandt's were distributed through a lifetime, van Gogh produced some thirty in all in the short space of five years --- from the end of the Brabant period (1885) to the last year of his life at St Rémy and Auvers. In each there is the same extraordinary intensity of expression concentrated in the eyes but otherwise there is a considerable variety. From the Paris period onwards he used different adaptations of Impressionist and Neo-Impressionist brushwork, separate patches of colour being applied with varying thickness and direction in a way that makes each painting a fresh experience.

Self-Portrait Dedicated to Paul Gauguin
1888 (130 Kb); Oil on canvas, 60.5 x 49.4 cm (23 3/4 x 19 1/2 in); Fogg Art Museum, Harvard University, Cambridge, MA

Self-Portrait in front of the Easel
1888 (200 Kb); 65 x 50.5 cm

Self-Portrait with Bandaged Ear
1889 (250 Kb); Oil on canvas, 60 x 49 cm; Courtauld Institute Galleries, London

Self-Portrait
1889 (250 Kb); Oil on canvas, 65 x 54 cm (25 1/2 x 21 1/4 in); Musee d'Orsay, Paris

Self-Portrait
1889 (250 Kb); Oil on canvas, 65 x 54 cm (25 1/2 x 21 1/4 in); Musee d'Orsay, Paris

(callout) narrative

(callout) click thumbnail image to open a larger image

This page, devoted to van Gogh's self-portraits, includes a narrative about these works; the title, date created, file size, media, size of the original; and information about the work's owner (if it is a public institution). You can click any of the small (or thumbnail) images to view a larger version of the image.

Finding image files on the Web was difficult in the past because the robots that gather information for search engines cannot read graphics files to identify their attributes. Search engines relied on HTML image tags that Web page builders include in their HTML documents that contain terms that describe the image. Today, however, many search engine and Web directory sites have improved their image classification databases and provide separate search functions that are dedicated to finding Web pages with graphics content. A list of search engines that include image search features is included in the Student Online Companion Additional Information section under the heading "Search Engines with Image Search Features."

Marti would like to see what types of images related to music are on the Web. She asks you to find some graphics and photos that include jazz-related subject matter.

To find jazz-related graphics and photos:

1. Return to the Student Online Companion page for Session 4.2, and then find the list of **Search Engines with Image Search Features**.

2. Choose one of the search engines and type **jazz** as the search term in the appropriate location on the page, then click the site's **Search** (or similar) button to start the search.

3. When you have found several images or photos that are about jazz, examine the Web page on which they are located and attempt to determine whether the images are protected by copyright.

4. Close your Web browser.

The results page of a Google Images search on the term "jazz" is shown in Figure 4-23. Each of the small images is a link to a page with a larger image. That page, in turn, is linked to the source of the image on the Web.

Results of a Google Images search on the term "jazz" | **Figure 4-23**

You can send the URLs of the pages you found that contain jazz images to Marti in an e-mail message along with a note about any copyright restrictions you found.

In addition to images, you can find sounds and movies on the Web. You will learn about this next.

Sound, Music, and Video on the Web

The animated GIF format has only a limited ability to present moving graphics and cannot store audio information along with the video animation. Many Web site designers include sound or video clips to enhance the information on their pages. Unlike graphics files, sound and video files appear on the Web in many different formats and often require that you add software extensions to your Web browser. These software extensions, or **plug-ins**, are usually available as free downloads. The firms that offer media players as free downloads earn their profits by selling encoding software to developers who want to include audio and video files in that format on their Web sites. Each firm that creates a format has an incentive to promote its use, so no clear standards for using audio or video files on the Web have emerged.

To play an audio file, your computer must be equipped with a sound card and either a speaker or earphones. The computers in your school's lab or in your employer's offices might not have a sound card installed; if that's the case, you will not be able to listen to sounds on those computers.

WAV Audio File Format

One widely used audio file format is the **Wave (WAV) format**, which was jointly developed by Microsoft and IBM. WAV files digitize audio waveform information at a user-specified sampling rate and can be played on any Windows computer that supports sound. WAV files recorded at a high sampling rate (the higher the sampling rate, the higher the sound quality) can be very large. A WAV file that stores one minute of CD-quality sound can be more than 1 megabyte in size. The size of WAV files limits their use on the Web to situations that require only short, lower-quality audio information. You can recognize a WAV file on the Web by its .wav file extension.

MIDI Audio File Format

Another commonly used Web file format is the MIDI format. The **MIDI (Musical Instrument Digital Interface) format** is a standard adopted by the music industry for controlling devices that create and read musical information. The MIDI format does not digitize the sound waveform; instead, it digitally records information about each element of the sound, including its pitch, length, and volume. Most keyboard synthesizers use MIDI so that music recorded on one synthesizer can be played on other synthesizers or on computers that have a MIDI interface. It is much easier to edit music recorded in the MIDI format than music recorded in the WAV format because you can manipulate the individual characteristics of the sound with precision. MIDI files are much smaller than WAV files and are, therefore, often used on the Web. Usually, MIDI files have either a .midi or .mid file extension.

AU Audio File Format

Because much of the Web was originally constructed on computers running the UNIX operating system, that system's audio file format still appears on the Web, although very few new audio files are created in this format today. Most Web browsers can read this format, which is known as the AU format because its file extension is normally .au. These files are approximately the same size as WAV files that store the same information.

Video File Formats

A very popular technique for transferring both sound and video files on the Web is called streaming transmission. In a **streaming transmission**, the Web server sends the first part of the file to the Web browser, which begins playing the file. While the browser is playing the file, the server is sending the next segment of the file. Streaming transmission allows you to access very large audio or video files in much less time than the download-then-play procedure requires because you start playing the file before you finish downloading. RealNetworks, Inc. has pioneered this technology and developed the RealAudio format for audio files and the RealVideo format for video files. To play these files, which you can recognize by their .ra, .ram, or .rmj file extensions, you must download and install one of the Real file players from the firm's Web site. The RealNetworks formats are compressed to further increase the efficiency with which they can be transferred over the Internet. For example, you can compress a 1-megabyte WAV file into a 30-kilobyte RealAudio file.

Video files are also available in older formats on the Web. Windows computers are able to play Microsoft's **AVI (Audio Video Interleaved) format** files and, with the proper software downloaded and installed, also can play Apple's **QuickTime format** files. One minute of video and sound recorded in either of these formats results in a file that is about 6 megabytes, which is a very large file to transmit over slower types of Internet connections. Because of the larger file sizes, development continues on better ways to transmit video files over the Internet. The International Standards Organization's **Moving Picture Experts Group (MPEG)** has created a series of standards for compressed file formats. As in JPEG graphic files, this compression technique deletes information from the file and can deteriorate quality.

Audio from Video: The MP3 File Format

The audio portion of the MPEG file format was responsible for one of the greatest revolutions in online music that has occurred in the history of the Web. The MPEG format's audio track, called **MPEG Audio Layer 3 (MP3)** became wildly popular just as disk storage on personal computers dropped in price and CD writers (also called CD burners) became affordable for home use. Files in the MP3 format are somewhat lower in quality than WAV format files, but they are 90 percent smaller. Thus, a CD that might hold 15 popular songs in high quality WAV format (about 40 megabytes per song) could instead hold 150 popular songs in MP3 format (about 4 megabytes per song).

Ethical and Legal Concerns: Sharing Audio Files

The smaller size of MP3 files made it easy to send them from one person to another through the Internet, and file sharing software, such as Napster and Kazaa, became very popular. People began copying music from CDs that they had purchased and converting that music into MP3 files, which they then exchanged with others on the Internet. This file-sharing activity is unethical because it deprives the creators of the audio works of their rights to control distribution and to profit from their work. It is also illegal in many countries, including the United States. Companies in the recording industry and the recording artists themselves were not very happy with the large number of MP3 files that were being transmitted on these file-sharing networks. Recording companies and artists filed suits against Napster and other file-sharing sponsors for violating copyright laws. The recording companies were generally successful in obtaining court orders or out-of-court settlements that prevent further copyright violations in many cases. Many individuals, however, still violate the law and share MP3 files that contain copyrighted works.

Legal MP3 File Distribution

More recently, a number of Web sites have been created to sell digital music in MP3 and other formats. These sites, which include Napster under new management, have obtained the legal right to distribute the musical works they offer for sale. Advances in flash memory technology have made it possible to create portable digital music players (such as Apple's iPod) that can store thousands of songs downloaded from music Web sites. Apple's iPod + iTunes Web site, which appears in Figure 4-24, has sold millions of songs since it opened in 2003.

Figure 4-24 | **Apple's iTunes home page**

A number of Web sites now offer music for download in MP3 and other, lesser known, formats. Some of these sites charge per song, while others charge a monthly fee that allows subscribers to download as many songs as they wish. Most of the sites that sell download-able music place restrictions on the number of copies you can make of each song. Some of the sites restrict you from converting downloaded song files into other formats, or they restrict the types of devices on which you are permitted to play the song. You should always check the site carefully for details about file formats and copying restrictions before you buy songs or sign up for a subscription. The Student Online Companion includes a list of these Web sites under the heading "Online Music Stores." The continuing developments in portable data storage technology and increasing bandwidth should ensure that digital music grows for many years.

Future of Electronic Publishing

One of the key changes that the Internet and the Web have brought to the world is that infor-mation can now be disseminated more rapidly than ever and in large quantities, but with a low required investment. The impact of this change is that firms in the public relations busi-ness—firms that spend great amounts of time and money trying to present their clients through the major media in the best possible light—might be facing a significantly changed business environment. Many industry analysts believe that the ease of publishing electronically on the Web might help reduce the concentration of media control that has been developing over the past three decades as newspapers and publishing companies merged with each other and, along with radio and television stations, were purchased by large media companies.

E-Zines

To be successful in print media publishing (such as publishing a monthly magazine), a publisher must have a large subscription market; the publisher can earn a profit only if the high fixed costs of composing and creating the magazine are spread over enough units. The costs of publishing a Web page are very low compared to those for printing magazines or newspapers. Therefore, the subscription market required for a Web publication to be successful can be very small or even nonexistent. If a Web-based magazine, or an **e-zine**, can attract advertisers, it can be financially successful with no subscribers and only a small number of readers. As a result, e-zines are appearing on the Web in increasing numbers. An e-zine does not require a large readership to be successful, so these elec-tronic publications can focus on very specialized, narrow interests. E-zines have become popular places for publishing new fiction and poetry, for example. The Additional Information section of the Student Online Companion page for this tutorial includes links to a number of e-zine Web sites under the heading "E-zines."

Blogs (Web Logs)

Most e-zines follow the general model used by print magazines for their layout, design, and structure. E-zines are usually managed by an editor who solicits manuscripts from other writers and then publishes some of those manuscripts after editing them. However, the Web has enabled an entirely new type of individual publication. Earlier in this tutorial, you learned about blogs (short for "Web logs"). Blogs are usually written by a single person (called the blogger) who wishes to express a particular point of view. Some blogs allow others to add comments or reactions to the blogger's statements, which may be edited or deleted by the blogger. Although blogs exist on a wide variety of topics, most blogs focus on political, religious, or other issues about which people have strong opinions.

When you need to use the Web to find information for your classes or your job, remember to return to the Additional Information section of the Student Online Companion page for Tutorial 4 for a comprehensive list of Web information resources.

Review

Session 4.2 Quick Check

1. Explain why it can be important to determine a Web page author's identity and credentials when you plan to use the page's information as a research resource.
2. What information about Web page authors can help you assess their objectivity with respect to the contents of their Web pages?
3. Briefly describe two ways that libraries use the Web.
4. What are the advantages of using online reference works, such as dictionaries or encyclopedias, instead of print editions?
5. For how long is a work copyrighted?
6. Briefly explain the concept of "fair use."
7. True or False: Music stored in a WAV file format would be of lower quality and would result in a smaller file than the same music stored in an MP3 formatted file.
8. Briefly explain the differences between a blog and an e-zine.

Review

Tutorial Summary

In this tutorial, you learned how to find current news stories, weather information, maps, and information about travel destinations on the Web by using specialized search engines and Web directories. Online library resources and other research and reference resources are also available on the Web.

You learned some basic facts about copyright protection, fair use, and avoiding plagiarism in the use of text, images, and multimedia files that you find on the Internet. You also learned how to access many of the graphics and multimedia resources on the Internet, and you learned which image, sound, and video file formats are common on the Web.

Key Terms

animated GIF file
AVI (Audio Video Interleaved) format
copyright
e-zine
fair use
Graphics Interchange Format (GIF)
intellectual property

Joint Photographic Experts Group (JPEG)
lossy compression
MIDI (Musical Instrument Digital Interface) format
Moving Picture Experts Group (MPEG)
MPEG Audio Layer 3 (MP3)
news search engine
plagiarism

plug-ins
public domain
QuickTime format
streaming transmission
Wave (WAV) format
Web logs (Weblogs or blogs)
Web news directory
white pages directory
wire service
yellow pages directory

Review Assignments

Marti is preparing to visit a new techno band that she would like to sign in Chicago, Illinois. While in Chicago, she would like to visit a number of clubs that feature blues artists.

1. Start your Web browser, open the Student Online Companion page at www.course.com/newperspectives/internet6, click the Tutorial 4 link, and then click the Review Assignments link.
2. Obtain weather forecasts for the Chicago area from two of the weather sites included in the list of links for this assignment (or use weather sites with which you are familiar). Print the forecasts from each site.
3. The band is renting practice space in a warehouse near the corner of West 35th Street and South Morgan Street on the South side of Chicago. Print two maps from one of the map Web sites included in the list of links for this assignment. Include at least one street-level map and one higher-level map that shows the surrounding area in Chicago.
4. Use one of the links to a travel destination guide site to locate information about restaurants in the Chicago area. Prepare a report that lists three restaurants you think would be good choices for Marti to entertain clients while in Chicago.
5. Use one of the travel destination guide sites to locate at least two blues clubs that Marti can visit while she is in Chicago.
6. Use one or more of the links to News Search Engines in the Student Online Companion to find an article in a Chicago area newspaper that discusses a local band or an area club that features live music. Summarize the article in a short memo to Marti and include a citation to the article in the memo.
7. When you are finished, close your Web browser.

Case Problem 1

Portland Concrete Mixers, Inc.   You are a sales representative for Portland Concrete Mixers, Inc., a company that makes replacement parts for concrete mixing equipment. This equipment is mounted on trucks that deliver ready-mixed concrete to buildings and other job sites. You have been transferred to the Seattle area and would like to plan your first sales trip there. Because you plan to drive to Seattle, you need information about the best route as well as a map of Seattle. You hope to generate some new customers on this trip and, therefore, need to identify sales-lead prospects in the Seattle area. Companies that manufacture concrete are good prospects for you.

1. Start your Web browser, open the Student Online Companion page at www.course.com/newperspectives/internet6, click the Tutorial 4 link, and then click the Case Problem 1 link.
2. Choose one of the map sites from the list provided in the Student Online Companion.
3. Obtain driving directions from the site you have chosen. Your starting address is Portland, OR, and your destination address is Seattle, WA.
4. Obtain a more detailed route from Portland to Seattle, and then print it.
5. Obtain a map of Seattle from the site you have chosen. You can adjust the map to the level of detail you desire.
6. To identify sales prospects in Seattle, return to the Student Online Companion page for Case Problem 1 in Tutorial 4, and use one or more of the directories listed under the Yellow Pages Directories heading to search for businesses in the Seattle area that sell concrete. The results pages for your searches should include contact information for a number of companies in the concrete business in Seattle. Copy the names and addresses of at least three sales prospects to a document that you will carry with you on your trip.
7. When you are finished, close your Web browser.

Research

Use specialized search engines and Web directories to find specific types of MIDI files. Examine information about copyright restrictions regarding your potential use of those files.

Case Problem 2

Midland Elementary School Music Classes You are a third-grade language skills teacher at Midland Elementary School. The school has closed its music program because the state has cut its budget severely over the past several years. Although the school no longer has any music teachers on staff, you believe that it is important to expose your third-graders to the music of the great composers, such as Beethoven and Mozart. You do not have a budget for buying CDs, but you do have a computer with an Internet connection in the classroom. You would like to find some music files to play on the computer, but you want to make sure that any use of these files complies with U.S. copyright law. You have heard that single musical instruments, particularly pianos, sound realistic when synthesized in the MIDI format and you would, therefore, like to find some music in that format to begin your collection for the class.

1. Start your Web browser, open the Student Online Companion page at www.course.com/newperspectives/internet6, click the Tutorial 4 link, and then click the Case Problem 2 link.
2. Click one or more of the MIDI music links provided for this Case Problem.
3. Evaluate the files offered on these Web pages or the pages to which they lead. Write a short report summarizing your experience. In your report, describe any copyright restrictions that apply to the files that you would like to use.
4. When you are finished, close your Web browser.

Research

Find news stories and pending legislation about child care, evaluate a child care information Web site, and create two evaluation reports.

Case Problem 3

Toddle Inn Headquartered in Minneapolis, Minnesota, Toddle Inn is a chain of day-care centers operating in several Midwestern states. The directors are interested in undertaking a national expansion program that will require outside financing and an effective public relations program that integrates with their strategic marketing plans. You are an intern in the office of Joan Caruso, a public relations consultant who does work for Toddle Inn. Joan has asked you to help her with some background research as she creates a proposal for Toddle Inn for integrating a Web site into its public relations program.

1. Start your Web browser, open the Student Online Companion page at www.course.com/newperspectives/internet6, click the Tutorial 4 link, and then click the Case Problem 3 link.
2. Follow the links provided there to one or more of the news search engines and directories to find at least three current (within the past three or four months) news reports about the child-care industry. Write a memo to Joan that summarizes the major issues identified in these reports.
3. Joan would like you to conduct an evaluation of the Child Care Parent/Provider Information Network Web site. Prepare an evaluation of that site that considers the author's or publisher's identity and objectivity, and the site's content, form, and appearance.
4. One of the things that any public relations campaign must consider is the impact of pending legislation. Joan asks you to see if there are any bills pending in the U.S. Congress that will affect the child-care industry. Return to the Student Online Companion page for Case Problem 3 in Tutorial 4, open the Thomas Legislative Information Web site, type "child care" (without quotation marks) in the Word/Phrase text box and then click the Search button. Read one of the bills listed and prepare a one-paragraph summary for Joan of the bill's likely effects on the child-care industry.
5. When you are finished, close your Web browser.

Create

Identify Web sites that present arguments for and against prison privatization. Evaluate the quality of each site and prepare a report that summarizes findings.

Case Problem 4

Arnaud for Senate Campaign You work for the campaign team of Lisa Arnaud, who is running for a seat in the state senate. One issue that promises to play a prominent role in the upcoming election campaign is privatization of the state prison system. It is important for Lisa to establish a clear position on the issue early in the campaign, and she has asked you to prepare a briefing document for her to consider. Lisa tells you that she has no particular preference on the issue and that she wants you to obtain a balanced set of arguments for each side. Once the campaign takes a position, however, she will need to defend it. Therefore, Lisa wants to have an idea of the quality of the information you gather. You decide to do part of your research on the Web.

1. Start your Web browser, open the Student Online Companion page at www.course.com/newperspectives/internet6, click the Tutorial 4 link, and then click the Case Problem 4 link.
2. Choose one of the listed search tools to conduct a search for "privatization prisons" (without the quotation marks).
3. Examine your search results for authoritative sites that include positions on the issue. You might need to follow a number of results page hyperlinks to find suitable Web pages. In general, you should avoid current news items that appear in the results list.
4. Find one Web page that states a clear position in favor of privatization and another that states a clear position against privatization. Print a copy of each.
5. Prepare a three-paragraph report that summarizes the content of the Web pages you chose. Include full citations for the pages.
6. When you are finished, close your Web browser.

Challenge

Find images that meet a particular need and determine the copyright limitations on the use of those images for a specific purpose.

Case Problem 5

Kim's Travel and Cruises You are an assistant to Kim Phong, the owner of Kim's Travel and Cruises. The Web site for the firm includes pages that describe many of the destinations featured in the cruises she books for her clients. Kim would like to include images of flags that correspond to the country of each destination. She would also like to have a local artist create replicas of the flags as gifts for her regular clients. She would like you to find images of the flags from which the artist can create the replicas. You decide to do your research on the Web.

1. Start your Web browser, open the Student Online Companion page at www.course.com/newperspectives/internet6, click the Tutorial 4 link, and then click the Case Problem 5 link.
2. Select one of the sites listed for this problem and use it to conduct a search for images of flags for Thailand, Singapore, Malaysia, the People's Republic of China, Korea, and Japan.
3. Repeat the search using another search engine.
4. Examine your list of search results for suitable flag images. You might need to follow a number of results page hyperlinks to find images that meet your needs.
5. When you find a Web page or pages with suitable images, examine the Web site to determine what copyright or other restrictions exist regarding your use of the images.
6. Prepare a one-paragraph report for each flag that describes the source you plan to use. Include the URL of the site where you found the flag image and a summary of the restrictions on Kim's use of that image. If the Web site does not include any description of restrictions, refer to the text and state your opinion regarding what restrictions might exist on Kim's use of the image.
7. Close your Web browser.

Quick Check Answers

Session 4.1

1. a major wire service (or press agency or news service) based in Great Britain
2. When you want to find information that has been released recently but might not have been published in a newspaper or magazine.
3. Different meteorologists often predict different weather conditions for the same location; gathering several forecasts provides a range of likely weather conditions.
4. You can change the map's scale, and you can e-mail the map or save it to a handheld computing device such as a personal digital assistant (PDA).
5. any three of: recommendations and reviews of restaurants, entertainment (or nightlife), sports, shopping, landmarks, and other visitor information
6. False
7. yellow pages directory
8. white pages directory

Session 4.2

1. Author identity and credentials help establish the credibility of Web page content.
2. their employment or other professional affiliations
3. by adding online resources to their collections and by making their collections accessible to remote users and other libraries
4. available 24 hours a day, seven days a week; can be easier and faster to search
5. A work is copyrighted for the life of the author plus 70 years; works copyrighted by corporations or not-for-profit organizations are protected for 95 years from the date of publication or 120 years from the date of creation, whichever is earlier.
6. You can copy small parts of a work for use in criticism, comment, news reporting, teaching, scholarship, or research.
7. False
8. A blog is usually written by one person who uses the Web to express strong personal opinions on a particular subject; an e-zine usually follows the format and structure of a printed magazine, in which an editor reviews manuscripts submitted by other authors and decides which manuscripts to publish after editing them.

Objectives

Session 5.1
• Learn what FTP is and how it works
• Explore how to use an FTP client program and Web browser to transfer files
• Navigate an FTP site using a Web browser
• Learn how to compress and decompress files and to check them for viruses

Session 5.2
• Download an FTP client program using a Web browser
• Download a compression program using an FTP client program
• Install and use a compression program
• Trace the connection between your computer and a remote computer

Session 5.3
• Explore storage options on the Internet
• Learn about emerging technologies for collaborative authoring on the Web

Lab

Keeping Your Computer Virus Free

Student Edition Labs

Student Data Files

Downloading and Storing Data

Using FTP and Other Services to Transfer and Store Data

Case

Sound Effects, Inc.

One of the things that Milt Spangler enjoys most about being a musician is being able to manipulate music electronically to create customized sounds. After graduating from the University of Southern California with a degree in business administration, Milt started Sound Effects, Inc., a company that produces sounds and voiceovers for local advertising agencies and other businesses that use digitally produced and created sounds. Soon Milt's business expanded sufficiently so that he could rent a warehouse with a built-in sound studio. As part of the expansion, Milt hired professional actors to do voiceover work and other speaking roles, such as recording characters' voices in CD-ROM games and educational programs for children. Milt soon began receiving contracts from out-of-state businesses, educational software manufacturers, and advertising agencies as his work became nationally recognized. As a result of his success, he needed to expand his pool of actor talent beyond the Los Angeles area.

Sound Effects operates with only a few permanent employees in the Los Angeles area. Many of the actors who provide voiceover work live elsewhere in the United States and in all provinces of Canada. These actors record their material for Milt in studios near their homes. Because their work is produced digitally, Milt needs a way to transfer files from studios in the actors' hometowns to the Los Angeles office, where he can edit and finalize the files for clients. The large sizes of digitally produced files and the high cost of sending files prohibit Milt from relying on e-mail attachments and overnight delivery services as options for transporting files. He asks you to help him find ways to send, manage, and store large files using other methods.

▼ **Tutorial.05**

▽ Tutorial folder	▽ Review folder	▽ Cases folder
Memorandum.doc	register.pdf	55.jpg
		56.jpg
		57.jpg
		58.jpg

Session 5.1

Understanding File Transfer Protocol

You already know that you can use e-mail attachments to send files over the Internet. E-mail is often a good way of transporting a file from one location to another, or even to yourself. For example, if you are working on a report in the university computer lab and forget to bring your disk, you can attach the report to an e-mail message you address to yourself; when you get home and download your e-mail messages the file arrives on your home computer. This method works for sending files to other people as well. However, many e-mail servers limit the sizes of files you can attach to a single e-mail message. E-mail servers might also limit the types of files you can send. For example, some servers will not accept file attachments that can execute programs to protect the e-mail server from viruses that might be hidden in those files.

To address storage issues and issues related to transmitting large files from one location to another and between multiple users, you can use FTP. **FTP**, or **File Transfer Protocol**, is the Internet protocol that transfers files between computers that are connected to the Internet. The site to which you are sending files and from which you are receiving files is called an **FTP site**, **FTP server**, or a **remote computer**; when it is connected to an FTP site, your computer is called the **local computer**. You can send any file type to an FTP site, including spreadsheet, picture, video, sound, program, and text files.

When you send a file using FTP, you **upload** the file to send it from your computer to the FTP site. When you receive a file, you **download** the file from the FTP site and receive it on your computer. When you want to upload or download a file, you connect to a remote computer and request it to either receive files from your computer or transfer files to your computer. The FTP server receives file transfer requests and then manages the details of transferring files between the local and remote computers.

FTP is operating system neutral. For example, your PC might use FTP and Windows XP to communicate with an FTP server running the UNIX operating system. (UNIX is a powerful operating system that runs on mainframe computers and workstations.) It makes no difference that the operating systems are different; FTP seamlessly transfers files between them. Whether files are uploaded or downloaded, FTP is the protocol that accomplishes the transfer.

Because you can use FTP to download almost any type of file, there are different types of file transfer modes and which one you use depends on the type of file you are downloading.

File Transfer Modes

Many files, including Web pages and e-mail messages, consist of ASCII (plain) text. **ASCII text** contains symbols typed from the keyboard but does not include any nonprintable, binary codes. Other files, such as pictures, movies, sound files, and graphics, are **binary**. Any file created by a word-processing program or containing character formatting, such as bold or italics, is binary. FTP can transfer both ASCII and binary files. Files are transferred using one of two **file transfer modes**; usually the FTP program chooses the file transfer mode for you automatically. **ASCII mode** is used to transfer plain-text files; **binary mode** is used to transfer everything else. If you download and open a file and it contains a bunch of codes, then you can suspect that the file was transferred in the wrong mode. Simply execute the FTP operation again using the correct transfer mode.

File Types and Extensions

The decision to transfer a file using binary or ASCII mode is largely determined by noting a file's type, much like Windows programs do. Programs such as Excel, Word, and

Internet Explorer determine a file's type by the file extension. It is helpful to understand the relationship between a file's extension and programs that manipulate that file type so you can determine a file's general use and assess your ability to read the file before you download it.

File extensions are added automatically by the program that created them based on a widely agreed-upon convention for associating files with programs. Your computer's operating system (Windows, for example) keeps track of most file extension associations and maintains a list of file extensions and programs that can open files with those file extensions. Each computer that you use maintains different information about the file types stored on that computer. You can use Windows Explorer to learn about the file extension associations on your computer.

To view Windows file extension associations:

▸ **1.** Click the **Start** button on the taskbar, point to **All Programs**, point to **Accessories**, and then click **Windows Explorer** to start the program.

▸ **2.** Click **Tools** on the menu bar, and then click **Folder Options**. The Folder Options dialog box opens.

▸ **3.** Click the **File Types** tab to see your computer's registered file types (file extensions) and the programs it uses to open those files. Figure 5-1 shows the registered file types for one user's computer; your list will probably differ. When you install a new software program on your computer, Windows registers the file type(s) associated with that program. Therefore, your list of registered file types depends on which programs are installed on your computer. Clicking a registered file type in the list displays more information about that file extension, including the program that opens the file and a description of the file's purpose.

Viewing registered file types ◂ **Figure 5-1**

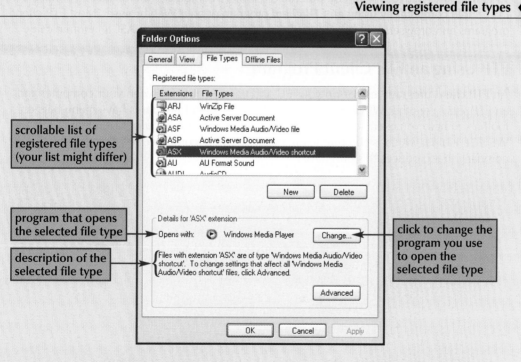

▸ **4.** Scroll down the list to view some of the registered file types, and then click the **Cancel** button to close the dialog box without making any changes.

▸ **5.** Close Windows Explorer by clicking its **Close** button.

Figure 5-2 shows several filenames with common file extensions, transfer modes, and programs that usually open them. Don't worry about remembering all the different file extensions; in practice, you might encounter only a few of them. Most often, you will see files on the Internet with extensions of .doc, .exe, .html, .txt, or .zip.

Figure 5-2	Common Internet file extensions, transfer modes, and associated programs

Filename and Extension	Extension	Transfer Mode	Type of File
picture.bmp	.bmp	Binary	Microsoft Paint picture
readme.doc	.doc	Binary	Word document
spinner.exe	.exe	Binary	Executable program
starship.gif	.gif	Binary	Picture
default.html or default.htm	.html or .htm	ASCII	HTML document (Web page)
employee.mdb	.mdb	Binary	Access database
b543215.mpg	.mpg	Binary	MPEG digitally compressed file
help.pdf	.pdf	Binary	Adobe Portable Document Format (PDF)
marketing.ppt	.ppt	Binary	PowerPoint presentation
readme.txt	.txt	ASCII	Text file
profit.xls	.xls	Binary	Excel worksheet
chapter1.zip	.zip	Binary	Compressed file

Connecting to an FTP Server

To transfer files between your computer and a remote computer, you must first connect to the remote computer by using an FTP client program or your Web browser. Most FTP client programs and browsers will select the file transfer mode of binary or ASCII automatically.

FTP Using an FTP Client Program

An **FTP client program** resides on your PC and transfers files between your computer and an FTP site. Like other Windows programs, most FTP client programs have menu bars or toolbars to help you execute commands. Figure 5-3 shows a popular FTP client program, WS_FTP Home, which is communicating with a remote computer at Ipswitch.com, the company that produces this program.

FTP client program ◄ **Figure 5-3**

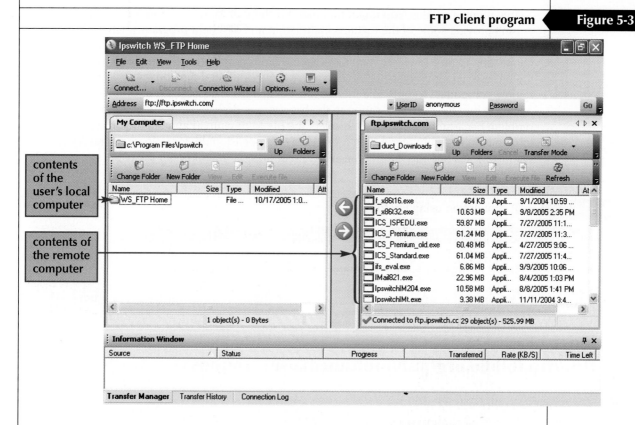

FTP client programs transfer files quickly and provide features that let you resume downloading a file when your connection is lost or interrupted. Many FTP client programs are either free or inexpensive. The features provided by an FTP client program vary from one program to another. When selecting an FTP client program, choose one that supports all or most of the following desirable features:

- Provides a multipane display so you can see both the local and remote computer directories simultaneously.
- Allows you to transfer multiple files in one FTP session. Some FTP clients restrict the number of files you can transfer at one time. If you need to transfer many files, this restriction can significantly increase the amount of time you will need to transfer the files.
- Permits drag and drop file transfers so you can use the mouse to drag and drop files between the local and remote computers.
- Simplifies the process of deleting directories and files on local and remote computers.
- Allows you to set up scheduled file transfers at a future date and time so you can transfer selected files unattended.
- Recovers interrupted file transfers by continuing the transfer process from the point where the connection was lost or interrupted.
- Reconnects automatically to sites that disconnect a transfer when your connection exceeds the maximum allotted time.

FTP Using a Web Browser

Most Web browsers, including Microsoft Internet Explorer and Mozilla Firefox, support FTP, but they have limited functionality when compared to FTP client programs. You can use a Web browser to upload and download files from FTP sites, but if you are transferring a large number of files, you might find that it is difficult to use a browser because it doesn't provide some of the features included in an FTP client program, such as file resume and reconnection features. Figure 5-4 shows how Milt might use Firefox to make a connection to an FTP site that includes sound files organized into categories. Notice that the browser window does not include a two-pane display of the contents of the local and remote computers. To upload a file, he must drag it from his desktop or Windows Explorer and drop it in the correct location in the browser window. Downloading a file poses no problem because he only needs to select the file to download and tell the browser where to save it on his computer. Using a Web browser occasionally for uploading and downloading files is fine, but if Milt transfers a lot of files, he might prefer the features of an FTP client program.

Figure 5-4 ▶ **FTP connection using Firefox**

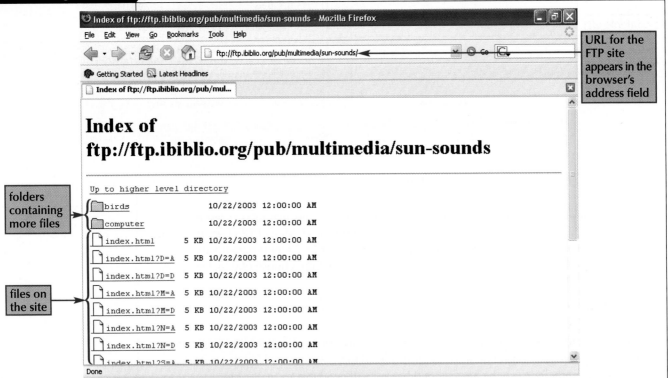

In Figure 5-4, notice that the protocol in the site's URL is ftp:// instead of http:// and that the site's URL indicates an FTP site (ftp) instead of a Web site (www).

Levels of Access for FTP Servers

To use a remote computer, regardless of how you access it, you must identify yourself, or **log on**, by supplying your user name and a password. Some FTP sites provide public access, which means anyone can connect to the FTP site. When you connect to a public FTP site, your access is restricted to only those files and folders designated for access by public users. Many software companies provide public FTP sites so users can download evaluation versions of their software and data to support their use of the program. Other FTP sites provide a combination of public and restricted access; some sites are completely restricted and do not allow public visitors. To access restricted FTP sites, you must have an account with the FTP site's owner or sponsor.

Anonymous FTP

Logging on to one of the many publicly accessible, remote computers connected to the Internet is known as an **anonymous login** because you use *anonymous* as your user name. You do not need a password to access a public computer; however, it is customary to enter your full e-mail address if you are prompted for a password. That way, the hosting organization can identify who is accessing the public areas of its FTP site. When you download or upload files using an anonymous login, you are participating in an **anonymous FTP session**. Figure 5-5 shows how Milt might use Internet Explorer to make an anonymous login to a public FTP site. Notice that Internet Explorer indicates the user name on the status bar; in this case, the user name is Anonymous. (Firefox does not display the user name in the browser window.) When you connect to a public FTP site using a Web browser, the browser might automatically supply the user name anonymous and an appropriate password to access the site. If the site requires you to enter a user name and password, the browser will prompt you for these items.

Anonymous FTP session using Internet Explorer ◄ **Figure 5-5**

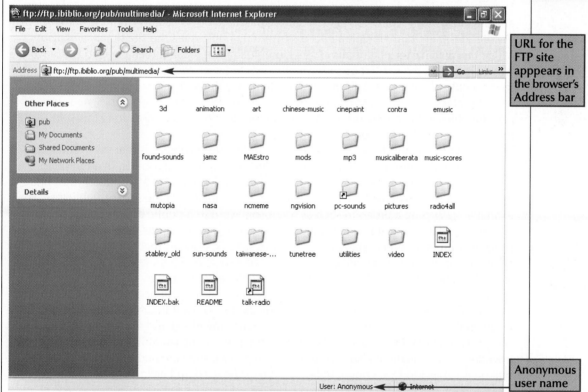

URL for the FTP site apppears in the browser's Address bar

Anonymous user name

You can use many of the anonymous FTP sites connected to the Internet to download files to your PC. In most cases, public FTP sites impose limits on uploading files or provide only one publicly accessible directory to which you can upload files. Public FTP sites also limit your access to selected directories and files on their systems. People using FTP sites with anonymous logins usually cannot open and view all the directories and files on the site. You can determine which directories you can access by experimenting. If you attempt to open directories or examine files that are not accessible to anonymous users, you will receive an error or warning message indicating that you do not have access to the requested file or directory. Experimenting with your access is allowable, but you should obey all rules and regulations regarding anonymous access. You can usually find information about the site's acceptable use rules and policies in the readme.txt file in the pub (public) directory. If you find a file by that or a similar name, be sure to read it carefully. Remember that you are using another person's or organization's FTP site at no cost to download files for your use.

Full-Privilege FTP

When you need to access an FTP site that is not public, such as one for your school or employer, you will use **full-privilege FTP**, where you are given access to its content with a user name and password. Even though you might have an account on a particular FTP site, your access might be limited to transferring files in a specific directory. When you log on to an FTP site with your user name and password, the system might automatically direct you to a particular directory on that FTP site in which you have been given rights to upload and download files. When you have an account on an FTP site, you can usually store files for longer periods than you can on a public FTP site.

Using a Public Directory

Some public FTP sites allow users with anonymous FTP access to view only one directory and any files or other directories it contains. That directory is usually named pub (for public). Besides permitting download access by anonymous users, the site's manager, also called the **Webmaster**, might allow users to upload files, making them available to anyone who connects to the site. Frequently, public directories provide a temporary location for users to upload and share data or programs that they think others might find useful. Most FTP sites place time limits, such as a few days or weeks, on how long anonymous users can store files in the public directory. The Webmaster determines how long files can remain in the public directory.

One problem with sites permitting users with upload privileges is that the Webmaster must monitor the files uploaded to a public directory on a regular basis. In addition to worrying about viruses that might be hidden in uploaded files, the Webmaster must find and delete any copyrighted files that were illegally uploaded to the site for public use. For example, uploading a program such as Microsoft Word to a public directory is a clear copyright violation because Microsoft's license agreement prohibits you from sharing the program with other users. Many FTP sites have specific policies that force you to acknowledge, before uploading any files, that you are the owner of the material or that its transfer to the FTP site will not violate any copyright or intellectual property restrictions.

Be sure to read the site's readme files to learn any rules about acceptable use when you enter an FTP site. Figure 5-6 shows the readme.txt file for Dell Inc. Notice that the language in this document indicates that the user must download and accept material on the site "as is" and that Dell makes no representations about the suitability of the material you download. The statement also includes a reminder that software and other written information is subject to U.S. copyright laws and must be used and acknowledged properly.

Readme file in Dell Inc.'s pub directory | **Figure 5-6**

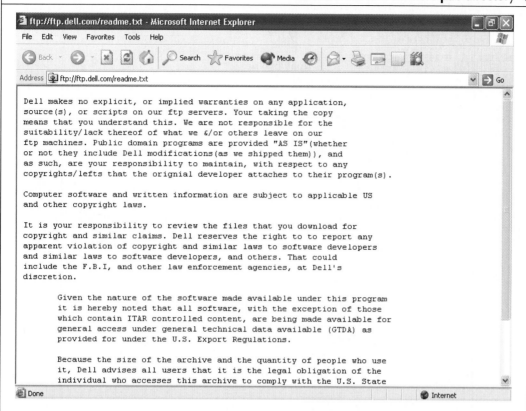

Now that you have reviewed some basic facts about FTP, Milt asks you to show him how to use a Web browser to navigate an FTP site. Sometimes Milt needs to obtain sound files of common sounds, such as a person laughing or a door closing, for use in the children's games that he produces. You will demonstrate the FTP site at ibiblio.org, a library on the Internet that stores an archive of sound files, to introduce him to this resource and also to show him how to navigate an FTP site.

Using a Web Browser to Navigate an FTP Site

Because most Internet users are adept at using a Web browser and know how hyperlinks work, they will have no difficulty navigating an FTP site in search of files. If you need to upload or download files to a site requiring full-privilege FTP access rights, the browser will prompt you for your user name and password.

When you visit an FTP site, your first goal should be to become familiar with its organization. FTP sites are organized hierarchically, much like the folders and files on a computer's hard drive. When you access an FTP site, you usually enter at the site's **root directory**, which contains other directories that contain files and other directories, such as those shown in Figure 5-7. Most sites prevent users with anonymous logins from accessing some files and directories in the root directory. When you enter a root directory for the first time, a message might appear indicating which file contains important information about navigating the site.

Figure 5-7 | **FTP site's hierarchical structure**

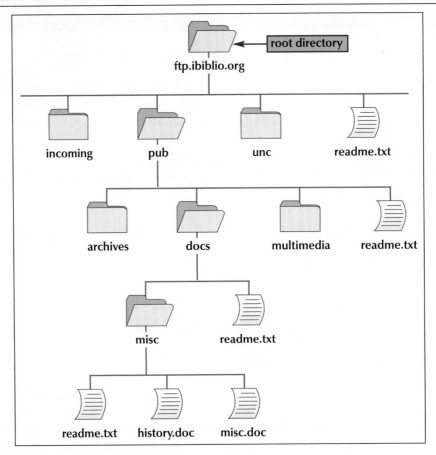

An FTP site usually stores two types of items—directories (folders) and files. Most Web browsers display directory and file links with different icons or notations so you can distinguish directories from files. In Figure 5-8, which shows an FTP connection in Internet Explorer, a yellow folder icon identifies a directory; a file is identified with a file icon that indicates the file's type. Double-clicking a file either opens the file in a new browser window or in a program window so you can view the file, or it begins downloading the file to your computer. Double-clicking a directory opens the directory and displays its contents. To move up (or back) one directory, you click the Up button.

Figure 5-8 | **FTP site in Internet Explorer**

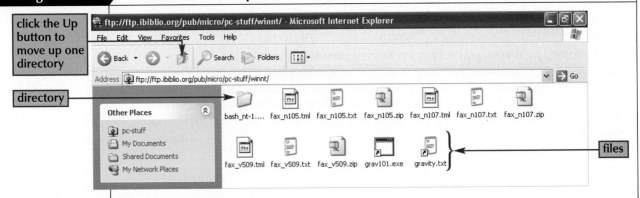

In Figure 5-9, which shows an FTP connection in Firefox, directories and files both appear as hyperlinks. A yellow folder icon usually indicates a directory and a white page icon indicates a file. Clicking a link to a file opens the file in a new browser window, starts the program associated with the file and opens the file, or begins downloading the file. Clicking a folder opens the directory and displays its contents. To move up (or back) one directory, you click the "Up to higher level directory" link at the top of the browser window.

FTP site in Firefox | **Figure 5-9**

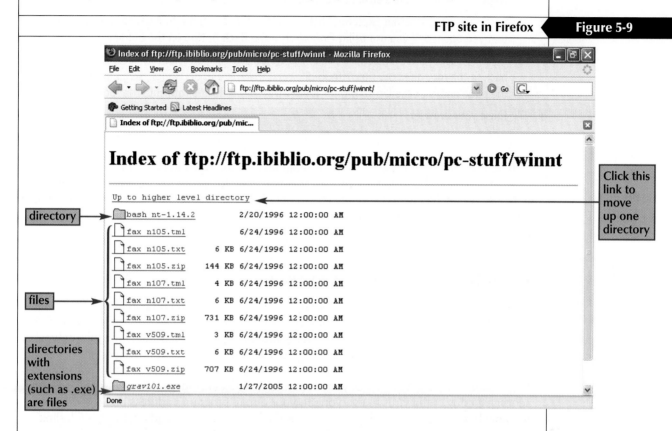

Milt asks you to show him how to use a Web browser to open and navigate an FTP site.

To open and navigate an FTP site using a Web browser:

▶ **1.** Start your Web browser, open the Student Online Companion page at **www.course.com/newperspectives/internet6**, click the **Tutorial 5** link, and then click the **Session 5.1** link. Click the **ibiblio.org** link and wait while the browser connects to the FTP site.

▶ **2.** If you are using Internet Explorer, double-click the **pub** folder to open it; if you are using Firefox, click the **pub** folder to open it. The pub (public) directory opens and displays several directories. If necessary, use the scroll bar to view the contents of this directory.

   When you are viewing files posted at an FTP site, the browser opens some files, such as text files (with a .txt file extension), and downloads other files, such as programs (files with a .exe file extension).

▶ **3.** If you are using Internet Explorer, double-click any folder to open it; if you are using Firefox, click any folder to open it.

   Trouble? If you try to open a folder that does not permit anonymous users, the browser will display an error message. Close the dialog box, and then try another folder until you open one successfully.

4. Explore several directories at this FTP site until you find a file named **readme.txt** (or **readme**) or **index.html** (or **index**). If you are using Internet Explorer, double-click the file to open it; if you are using Firefox, click the file to open it, and then read the file that opens. Sometimes you might find site information in the readme.txt, about.txt, or welcome.txt file. You might encounter other names, but they all serve the same function; that is, to provide an overview of the site's structure and file locations.

5. If you are using Internet Explorer, click the **Close** button on the title bar to close the file that you opened; if you are using Firefox, click the **Back** button on the toolbar.

6. If you are using Internet Explorer, click the **Up** button on the toolbar as necessary to move back to the root directory (ftp://ftp.ibiblio.org); if you are using Firefox, scroll to the top of the page and click the **Up to higher level directory** until you return to the root directory.

7. Close your browser.

Before you open or install any file or program that you downloaded from another computer, you must first check it for viruses. Milt will want to ensure the security of the computers at Sound Effects, so he wants you to help him locate several options for checking its computers before he starts transferring files and for checking downloaded files or programs before opening or installing them.

Checking Files for Viruses

For everyone using the Internet, computer viruses pose a real and potentially costly threat. Computer viruses are programs that "infect" your computer and cause harm to your disk or programs. People create viruses by coding programs that hide by attaching themselves to other programs on a computer. Some viruses simply display an annoying or silly message on your screen and then go away, whereas others can cause real harm by reformatting a hard drive, changing all of your computer's file extensions and their associations, or sending a copy of the virus to everyone in your e-mail program's address book. You have to know how to detect and eradicate viruses if you plan to download anything, including data, programs, or e-mail attachments, from any Internet server.

Virus detection software, also called **antivirus software**, regularly scans the files on your computer and the files being downloaded to your computer and compares them to a signature that known viruses carry. A **virus signature** (also called a **virus pattern** or a **virus definition**) is a sequence (string) of characters that is always present in a particular virus. A virus detection program can scan a single file or folder or your entire computer to search for infected files. When the antivirus program finds a virus signature, it warns you. You can either delete the file containing the virus or ask the antivirus program to remove the virus. Most antivirus programs can clean infected files by removing the virus.

Dell Inc., IBM, Gateway, and other well-known manufacturers load most new personal computers with an antivirus program. If your PC does not have an antivirus program, you can follow the links in the Virus Detection Software section of the Student Online Companion page for Tutorial 5 to find resources for obtaining and using a virus detection program. Two popular choices for protecting PCs are Norton AntiVirus and McAfee VirusScan. Both programs protect your computer from viruses, but only when they are turned on, properly configured, and include current virus patterns. When you first start your antivirus program, it will ask you to make a connection to its server, where the program will download the most recent virus patterns. You must regularly download virus patterns from the server to keep your computer safe. Some programs include features that automatically download the patterns for you on a weekly or bi-weekly basis; other programs require you to connect to the server and initiate the download. When you install an antivirus program, you usually receive a free trial subscription for downloading current virus patterns. After this initial period ends, you must pay the software producer an annual fee to continue downloading current virus patterns. In either case, your antivirus software can protect you only from viruses that it recognizes. If you install an antivirus program and do not regularly download new patterns, your computer isn't protected from new virus threats. In addition, if your antivirus software isn't turned on or isn't set to scan downloaded files, it cannot protect your computer.

Figure 5-10 shows the configuration screen for Norton AntiVirus. Notice that the user's system is set to auto-protect, meaning that the antivirus software starts automatically when Windows starts; the software automatically scans all incoming e-mail messages; the user has completed a full system scan; and the virus definitions are current. Automatic LiveUpdate is a feature that, when enabled, automatically checks for and downloads new virus patterns on a timetable set by the user. The options shown in this window are global and you usually need to set them only once.

Configuring Norton AntiVirus | **Figure 5-10**

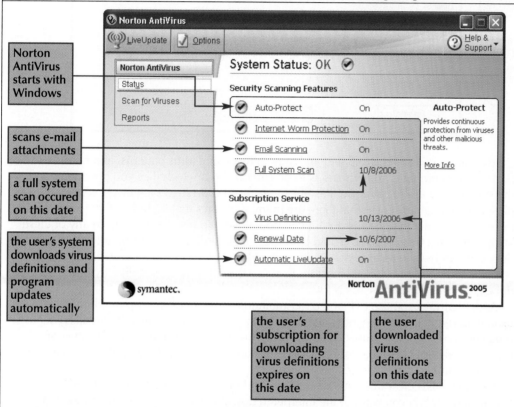

Norton AntiVirus starts with Windows

scans e-mail attachments

a full system scan occured on this date

the user's system downloads virus definitions and program updates automatically

the user's subscription for downloading virus definitions expires on this date

the user downloaded virus definitions on this date

Because any file that you download from the Internet can contain a virus, it is important to use your antivirus software as directed. Just downloading a file with a virus usually will not cause any harm to your computer, unless you open it. Before downloading any file, make sure that your antivirus software is turned on, enabled, and uses current virus patterns. After downloading the file, use the antivirus software to scan it for viruses. Most antivirus programs let you select which types of files to scan; the safest course is to scan all files, as shown in Figure 5-11. Most antivirus programs let you initiate a scan by right-clicking a file and then choosing an option on the shortcut menu to scan the file. If the file is free of known viruses, a dialog box will open and tell you that no viruses were found. In addition, you might be able to request a full system scan, in which all of the files on your computer are scanned and checked for viruses; many antivirus software programs also allow you to set up a schedule for automatically performing full system scans on a regular basis. If the program finds a virus, it will present you with options for handling the file. You can choose to ignore the virus (which is not recommended), repair the infected file, quarantine the file in an isolated folder on your hard drive, or delete the infected file.

Figure 5-11 ▶ Norton AntiVirus Options dialog box

auto-protect options

options for handling detected viruses

identifies which files to scan

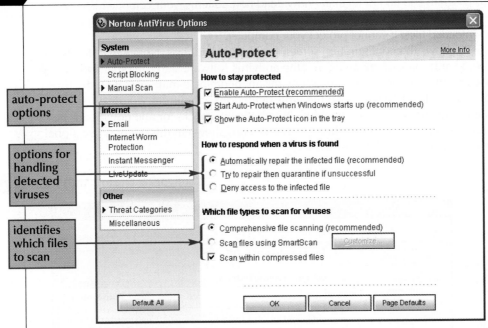

In addition to installing updated antivirus software and virus patterns, another way to protect your computer from viruses is to be careful about which files you download and the sources you use to get those files. If Milt wants to download the newest version of a program, he might discover that there are many Web sites that include a link to download the executable file that installs it. Milt can download and install the file from any of these Web sites, but a better choice would be to download it directly from the software's producer. Not only is he assured of a valid copy of the program, but he can make sure that he is downloading its most recent version. Because the software comes directly from its producer, the likelihood of a virus is low.

And, finally, as you use FTP and other methods to obtain files, keep in mind that you usually have to open or execute a file to unleash any virus it contains. By regularly scanning your computer for viruses, keeping your virus patterns current, configuring your antivirus program to work automatically, and scanning all downloaded files, you can protect your computer from viruses.

Milt now has a clear understanding of FTP and the tools he needs to transfer files using FTP. In Session 5.2, you will use the Internet to download an FTP client program that Milt and his contractors can use to transfer files between the Los Angeles studio and different areas of the United States and Canada. You will also download a file compression program.

Review

Session 5.1 Quick Check

1. What is the primary difference between using an FTP client program and a Web browser for file uploads to an FTP site?
2. When a user logs on to a publicly accessible computer connected to the Internet, what customary password should the user supply?
3. True or False: Some FTP client programs automatically determine the transfer mode for files that you download.
4. What two types of items might you find in the root directory of an FTP site?

5. What would you type in your browser's address field to open the FTP site at zdnet.com?

6. Which file transfer mode should you use for a file with a .ppt file extension? For a file with a .txt file extension?

Session 5.2

Visiting and Using a Download Site

Now that Milt understands how FTP works, he is ready to learn how to use it. The computers in the Los Angeles office use Windows XP Professional. Because Milt will need to upload and download files, he is most interested in obtaining an FTP client program that can handle both transactions. To help Milt make his decision about an FTP client program, your first goal is to make sure that the software you will download and install is reliable. Perhaps equally important is how various software tools compare to each other, so you need to find some sort of ratings system that will guide you in making good decisions about which software to choose. Finally, cost is a consideration because Milt will need to provide this software to employees in his studio and ask his contractors to obtain it.

A good way to locate software on the Internet is to use one or more Internet search engines. If you are searching for FTP client programs, you can look for reviews or comparisons of the software by users or vendors. For example, several popular computer magazines feature articles comparing Internet utility programs and designating one or more programs as superior. The criteria these sites use to judge which program is best might be different from your own criteria. However, it never hurts to review the ratings when you can.

Computer magazines frequently review software using their specially designed software testing laboratories, conduct product comparisons, and report the results. They should not have a vested interest in the outcome, but always view the results with a critical eye to identify any biases. The Computer Magazines and Download Sites section of the Student Online Companion page for Tutorial 5 contains links to publishers of software and hardware product reviews and sites that provide downloads of popular programs.

Several Web sites provide links to freeware and shareware programs; some of these same sites also allow you to download programs directly. Download sites are helpful as you search for new software because they frequently include program descriptions and ratings by current users. To find a list of FTP client programs and reviews about their usage, you decide to visit Download.com, which contains many freeware and shareware programs organized in different categories.

To browse the Download.com Web site:

1. Start your Web browser, open the Student Online Companion page at **www.course.com/newperspectives/internet6**, click the **Tutorial 5** link, and then click the **Session 5.2** link. Click the **Download.com** hyperlink and wait while your Web browser loads the Web page.

2. Locate the Search text box, and then type **FTP client** in the Search text box. Alternatively, you could select a category in which to search, such as Internet. Each category contains subcategories so you can narrow your search.

3. Click the **Go** button to search for FTP client programs. The search returns the date when the files were uploaded to the site and the current number of times each file has been downloaded. Sometimes the download count is a good resource for discovering popular and useful programs because these programs usually have larger download counts.

4. Scroll down and to the right, if necessary, and then click the **Total downloads** link in the search results to sort the list by the number of downloads. Figure 5-12 shows the search results after resorting the list by the number of downloads. (Your list might differ.)

Figure 5-12 **FTP client programs sorted by the number of downloads**

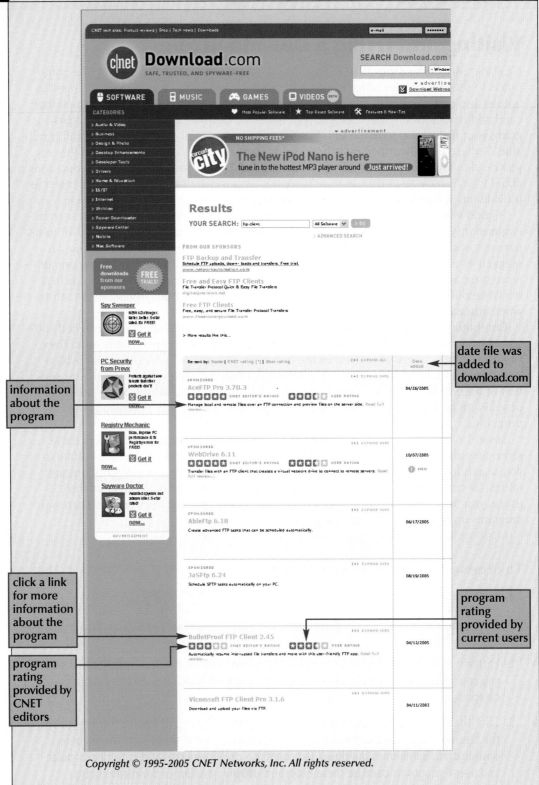

information about the program

click a link for more information about the program

program rating provided by CNET editors

date file was added to download.com

program rating provided by current users

5. If you see a link to the WS_FTP Home program in the list, click the **WS_FTP Home** link. If you do not see the WS_FTP Home link, scroll to the bottom of the page, click in the **Search Again** text box, type **WS_FTP Home**, click the **Go** button, and then click the **WS_FTP Home** link.

Trouble? If you cannot find the link to the WS_FTP Home program, click a link to another popular FTP client program to learn more about it.

6. Read the Web page that opens and describes this program's features.

7. Return to the Student Online Companion page for Session 5.2.

After reading several other reviews, Milt has decided to install WS_FTP Home and use it for several weeks to determine its usefulness for Sound Effects. To make sure that Milt downloads the latest version of WS_FTP Home, you will use the information you obtained from Download.com to obtain the executable file from the program's vendor, Ipswitch.

Downloading Programs

Internet users are often pleasantly surprised to discover that many programs are available for download at little or no cost. There are four general types of downloaded software: freeware, shareware, limited edition, and licensed (or full version).

Developers often make their software available for free in exchange for user feedback. After collecting user feedback and improving the free software, many developers provide an upgrade of the free version for a nominal fee. Software that is available to users at no cost and with no restrictions is called **freeware**. Freeware users must accept the implicit or explicit warning that the software might contain errors, called **bugs**, which could cause the program to halt or malfunction or even damage the user's computer. The main risk associated with using freeware is that its limited testing sometimes results in a program that contains bugs, and the software's developer is rarely liable for any damage that the freeware program might cause. On the other hand, a lot of good-quality commercial software started as freeware. To see what kinds of successes and problems its users have reported, you should use a Web search engine to locate reviews before you download, install, virus check, and use any freeware program.

Shareware is similar to freeware, but it is usually available for free only for a short evaluation period. After that evaluation period expires—usually after a specified number of days or a specific number of uses—shareware stops functioning. Shareware users are expected to stop using the shareware after the specified initial trial period and uninstall it from their computers. Otherwise, anyone who likes the program and wants to continue using it can purchase a license. There are three popular ways to turn shareware users into paying customers. The first way is to build a counter into the program that keeps track of the number of times they have used a program. After users have reached a usage limit, the software is disabled. The second way inserts an internal date checker that causes the shareware to stop working after a specific time period from the installation date has elapsed, such as 30 days. Third, many shareware developers use a "nag" screen that appears each time you start the program to encourage those users who do not purchase a license to stop using the shareware, although the program might continue to work. The screen usually displays a message with the developer's name and Web address and asks users to abide by the licensing agreement and to submit payment for the shareware version of the product.

Shareware is usually more reliable than freeware because the shareware developer is sometimes willing to accept responsibility for the program's operation. Usually, shareware developers have an established way for users to report any bugs and receive free or low-cost software upgrades and patches.

Some developers distribute restricted versions of their software for free to let people use it without cost. A restricted version of a program is called a **limited edition** (often abbreviated as LE) or an **evaluation version**, and it provides most of the functionality of the full version that is for sale. However, limited edition software omits one or more useful features of the full version. You can sometimes download a limited edition version and use it for free. If you like the limited edition, you can purchase the full version. The FTP client program WS_FTP Home is a free limited edition of the full WS_FTP program. The limited edition performs standard FTP tasks but disables or omits some of the advanced features that make the full product especially attractive. Because the complete versions of limited edition software are inexpensive, most users of the limited edition will purchase the upgraded, comprehensive version so they can use its additional capabilities.

Regardless of which type of software you use to evaluate a product, most developers provide you with a means of contacting them to purchase a license to use the full version of the evaluation copy. Purchasing a license usually involves paying a fee to get a code to unlock the software and render it fully functional.

Using a Web Browser to Download an FTP Client Program

Milt has decided that the WS_FTP Home FTP client program is the best choice for Sound Effects, so you will use a browser to download it next.

Reference Window

Using a Browser to Download a Program

- Open the FTP site from which you will download the program.
- Navigate the FTP site to find the program's executable file, and then double-click the file (Internet Explorer) or click the file (Firefox).
- In Internet Explorer, click the Save button, use the Save in list arrow to navigate to the drive or folder in which to store the file, and then click the Save button. If necessary, click the Close button to close the dialog box.
- In Firefox, click the Save it to disk option button (if necessary), click the OK button, use the Save in list arrow to navigate to the drive or folder in which to store the file, and then click the Save button. If necessary, click the Close button to close the dialog box.

To use a browser to download the WS_FTP Home program:

1. On the Student Online Companion Web page for Session 5.2, click the **Ipswitch** link and wait while your Web browser opens the Ipswitch FTP site.

2. Open the **ipswitch** directory, and then open the **Product_Downloads** directory. The WSFTP_HomeT40_ Install.exe file is the limited edition version of WS_FTP Home. You will download this file to your Tutorial.05\Tutorial folder.

   Trouble? The Ipswitch FTP site might change over time. If you cannot find the ipswitch directory or the WSFTP_HomeT40_Install.exe file, open other directories at the site and examine their contents. If you cannot find this file, return to the Student Online Companion page for Session 5.2, click the FTPplanet.com link, and use the instructions at this Web site to download the WS_FTP Home program.

3. Locate the **WSFTP_HomeT40_Install.exe** file. If you are using Internet Explorer, double-click the file; if you are using Firefox, click the file. Figure 5-13 shows the dialog box that opens in Internet Explorer.

Downloading a file in Internet Explorer ◄ **Figure 5-13**

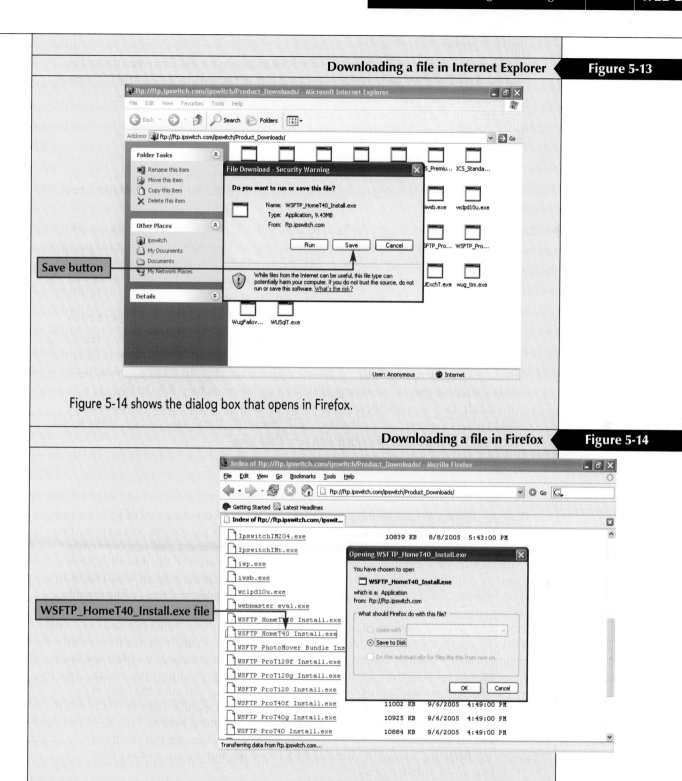

Figure 5-14 shows the dialog box that opens in Firefox.

Downloading a file in Firefox ◄ **Figure 5-14**

4. If you are using Internet Explorer, click the **Save** button in the File Download dialog box, use the **Save in** list arrow in the Save As dialog box to navigate to the Tutorial.05\Tutorial folder included with your Data Files, and then click the **Save** button. When the download is complete, the File Download dialog box will close.

Trouble? If the Download complete dialog box is open, click its Close button.

Trouble? To complete this tutorial, you must have access to a folder on your computer's hard drive or a personal network drive. You cannot complete this tutorial using a floppy disk. See the "Read This Before You Begin" on page WEB 152 for more information about the data files.

5. If you are using Firefox, click the **Save to Disk** option button, if necessary, click the **OK** button, use the **Save in** list arrow in the Enter name of file to save to dialog box to navigate to the Tutorial.05\Tutorial folder included with your Data Files, and then click the **Save** button. A dialog box opens displaying the progress of the download. You return to the FTP site for Ipswitch.

Trouble? If the Downloads dialog box is still open on the screen, click its Close button.

Trouble? If the Enter name of file to save to dialog box does not open and only the dialog box displaying the progress of the download opens, a default download folder is set in Firefox on your computer. After the file has downloaded, click the Close button in the Downloads dialog box (if necessary), click Tools on the menu bar, click Options, click Downloads, then click the Show Folder button to open the default folder for downloads. Use Windows Explorer to copy the file WSFTP_HomeT40_Install.exe from this folder to the Tutorial.05\Tutorial folder included with your Data Files.

6. Close your browser.

The time it takes to transfer the program file varies based on the speed of your Internet connection. If you are on a local area network (LAN) with a T1 Internet connection, then the transfer time is a few seconds. If you are using a modem and a dial-up connection, then the transfer time could take several minutes. Another factor in the download time is the amount of traffic at the FTP site. Many simultaneous users (more than 4,000 for example) can directly affect the download process. If you encounter problems while downloading a file, stop the process by clicking the Cancel button and try again later.

After downloading anything from the Internet—even files from reputable sources—your first priority is to scan the file for viruses. You can download many high quality antivirus programs from the Internet and install and use them for a limited time to determine their appropriateness for your own security needs. Because most antivirus programs are large in size, you won't download a program in this tutorial, but you can click the links in the Virus Detection Software section of the Student Online Companion page for Tutorial 5 to download trial versions of antivirus programs for your operating system.

You must install the program on your computer to use it. You can use Windows Explorer to check the Tutorial.05\Tutorial folder to make sure that it contains the WSFTP_HomeT40_Install.exe file.

Note: If your instructor or technical support person permits you to install and use the program, complete the next set of steps to install the software. If your lab policy prohibits you from installing the program, read the following steps so you know how to install the software, but do *not* complete the steps at the computer.

To install WS_FTP Home on your computer:

1. Start Windows Explorer, and then navigate to the Tutorial.05\Tutorial folder included with your Data Files.

   Trouble? If required to do so by your instructor, scan the WSFTP_HomeT40_Install.exe file that you downloaded for viruses following the instructions provided before proceeding to Step 2.

2. Double-click the **WSFTP_HomeT40_Install.exe** file to start the installation process. An installation screen appears.

   Trouble? If the on-screen instructions for WS_FTP Home differ from those shown in the steps, follow the on-screen instructions.

3. Click the **Next** button.

4. Read the license agreement, click the **I accept the terms of the license agreement** option button to indicate that you accept the terms of the agreement, and then click the **Next** button. (If you do not accept the terms of the license agreement, then the installation process stops.)

5. If necessary, click the **Browse** button to change the default folder in which to install the program, and then click the **Next** button.

6. If necessary, change the default program folder in which to install the program's shortcut, and then click the **Next** button.

7. Click the **Next** button to confirm your settings.

8. Click the **Next** button to install the program.

9. If necessary, click the **Launch Ipswitch WS_FTP Home now** and **View Release Notes** check boxes so they do not contain check marks, and then click the **Finish** button.

After you are finished installing the program, you might want to read the WS_FTP Home Release Notes file to learn how to use the program, or you can use the program's Help files for program instructions. After installing the product, Milt can use it to transfer files.

After installing any program, you can delete the downloaded files from the drive and folder to which you downloaded it, or you can keep it in case you need to reinstall the program. Some programs automatically delete downloaded files to save space on your drive.

Using an FTP Client Program to Download WinZip

Milt is very interested in compressing files to decrease the amount of space they require and also to decrease the time it takes to upload and download files. Many file compression programs available on the Internet are reliable and easy to use. One popular program is WinZip, which is available for free during its evaluation period. WinZip has been downloaded by millions of users and has received many awards from computer magazines and other sources.

To test the FTP client program that you downloaded for Milt earlier, you will use it to connect to the WinZip FTP site so you can download an evaluation copy of the program. When you establish a connection to an FTP site, you can save the site's address and your user name and password so you can easily return to the site later. When you use an FTP client program to save this information, you are creating an **FTP session profile**.

Note: In the following steps, you will use the WS_FTP Home program to download the WinZip program. If you do not have an FTP client or cannot install one on your school's computer, then read the steps without completing them at the computer.

To establish and save an FTP session profile:

1. Click the **Start** button on the taskbar, point to **All Programs**, point to **Ipswitch WS_FTP Home**, and then click **WS_FTP Home** to start the WS_FTP Home program. The Ipswitch WS_FTP Home Product Activation dialog box opens. You can activate the product by purchasing a license key or you can use the software for 30 days without activating it. You will choose the option to activate the product later.

   Trouble? If you do not see Ipswitch WS_FTP Home on the All Programs menu, make sure that you downloaded and installed the WS_FTP Home program earlier in this session.

2. Click the **Activate Later** option button, and then click the **Next** button. The Connection Wizard dialog box opens. You can click the link to view the Getting Started Tour or use the Connection Wizard to quickly connect to an FTP site. You will choose the second option.

3. Click the **Next** button, and then type **WinZip** in the Site Name text box.

4. Click the **Next** button, click the **Next** button again to accept FTP as the Connection Type, click the **Server Address** text box, and then type **ftp.winzip.com**. This address is the URL to the FTP site for WinZip. You can usually find the FTP address for an FTP site by replacing the "www" in a site's Web address with "ftp." Some companies include hyperlinks on their Web sites to their FTP sites.

5. Click the **Next** button, and then type **anonymous** in the User Name text box. Because you are making an anonymous connection to the WinZip FTP site, you do not need to supply a password. Some users change the default password to their e-mail address to identify their use of the site, but this custom is not required.

6. Click the **Next** button. Figure 5-15 shows the last dialog box of the Connection Wizard, which creates an anonymous login to the WinZip FTP site.

| Figure 5-15 | Final Connection Wizard dialog box for WinZip FTP site |

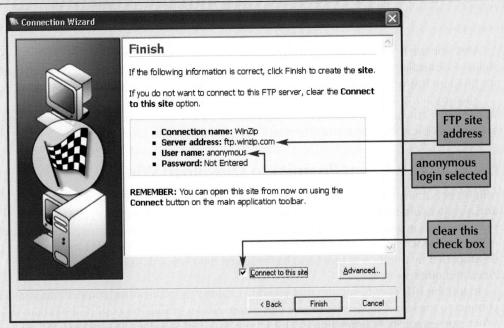

7. Click the **Connect to this site** check box to clear it, and then click the **Finish** button to save the WinZip session profile without connecting to the WinZip FTP site.

8. If the Tip of the Day dialog box opens, click the **Close** button to close it. WS_FTP Home starts and displays the contents of your computer in the pane on the left and a blank connection pane on the right.

With the URL and user information entered, you are ready to log on to the FTP site anonymously and download the WinZip program.

Reference Window

Downloading a File Using an FTP Client Program

- Log on to the remote computer by supplying its URL, your user name or *anonymous*, and your password.
- Navigate to the file you want to download.
- Click the filename on the remote computer to select it.
- If necessary, select binary or ASCII transmission mode.
- Execute the command that downloads the file from the FTP site to your computer.
- End the FTP session by disconnecting from the remote computer.

Note: You cannot download the WinZip program to a floppy disk because the program's file size (approximately six megabytes) exceeds the disk's storage capacity. Your instructor might ask you to download the program to your hard drive or to read the following steps without actually downloading the file.

To log on anonymously and download the file:

1. Click the **list arrow** for the Connect button on the toolbar, and then click **Site Manager**. The Site Manager dialog box opens.

2. Click **WinZip** in the list of sites, and then click the **Connect** button to log on to the WinZip FTP site.

   Trouble? If you cannot establish a connection with the WinZip FTP server, click the list arrow for the Connect button on the toolbar, click Site Manager, click WinZip in the Site Manager dialog box, and then click the Edit button. Make sure you entered ftp.winzip.com in the Host name text box. Click the OK button to connect.

   Trouble? If you tried more than once to connect to the WinZip site without success, the site might be busy. When the number of anonymous logins exceeds a large number, the WinZip site rejects all subsequent anonymous FTP sessions. Try again later, or just read the steps so you understand how to use an FTP client to download files.

3. If necessary, click the **Maximize** button to maximize the program window. See Figure 5-16. The pane on the left displays the drives and folders on your computer (the local computer) and the pane on the right displays the contents of the WinZip FTP site (the remote computer). You use the buttons in each pane to change, make, view, rename, delete, and refresh the directories and files.

Figure 5-16 **WS_FTP Home program window**

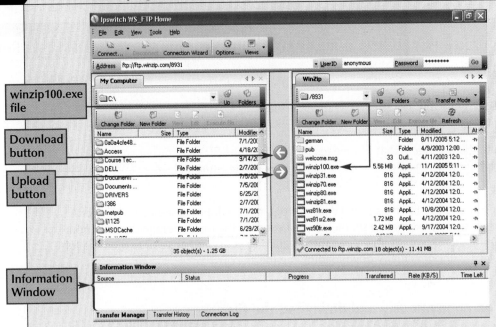

4. Click the **Change Folder** button in the pane on the left. The Change directory dialog box opens and requests the local folder name that you would like to display.

5. Type the drive letter and folder for the Tutorial.05\Tutorial folder included with your Data Files in the Enter directory to change to text box, and then click the **OK** button. The pane on the left changes and displays the files and folders on the drive you selected. By changing the drive and folder on the local computer, files you download will be stored in that location.

   The file you want to download, winzip100.exe, is listed in the pane on the right.

6. In the pane on the right, locate and then click **winzip100.exe** to select it.

7. Click the **Download** button between the two panes (see Figure 5-16) to begin downloading the file from the WinZip FTP site to the location you specified. As shown in Figure 5-17, the Information Window at the bottom of the screen displays information about the status of the download. The download is complete when the Information Window is empty and the file is transferred to the pane on the left.

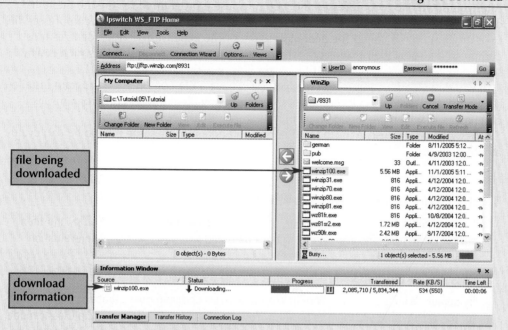

8. Click **File** on the menu bar, and then click **Exit** to log off the WinZip FTP site and to close the WS_FTP Home program.

9. If you are allowed to install the WinZip program, open Windows Explorer, navigate to the Tutorial.05\Tutorial folder included with your Data Files, scan the downloaded file for viruses, double-click **winzip100.exe**, and then follow the on-screen instructions. When prompted to select a start interface, make sure that the **Start with the WinZip Wizard** option button is selected and select the **Quick Search (faster)** option button when prompted to search for zip folders, click the **Close** button, and then click the **Yes** button, if necessary, to exit the setup program.

Trouble? Ask your instructor or technical support person first before installing the program.

The WinZip file that you downloaded is an evaluation version that you can use to evaluate the software at no charge. Each time you start the program, it will remind you about your use of an evaluation copy that has not yet been registered. If you continue using the software, you can click a button in the reminder screen to purchase a license to use the full version. Milt will use WinZip frequently to compress the sound files he produces, so he wants to use the program during the evaluation period to see how it works.

Compressing and Decompressing Files

Internet files of all types are frequently stored in compressed form. **Compressed files** use less space when stored and they take less time to be transferred from one computer to another. Some files are compressed automatically in their native file formats, such as JPEG and MPEG files. For files that are not compressed automatically, you can use a program to reduce the file size and thereby significantly decrease the transmission time. Compression will be especially important to Milt, because many of his contractors live in areas that do not have broadband service and must connect to the Internet using dial-up connections with slow upload and download times. In addition, by compressing sound files, they will require less space on his hard drive and on the FTP site he selects to store the files.

You can use a **file compression program** to decrease the original size of most files. After you download a compressed file, you must use a program to restore the file to its original state before you can open or execute it. The process of restoring a compressed file to its original state is called **file decompression**, or **file expansion**. FTP recognizes most compressed files by their extensions. The most common extension is .zip, which is why some people refer to compressed files as **zip files** or a **zip archive**.

If you download a compressed file, you must have a file compression program installed on your computer to view its contents. There are many file compression programs available, many of which are inexpensive or free.

Milt wants you to use WinZip to compress and decompress some files so he can evaluate the software.

To start WinZip and compress files:

1. Click the **Start** button on the taskbar, point to **All Programs**, point to **WinZip**, and then click **Winzip 10.0**. The WinZip dialog box opens and tells you that this is an evaluation copy of the software.

2. Click the **Use Evaluation Version** button to close the dialog box and to start WinZip.

   By default, WinZip starts the WinZip Wizard, a series of dialog boxes that will prompt you for the activity that you want to perform. You can also start WinZip in WinZip Classic mode, where you use the program's menu bar and toolbar to execute commands. Both methods accomplish the same tasks.

3. Click the **Next** button, click the **Create a new Zip file** option button, and then click the **Next** button. The WinZip Wizard – Choose Zip Name dialog box opens. You can type a filename in the File name text box or use the Browse button to locate the folder in which to store the zip file.

4. Click the **Browse** button, navigate to the Tutorial.05 folder included with your Data Files, type **zipfile.zip** in the File name text box, and then click the **OK** button.

5. Click the **Next** button. The WinZip Wizard – Select Files dialog box opens and prompts you for the location from which to add files to the zip file you just created.

6. Click the **Add folders** button, select the **Tutorial** folder in the Tutorial.05 folder included with your Data Files, click the **OK** button, and then click the **Zip Now** button. WinZip searches for the files you selected, creates a zip file named zipfile.zip, and displays the dialog box shown in Figure 5-18 when the zip operation is complete.

| Figure 5-18 | **WinZip Wizard - Zip Complete dialog box** |

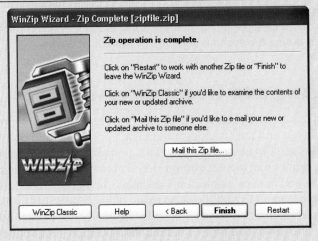

7. Click the **Finish** button to close the WinZip Wizard. The file zipfile.zip appears in Windows Explorer in the Tutorial.05 folder.

The WinZip Wizard made it easy to compress files. After you become more familiar with WinZip, you might want to use the WinZip Classic setting to compress and decompress files. To compress files using the WinZip Classic interface, follow these steps:

1. In Windows Explorer, select the folders and/or files that you want to compress.
2. Right-click the selected items to compress, point to WinZip on the shortcut menu, click Add to Zip file, and then click the Use Evaluation Version button.
3. In the Add dialog box, type the location in which to save the compressed file in the Add to archive text box. Make sure to include the drive letter, folder, and filename of the compressed file. Figure 5-19 shows the Add dialog box after the user selected a folder to compress in a file named zipfile.zip in the Tutorial.05 folder on drive C.

WinZip Add dialog box ◄ **Figure 5-19**

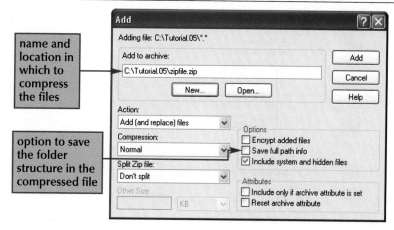

4. Click the Save full path info check box to save the files with the original folder structure that you have on your PC. To save the files without any folder structure, clear this check box.
5. Click the Add button. WinZip compresses the files.
6. Close WinZip.

When you want to decompress a zipped file, you simply double-click it to start WinZip and the WinZip Wizard.

To decompress the file:

1. With the contents of the Tutorial.05 folder open in Windows Explorer, double-click the **zipfile.zip** file, and then click the **Use Evaluation Version** button. The WinZip Wizard – Welcome dialog box opens.

2. Click the **Next** button, click the **No** button if you are asked to add the folder to your Favorite Zip Folders, make sure that the **Unzip or install from "zipfile.zip"** option button is selected, and then click the **Next** button. The WinZip Wizard – Unzip dialog box opens.

   Trouble? If a WinZip Caution dialog box opens, read the information it contains, and then click the Yes button.

3. Click the **Select different folder** button, select the **Tutorial.05** folder, click the **OK** button, make sure that the **Overwrite matching files automatically** check box is selected and the Display file icons after unzipping check box is cleared, and then click the **Unzip Now** button. WinZip decompresses the zipfile.zip file and overwrites the files with the same names.

4. Click the **Finish** button to close the WinZip Wizard dialog box, and then close Windows Explorer.

You can also decompress files using the WinZip Classic interface. You can do this by performing the following steps:

1. Locate the .zip file in Windows Explorer and double-click it.
2. Click the Use Evaluation Version button in the dialog box, and then click the WinZip Classic button.
3. Click the Extract button on the WinZip toolbar. The Extract dialog box opens.
4. Select the drive and folder into which you want to extract (decompress) the files. Figure 5-20 shows that the files will be extracted to C:\Temp.

Figure 5-20 ⟩ **Extract dialog box in WinZip**

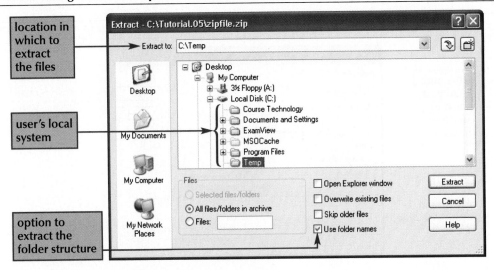

5. To use the folder structure saved in the .zip file, select the Use folder names check box. To extract just the files, without any folder structure, clear this check box.
6. Click the Extract button.
7. Close WinZip.

The File Compression Programs section of the Student Online Companion page for Tutorial 5 contains links to other file compression programs that you can download and examine at no cost during the program's evaluation period.

Tracing an Internet Route

When downloading software from a Web site, you might be asked to select a download location, also known as a mirror site, from which to download a file. A **mirror site** is a replica of an existing server that provides an alternate location for downloading files. When you select a mirror site, you will usually select a site close to you; for example, if you live in Tallahassee, Florida, you might choose a mirror site in Atlanta, Georgia, rather than a site in Seattle, Washington. Because the Internet makes it feel as though you are accessing sites from very long distances in just a few seconds, you might not think that the physical distance between you and another Internet site is important, but it is. Remember, the Internet is a complex network of interconnected computers. Just as the distance between your PC and a remote computer might be measured in miles, the distance between your PC and a remote computer on the Internet is measured in hops. A **hop** is a connection between two computers. If a file travels through 15 computers before arriving at your PC, then the file has made 14 hops (the number of computers in the path minus one). Minimizing the number of hops between a remote computer and your PC reduces the total download time to transfer files between computers.

You can count the hops and identify the computers between your PC and a remote computer using the Windows **tracert** (for *trace route*) program. You can use the tracert program to make an informed choice when selecting a download site. Tracert will show you up to 30 hops and indicate the response time, the site name, and the IP address of each hop along the route. (If you do not have tracert installed on your computer, use a Web search engine to search for **ping**, or **Packet Internet Groper**, which is a program that tests a computer to determine if it is connected to the Internet. You can find several freeware and shareware ping programs that accomplish the same thing as tracert. In addition, the Packet Internet Groper section of the Student Online Companion page for Tutorial 5 includes links to programs that trace routes.)

As Milt reviews additional software programs, he might be given a list of mirror sites from which to download files; he can use tracert to determine if one mirror site might provide a more direct connection over others. Because many of the actors who provide voiceovers live in New York City, Milt asks you to use tracert to view the hops between your PC and the FTP site at New York University.

To view the hops between your PC and a remote computer:

1. Click the **Start** button on the taskbar, click **Run**, type **command** in the Open list box, and then click the **OK** button. A DOS program window opens. If necessary, click the **Maximize** button on the program window's title bar to maximize it.

2. Type **tracert ftp.nyu.edu** at the command prompt, and then press the **Enter** key to list the hops between your PC and the server at the New York University in New York. Tracert produces a list of each computer's IP address on the path between your PC and the specified URL. When the trace is complete, the "Trace complete" message appears at the bottom of the site trace list. Figure 5-21 shows a path with 22 hops between a user located in Texas and the FTP site at New York University; your trace will be different.

Figure 5-21 ▸ **Tracert command**

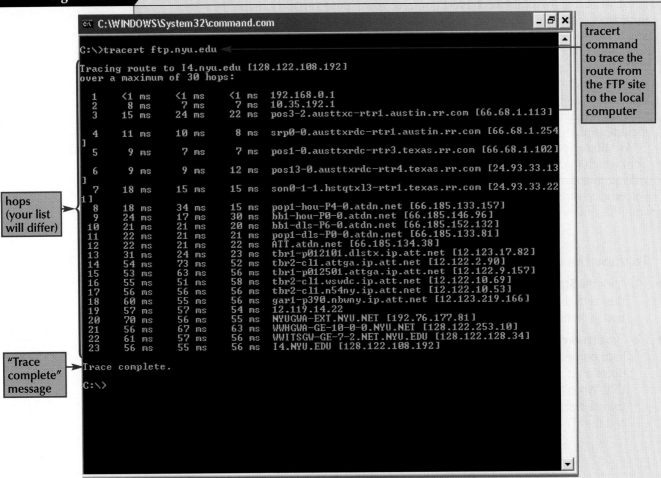

Trouble? If you receive the error message "Unable to resolve target system name ftp.nyu.edu," type exit at the command prompt, press the Enter key, connect to the Internet, and then repeat Steps 1 and 2.

Trouble? If the tracert program pauses for a long time or stops, press Ctrl + C to display the DOS command prompt and then repeat Step 2 to try tracing the route again. If you still have problems, ask your instructor or technical support person for help.

3. Type **exit** at the command prompt, and then press the **Enter** key to close the DOS window.

When you are downloading very large files, you can use the tracert command any time—even while your browser is running—to find the path with the fewest hops, because that path might reduce your download time significantly. You can also use the tracert command to determine where a problem exists when you cannot successfully transfer files to or from another computer. To trace a route while your browser is running, write down or copy the URL to the target site, click the Start button on the taskbar, click Run, and then type *tracert* followed by the URL of the target site. Click the OK button to trace the route. Once the trace is complete, the tracert window closes immediately, so look quickly!

You successfully downloaded an FTP client program and a compression software program for Milt. After testing the programs to make sure that they will satisfy the requirements at Sound Effects, Milt will fulfill any licensing agreements so he can install the full versions of the programs you downloaded on the office computers. In addition to its utility in transferring files between computers, FTP is an excellent way to share files with other users and to store files temporarily and permanently.

In Session 5.3, you will learn about online storage providers and collaboration on the Web.

Session 5.2 Quick Check

Review

1. What is freeware, shareware, and limited edition software?
2. After downloading a program from the Internet, what should you do prior to installing it?
3. What are the three most important considerations when using antivirus software to ensure that a virus does not infect your computer?
4. What information is stored in an FTP session profile?
5. What is a hop?
6. Which Windows program determines the distance between computers connected to the Internet?

Session 5.3

Using Online Storage Services

Now that you have provided Milt with the tools he needs to transfer files on the Internet, he needs a place to store those files. He cannot upload his proprietary data and other sensitive information to a public directory on a publicly accessible FTP site, nor can he ask his contractors to do the same. Milt needs access to a site that is both secure and password protected, with enough storage space so that files can remain on the site for as long as necessary. He also needs to provide access to this site to his contractors so they can upload and download files.

When you use an ISP for your Internet connection and e-mail services, you might also receive some free space to use to store a Web site or files. This space is useful to you because your user name and password control access to the site. However, you probably won't want to share this space with other users, because by doing so you will need to give those other users full access to your account, including your e-mail messages. You would have no way of controlling access to the site or securing important data from other users.

Because FTP is an easy-to-use and efficient way of transferring files across the Internet, many services have evolved to meet the increased need for ways to store and share files. FTP sites are one way of sharing and storing files, but not everyone has full-privilege access to an FTP server. From this need, the creation of a new business model formed, where ISPs and other entities started providing storage space on their servers, either for free or for a small monthly fee, with an option to purchase additional storage space later. Users access the online storage space using an FTP client program, a program or other interface provided by the provider, or a Web browser. The space is secured with an account name and password and permits the sharing of files by many users. Many businesses rely on these online storage services to send and receive large files while employees are traveling or as a normal course of business. Many individuals use these online storage services to store computer backup files, collections of sound files, personal Web sites, pictures, and other data. In addition, the proliferation of large data files moving across the Internet has the potential to overload many networks and mail servers when these files are attached to e-mail messages, so these online storage providers provide an alternate to consuming a company's network resources.

As more registered users started using these services, and as those users started storing large files and increasing the number of daily transfers, many sites experienced conflicts with users competing for the company's resources. As a result of bandwidth problems, many online storage providers changed their policies to limit the number of transfers and amount of space provided, to charge a small monthly fee for use of the space, or a combination of both. Most providers of free services offer an option to purchase additional space and transfers for a fee.

Using an online storage provider might be a good opportunity for Milt. As he reviews his requirements, he decides that he needs at least 30 to 50 megabytes of space and the capability to allow restricted and full access, depending on the user. Because the cost of maintaining his own FTP server would be an impediment to his overall operating budget, Milt is willing to pay a monthly fee for use of whichever provider best meets his needs. In addition, because Milt works with only a few contractors at a time, his space will not have a high number of transfers each day. Milt and his contractors will perform upload and download transfers, so they will need to use an FTP client program or an easy-to-use Web page interface to execute the transfers. Being able to use any FTP client program or a Web browser to log on to the site will make it easier for Milt and his contractors to access and use the site. Finally, Milt wants to make sure that the provider will ensure the security of his data from unauthorized use.

Like other free services found on the Internet, some online storage providers come and go on a regular basis. For this reason, most individuals and businesses that rely on these types of services are careful to back up important files and keep a copy of them locally in case the provider experiences a technical problem or suddenly ceases its operations. In addition, some businesses rely on two online storage providers to store their files, so they have a primary and secondary set of files in case of a problem.

Online Storage Providers

Xdrive Technologies has several online storage space plans to serve users in many categories, from large corporations to individuals. Many individuals use Xdrive to store and share large files, such as sound files, that would otherwise be difficult to store locally and distribute over the Internet. Corporations use Xdrive to reduce the amount of traffic generated by large e-mail attachments on their network servers. Xdrive is also a simple way for people employed in satellite and home offices to transfer files to people working in corporate offices. Figure 5-22 shows the home page for Xdrive.

Xdrive Technologies home page | **Figure 5-22**

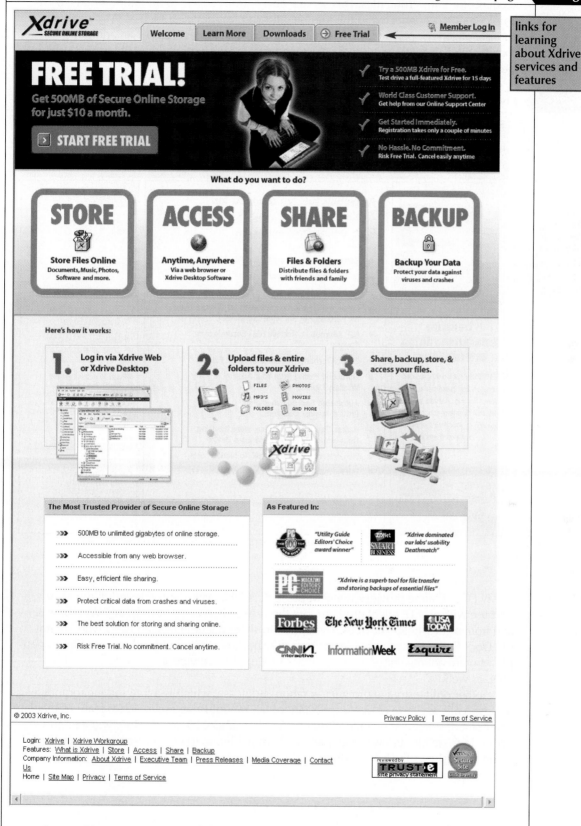

links for learning about Xdrive services and features

Xdrive might be a good option for Milt. It includes security features, individualized accounts, and file storage capabilities.

Another online storage provider is My Docs Online, which provides individual accounts for transferring files. This service also permits access to an online storage drive from computers connected to the Internet and wireless devices, such as Web-enabled phones, pagers, or personal digital assistants such as a Palm Pilot. For an additional charge, you can send, print, or fax documents from your online drive. Figure 5-23 shows the home page for My Docs Online.

Figure 5-23 ▶ **My Docs Online home page**

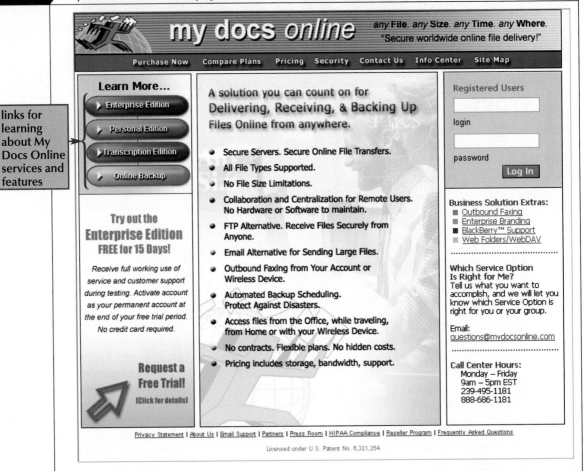

links for learning about My Docs Online services and features

My Docs Online provides many of the features that Milt has requested. It does not support use with an FTP client program, but the service is accessible from any Web browser and from most wireless devices. The option to share documents with users who are not My Docs Online account holders is attractive because Milt could still transfer files to people who are not regular users of My Docs Online. This service seems to be very affordable, as well.

Another online storage provider is Yahoo! Briefcase, which is a free service for individuals who already have or apply for a Yahoo! ID. Yahoo! Briefcase includes features that let you upload, store, and download files using your Yahoo! ID. In addition, you can provide access to these files to everyone, making them public, or to only those users you specify. Figure 5-24 shows the Yahoo! Briefcase home page.

Yahoo! Briefcase home page | **Figure 5-24**

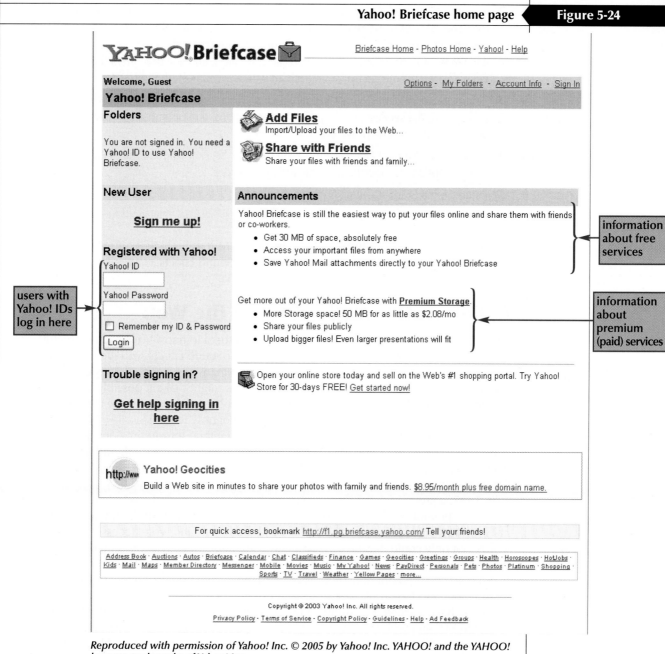

Reproduced with permission of Yahoo! Inc. © 2005 by Yahoo! Inc. YAHOO! and the YAHOO! logo are trademarks of Yahoo! Inc.

Milt wants you to gather some information about these and other online storage providers so he can select one to manage file transfers between the Sound Effects studio and its contractors. You'll explore the Web sites of three online storage providers for Milt next.

To find information about online storage providers:

▶ **1.** Start your Web browser, open the Student Online Companion page at **www.course.com/newperspectives/internet6**, click the **Tutorial 5** link, and then click the **Session 5.3** link.

   2. Click one of the online storage providers to open its home page, and then use the links on the home page to learn more about the services the company offers. As you explore the site, pay attention to pricing options, file storage limits (in terms of file sizes, transfer restrictions and limits, and the amount of time you can store files), and any trial offers the service provides. (*Note:* Do not sign up for an account with any online storage provider at this time.)

   3. Return to the Student Online Companion page for Session 5.3, and then click another link and explore the services, pricing, file storage options, and potential trial periods for another online storage provider.

   4. Return to the Student Online Companion page for Session 5.3, and then explore the Web site and options for your final online storage provider.

   5. Return to the Student Online Companion page for Session 5.3.

The information you collected will be helpful to Milt as he makes a final decision about which online storage provider to choose for Sound Effects.

Collaborative Authoring on the Web

As you finish your exploration of using the FTP protocol to transfer files across the Internet and using online storage services for storing files for Sound Effects, you are probably aware that the Internet is an evolving medium with many new technologies on the horizon. In a couple of years, technology improvements might make it possible for Milt to do business in many different ways. One topic that has been discussed since the first Web browser was created in 1994 is using the Internet not only to transfer files, but also to collaborate on files. In this context, **collaboration** is a method for multiple developers or authors to work on the same file without having to download it, edit it, and transfer it back to the original author(s). The goal of many Web developers has always been to make the Internet a true read-write medium.

In 1995, a group of developers began working together to find a way to make such collaboration possible by using or expanding the existing protocols of the Internet. The original goal was to create a way to share files with both read and write access—in other words, not only could files be sent between computers, but those files could also be edited. The method of choice for this collaboration was expanding the HTTP protocol so that it could be used not only to transfer files between computers connected to the Internet, but also to permit the editing of those files.

As you have learned, FTP transfers files between computers connected to the Internet using the FTP protocol. However, FTP has some disadvantages. The most significant disadvantages are that FTP requires a direct connection to the server for each file that you transfer; during the transfer, there is no built-in security mechanism; and FTP cannot penetrate many firewalls. Any extension to the HTTP protocol instantly has these features because the HTTP protocol already provides them.

The desire for a means of transferring and editing files over the Internet using the HTTP protocol has led to a new protocol for the Internet, **WebDAV** (sometimes called **DAV**), which stands for **Web Distributed Authoring and Versioning**. This protocol is a standard extension of the original HTTP 1.1 protocol that is used to transfer Web pages over the Internet. Because HTTP has built-in features that provide security and other desirable features during file transfers, it provides collaboration features on the Internet. In many ways, WebDAV is transparent; you might have used it without even realizing it.

The WebDAV Working Group, which is the group of individuals who are actively working on defining this new protocol, is dedicated to developing and improving the WebDAV protocol on the Internet to create an operating-system neutral form of collaborative authoring so that people can transfer files, much like they do with a Web browser or FTP client program, using features built into many operating systems and browsers. The group's progress is well documented on the Internet Engineering Task Force (IETF) Web site. The IETF is a large group of individuals who contribute to the evolution of new and existing Internet technologies. Membership in the IETF is open to all interested parties and members represent countries from around the world. The WebDAV Working Group has identified four important features that make the WebDAV protocol desirable:

- **Locking** prevents users from simultaneously editing files. Some programs, such as Microsoft FrontPage, have source control features that prevent two authors from concurrently editing the same Web page in the same Web site. This feature, however, has limitations: it must be enabled and it works only in a Web site created by that program. The locking feature of the WebDAV protocol automatically prevents users from simultaneously editing files. Because the locking feature is built into the WebDAV protocol, it overrides any other lock that might be in place, such as a lock from a software program or network.
- **Properties** enable a developer to store, delete, and revise information about Web pages, including the page's creator and last revision date. Because these properties are stored with the Web page, a developer can search for information about these details.
- **Name space management** is a feature that lets a developer copy, move, and rename files.
- **Collections** allow a developer to retrieve a directory listing of the files on the server.

The WebDAV protocol continues to evolve, but is already available for use on many Internet Web servers and in current Microsoft Office, Macromedia, and other programs. The Web Publishing Wizard, which is part of the Windows XP operating system, lets you transfer files directly to an Internet server using the HTTP protocol. Windows refers to WebDAV as "Web folders;" you might encounter both terms as you expand your knowledge of the WebDAV protocol. Two services, Xdrive and MSN, provide space on their servers for transferring files in this way. My Docs Online also supports WebDAV files transfers. (The Web Folders & WebDAV section of the Student Online Companion page for Tutorial 5 contains links to other services and resources that you can explore.) What this means to Milt is that he could use Windows XP, which includes the WebDAV protocol, to transfer files to a storage provider's server. Instead of using the storage provider's interface to upload and download files, Milt could use the Web Publishing Wizard in Windows XP for uploading files, and the My Network Places shortcut for downloading files. The online storage service he selects would let him control access to the files.

To learn more about WebDAV and the potential it might have for Sound Effects, you will start the Web Publishing Wizard in Windows XP to see how you can use this feature to upload a file.

To start the Web Publishing Wizard:

1. Start Windows Explorer and make sure that the **Folders** button on the toolbar is selected.

   Trouble? You must have Windows XP installed on your computer to complete this set of steps.

2. In the pane on the left, open the drive or folder that contains the Tutorial.05 folder, open the **Tutorial.05** folder, and then select the **Tutorial** folder.

3. Click the **Folders** button on the toolbar. Your screen should look like Figure 5-25.

Figure 5-25 | **Tutorial folder in Windows Explorer**

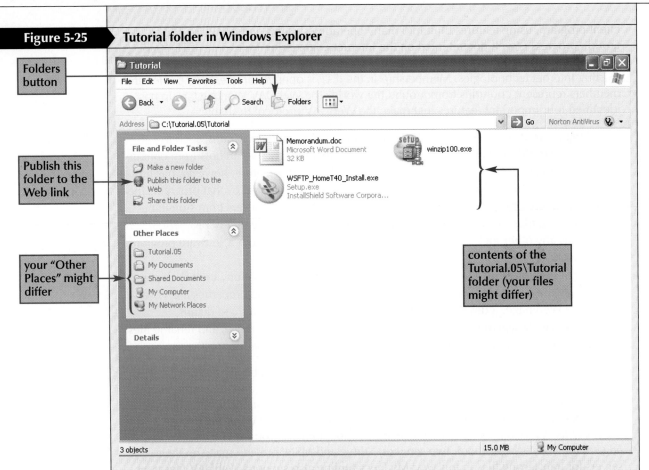

Trouble? If you click the Folders button and your screen does not look like Figure 5-25, Windows Explorer is set to use classic folders. Click Tools on the menu bar, click Folder Options, click the Show common tasks in folders option button, and then click the OK button. If neccessary, click the Folders button on the toolbar so your screen looks like Figure 5-25.

4. In the Folders pane on the left, click **Publish this folder to the Web** link. The Web Publishing Wizard starts.

5. Click the **Next** button. The Tutorial folder contains several files, all of which contain check marks to indicate that they will be published. If you clear a check mark for a file, it will not be published.

6. Click the check boxes for the winzip90.exe and WSFTP_HomeT40_Install.exe to clear them (click the icon for each file once to select it, and then click the check box to clear it). Only the Memorandum.doc file should contain a check mark, as shown in Figure 5-26.

Changing the file selection ◀ **Figure 5-26**

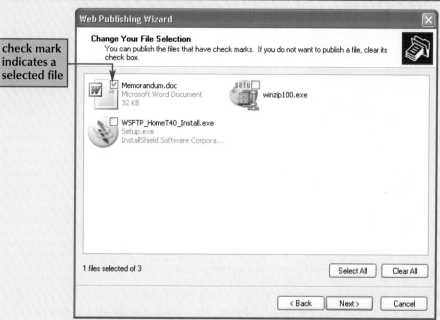

7. Click the **Next** button. The Wizard will make a connection to the Internet and identify service providers (the term Microsoft uses to mean storage providers) that can host your Web site. (In this case, a "Web site" is any collection of files, and not just HTML documents.) Figure 5-27 shows one provider: MSN Groups. If you do not already have an account for the provider you select, the Wizard will create one for you. MSN Groups is free after registering for a Passport account. If you already have a Hotmail address, all you need to do is register that address as a Passport account.

Selecting a service provider ◀ **Figure 5-27**

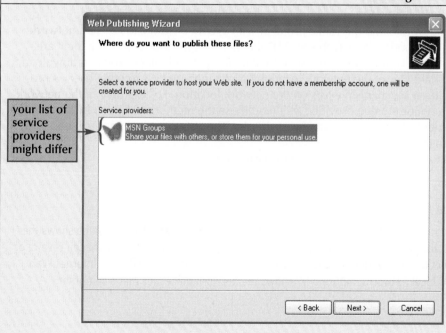

8. If necessary, select **MSN Groups** in the list of service providers, and then click the **Next** button. The dialog box shown in Figure 5-28 opens.

Figure 5-28 .NET Passport Wizard dialog box

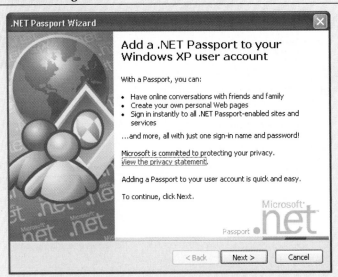

Trouble? If you or another user has already used the Web Publishing Wizard on your computer to create an MSN Group, the Web Publishing Wizard will display a list of groups that have been created with an option to create a new MSN Group. Click the Cancel button and continue with Step 10.

If you have a .NET Passport account from MSN, you would sign in using your e-mail address and password. To get a .NET Passport, you would click the Next button to create one. You will not create an account for Milt now, so you will cancel the Wizard.

9. Click the **Cancel** button in the .NET Passport Wizard dialog box.

10. Click the **Cancel** button in any open dialog boxes to close the Wizard.

The Web Publishing Wizard only allows you to upload files to a server. To download a file using Windows XP and the HTTP protocol with WebDAV, you can create a **network place**, which is a shortcut to a Web site, FTP site, network location (such as a local area network), or online storage provider. After creating the network place, you can download, upload, and share files at the network location you defined. Access to other users is provided by whatever mechanism exists on the network location. For example, if the network location is an online storage provider, Milt would use the methods provided by the online storage provider to control who can access the site. The network place makes it easier to upload and manage the files.

You will show Milt how to create a network place next.

To create a network place:

1. In the left pane in Windows Explorer, click **My Network Places**. The right pane shows the local and Internet network places (connections) for your computer. You might see several or no connections, depending on the connections you have made to FTP sites, Internet Web sites, and local networks. Figure 5-29 shows the network places for Milt's computer.

My Network Places ◀ **Figure 5-29**

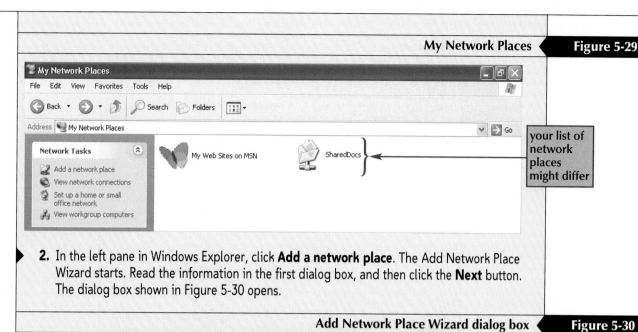

your list of
network
places
might differ

2. In the left pane in Windows Explorer, click **Add a network place**. The Add Network Place
   Wizard starts. Read the information in the first dialog box, and then click the **Next** button.
   The dialog box shown in Figure 5-30 opens.

Add Network Place Wizard dialog box ◀ **Figure 5-30**

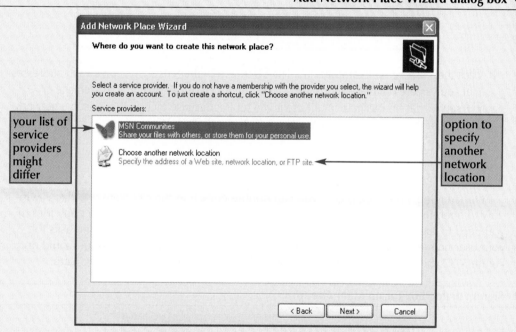

your list of
service
providers
might
differ

option to
specify
another
network
location

3. Make sure that **Choose another network location** is selected, and then click the **Next** button. The dialog box shown in Figure 5-31 opens. You use this dialog box to enter the
   address of the Web site, FTP site, or network location that this network place will open.

Figure 5-31 | **Adding a network place**

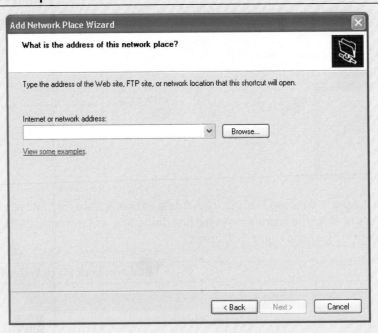

4. Click the **View some examples** link. The ScreenTip that opens shows some valid addresses that you can use to create your shortcut. Milt might create a shortcut to a Web site or FTP server that his business might use in the future. Because Milt does not need a network shortcut at this time, you will cancel the Add Network Place Wizard.

5. Click the **Cancel** button.

After creating a network place, you can double-click it in the My Network Places window to open the location. After that, you can download, upload, move, and copy files. If you need to log on to the network, a Connect or Sign In dialog box opens and asks for your user name and password, just like a Web browser or FTP client program would do. Figure 5-32 shows the dialog box that opens when Milt logs on to his MSN Group.

Figure 5-32 | **Sign In dialog box for an MSN Group**

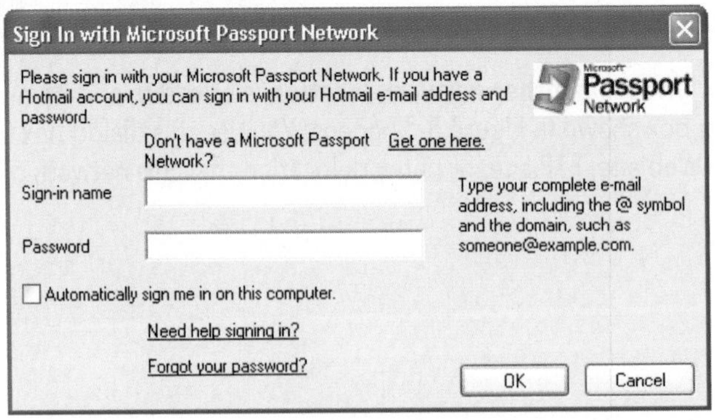

Milt is pleased with the information that you have provided. His goal of finding the perfect online storage provider will be much easier now that he has resources he can evaluate. He is confident that he will be able to find a suitable provider for him and his contractors.

Review

Session 5.3 Quick Check

1. How might an online storage provider help a company reduce its network activity and increase its productivity?
2. True or False: Some online storage providers offer free online storage for registered users.
3. True or False: Some online storage providers offer the ability to share files between registered and unregistered users.
4. What does collaboration mean in the context of the Internet and file sharing?
5. When did developers begin working on WebDAV?
6. What are the four important features that make the WebDAV protocol desirable?
7. What is a network place in Windows XP?

Review

Tutorial Summary

In this tutorial, you learned how to use a Web browser and an FTP client program to transfer files between computers connected to the Internet. You also learned how to use a download site to evaluate freeware, shareware, limited edition, and full use programs. Finally, you learned how to use online storage providers to store files that you can share with other users.

You might already have many needs for file storage on the Web—perhaps you have a large collection of MP3 files that you want to share with your friends or you need to set up a Web site to use as a central point for collaboration with a study group to prepare a term project. In any case, using the skills you learned in this tutorial will prepare you to evaluate and download the best FTP program for your needs; set up an online storage provider at which to store the files; and use your computer to upload, download, and manage your files.

Key Terms

anonymous FTP session	file transfer mode	properties
anonymous login	File Transfer Protocol (FTP)	remote computer
antivirus software	freeware	root directory
ASCII mode	FTP client program	shareware
ASCII text	FTP server	tracert
binary file	FTP session profile	upload
binary mode	FTP site	virus definition
bugs	full-privilege FTP	virus detection software
collaboration	hop	virus pattern
collections	limited edition	virus signature
compressed file	local computer	Web Distributed Authoring
DAV	locking	and Versioning
download	log on	(WebDAV)
evaluation version	mirror site	Webmaster
file compression program	name space management	zip archive
file decompression	network place	zip file
file expansion	ping (Packet Internet Groper)	

Review Assignments

Data File needed for the Review Assignments: register.pdf

Milt just received an e-mail message with an attachment saved with a .pdf file extension, and he needs to install a program to read it. Portable Document Format (PDF), developed by Adobe Corporation, provides a convenient, self-contained package for delivering and displaying documents containing text, graphics, charts, and other objects. To create a PDF file, you need to purchase and learn how to use a program called Adobe Acrobat. When you download a PDF file, you do not need the same program as the file's creator to display, browse, and print the document; you can use the free Adobe Reader program to view the document. For example, if you download a PDF file that was created from a Microsoft Word document, you can use Adobe Reader to view the document, even if you don't have Word installed on your computer. Adobe Reader is a free, simple to install program. You will download Adobe Reader so Milt can read the PDF file he received.

Note: You cannot download the Adobe Reader program to a floppy disk because the program's size (over 27 megabytes) exceeds the disk's storage capacity. Your instructor might ask you to download the program to your hard drive or to simply read the following steps without actually downloading the file.

1. Start your Web browser, open the Student Online Companion page at www.course.com/newperspectives/internet6, click the Tutorial 5 link, and then click the Review Assignments link. Click the Adobe link and wait while the browser opens the home page of the Adobe Web site.
2. Explore the Adobe home page and click the link to learn more about products in the Acrobat family. Then read about Adobe Reader and Adobe Acrobat so you understand how both programs are used to make Internet file transfers easier for users and developers.
3. Find the link to download the free Adobe Reader program, and then click it. Read the instructions provided and download the Adobe Reader program for your platform (operating system). Save the file in the Tutorial.05\Review folder included with your Data Files.
4. When the download is complete, follow the on-screen instructions to install Adobe Reader, and then close your browser. (*Note:* Check with your instructor or technical support person before installing any program on your computer.)
5. Open Windows Explorer, and then locate and double-click the **register.pdf** file in the Tutorial.05\Review folder. Adobe Reader starts and opens the file.
6. Print the document. (*Hint:* Use the Print button on the Adobe Reader toolbar.)
7. Close Adobe Reader and Windows Explorer.

Research

Use the Internet to locate reviews of appropriate ping programs to use to trace the route between computers connected to the Internet.

Explore

Case Problem 1

There are no Data Files needed for this Case Problem.

County Assessor's Office Will Hoenig is the County Assessor for Lancaster County in eastern Nebraska. The county assessor's property office has a large database of information stored on an FTP site that the public can access for a small fee. Realtors and real-estate appraisers are the primary users of this information. However, many other businesses are taking advantage of this online access to Lancaster County property records. Will has received complaints from customers in the southern part of the county about long delays in accessing the system. You are Will's chief architect of the information system that supports the entire county assessor's online database. Will wants you to investigate the system's processing delays. You realize that because the Lancaster system is stored on a network server, some delays are caused by general Internet traffic and, therefore, are not solvable. Will wants you to see if the problem is with one of the computer systems that is connected to the main computer that stores the county assessor's files.

You decide to begin your research by installing an Internet ping program to test the Internet connections for delays. You will complete the following steps to research and find programs that can identify processing problems, and then you will download the program.

1. Start your Web browser, open the Student Online Companion page at www.course.com/newperspectives/internet6, click the Tutorial 5 link, and then click the Case Problem 1 link. Click the Tucows link to open the Tucows home page.
2. Search for ping software programs.
3. Explore the links to programs to learn more about the programs you can download. Use the resources you learned about in this tutorial to see if you can find a review of the programs. If you find a review, use your browser's Print dialog box to print the first page.
4. Based on your research, locate a program on the Tucows Web site that will help Will with his problem as described in the case problem description. Use your browser's Print dialog box to print the page that describes the program you are recommending.
5. If you have permission to do so, download to the Tutorial.05\Cases folder included with your Data Files the ping program you are recommending. (*Note:* Check with your instructor before downloading any files from the Internet. Before downloading the file, make sure that you have enough disk space to save it in the location you specify.)
6. If you are able to do so, scan the file you downloaded for viruses.
7. Close your browser.
8. On a separate piece of paper, write a short memo to Will that explains why you have chosen the program you selected and list some advantages it has over other shareware programs you evaluated on the Tucows Web site.

Research

Use the skills you learned in this tutorial and a Web browser to navigate an FTP site to find and download three PDF files at the FTP site for the Internal Revenue Service.

Case Problem 2

There are no Data Files needed for this Case Problem.

Englewood Health Club   John Rowe owns the Englewood Health Club in Englewood, Colorado. His business transmits all of its employment data on tape to the Internal Revenue Service (IRS) and uses a wire transfer to deposit its employees' federal tax payments into the correct accounts. John just received a letter from the IRS indicating that the tape with his company's federal unemployment data for the third quarter of the year 2003 was lost or damaged by the IRS, and that he needs to submit this form again manually. Because this error was due to an IRS error, neither John nor the club will incur any penalty. John needs to download the correct forms to use from the IRS FTP site. The letter indicated that he could use the IRS's FTP site to download forms from the year 2003. He asks you to help him find the forms using a browser.

1. Start your Web browser, open the Student Online Companion page at www.course.com/newperspectives/internet6, click the Tutorial 5 link, and then click the Case Problem 2 link. Click the Internal Revenue Service link and wait while the browser opens the FTP site at the Internal Revenue Service.

Explore
2. Find and open the directory that stores forms from the year 2003. If this directory contains a file with instructions or directions for retrieving files, open and read it using your browser, and then close it. (*Note:* There might not be a file of this type stored in the directory.)

Explore
3. Scroll the directory's contents to find the PDF files for the following forms: Form 940 (Employer's Annual Federal Unemployment (FUTA) Tax Return), Form 940EZ (Employer's Annual Federal Unemployment (FUTA) Tax Return), and Form 1120 (U.S. Corporation Income Tax Return). (*Hint:* Open the PDF files to view and confirm their contents before downloading them in the next step. You must have Adobe Reader to view the files.)

4. Save these three files in the Tutorial.05\Cases folder included with your Data Files. (*Hint:* In Internet Explorer, press and hold the Ctrl key, click each file, release the Ctrl key, click File on the menu bar, and then click Copy to Folder to save the files. In Firefox, right-click a file and click Save Link As on the shortcut menu to save each file individually.)

Explore
5. Open the PDF file for Form 1120 that you saved. (*Note:* Double-click the file in Windows Explorer to open it.) Use the Print button on the Adobe Reader toolbar to print page 1 of the PDF file.

6. Close Adobe Reader, and then close your browser.

Explore

Use the skills you learned in this tutorial to browse an FTP site to find specific information on current virus patterns.

Case Problem 3

There are no Data Files needed for this Case Problem.

Midwestern University Marco Lozario is director of computing at Midwestern University. He and his staff of three people ensure that the school's computer lab of 45 Windows-based computers function properly. Last week, a virus infected every computer in the lab, and Marco had to close the lab to prevent the virus from spreading to students' disks and to other computers. Some of the lab computers have McAfee VirusScan software installed and others have Norton AntiVirus, but the installed versions of both programs do not recognize and cannot eradicate the new virus pattern. Complete the following steps to locate the latest virus data files from McAfee and Symantec (the company that produces Norton AntiVirus) so Marco can clean the infected computers.

1. Start your Web browser, open the Student Online Companion page at www.course.com/newperspectives/internet6, click the Tutorial 5 link, and then click the Case Problem 3 link. Click the McAfee link and wait while the browser opens the FTP site at McAfee.
2. Use your browser to navigate to the **readme.txt** file at ftp.mcafee.com/pub/antivirus/datfiles/4.x. (*Note:* If this directory or file no longer exists, browse the site until you find another readme.txt file or a file that explains the contents of another directory.)
3. Open the **readme.txt** file in this folder and view its contents.
4. Return to the Student Online Companion page for Case Problem 3, and then click the Symantec link and wait while your browser opens the FTP site at Symantec.
5. Use your browser to navigate to the **update.txt** file at ftp.symantec.com/public/english_us_canada/antivirus_definitions/norton_antivirus. (*Note:* If this directory or file no longer exists, browse the site until you find another text file that explains the contents of another directory.)
6. Open the **update.txt** file in this folder and review its contents. Use your browser or the program that opens to print the first page of this document.

Explore

7. Marco needs some information about the Live Update product from Symantec so he can look into installing it on the lab's computers. He asks if you can find a text file that describes the Live Update setup. Browse the FTP site at ftp.symantec.com to find this file, and then save the file in the Tutorial.05\Cases folder included with your Data Files.
8. Close your browser.

Case Problem 4

There are no Data Files needed for this Case Problem.

Biehle Clipping Service When Blake Biehle was in college, he did a brief internship at an advertising agency and soon discovered a need for a clipping service that would record televised commercials so companies could monitor the marketing campaigns prepared by their competitors. The advertising agency had a staff member who tried to assimilate marketing information from estimating the number of 30-second commercials purchased by businesses in certain industries, such as grocery stores, and using that data to estimate the cost of the commercials. This system worked well but it suffered because most of the data was estimated.

After Blake completed his internship and during his last year of college, he approached the largest grocery store and department store in the area and offered to use a video recorder to record all three local television networks, 24 hours a day. He proposed that he could provide these businesses with exact information about their competitors' marketing campaigns. Both businesses accepted Blake's proposal and other businesses in other areas soon hired him for the same role. After graduating from college, he expanded his business to news clipping and recording radio broadcast services and hired several monitors and editors to help him collect and process the data.

Blake needs a way to store the marketing data he prepares in PDF format for his clients. He has a Web site but the host doesn't provide any online storage space. He asks you to do some research on online storage providers and prepare a report of your findings, with a recommendation for which provider to use.

1. Start your Web browser, open the Student Online Companion page at www.course.com/newperspectives/internet6, click the Tutorial 5 link, and then click the Case Problem 4 link.

Explore

2. Visit four sites listed in this section. When you are exploring each site, try to find answers to questions that Blake might ask, such as why using an online storage provider is better than using e-mail attachments, how to create and log in to an account, how to share files with other users, how much space is provided and at what cost, security features, and ease of use. For each site that you visit, print one page that contains answers to some of these questions. (*Note:* Do not sign up for an account at any of these sites.)

3. Close your browser.

Explore

4. On a separate piece of paper, write a memo to Blake that identifies the online storage providers you examined and explains the pros and cons of using each one. In the final paragraph, recommend one provider for Blake and give the reasons for your selection and why the provider you are recommending would work well for Blake's clipping service.

Explore

Discover more about online storage providers so you can expand your knowledge of this Internet resource.

Case Problem 5

Data Files needed for this Case Problem: 55.jpg, 56.jpg, 57.jpg, and 58.jpg

Mooney Genealogy Services   Maureen Mooney's interest in genealogy began with research about her own family tree. After tracing her family's roots back to the late 1300s, she realized that she could turn her friends' requests for help with their own family trees into a second career. She soon opened an office and hired an assistant to help her with her friends and her new clients, many of whom were searching for connections to lost relatives or were just curious about their family's roots.

As Maureen travels, she takes pictures of grave markers to document the birth and death dates and names of people born before modern records recorded these events. Sometimes she is able to send these digital photos to her assistant via e-mail, but she lacks a place to store the pictures in a central location. More important, she doesn't have a way to share pictures with other researchers or her clients.

Maureen wants you to set up an account with an online storage provider so she can post pictures and other types of files to it. As she begins working with other researchers, she will give them access to her files and provide space for them to post their files. Because her business is small, she does not require a lot of space, so she asks you to locate a free provider that does not charge a fee.

Note: You must have Windows XP to complete this case problem. If you have problems using the Web Publishing Wizard to connect to MSN Groups, cancel the Wizard, start your Web browser, open the Student Online Companion page at www.course.com/newperspectives/internet6, click the Tutorial 5 link, and then click the Case Problem 5 link. Click the MSN Groups link and use the links on the page that opens to create the MSN group and upload files to it.

1. Start Windows Explorer. If necessary, select My Documents in the Folders pane, and then click the Folders button on the toolbar so it is not selected.
2. Use the My Computer link in the Other Places section to display the files stored on your computer, and then open the Tutorial.05\Cases folder included with your Data Files.
3. Start the Web Publishing Wizard. In the second dialog box, make sure that the only files selected are four pictures: **55.jpg**, **56.jpg**, **57.jpg**, and **58.jpg**. (If you completed another case problem, deselect any files that you stored in the Cases folder.)
4. Choose the option to create an MSN Group.
5. If you have a Hotmail address, use the .NET Passport Wizard dialog boxes to enter your Hotmail address and password; if the .NET Passport Wizard does not open, type your complete e-mail address, including the host name, in the E-mail address text box, and then type your password in the Password text box. If you do not have a Hotmail address or a .NET Passport, click the link to get one and follow the on-screen instructions. Use the Help link as necessary to get more information about creating your MSN Group.
6. When prompted to select the location where you want your files stored, click the option to share your files.
7. Use the group name "Mooney Genealogy Services" and your first and last names (such as "Mooney Genealogy Services Jay Johnston"), type your e-mail address in the appropriate text box (if necessary), and then click the link to read the code of conduct. After reading this information, click the option to accept its terms.
8. Enter a description for your new group, choose English as the language, and choose the option to omit your group from being listed in the directory.

9. Choose the option to add your group's URL to your browser's Favorites list, and then click the Next button until you see the dialog box that offers to resize your pictures. Select the options to resize pictures to small.

10. Click the Next button and wait while the Wizard uploads the files to your MSN group. When the copy is complete, a message will appear to tell you that the upload was successful.

11. Finish the Wizard and choose the option to open your MSN Group when the Wizard closes. Your Web browser starts and opens your site.

Explore

12. Explore the MSN site to learn more about this service. You can use any files in the Tutorial.05 folder included with your Data Files to practice uploading documents and pictures to the site. Experiment by creating and deleting folders and files until you are comfortable using this service. In addition, learn how to send e-mail messages to group members, how to invite other users to join, and how to promote your group. Use the Help link on your group's home page as necessary to learn more about these features.

Explore

13. Return to Windows Explorer and examine My Network Places. Windows should have created a network shortcut to your MSN Group. (This shortcut might appear in the "My Web Sites on MSN" shortcut, which you can double-click to open.) Use the shortcut to access the files in your group, and then locate and delete the file **56.jpg**.

14. Use the favorite you created to access your MSN Group using your browser. (If your browser did not create this favorite, open the Student Online Companion page at www.course.com/newperspectives/internet6, click the Tutorial 5 link, and then click the Case Problem 5 link. Click the MSN Groups link, and then click the My Groups link.)

15. Confirm that the **56.jpg** file was deleted, and then close your Web browser.

Explore

16. Write a two-paragraph memo to Maureen about your experience working with MSN Groups and Windows Explorer to upload files. Be as specific as possible about the service's ease of use, Help system, and other features that Maureen might find helpful. Finally, make a recommendation about the easiest way to upload files to the site and defend your choice with details about using each method.

Student Edition Labs

Lab Assignments

The interactive Student Edition Lab on **Keeping Your Computer Virus Free** is designed to help you master some of the key concepts and skills presented in this tutorial, including:

- using FTP and a browser to download files
- using an FTP client program to download files
- using a file compression program to compress and decompress files

This lab and lab assignment are available online and can be accessed from the Tutorial 5 Web page on the Student Online Companion at www.course.com/newperspectives/internet6.

Quick Check Answers

Session 5.1

1. An FTP client program provides a multipane display and multiple features that a browser does not include. Because of these features, an FTP client program is easier to use than a Web browser for uploading files.
2. an e-mail address
3. True
4. directories (folders) and files
5. ftp://ftp.zdnet.com
6. binary, ASCII

Session 5.2

1. Freeware is free software that has no restrictions on its use or guarantees for its performance; shareware is free or for-fee software that usually is operable for a limited time period; limited edition software is a limited version of a complete program that either functions for a limited time or includes only core features.
2. scan it for viruses
3. Make sure that the antivirus software program is turned on, configured properly to scan all downloaded files, and that it uses current virus definitions
4. the site's address, your user name, and your password
5. A hop is a connection between two computers.
6. tracert

Session 5.3

1. A company can reduce its network activity by encouraging its employees to use an online storage provider instead of e-mail attachments to transport large files. A company can increase its productivity by offering online storage for traveling employees or those employees in satellite offices.
2. True
3. True
4. Collaboration is a method for multiple developers or authors to work on the same file without having to download it, edit it, and send it back to the original author.
5. 1995
6. locking, properties, name space management, and collections
7. a shortcut to a Web site, FTP site, or any other network location that when clicked, opens the site

New Perspectives on
The Internet

Appendix A   App 3
The Internet and the World Wide Web

History, Structure, and Technologies

The Internet and the World Wide Web

History, Structure, and Technologies

The Internet and the World Wide Web: Amazing Developments

The Internet—a large collection of computers all over the world that are connected to one another in various ways—is one of the most amazing technological developments of the 20th century. Using the Internet you can communicate with other people throughout the world through electronic mail (or e-mail) or instant messaging software; read online versions of newspapers, magazines, academic journals, and books; join discussions on almost any conceivable topic; participate in games and simulations; and obtain free computer software. In recent years, the Internet has allowed commercial enterprises to connect with customers and each other. Today, all kinds of businesses provide information about their products and services on the Internet. Many of these businesses use the Internet to market and sell their products and services. The part of the Internet known as the World Wide Web (or the Web), is a subset of the computers on the Internet that are connected to each other in a specific way that makes those computers and their contents easily accessible to all computers in that subset. The Web has helped to make Internet resources available to people who are not computer experts.

Student Data Files

There are no student data files needed for this tutorial.

Exploring Uses for the Internet

The Internet and the Web give people around the world new ways to communicate with each other, obtain information resources and software, conduct business transactions, and find entertainment.

New Ways to Communicate

In the 1970s, e-mail and other messaging systems were developed within large companies and government organizations. These systems let people in a particular organization send messages to other people in that organization. Very few organizations allowed their computers to be connected to the computers in other organizations and there were many different messaging systems, most of which were not compatible with each other.

The Internet provided a common set of rules for e-mail and allowed persons in different organizations (and even persons who were not in any organization at all) to send messages to each other. In addition to e-mail, the Web offers other ways to communicate. Electronic discussions are hosted on many Web sites and many people use instant messaging software to chat with each other over the Internet. In Tutorial 2, you will learn more about how e-mail works and how you can use it most effectively.

Information Resources and Software

The amount of information that is available online today is staggering. Millions of Web sites offer an amazing variety of useful information on almost any imaginable topic. Online versions of newspapers, magazines, government documents, research reports, and books offer a wealth of information greater than the holdings of any library.

Some sites are like encyclopedias; they offer a wide range of information on many different topics. Figure A-1 shows a small part of one such site, which is named "How Stuff Works." The figure shows the information available in the Science category.

Science page on the How Stuff Works Web site | **Figure A-1**

Other Web sites specialize in specific types of information. For example, you can find Web sites that offer DVD player reviews, recipes for Mexican food, or instructions for growing house plants. Many of the first resources to appear on the Internet were collections of computer software. This is not surprising, since many of the earliest users of the Internet were computer enthusiasts. Today there are many Web sites that offer software you can download and install on your computer. Many of these software products are free, others are trial or demo versions (versions that you can use for a limited amount of time or without all of the features of the full versions) that allow you to try the software for a period of time before buying a license that allows you to continue using the software. Figure A-2 shows one Web site, Tucows, that offers free software, trial version software, and demo version software.

Tucows Web site **Figure A-2**

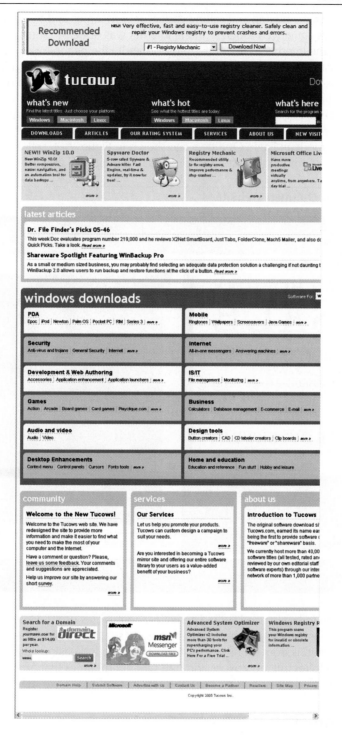

Doing Business Online

The Web can make buying and selling easier for companies and their customers. The first major business activity conducted on the Internet was done by large companies who started using the Internet in the mid-1990s to handle the paperwork on purchases and sales of industrial goods. Soon thereafter, individuals began buying significant amounts of items such as books, music CDs, and clothing on the Web. Today, billions of dollars in business and consumer transactions occur each year on the Web. Some companies, such as Amazon.com, exist only on the Web, while others, such as American Eagle Outfitters, maintain a Web site to supplement sales in their physical stores. Electronic storefronts, such as the American Eagle Outfitters site shown in Figure A-3, sell everything that you would expect to find in their store in a major shopping mall and more.

Figure A-3	American Eagle Outfitters Web site

In addition to buying and selling activities, companies use the Internet to coordinate their operations throughout the world, managing supplies, inventories, and factory production operations from thousands of miles away. An increasing number of companies use the Web to recruit employees and find other companies that are potential partners in opening new markets or finding new sources of supplies.

Entertainment

Many Web sites offer reviews of restaurants, movies, theater, musical events, and books. You can download music or play interactive games with people around the world using the Internet. The Calabash Music Web site, shown in Figure A-4, allows members to download music from all over the world. The Web provides a good way to follow your favorite sports teams, too. All of the major sports organizations have Web sites with current information about the teams in their leagues. In fact, the Web gives you a way to follow sports teams around the world in a variety of languages.

Computer Networks

As you know, computers that are connected to each other form a network. Each computer on a network has a network interface card installed inside it. A **network interface card** (often called a **NIC** or simply network card) is a card (circuit board) or other device used to connect a computer to a network of other computers. Many newer personal computers have a network interface device built into them, so that it is not necessary to add a separate NIC to make the computer networkable. These cards are connected to cables that are, in turn, connected to the company's main computer, called a server. A **server** is a general term for any computer that accepts requests from other computers that are connected to it and shares some or all of its resources, such as printers, files, or programs, with those computers.

Client/Server Local Area Networks

The server runs software that coordinates the information flow among the other computers, which are called **clients**. The software that runs on the server computer is called a **network operating system**. Connecting computers this way, in which one server computer shares its resources with multiple client computers, is called a **client/server network**. Client/server networks commonly are used to connect LANs. Figure A-5 shows a typical client/server LAN.

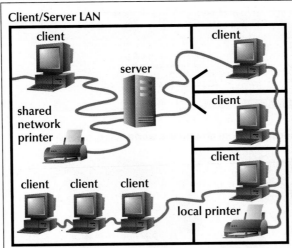

Each computer, printer, or other device attached to a network is called a **node** or **network node**. The server can be a powerful personal computer (PC) or a larger, more expensive computer. Until recently, these larger computers were called minicomputers, midrange computers, or mainframe computers. You might still hear people using these terms, but they are generally considered to be dated terminology. Today, most of these larger computers use similar designs and are all called "servers" to distinguish them from desktop or notebook computers. Likewise, most PCs can handle server duties if they are equipped with enough memory and large enough disk drives. Companies that need large amounts of computing power often connect hundreds or even thousands of PCs together to perform as servers.

Servers have operating systems just as any personal computer; however, they also can run network operating systems software. Although network operating systems software can be more expensive than the operating system software for a standalone computer, having computers connected in a client/server network can provide cost savings. For example, by connecting each computer to the server, each computer can share the network printer and one tape drive for backups because a client/server network lets any computer on the network use a printer connected to the server and tape drives that are installed in the server.

Some personal computer operating systems, such as Microsoft Windows XP, have networking capabilities built in. Macintosh computer operating systems have included built-in networking capabilities for many years. Also, some personal computer operating systems that can serve as network operating systems, such as Linux, are available on the Internet and can be downloaded and used at no cost.

Connecting Computers to a Network

Not all LANs use the same kind of cables to connect their computers. The oldest cable type is called **twisted-pair cable**, which is the type of cable that telephone companies have used for years to wire residences and businesses. Twisted-pair cable has two or more insulated copper wires that are twisted around each other and enclosed in another layer of plastic insulation. A wire that carries an electric current generates an electromagnetic field around itself. This electromagnetic field can induce a small flow of electricity in nearby objects, including other wires. This induced flow of unwanted electricity is called **electrical interference** because it can interfere with the signal that is carried by the wire that picks up the unwanted electricity flow. In twisted-pair wiring, the wires are twisted because the wrapping of the two wires around each other tends to reduce the amount of electrical interference that each wire in the pair might pick up from other nearby current-carrying wires. The type of twisted-pair cable that telephone companies have used for years to transmit voice signals is called **Category 1 cable**. Category 1 cable transmits information more slowly than the other cable types, but it is also much less expensive.

Coaxial cable is an insulated copper wire that is encased in a metal shield that is enclosed with plastic insulation. The signal-carrying wire is completely shielded, so it resists electrical interference much better than twisted-pair cable. Coaxial cable also carries signals about 20 times faster than Category 1 twisted-pair; however, it is considerably more expensive. Because coaxial cable is thicker and less flexible than twisted-pair, it is harder for installation workers to handle and thus is more expensive to install. You probably have seen coaxial cable because it is the type of cable used for most cable television connections. You might hear this type of cable called "coax" (koh-axe) by network technicians.

In the past 20 years, cable manufacturers have developed better versions of twisted-pair cable. The current standards for twisted-pair cable used in computer networks are Category 5 and Category 5e cable. **Category 5 cable** carries signals between 10 and 100 times faster than coaxial cable and is just as easy to install as Category 1 cable. **Category 5e cable** (the "e" stands for "enhanced") looks exactly like regular Category 5 cable, but it is constructed of higher quality materials so it can carry more signals even faster—up to 10 times faster—than regular Category 5 cable. Many businesses have Category 5 cable installed, but they are gradually replacing it with Category 5e. You might hear either of these cable types called "Cat-5" cable by network technicians.

The most expensive cable type is fiber-optic cable, which does not use an electrical signal at all. **Fiber-optic cable** (also called simply fiber) transmits information by using lasers to pulse beams of light through very thin strands of glass. Fiber-optic cable transmits signals much faster than either coaxial cable or Category 5 twisted-pair cable. Because it does not use electricity, fiber-optic cable is completely immune to electrical interference. Fiber-optic cable is lighter and more durable than coaxial cable, but it is harder to work with and more expensive than either coaxial cable or Category 5 twisted-pair cable. The price of fiber-optic cable and the laser sending and receiving equipment needed at each end of the cable has dropped dramatically in the past few years. Thus, companies are using fiber-optic cable in more and more networks as the cost becomes more affordable. Figure A-6 shows these three types of cable.

Twisted-pair, coaxial, and fiber-optic cables **Figure A-6**

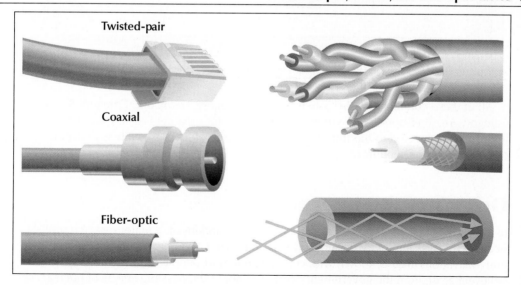

Perhaps the most intriguing way to connect computers in a LAN is to avoid cable completely. **Wireless networks** are becoming more common as the cost of the wireless transmitters and receivers that plug into or replace network cards continues to drop. Wireless LANs are especially welcome in organizations that occupy old buildings. Many cities have structures that were built before electricity and telephones were widely available. These buildings have no provision for running wires through walls or between floors, so a wireless network can be the best option for connecting resources.

Wireless connections are especially popular with companies whose employees use laptop computers and take them from meeting to meeting. A wireless network can help workers be more effective and productive in flexible team environments. An increasing number of schools are adding wireless network access points so that students can use their wireless-equipped laptop computers in classrooms, in libraries, and in study lounges. Some schools have even placed network access points on the outside edges of their buildings so that students can use their computers in patios and other outdoor areas such as parking lots. The cost of wireless networks is dropping, and many people are even installing them in their homes. Figure A-7 depicts a wireless home network that includes two desktop PCs, two laptop PCs, and a shared printer.

Figure A-7 ▶ **A wireless home network**

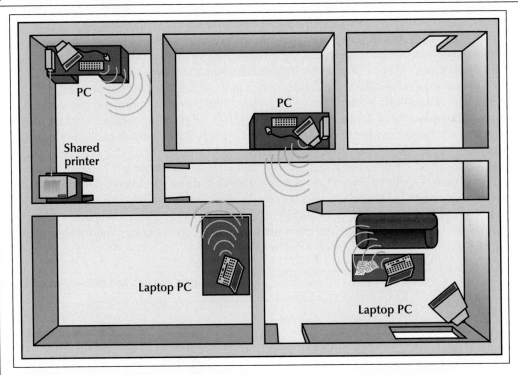

All of these connection types—twisted-pair, Category 1, coaxial, Category 5, Category 5e, fiber-optic, and wireless—are options for creating LANs. These LANs can, in turn, be connected to the Internet or to other, larger networks, such as those discussed in the next section.

Origins of the Internet

In the early 1960s, the U.S. Department of Defense undertook a major research project. Because this was a military project and was authorized as a part of national security, the true motivations are not known with certainty, but most people close to the project believe it arose from the government's concerns about the possible effects of nuclear attack on military computing facilities. The Department of Defense realized that the weapons of the future would require powerful computers for coordination and control. The powerful computers of that time were all large mainframe computers, so the Department of Defense began examining ways to connect these computers to each other and to weapons installations that were distributed all over the world.

The agency charged with this task was the **Advanced Research Projects Agency (ARPA)**. (During its lifetime, this agency has used two acronyms, ARPA and DARPA; this book uses its current acronym, **DARPA**, for **Defense Advanced Research Projects Agency**.) DARPA hired many of the best communications technology researchers and for many years funded research at leading universities and institutes to explore the task of creating a worldwide network of computers. A photo of these dedicated computer networking pioneers appears in Figure A-8.

DARPA computer scientists | **Figure A-8**

©1969, BBN Technologies

Courtesy of BBN Technologies

DARPA researchers soon became concerned about computer networks' vulnerability to attack because networks at that time relied on a single, central control function. If the network's central control point were damaged or attacked, the network would be unusable. Consequently, they worked hard to devise ways to eliminate the need for network communications to rely on a central control function.

Connectivity: Circuit Switching vs. Packet Switching

One of the first networking-related topics to be researched by the DARPA scientists was connectivity, or methods of sending messages over networks.

The first computer networks were created in the 1950s. The models for those early networks were the telephone companies because most early WANs used leased telephone company lines to connect computers to each other. In telephone company systems of that time, a telephone call established a single connection between sender and receiver. Once the connection was established, all data then traveled along that single path. The telephone company's central switching system selected specific telephone lines, or circuits, that would be connected to create the single path. This centrally controlled, single-connection method is called **circuit switching**. Most local telephone traffic today is still handled using circuit-switching technologies.

Although circuit switching is efficient and economical, it relies on a central point of control and a series of connections that form a single path. This makes circuit-switched communications vulnerable to the destruction of the central control point or any link in the series of connections that make up the single path that carries the signal.

Packet switching is an alternative means for sending messages. In a packet-switching network, files and messages are broken down into packets that are labeled electronically with codes for their origin and destination. The packets travel from computer to computer along the network until they reach their destination. The destination computer collects the packets and reassembles the original data from the pieces in each packet. Each computer that an individual packet encounters on its trip through the network determines the best way to move the packet forward to its destination. Computers and other devices that perform this function on networks are often called routing computers, or **routers**, and the programs they use to determine the best path for packets are called **routing algorithms**. Thus, packet-switched networks are inherently more reliable than circuit-switched networks because they rely on multiple routers instead of a central point of control and because each router can send individual packets along different paths if parts of the network are not operating.

By 1967, DARPA researchers had published their plan for a packet-switching network, and in 1969, they connected the first computer switches at the University of California at Los Angeles, SRI International, the University of California at Santa Barbara, and the University of Utah. This experimental WAN was called the **ARPANET**. Figure A-9 shows a famous hand-drawn sketch of the Internet as it existed in 1969.

Figure A-9	The Internet's humble beginning as ARPANET, 1969

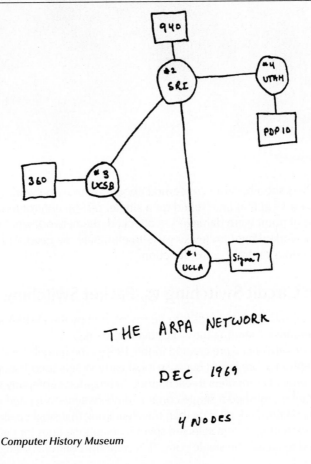

Computer History Museum

ARPANET grew over the next three years to include more than 20 computers. ARPANET used the **Network Control Protocol (NCP)** to enable each of those computers to communicate with other computers on the network. A **protocol** is a collection of rules for formatting, ordering, and error-checking data sent across a network.

Open Architecture Philosophy

As more researchers connected their computers and computer networks to the ARPANET, interest in the network grew in the academic community. One reason for increased interest in the project was its adherence to an **open architecture** philosophy; that is, each network could continue using its own protocols and data-transmission methods internally. This open approach was quite different from the closed architecture designs that companies such as IBM and Digital Equipment Corporation were using to build computer networks for their customers during this period. The open architecture philosophy includes four key points:

- Independent networks should not require any internal changes to be connected to the Internet.
- Packets that do not arrive at their destinations must be retransmitted from their source network.
- Router computers do not retain information about the packets they handle.
- No global control will exist over the network.

This open architecture philosophy was revolutionary at the time. Most companies that built computer networking products at that time tried hard to make their networks incompatible with other networks. These manufacturers believed that they could lock out competitors by not making their products easy to connect with products made by other companies. The shift to an open architecture approach is what made the Internet of today possible.

In the early 1970s, Vincent Cerf and Robert Kahn developed a set of protocols that implemented the open architecture philosophy better than the NCP. These new protocols were the **Transmission Control Protocol** and the **Internet Protocol**, which usually are referred to by their combined acronym, **TCP/IP**. TCP includes rules that computers on a network use to establish and break connections; IP includes rules for routing of individual data packets. TCP/IP continues to be used today in LANs and on the Internet. The term "Internet" was first used in a 1974 article about the TCP protocol written by Cerf and Kahn. The importance of the TCP/IP protocol in the history of the Internet is so great that many people consider Vincent Cerf to be the father of the Internet.

A number of TCP/IP-based networks—independent of the ARPANET—were created in the late 1970s and early 1980s. The National Science Foundation (NSF) funded the **Computer Science Network (CSNET)** for educational and research institutions that did not have access to the ARPANET. The City University of New York started a network of IBM mainframes at universities, called the **Because It's Time** (originally, "Because It's There") **Network (BITNET)**.

Birth of E-Mail: A New Use for Networks

Although the goals of ARPANET were still to control weapons systems and transfer research files, other uses for this vast network began to appear in the early 1970s. In 1972, an ARPANET researcher named Ray Tomlinson wrote a program that could send and receive messages over the network. E-mail had been born and rapidly became widely used in the computer research community. In 1976, the Queen of England sent an e-mail message over the ARPANET. The ARPANET continued to develop faster and more effective network technologies; for example, ARPANET began sending packets by satellite in 1976.

More New Uses for Networks Emerge

By 1981, the ARPANET had expanded to include more than 200 networks. The number of individuals in the military and education research communities that used the network continued to grow. Many of these new participants used the networking technology to transfer files and access computers remotely. The TCP/IP suite included two tools for performing these tasks. **File Transfer Protocol (FTP)** enabled users to transfer files between computers, and **Telnet** let users log in to their computer accounts from remote sites. Both FTP and Telnet still are widely used on the Internet today for file transfers and remote logins, even though more advanced techniques facilitate multimedia transmissions such as real-time audio and video clips. The first e-mail mailing lists also appeared on these networks. A **mailing list** is an e-mail address that takes any message it receives and forwards it to any user who has subscribed to the list.

Although file transfer and remote login were attractive features of these new TCP/IP networks, their improved e-mail and other communications facilities attracted many users in the education and research communities. Mailing lists (such as BITNET's **LISTSERV**), information posting areas (such as the **User's News Network**, or **Usenet**, **newsgroups**), and adventure games were among the new applications appearing on the ARPANET.

Although the people using these networks were developing many creative applications, relatively few people had access to the networks. Most of these people were members of the research and academic communities. From 1979 to 1989, these new and interesting network applications were improved and tested with an increasing number of users. TCP/IP became more widely used as academic and research institutions realized the benefits of having a common communications network. The explosion of PC use during that time also helped more people become comfortable with computing.

Interconnecting the Networks

The early 1980s saw continued growth in the ARPANET and other networks. The **Joint Academic Network (Janet)** was established in the United Kingdom to link universities there. Traffic increased on all of these networks, and in 1984, the Department of Defense split the ARPANET into two specialized networks: ARPANET would continue its advanced research activities, and **MILNET** (for **Military Network**) would be reserved for military uses that required greater security. By 1987, congestion on the ARPANET caused by a rapidly increasing number of users on the limited-capacity leased telephone lines was becoming severe. To reduce the traffic load on the ARPANET, a network run by the National Science Foundation, called NSFnet, merged with another NSF network, called CSNet, and with BITNET to form one network that could carry much of the network traffic that had been carried by the ARPANET. The resulting NSFnet awarded a contract to Merit Network, Inc., IBM, Sprint, and the state of Michigan to upgrade and operate the main NSFnet backbone. A **network backbone** includes the long-distance lines and supporting technology that transports large amounts of data between major network nodes. By the late 1980s, many other TCP/IP networks had merged or established interconnections. Figure A-10 summarizes how the individual networks described in this section combined to become the Internet as it is known today.

Networks that became the Internet ◀ **Figure A-10**

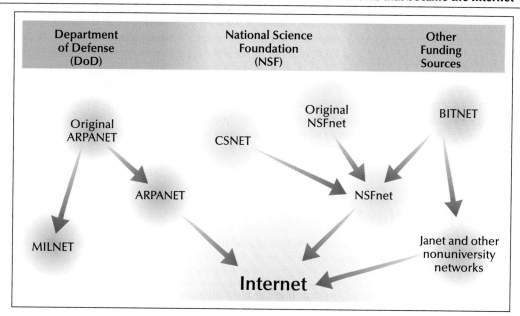

Commercial Interest Increases

As PCs became more powerful, affordable, and available during the 1980s, companies increasingly used them to construct LANs. Although these LANs included e-mail software that employees could use to send messages to each other, businesses wanted their employees to be able to communicate with people outside their corporate LANs. The National Science Foundation (NSF) prohibited commercial network traffic on the networks it funded, so businesses turned to commercial e-mail services. Larger firms built their own TCP/IP-based WANs that used leased telephone lines to connect field offices to corporate headquarters. Today, people use the term **intranet** to describe LANs or WANs that use the TCP/IP protocol but do not connect to sites outside the firm. Although most companies allow only their employees to use the company intranet, some companies give specific outsiders, such as customers, vendors, or business partners, access to their intranets. These outside parties agree to respect the confidentiality of the information on the network. An intranet that allows selected outside parties to connect is often called an **extranet**.

In 1989, the NSF permitted two commercial e-mail services, MCI Mail and CompuServe, to establish limited connections to the Internet that allowed their commercial subscribers to exchange e-mail messages with the members of the academic and research communities who were connected to the Internet. These connections allowed commercial enterprises to send e-mail directly to Internet addresses and allowed members of the research and education communities on the Internet to send e-mail directly to MCI Mail and CompuServe addresses. The NSF justified this limited commercial use of the Internet as a service that would primarily benefit the Internet's noncommercial users.

People from all walks of life—not just scientists or academic researchers—started thinking of these networks as a global resource that we now know as the Internet. Information systems professionals began to form volunteer groups such as the **Internet Engineering Task Force (IETF)**, which first met in 1986. The IETF is a self-organized group that makes technical contributions to the engineering of the Internet and its technologies. IETF is the main body that develops new Internet standards.

Just as the world was coming to realize the value of these interconnected networks, however, it also became aware of the threats to privacy and computer security posed by these networks. In 1988, Robert Morris, Jr., a graduate student in Computer Science at Cornell University, launched a program called the **Internet Worm** that used weaknesses in e-mail programs and operating systems to distribute itself to more than 6,000 of the 60,000 computers that were then connected to the Internet. The Worm program created multiple copies of itself on the computers it infected. The large number of program copies consumed the processing power of each infected computer and prevented it from running other programs. This event brought international attention and concern to the Internet. Unfortunately, worms and other malicious programs such as viruses still appear regularly on the Internet today, and they continue to do considerable damage to individual computers and networks.

Although the network of networks that is now known as the Internet had grown from four computers on the ARPANET in 1969 to more than 300,000 computers on many interconnected networks by 1990, the greatest growth in the Internet was yet to come.

Growth of the Internet

A formal definition of Internet, which was adopted in 1995 by the Federal Networking Council (FNC), appears in Figure A-11.

| Figure A-11 | The FNC's October 1995 resolution to define the term Internet |

RESOLUTION: The Federal Networking Council (FNC) agrees that the following language reflects our definition of the term Internet. Internet refers to the global information system that

(i) is logically linked together by a globally unique address space based on the Internet Protocol (IP) or its subsequent extensions/follow-ons;

(ii) is able to support communications using the Transmission Control Protocol/Internet Protocol (TCP/IP) suite or its subsequent extensions/follow-ons, and/or other IP-compatible protocols; and

(iii) provides, uses or makes accessible, either publicly or privately, high level services layered on the communications and related infrastructure described herein.

Source: http://www.nitrd.gov/fnc/Internet_res.html

The researchers who had been so involved in the creation and growth of the Internet accepted it as part of their working environment, but people outside the research community were largely unaware of the potential offered by a large interconnected set of computer networks until the 1990s.

From Research Project to Information Infrastructure

Realizing that the Internet was becoming much more than a scientific research project, the U.S. Department of Defense finally closed the research portion of its network, the ARPANET, in 1995. The NSF also wanted to turn over the Internet to others so it could return its attention and funds to other research projects.

The process of shutting down the ARPANET and privatizing the Internet began in 1991 when the NSF eased its restrictions on Internet commercial activity. Businesses and individuals continued to connect to the Internet in ever-increasing numbers. Although nobody really knows how big the Internet is, one commonly used measure is the number of Internet hosts. An **Internet host** is a computer that connects a LAN or a WAN to the Internet. Each Internet host might have any number of computers connected to it. Figure A-12 shows the rapid growth in the number of Internet host computers. As you can see, the growth has been dramatic.

Growth in the number of Internet hosts | **Figure A-12**

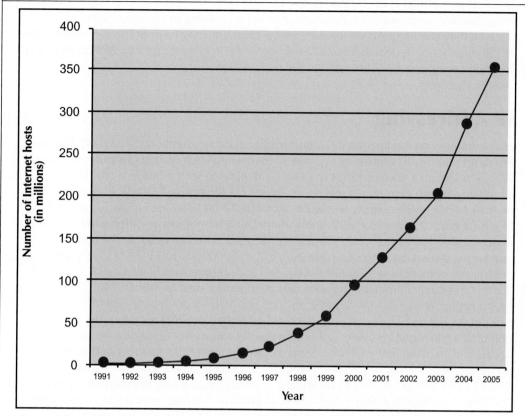

Source: Adapted from Internet Systems Consortium (http://www.isc.org/) and other sources

The numbers in the figure probably understate the true growth of the Internet in recent years for two reasons. First, the number of hosts connected to the Internet includes only those computers that are directly connected to the Internet. In other words, if a LAN with 100 PCs is connected to the Internet through only one host computer, those 100 computers appear as one host in the count. Because the number and size of LANs have increased in recent years, the host count probably understates the growth in the number of all computers that have access to the Internet. Second, the number of computers is only one measure of growth. Internet traffic now carries more files that contain graphics, sound, and video, so Internet files have become larger. A given number of users sending video clips will use much more of the Internet's capacity than the same number of users will use by sending e-mail messages or text files.

The Internet has no central management or coordination, and the routing computers do not retain copies of the packets they handle. Some companies and research organizations estimate the number of regular users of the Internet today to be more than 800 million, but no one knows how many individual e-mail messages or files travel on the Internet, and no one really knows how many people use the Internet today.

New Structure for the Internet

As NSFnet converted the main traffic-carrying backbone portion of its network to private firms, it organized the network around four **network access points (NAPs)**, which were operated by four different telecommunications companies. These four companies and their successors sell access to the Internet through their NAPs to organizations and businesses. The NSFnet still exists for government and research use, but it uses these same NAPs for long-range data transmission.

With more than 350 million connected Internet host computers and more than 800 million worldwide Internet users, the Internet faces some challenges. The firms that sell network access have enough incentive to keep investing in the network architecture because they can recoup their investments by attracting new Internet users. However, the TCP/IP numbering system that identifies users on the Internet is running short of numbers. This numbering system is discussed in the next section.

IP Addressing

Each computer on the Internet has a unique identification number, called an **IP (Internet Protocol)** address. IP addressing is a way of identifying each unique computer on the Web, just like your home address is a way of identifying your home in a city. The IP addressing system currently in use on the Internet is **IP version 4 (IPv4)**. IPv4 uses a 32-bit number to label each address on the Internet. The 32-bit IP address is usually written in four 8-bit parts. In most computer applications, an 8-bit number is called a **byte**; however, in networking applications, an 8-bit number is often called an **octet**. In the binary (base 2) numbering system, an octet can have values from 00000000 to 11111111; the decimal equivalents of these binary numbers are 0 and 255, respectively. Each part of a 32-bit IP address is separated from the previous part by a period, such as 106.29.242.17. You might hear a person pronounce this address as "one hundred six dot twenty-nine dot two four two dot seventeen." This notation is often called **dotted decimal notation**. The combination of these four parts provides 4.2 billion possible addresses ($256 \times 256 \times 256 \times 256$). Because each of the four parts of a dotted decimal number can range from 0 to 255, IP addresses range from 0.0.0.0 (which would be written in binary as 32 zeros) to 255.255.255.255 (which would be written in binary as 32 ones). Although many people find dotted decimal notation to be somewhat confusing at first, most do agree that writing, reading, and remembering a computer address as 216.115.108.245 is easier than 11011000011100110110110011110101 or its full decimal equivalent, which is 3,631,443,189.

In the mid-1990s, the accelerating growth of the Internet created concern that the world could run out of IP addresses within a few years. In the early days of the Internet, the 4 billion addresses provided by the IPv4 rules certainly seemed to be more addresses than an experimental research network would ever need. However, about 2 billion of those addresses today are either in use or unavailable for use because of the way blocks of addresses were assigned to organizations. The addition of new kinds of devices to the Internet's many networks, such as wireless personal digital assistants and mobile phones that can access the Web, promises to keep the demand for IP addresses high.

Network engineers have devised a number of stop-gap techniques, such as **subnetting**, which is the use of reserved private IP addresses within LANs and WANs to provide additional address space. **Private IP addresses** are series of IP numbers that have been set aside for subnet use and are not permitted on packets that travel on the Internet. In subnetting, a computer called a **network address translation (NAT) device** converts those private IP addresses into normal IP addresses when the packets move from the LAN or WAN onto the Internet.

The IETF worked on several new protocols that could solve the limited addressing capacity of IPv4 and, in 1997, approved **IP version 6 (IPv6)** as the protocol that would replace IPv4. The new IP is being implemented gradually because the two protocols are not directly compatible. However, network engineers have devised ways to run both protocols together on interconnected networks. The major advantage of IPv6 is that the number of addresses is more than a billion times larger than the four billion addresses available in IPv4. The new IP also changes the format of the packet itself. Improvements in networking technologies over the past 20 years have made many of the fields in the IPv4 packet unnecessary. IPv6 eliminates those fields and adds new fields for security and other optional information.

In just over 30 years, the Internet has become one of the most amazing technological and social accomplishments of the century. Millions of people use a complex, interconnected network of computers that run thousands of different software packages. The computers are located in almost every country in the world. Billions of dollars change hands every year over the Internet in exchange for all kinds of products and services. All of the Internet's activity occurs with no central coordination point or control. Even more interesting is that the Internet began as a way for the military to maintain control while under attack.

The opening of the Internet to business enterprise helped increase its growth dramatically in recent years. However, another development worked hand in hand with the commercialization of the Internet to spur its growth. That development was the technological advance known as the World Wide Web.

World Wide Web

The World Wide Web (Web) is more a way of thinking about information storage and retrieval than it is a technology. Many people use "the Web" and "the Internet" interchangeably, but they are not the same thing. As you will learn in this section, the Web is software that runs on some of the computers that are connected to each other through the Internet. Because of this, its history goes back many years. Two important innovations played key roles in making the Internet easier to use and more accessible to people who were not research scientists: hypertext and graphical user interfaces (GUIs).

Origins of Hypertext

In 1945, Vannevar Bush, who was director of the U.S. Office of Scientific Research and Development, wrote an *Atlantic Monthly* article about ways that scientists could apply the skills they learned during World War II to peacetime activities. The article included a number of visionary ideas about future uses of technology to organize and facilitate efficient access to information. Bush speculated that engineers eventually would build a machine that he called the **Memex**, a memory extension device that would store all of a person's books, records, letters, and research results on microfilm. Bush's Memex would include mechanical aids to help users consult their collected knowledge fast and in a wide variety of ways. In the 1960s, Ted Nelson described a similar system in which text on one page links to text on other pages. Nelson called his page-linking system **hypertext**. Douglas Engelbart, who also invented the computer mouse, created the first experimental hypertext system on one of the large computers of the 1960s. In 1976, Nelson published a book, *Dream Machines*, in which he outlined project Xanadu, a global system for online hypertext publishing and commerce. Figure A-13 includes photos of Bush, Nelson, and Engelbart, three forward-looking thinkers whose ideas laid the foundation for the Web.

Left to right: Vannevar Bush, Ted Nelson, and Douglas Engelbart ▶ **Figure A-13**

MIT Museum

Courtesy of Ted Nelson/Project Xanadu

Courtesy of the Bootstrap Institute

Hypertext and Graphical User Interfaces Come to the Internet

In 1989, Tim Berners-Lee and Robert Calliau were working at CERN—the European Laboratory for Particle Physics. (The acronym, CERN, comes from the French of the original name of the laboratory, the *Conseil Européen pour la Recherche Nucléaire*.) Berners-Lee and Calliau were trying to improve the laboratory's research document-handling procedures. CERN had been using the Internet for two years to circulate its scientific papers and data among the high-energy physics research community throughout the world; however, the Internet did not help the agency display the complex graphics that were important parts of its theoretical models. Independently, Berners-Lee and Calliau each proposed a hypertext development project to improve CERN's document-handling capabilities.

Over the next two years, Berners-Lee developed the code for a hypertext server program and made it available on the Internet. A **hypertext server** is a computer that stores files written in the hypertext markup language and lets other computers connect to it and read those files. **Hypertext Markup Language (HTML)** is a language that includes a set of codes (or **tags**) attached to text. These codes describe the relationships among text elements. For example, HTML includes tags that indicate which text is part of a header element, which text is part of a paragraph element, and which text is part of a numbered list element. One important type of tag is the hypertext link tag. A **hypertext link**, or **hyperlink**, points to another location in the same or another HTML document. HTML documents can also include links to other types of files, such as word processing documents, spreadsheets, graphics, audio clips, and video clips.

You can use several different types of software to read HTML documents, but most people use a Web browser such as Netscape Navigator or Microsoft Internet Explorer. A **Web browser** is software that lets users read (or browse) HTML documents and move from one HTML document to another through the text formatted with hypertext link tags in each file. If the HTML documents are on computers connected to the Internet, you can use a Web browser to move from an HTML document on one computer to an HTML document on any other computer on the Internet. HTML is a subset of **Standard Generalized Markup Language (SGML)**, which organizations have used for many years to manage large document-filing systems. An HTML document differs from a word-processing document because it does not specify *how* a particular text element will appear. For example, you might use word-processing software to create a document heading by setting the heading text font to Arial, its font size to 14 points, and its position to centered. The document displays and prints these exact settings whenever you open the document in the word processor. In contrast, an HTML document surrounds the text with a pair of **heading tags** to indicate that the text should be considered a heading. Many programs can read an HTML document. The programs recognize the heading tags and display the text in whatever manner that program normally displays headings. Different programs might display the heading text differently.

A Web browser presents an HTML document in an easy-to-read format in its graphical user interface. A **graphical user interface** (**GUI**, pronounced "gooey") is a way of presenting program output using pictures, icons, and other graphical elements instead of just displaying text. Almost all PCs today use a GUI such as Microsoft Windows or the Macintosh user interface. Researchers have found that computer users—especially new users—learn new programs more quickly when they have a GUI interface instead of a text interface. Because each Web page has its own set of controls (hyperlinks, buttons to click, and blank text boxes in which to type text), every person who visits a Web site for the first time becomes a "new user" of that site. Thus, the GUI presented in Web browsers has been an important element in the rapid growth of the Web. Figure A-14 shows the same Web page displayed in two different browsers. The page displayed in the top half of the figure was rendered by a text-based browser. The page in the bottom half of the figure was rendered by a GUI browser. Most people find the GUI browser version to be much easier to use.

Web page rendered in a text-based browser and a GUI browser ◄ **Figure A-14**

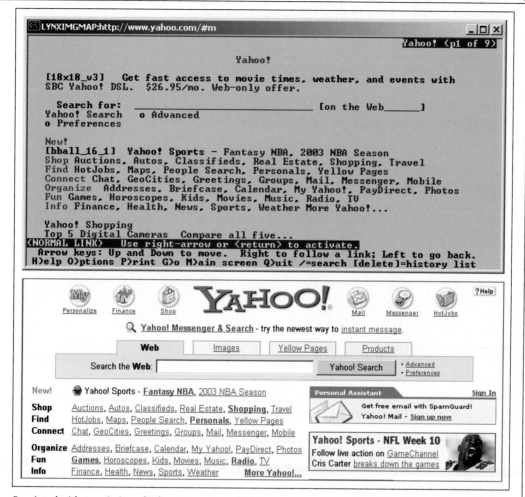

Reprinted with permission of Yahoo! Inc. © 2005 by Yahoo! Inc. YAHOO! and the YAHOO! logo are trademarks of Yahoo! Inc.

Berners-Lee called his system of hyperlinked HTML documents the World Wide Web. The Web caught on rapidly in the scientific research community, but few people outside that community had software that could read the HTML documents. In 1993, a group of students led by Marc Andreessen at the University of Illinois wrote **Mosaic**, the first GUI program that could read HTML and use HTML documents' hyperlinks to navigate from page to page on computers anywhere on the Internet. Mosaic was the first Web browser that became widely available for PCs. Figure A-15 shows a 1993 Web page displayed in an early version of the Mosaic Web browser.

Figure A-15 Mosaic, the first widely available Web browser

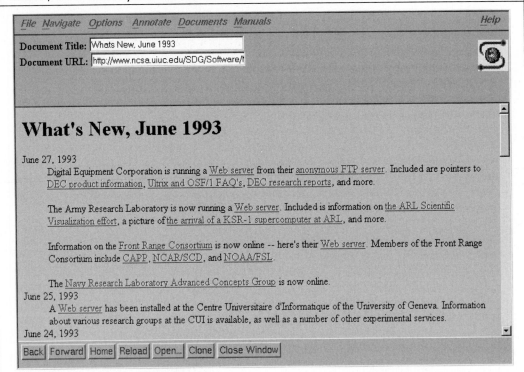

Source: http://www.dejavu.org/emulator.htm

The Web and Commercialization of the Internet

Programmers quickly realized that a functional system of pages connected by hyperlinks would provide many new Internet users with an easy way to locate information on the Internet. Businesses quickly recognized the profit-making potential offered by a world-wide network of easy-to-use computers. In 1994, Andreessen and other members of the University of Illinois Mosaic team joined with James Clark of Silicon Graphics to found Netscape Communications. The university was not too happy when the team decided to leave the school and develop a commercial product. The university refused to allow the team to use the name "Mosaic." Netscape's first browser was, therefore, called the "Mosaic Killer" or "Mozilla." Shortly after its release, the product was renamed Netscape Navigator. The program was an instant success. Netscape became one of the fastest grow-ing software companies ever.

Microsoft created its Internet Explorer Web browser and entered the market soon after Netscape's success became apparent. Microsoft offered its browser at no cost to computer owners who used its Windows operating system. Within a few years, most users had switched to Internet Explorer, and Netscape was unable to earn enough money to continue in business. Microsoft was accused of wielding its monopoly power to drive Netscape out of business; these accusations led to the trial of Microsoft on charges that it violated U.S. anti-trust laws. These charges were settled in a consent decree, but other violations by Microsoft led to a second trial in which the company was found guilty. Parts of Netscape were sold to America Online, but the Netscape Navigator browser became open-source software. **Open-source software** is created and maintained by volunteer programmers, often hundreds of them, who work together using the Internet to build and refine a pro-gram. The program is made available to users at no charge. The current open-source release of this browser is called Mozilla, which recalls the name of the original Netscape product. In an interesting turn of Web history, the Netscape Navigator browser that is available today is based on the Mozilla open-source software.

The number of **Web sites**, which are collections of HTML documents stored on computers that are connected to the Internet, has grown even more rapidly than the Internet itself. Figure A-16 shows the growth in the Web during its lifetime.

Growth of the World Wide Web ◄ **Figure A-16**

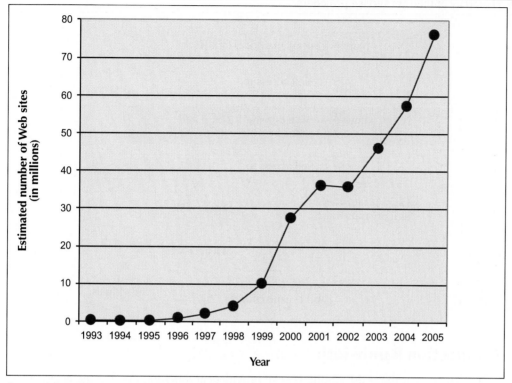

Source: Adapted from Netcraft Web Survey (http://www.netcraft.com/survey/Reports)

After a brief dip between 2001 and 2002, growth in the number of Web sites resumed at its formerly rapid rate. As individual Web sites become larger, they each have many more pages. Most experts agree that the number of pages available on the Web today is greater than 1 billion and that number is increasing faster than ever. Thus, the size of the Web is truly astounding. As more people obtain access to the Web, commercial uses of the Web and the variety of non business uses will continue to increase.

Business of Providing Internet Access

As you continue your research, you learn more about the NAPs (network access points) that maintain the core operations and long-haul backbone of the Internet. You find that they do not offer direct connections to individuals or small businesses. Instead, they offer connections to large organizations and businesses that, in turn, provide Internet access to other businesses and individuals. These firms are called **Internet access providers (IAPs)** or **Internet service providers (ISPs)**. Most of these firms call themselves ISPs because they offer more than just access to the Internet. ISPs usually provide their customers with the software they need to connect to the ISP, browse the Web, send and receive e-mail messages, and perform other Internet-related functions such as file transfer and remote login to other computers. ISPs often provide network consulting services to their customers and help them design Web pages. Some ISPs have developed a full range of services that include network management, training, and marketing advice. Large ISPs that sell Internet access along with other services to businesses are often called **commerce service providers (CSPs)** because they help businesses conduct business activities (or commerce) on the Internet. The larger ISPs also sell Internet access to smaller ISPs, which in turn sell access and services to their own business and individual customers. This hierarchy of Internet service providers appears in Figure A-17.

Figure A-17 | **Hierarchy of Internet service providers**

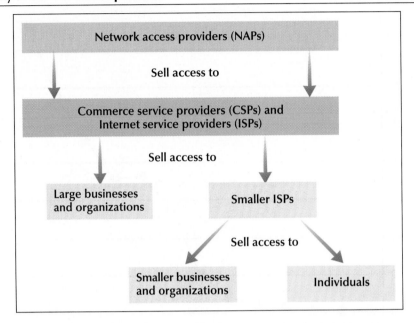

Connection Bandwidth

Of the differences that exist among service providers at different levels of the access hierarchy, one of the most important is the connection bandwidth that an ISP can offer. **Bandwidth** is the amount of data that can travel through a communications circuit in one second. The bandwidth that an ISP can offer you depends on the type of connection it has to the Internet and the kind of connection you have to the ISP.

The available bandwidth for any type of network connection between two points is limited to the narrowest bandwidth that exists in any part of the network. For example, if you connect to an ISP through a regular telephone line, your bandwidth is limited to the bandwidth of that telephone line, regardless of the bandwidth connection that the ISP has to the Internet. Bandwidth for Internet connections is measured the same way as bandwidth for connections within networks, in multiples of **bits per second (bps)**. Discussions of bandwidth often use the terms **kilobits per second (Kbps)**, which is 1,024 bps; **megabits per second (Mbps)**, which is 1,048,576 bps; and **gigabits per second (Gbps)**, which is 1,073,741,824 bps.

Sometimes computer users become confused by the use of bits to measure bandwidth because file sizes are measured in bytes. As explained earlier in this appendix, a byte is eight bits; it is abbreviated using an uppercase "B." Thus, a **kilobyte (KB)** is 1,024 bytes, or 8,192 bits. Similarly, a **megabyte (MB)** is 1,048,576 bytes (or 8,388,608 bits) and a **gigabyte (GB)** is 1,073,741,824 bytes (or 8,589,934,592 bits).

Most LANs today run either Fast Ethernet, which operates at 100 Mbps, or Gigabit Ethernet, which operates at 1 Gbps. Some older LANs still use an older version of Ethernet that operates at about 10 Mbps. The effective bandwidth of wireless LANs depends on the distance between computers and what types of barriers the wireless signals must pass through (for example, wireless signals travel more easily through glass than steel). Most wireless LANs operate at a bandwidth of between 2 Mbps and 10 Mbps, although newer wireless devices capable of 50 Mbps are now available. Figure A-18 shows some examples of typical times required to send different types of files over different types of LANs.

Typical file transmission times for various types of LANs ◄ **Figure A-18**

Type of File	Typical File Size	Wireless (7 Mbps)	Ethernet (10 Mbps)	Fast Ethernet (100 Mbps)	Gigabit Ethernet (1 Gbps)
One paragraph text message	5 KB	Less than .1 second	Less than .1 second	Less than .1 second	Less than .1 second
Word processing document, 20 pages	100 KB	.1 second	Less than .1 second	Less than .1 second	Less than .1 second
Web page containing several small graphics	200 KB	.2 second	.2 second	Less than .1 second	Less than .1 second
Presentation file with 20 slides and several large graphics	800 KB	1 second	.7 second	Less than .1 second	Less than .1 second
Color brochure, five pages with several color photos	2 MB	3 seconds	2 seconds	.2 second	Less than .1 second
Compressed music file (MP3 format) containing a four-minute song	5 MB	6 seconds	4 seconds	.4 second	Less than .1 second
Uncompressed music file containing a four-minute song	60 MB	1 minute	50 seconds	5 seconds	.5 second
Compressed video file containing a ten-minute interview	200 MB	4 minutes	4 minutes	17 seconds	2 seconds
Compressed video file containing a feature-length film	4 GB	1.5 hours	1 hour	6 minutes	35 seconds

When you extend your network beyond a local area, either through a WAN or by connecting to the Internet, the speed of the connection depends on what type of connection you use.

One way to connect computers or networks over longer distances is to use regular telephone service (sometimes referred to as **dial-up**, **POTS**, or **plain old telephone service**). Regular telephone service to most U.S. residential and business customers provides a maximum bandwidth of between 28.8 Kbps and 56 Kbps. These rates vary because the United States has a number of different telephone companies that do not all use the same technology. When you connect your computer, which communicates using digital signals, to another computer through a telephone line, which uses analog signals, you must convert the signals from one form to the other. The device that performs this signal conversion is called a **modem**, which is short for modulator-demodulator. Converting a digital signal to an analog signal is called **modulation**; converting that analog signal back into digital form is called **demodulation**. A modem performs both functions; that is, it acts as a modulator and demodulator.

Some telephone companies offer a higher grade of service that uses one of a series of protocols called **Digital Subscriber Line** or **Digital Subscriber Loop (DSL)**. The first technology that was developed using a DSL protocol is called **Integrated Services Digital Network (ISDN)**. ISDN service has been available in various parts of the United States since 1984. Although considerably more expensive than regular telephone service, ISDN offers bandwidths of up to 256 Kbps. ISDN is much more widely available in Australia, France, Germany, Japan, and Singapore than in the United States because the regulatory structure of the telecommunications industries in those countries encouraged rapid deployment of this new technology.

All technologies based on the DSL protocol require the implementing telephone company to install new equipment at its switching stations, which can be very expensive. New technologies that use the DSL protocol are currently being implemented around the world. One of those, **Asymmetric Digital Subscriber Line** (**ADSL**, also abbreviated **DSL**), offers transmission speeds ranging from 16 to 640 Kbps from the user to the telephone company and from 1.5 to 9 Mbps from the telephone company to the user.

Businesses and large organizations often obtain their connection to the Internet by connecting to an ISP using higher-bandwidth telephone company connections called **T1** (1.544 Mbps) and **T3** (44.736 Mbps) connections. (The names T1 and T3 were originally acronyms for Telephone 1 and Telephone 3, respectively, but very few people use these terms any longer.) Companies with operations in multiple locations sometimes lease T1 and T3 lines from telephone companies to create their own WANs that connect their locations to each other.

T1 and T3 connections are much more expensive than POTS or ISDN connections; however, organizations that must link hundreds or thousands of individual users to WANs or to the Internet require the greater bandwidth of T1 and T3 connections. Smaller firms can save money by renting access to a partial T1 connection from a telephone company. In a partial T1 rental, the connection is shared with other companies.

The NAPs operate the Internet backbone using a variety of connections. In addition to T1 and T3 lines, the NAPs use newer connections that have bandwidths of more than 1 Gbps—in some cases exceeding 10 Gbps. These new connection options use fiber-optic cables, and they are referred to as OC3, OC12, and so forth. **OC** is short for **optical carrier**. NAPs also use high-bandwidth satellite and radio communications links to transfer data over long distances.

A group of research universities and the National Science Foundation (NSF) now operates a network called **Internet2** that has backbone bandwidths greater than 10 Gbps. The Internet2 project continues the tradition of the DARPA scientists by sponsoring research at the frontiers of network technologies.

A connection option that is increasingly available in the United States and some other countries is to connect to the Internet through a cable television company. The cable company transmits data in the same cables it uses to provide television service. Cable can deliver up to 10 Mbps to an individual user and can accept up to 768 Kbps from an individual user. In practice, cable connections usually deliver speeds between 500 Kbps and 3 Mbps, although some cable companies offer guarantees of higher speeds (for higher monthly fees, of course). These speeds far exceed those of existing POTS and ISDN connections and are comparable to speeds provided by the ADSL technologies currently being implemented by telephone companies and other companies that rent facilities from the telephone companies.

An option that is particularly appealing to users in remote areas is connecting by satellite. Using a satellite-dish receiver, you can download at a bandwidth of approximately 400 Kbps. Until recently, you could not send information to the Internet using a satellite-dish antenna, so you needed to also have an ISP account to send files or e-mail. Two satellite companies have recently introduced a satellite transmitter that can be installed on the dish antenna. This allows them to now offer two-way satellite connections to the Internet.

The actual bandwidth provided by all these Internet connection methods varies from provider to provider and with the amount of traffic on the Internet. During peak operating hours, the Internet can become congested. Remember that the bandwidth obtained is limited to the lowest amount of bandwidth available at any point in the network.

Figure A-19 shows typical file transmission times for various types of Internet connection options. The speeds shown are examples of what a user can expect on average during download operations. Any Internet connection that is faster than POTS is generally called a **broadband** connection.

Typical file transmission times for various types of Internet connections ◀ **Figure A-19**

Type of File	Typical File Size	POTS (25 Kbps)	ISDN or Satellite (100 Kbps)	Residential Cable or DSL (300 Kbps)	Business Leased T-1 (1.4 Mbps)
One paragraph text message	5 KB	2 seconds	.4 second	.2 second	Less than .1 second
Word processing document, 20 pages	100 KB	33 seconds	8 seconds	3 seconds	Less than .1 second
Web page containing several small graphics	200 KB	1 minute	16 seconds	6 seconds	Less than .1 second
Presentation file with 20 slides and several large graphics	800 KB	4 minutes	1 minute	22 seconds	Less than .1 second
Color brochure, five pages with several color photos	2 MB	11 minutes	3 minutes	1 minute	Less than .1 second
Compressed music file (MP3 format) containing a four-minute song	5 MB	28 minutes	7 minutes	2 minutes	Less than .1 second
Uncompressed music file containing a four-minute song	60 MB	6 hours	1.5 hours	28 minutes	.4 second
Compressed video file containing a ten-minute interview	200 MB	19 hours	5 hours	2 hours	1 second
Compressed video file containing a feature-length film	4 GB	16 days	4 days	1.5 days	25 seconds

Of course, faster Internet connections cost significantly more money than slower connections. Figure A-20 summarizes the bandwidths, costs, and typical uses for the most common types of connections currently in use on the Internet. Some companies are beginning to offer **fixed-point wireless** connections, which use technology similar to wireless LANs, but these offerings are in limited areas and prices are still highly variable.

| Figure A-20 | Types of Internet connections |

Service	Upstream Speed (Kbps)	Downstream Speed (Kbps)	Capacity (Number of Simultaneous Users)	One-time Startup Costs	Continuing Monthly Costs
Residential-Small Business Services					
POTS	28–56	28–56	1	$0–$20	$12–$20
ISDN	128–256	128–256	1–3	$60–$300	$50–$90
ADSL	100–640	4,500–9,000	1–4	$50–$100	$40–$90
Cable	300–1,000	500–10,000	1–4	$0–$100	$40–$100
Satellite	125–150	400–500	1–3	$0–$800	$40–$100
Business Services					
Leased digital line (DS0)	64	64	1–10	$50–$200	$40–$150
Fractional T1 leased line	128–1,544	128–1,544	5–180	$50–$800	$100–$1,000
T1 leased line	1,544	1,544	100–200	$100–$2,000	$900–$1,600
T3 leased line	44,700	44,700	1,000–10,000	$1,000–$9,000	$5,000–$12,000
Large Business, ISP, NAP, and Internet2 Services					
OC3 leased line	156,000	156,000	1,000–50,000	$3,000–$12,000	$9,000–$22,000
OC12 leased line	622,000	622,000	Backbone	Negotiated	$25,000–$100,000
OC48 leased line	2,500,000	2,500,000	Backbone	Negotiated	Negotiated
OC192 leased line	10,000,000	10,000,000	Backbone	Negotiated	Negotiated

Review

Appendix Summary

In this appendix, you learned that the Internet is a truly amazing phenomenon. From its birth as a scientific research project to its current role as a global communications network that links more than a billion persons, businesses, organizations, and governments, the Internet has made information available on a scale never before imagined. You learned how client/server networks work when they are interconnected. You also learned something about the people who played important roles in the development of the technologies and philosophies that underlie the success of the Internet.

The Internet grew rapidly, especially after the Web became available as a new way of using the Internet. You learned how the business of providing Internet access works and what bandwidth and pricing choices are available for connecting to the Internet.

Key Terms

Advanced Research Projects
   Agency (ARPA)
ARPANET
Asymmetric Digital
   Subscriber Line
   (ADSL or DSL)
bandwidth
Because It's Time Network
   (BITNET)
bits per second (bps)

broadband
byte
Category 1 cable
Category 5 cable
Category 5e cable
circuit switching
client
client/server network
coaxial cable
commerce service
   provider (CSP)

Computer Science Network
   (CSNET)
Defense Advanced
   Research Projects
   Agency (DARPA)
demodulation
dial-up
Digital Subscriber Line (DSL)
Digital Subscriber Loop (DSL)
dotted decimal notation
electrical interference

extranet
fiber-optic cable
File Transfer Protocol (FTP)
fixed-point wireless
gigabits per second (Gbps)
gigabyte (GB)
graphical user interface (GUI)
heading tag
hypertext
hypertext link (hyperlink)
Hypertext Markup
    Language (HTML)
hypertext server
Integrated Services Digital
    Network (ISDN)
Internet access provider (IAP)
Internet Engineering Task
    Force (IETF)
Internet host
Internet Protocol
Internet service provider (ISP)
Internet Worm
Internet2
intranet
IP (Internet Protocol)
    address

IP version 4 (IPv4)
IP version 6 (IPv6)
Joint Academic Network
    (Janet)
kilobits per second (Kbps)
kilobyte (KB)
LISTSERV
mailing list
megabits per second (Mbps)
megabyte (MB)
Memex
MILNET (Military Network)
modem
modulation
Mosaic
network access point (NAP)
network address translation
    (NAT) device
network backbone
Network Control
    Protocol (NCP)
network interface card (NIC)
network operating system
node (network node)
octet
open architecture
open-source software

optical carrier (OC)
packet switching
plain old telephone
    service (POTS)
private IP address
protocol
router
routing algorithm
server
Standard Generalized
    Markup Language
    (SGML)
subnetting
T1
T3
tag
TCP/IP
Telnet
Transmission Control
    Protocol (TCP)
twisted-pair cable
User's News Network
    (Usenet) newsgroups
Web browser
Web site
wireless network

New Perspectives on
The Internet

Additional Research Assignments   ADD 3
**Locating and Evaluating Health
Care Information on the Internet**   ADD 4
Telemedicine   ADD 6
Advances in Distance Learning   ADD 8
The Future of the Semantic Web   ADD 9

Objectives

- Research a disease or medical condition
- Discover the advantages and disadvantages of telemedicine
- Uncover distance learning opportunities
- Research the Semantic Web and evaluate the resources found

Additional Research Assignments

These additional research assignments allow you the opportunity to practice the skills you learned in the tutorials as you further explore what the Internet has to offer. As you research and learn about these additional topics, you will also be asked to consider how the Internet impacts your life.

Student Data Files

There are no Student Data Files needed for this section.

Objectives

- Visit Web sites to find information about a disease or medical condition
- Use the skills you learned in this book to evaluate the resources you find
- Examine the resources provided by a credentialing site to evaluate health care information on the Web

In this assignment, you will use and expand the skills you learned in Tutorials 3 and 4.

Locating and Evaluating Health Care Information on the Internet

Many Web sites provide information about medical care, prescription drugs, and related health topics. An increasing number of doctors and other health care professionals have concerns about the quality of medical and health resources available on the Internet because anyone can post anything on the Web—there are no requirements for or restrictions on giving medical advice in this manner. Thus, it is not surprising that recent surveys have shown that a significant number of health information Web sites include information that is incorrect.

When you need information about a specific disease or medical condition, you can use one of the many sites on the Internet to conduct your research. In some cases, you might visit sites with connections to research institutions, medical facilities, and universities. Sites in these categories include the Medical College of Wisconsin HealthLink, WebMD, and the Mayo Clinic. When you visit the sites of these organizations, you can read about the specific disease or medical condition that interests you, and often you will find links to other sites that provide more information. For example, if you are trying to learn about emphysema, a condition commonly associated with smoking cigarettes, one of these sites might provide information about the condition and links to other Web sites, such as the American Lung Association, where you can get more detailed information.

Just like any other Web site, it's up to you to evaluate the quality of the resources and information it provides. Sometimes you can make these determinations easily. For example, the American Lung Association is a well-known health organization that was founded in 1904 to fight tuberculosis and other lung diseases through donations and resources from public and private sources, foundations, and government agencies. Other resources, however, might be more difficult to evaluate because you might not be familiar with them. Fortunately, accrediting agencies that evaluate health information sites have Web sites that provide information about medical sites. Two of these sites are the Health on the Net (HON) Foundation and the URAC Health Web Site Accreditation. You can use the resources at these sites and other credentialing sites to evaluate health resources you find on the Internet. In some cases, the credentialing site might let you search its database to locate sites that it has already deemed credible using its own sets of rules, guidelines, and quality standards.

Student Data Files

There are no student Data Files needed for this assignment.

In this assignment, you will select a specific disease or medical condition that interests you (or your instructor might provide one for you to use), find information about it, and then use a credentialing site to evaluate its resources.

1. Visit at least two health information sites to obtain information about the disease or medical condition you selected. You can use your favorite search engine or directory to find the sites. Gather the information and evaluate the quality of the information and the quality of the Web site from which you obtained it.
2. Visit at least one credentialing or accreditation site and review its contents. Write a summary that describes how the site operates and evaluate whether the site accomplishes its goals.
3. Visit a site maintained by the U.S. government that offers health care information, such as the U.S. Centers for Disease Control and Prevention (CDC) or the U.S. National Institutes of Health MedlinePlus. Explore the site you selected and then write a review of the site in which you describe how the government-sponsored site is different from the privately operated sites you already visited.

Objectives

- Explore the hardware and software required to conduct telemedicine
- Examine the advantages and disadvantages for patients and health care providers participating in telemedicine
- Examine some legal issues for health care providers who participate in telemedicine

In this assignment, you will use and expand the skills you learned in Tutorials 3, 4, and 5.

Telemedicine

Telemedicine (also called **telehealth** or **e-health**) is a way of providing medical care for consumers through the use of telecommunications technology. Telemedicine can enhance and expedite consultations with other doctors and specialists for patients and provide medical care for people in remote areas. Health care providers who utilize telemedicine must have access to the Internet and specialized equipment to conduct their interviews with patients. Some of the technologies that are used are video conferencing (to evaluate a person's mental health or movements), electronic stethoscopes (for listening to a patient's heartbeat), electronic otoscopes (for looking into a patient's ear, nose, or throat), and specialized cameras that are capable of focusing on and magnifying images, usually for dermatological (skin) examinations. In most cases, the data from these specialized technologies are transmitted to another location via a broadband connection to the Internet.

There are many ways that patients and health care providers can benefit from telemedicine. However, there are also some disadvantages, mostly related to cost and legal matters. Most states have individual licensing requirements for physicians practicing in a particular state. For example, current California law prohibits a doctor who is not licensed to practice medicine in California from being directly involved in a telemedicine interaction with a patient located in California. Doctors who are not licensed to practice medicine in Florida can participate in telemedicine interviews with patients located in Florida as long as the telemedicine interview is limited to electronic images. If the out-of-state doctor orders electronic communications, diagnostic imaging, or treatment services for that patient, he or she must have a license to practice medicine in Florida. Other states have exceptions to the in-state rules for out-of-state consultations, and some states have adopted specific laws that affect the use of telemedicine with doctors who are not licensed to practice in their states.

In this assignment, you will use the Internet to learn more about the technology that makes telemedicine possible, the impact of telemedicine on patients and doctors located in the United States, and the legal environment of practicing medicine in this way.

1. Use your favorite search engine or directory to learn more about the Internet and medical technologies that make telemedicine possible. Some good resources include the NLM (National Library of Medicine) National Telemedicine Initiative, the Kansas University Center for Telemedicine and TeleHealth, the Medical College of Georgia Center for Telehealth, and HealthWeb.
2. Select one or more medical specialties, such as dermatology (diseases of the skin), psychiatry (mental health), otolaryngology (ear, nose, and throat), or physical therapy (the treatment or recovery from an injury or other condition that affects mobility). Use your search engine or directory to learn more about how telemedicine is used by health care providers in the medical specialty you selected.

Student Data Files

There are no student Data Files needed for this assignment.

3. Use your search engine or directory to get an overall sense of some of the current and proposed laws that affect telemedicine in the United States. Some potential resources are Telemedicine Today and the Telemedicine Information Exchange. If you were a health care provider, would you feel comfortable using telemedicine to evaluate a patient located in another state? Why or why not? Support your answer with information you learned from your research.

4. Would you participate in telemedicine as a patient if this option were available for treatment? If you were a health care provider, would you participate in telemedicine? Why or why not? Support your answers with information you learned from your research.

Objectives

- Learn about the Mars Student Imaging Project
- Find distance learning programs at your school or in your area
- Consider ways that distance learning can enhance education

In this assignment, you will use and expand the skills you learned in Tutorials 3, 4 and 5.

Advances in Distance Learning

The Internet has enhanced the way that students in grades kindergarten through 12 learn about and participate in scientific research. The National Aeronautics and Space Administration (NASA) began its historic Mars Exploration Rover Mission, which is a long-term robotic exploration of the planet Mars, in June, 2003 and successfully landed a rover on the planet surface in January, 2004. NASA teamed with the Mars Education Program at Arizona State University to offer students in the United States the opportunity to participate in the Mars Student Imaging Project (MSIP), in which students in grades 5 though 10 work in teams with scientists on the Mars project and choose a site on the Mars planet that they would like to map (photograph) from an orbiting rover. Archived data is also available for students to use in research projects. Students participate in the project via distance learning, which is made possible through video conferencing, chats, and teleconferencing. Students complete their projects by writing and submitting a final scientific report for publication in the online MSIP Science Journal.

In this assignment, you will explore the Mars Student Imaging Project site and other distance learning sites that you find on the Internet. Then you will consider the future of using distance learning to enhance education of grade school and college students.

1. Use your favorite search engine or directory to locate the Mars Student Imaging Project Web site, and then spend some time exploring the site to become more familiar with the project. Which Internet technologies make this project possible for students located in the United States?
2. Use your search engine or directory to explore distance learning opportunities at your own school or at other colleges and universities in your area. How do these programs compare to the Mars Student Imaging Project? Which Internet technologies make these programs possible? Are all students able to participate in distance learning programs? Why or why not?
3. Based on your findings, in which other ways can schools use the Internet to enhance the education of grade school and college students? Are there technological impediments that prevent this method of learning? If so, what are they? What advantages do these types of programs offer students and educators?

Student Data Files

There are no student Data Files needed for this assignment.

Additional Research Assignment 4

Objectives

- Use a search tool to find Web sites with information about the Semantic Web
- Use the skills you learned in this book to evaluate the resources you find
- Draw conclusions about the future of the Semantic Web based on your research

In this assignment, you will use and expand the skills you learned in Tutorials 1, 3, and 4.

The Future of the Semantic Web

Tim Berners-Lee, widely regarded as the founding father of the World Wide Web, has been active in promoting and developing a project that blends technologies and information to create a next-generation Web, which he calls the **Semantic Web**. Today, people are the primary users of the Web as a communication medium. An increasing portion of the traffic on the Internet, however, is computers communicating with other computers. The Semantic Web is intended to facilitate automated computer-to-computer communication that can support all types of human activity.

The Semantic Web project, as currently conceived, would result in words on Web pages being tagged with their meanings (the meanings of words are called **semantics**, thus the name "Semantic Web"). These tags would turn the Web into a huge computer-readable database. People could use intelligent programs called **software agents** to read the Web page tags to determine the meaning of the words in their contexts. For example, a software agent could be given an instruction to find an airline ticket with certain terms (such as a specific date, destination city, and a cost limit). The software agent would launch a search on the Web and return an electronic ticket that meets the criteria. Instead of a user having to visit several Web sites to gather information, compare prices and itineraries, and make a decision, the software agent would automatically do the searching, comparing, and purchasing.

The key elements that must be added to Web standards so that software agents can perform these functions (and thus create the Semantic Web) include a well-defined tagging system and a set of standards called an ontology. Many researchers working on the Semantic Web project believe that Extensible Markup Language (XML) could work as a tagging system. Unlike HTML, which has a common set of defined tags (for example, <h1> is the tag for a level-one heading), XML tags are defined by users. Different users can create different definitions for the same XML tag. If a group of users agrees on a common set of definitions, they can all use the same XML tags. For the Semantic Web to work, everyone must agree on a common set of XML tags that will be used on the Web. Semantic Web researchers call this common set of tag definitions a **resource description framework (RDF)**. An **ontology** is a set of standards that defines, in detail, the relationships among RDF standards and specific XML tags within a particular knowledge domain. For example, the ontology for cooking would include concepts such as ingredients, utensils, and

Student Data Files

There are no student Data Files needed for this assignment.

ovens; however, it would also include rules and behavioral expectations, such as identifying ingredients that can be mixed using utensils, the resulting product that can be eaten by people, and ovens that generate heat within a confined area. Ontologies and the RDF would provide the intelligence about the knowledge domain so that software agents could make decisions as humans would.

In this assignment, you will search for information about the Semantic Web and evaluate its potential for future use.

1. Use your favorite search engine or Web directory to find sites with information about the Semantic Web, XML, RDF, and the term "ontology" as it is used in this area of research (the term "ontology" is used in philosophy and other disciplines, so you will need to use some of the techniques you learned in Tutorial 3 to narrow your results). Prepare a report of about 800 words that summarizes your findings on each of the four topics. Include citations to at least two Web pages for each of the four topics in your report.

2. For each of the eight (or more) Web pages you cited in the report required by the previous step, evaluate the quality of the information you obtained and evaluate the overall quality of the Web site from which you obtained it. Summarize your evaluations in your report. Be sure to include the reasons for your evaluations and explain how you performed the evaluations.

3. Using the information you have gathered about the Semantic Web, evaluate the likelihood that it will become a useful part of the Web within the next ten years. Include a summary of your evaluation in your report and cite at least four Web sources that support your arguments.

Glossary/Index

Note: Boldface entries include definitions.

Special Characters

\ (backslash), WEB 9

/ (forward slash), WEB 10

A

Account Wizard dialog box, Thunderbird, WEB 82

AccuWeather, WEB 213

address

e-mail, WEB 72–73, WEB 123

e-mail group, WEB 74. *See also* address book *entries*

Hotmail, creating, WEB 123

IP, APP 20–21, WEB 8

Address bar (Internet Explorer) The toolbar in Internet Explorer into which you can enter URLs directly. WEB 25–27

address book The collection of e-mail addresses maintained by an e-mail program. WEB 81

Address Book window, Thunderbird, WEB 86

address book (Hotmail), WEB 138–142

adding contacts, WEB 138–140

adding groups of contacts, WEB 140–141

addressing messages to groups, WEB 141–142

address book (Outlook Express), WEB 115–119

adding contacts, WEB 115–117

adding groups of contacts, WEB 117–118

addressing messages to groups, WEB 118–119

Advanced Research Projects Agency (ARPA) The agency charged with the task of connecting Department of Defense computers to each other and to weapons installations distributed all over the world. *Also called* Defense Advanced Research Projects Agency (DARPA), APP 13

aggregator A program that lets you read newsfeed content. WEB 88

AlltheWeb, WEB 205–206

AltaVista, WEB 181–182, WEB 204–205

America Online (AOL)

efforts to limit spam, WEB 99

Mozilla Suite, WEB 17

Andreessen, Marc, APP 23, APP 24

animated GIF file A file that combines several Graphics Interchange Format (GIF) images into a single GIF file. WEB 232

anonymous FTP session The process of downloading and uploading files between your computer and a remote Web site while logged on using "anonymous" as your user name. WEB 251–252

anonymous login The process of logging on to a publicly accessible remote computer by specifying the user name "anonymous" and your e-mail address as the password. WEB 251

antivirus software. *See* virus detection software

AOL. *See* America Online (AOL)

appearance of Web resources, WEB 193

ARPA. *See* Advanced Research Projects Agency (ARPA)

ARPANET The wide area network (WAN) created by DARPA in 1969 that grew to become the Internet. APP 14, APP 16, APP 18. *See also* Advanced Research Projects Agency (ARPA)

ASCII mode A file transfer setting in which all data being transferred consists of plain text. WEB 246

ASCII text Text containing only symbols typed from the keyboard. WEB 246

Ask Jeeves, WEB 183–185

Asymmetric Digital Subscriber Line (ADSL). *See* Digital Subscriber Line (DSL)

attachment A file encoded so that it can be carried over the Internet safely with an e-mail message. WEB 74, WEB 75–76

Hotmail, WEB 133–134

Opera M2, WEB 93

Outlook Express, WEB 108–110

saving. *See* saving attached files

Thunderbird, WEB 85

viewing. *See* viewing attached files

viruses in, WEB 75

AU audio file format, WEB 236

audio files on Web, WEB 236, WEB 237–239

AVI (Audio Video Interleaved) format A file format used for video and audio files on the Web that was developed by Microsoft. WEB 237

B

Back button The button you click on a toolbar in a browser to retrace your path through the hyperlinks you have followed. WEB 11, WEB 12, WEB 15

bandwidth The amount of data that can travel through a communications circuit in one second. APP 26–30

banner ad Advertising that appears in a box on a Web page, usually at the top, but sometimes along the side or at the bottom of the page. WEB 161

Bartleby.com, WEB 226

Bcc. *See* blind courtesy copy (Bcc)

Because It's Time Network (BITNET) A network of university computers that eventually became part of the Internet. APP 15

Bergman, Michael, WEB 191

Berners-Lee, Tim, APP 22, APP 23

binary file A file type that can contain text, pictures, movies, sound files, and graphics. WEB 246

binary mode A file transfer setting for files containing graphics, word-processed documents, spreadsheets, and other formatted files. WEB 246

BITNET. *See* Because It's Time Network (BITNET)

bits per second (bps) The basic increment in which bandwidth is measured. APP 26–30

blind courtesy copy (Bcc) The copy of an e-mail message sent to a recipient without that recipient's address appearing in the message so that the message's other recipients are unaware that the Bcc recipient received the message. WEB 74

blog A Web site that contains commentary on current events written by an individual. *Also called* Web log; Weblog, WEB 97–98, WEB 211, WEB 239

body, e-mail message, WEB 73, WEB 74, WEB 76

bookmark, WEB 15

bookmark (Firefox) The URL of a site you have visited that is saved in a special folder in Firefox so you can later return to the site easily without having to remember the URL or search for the page again.

creating, WEB 48–52

saving, WEB 50–51

Bookmarks Sidebar, Mozilla Firefox, WEB 44

Boolean algebra A branch of mathematics and logic in which all values are reduced to one of two values; in most practical applications of Boolean algebra, these two values are true and false. WEB 178

Boolean operator In Boolean algebra, an operator that specifies the logical relationship between the elements it joins, just as the plus sign arithmetic operator specifies the mathematical relationship between the two elements it joins. Most search engines recognize three basic Boolean operators: AND, OR, and NOT. *Also called* logical operator, WEB 178–179

bot. *See* Web robot

bps. *See* bits per second (bps)

broadband Any Internet connection that is faster than POTS. APP 28

browser rendering engine The internal workings of the browser. WEB 17

bug An error in software that can cause a program to halt, malfunction, or damage the user's computer. WEB 261

bulk mail. *See* junk mail

Bush, George W. WEB 98

Bush, Vannevar, APP 21

business activity on Internet, APP 8

businesses, finding on Web, WEB 220–221

byte The basic increment in which file sizes are measured; it contains 8 bits. APP 20

C

cache (or cache folder) The folder on a computer in which a Web browser stores copies of Web pages and Web page elements so it can redisplay those pages faster than if it were to request the pages from the Web server each time they were opened in the browser. WEB 16

Calendar tab (Hotmail) A Web page in Hotmail that contains options for organizing your scheduled appointments and daily calendar.

Hotmail, WEB 129

Calliau, Robert, APP 22

CAN-SPAM law, WEB 99–100

Category 1 cable A type of twisted-pair cable that telephone companies have used for years to carry voice signals; Category 1 cable is inexpensive and easy to install but transmits information much more slowly than other types of cable. APP 11

Category 5 (Cat-5) cable A type of twisted-pair cable developed specifically for carrying data signals rather than voice signals; Category 5 cable is easy to install and carries signals between 10 and 100 times faster than coaxial cable. APP 11

Category 5e (Cat-5e) cable An enhanced Category 5 cable that is constructed of higher quality materials so it can carry signals about ten times faster than regular Category 5 cable. APP 11

CERN, APP 22

circuit switching A centrally controlled, single-connection method for sending information over a network. APP 14

citing Web research resources, WEB 227–229

Clark, James, APP 24

clearinghouse. *See* Web bibliography

client A computer connected to a server computer that can share the resources of the server computer. APP 9

client/server network A way of connecting multiple client computers to a server computer to allow the client computers to share the server computer's resources, such as printers, files, and programs. APP 9–10

Close button The button on the right side of the title bar in a program window that closes the window when clicked.

browser windows, WEB 12

coaxial cable An insulated copper wire encased in a metal shield and then enclosed in plastic insulation; coaxial cable carries signals about 20 times faster than twisted-pair cable, but is considerably more expensive. APP 11

collaboration In the context of sharing documents over the Internet, the method used by multiple developers that allows them to work on the same file without having to download it, edit it, and transfer it back to the original author(s). WEB 280–286

collections In WebDAV, the feature that allows a developer to retrieve a directory listing of files on a server. WEB 281

commerce service provider (CSP) A firm that purchases Internet access from network access points and sells it to businesses, individuals, and smaller ISPs. APP 25–26

communication, Internet, APP 4

complex search, WEB 180–191

AltaVista, WEB 181–182

Ask Jeeves, WEB 183–185

future of Web search tools, WEB 190–191

Google filtered search, WEB 186–188

people to enhance Web directories, WEB 191

search engines with clustering features, WEB 189–190

Compose message tab, Opera, WEB 92

Compose window, Thunderbird, WEB 84

compressed file A file saved in a special format that makes its file size smaller to conserve space and decrease the transfer time from one computer to another. *Also called* zip file, WEB 269–272

computer

connecting to networks, APP 10–12

host, WEB 73

local, WEB 246

Computer Science Network (CSNET) An internet funded by the NSF for educational and research institutions that did not have access to the ARPANET. APP 15

configuring e-mail, Outlook Express, WEB 102–104

connectivity, APP 13–15

Contacts list (Outlook Express) Contains the e-mail addresses in an Outlook Express address book.

Outlook Express, WEB 101

Contacts tab (Hotmail) A Web page in Hotmail that contains options for managing the address book.

Hotmail, WEB 129

content of Web resources, WEB 193

cookie A small file written on a user's computer by a Web server; the Web server reads the cookie when the user revisits the Web site. WEB 15–16

Mozilla Firefox, WEB 56–57

copying text from Web page to WordPad document, WEB 40–41

copyright A right granted by a government to the author or creator of a literary or artistic work that protects the tangible expression of an idea for the specific length of time provided in the copyright law and gives the author or creator the sole and exclusive right to print, publish, or sell the work. WEB 21

fair use, WEB 230–232

ideas, WEB 230

protection, WEB 230

Web resources, WEB 229–232

courtesy copy (Cc) An e-mail message sent to other people in addition to the primary recipient(s). WEB 74

CSNET. *See* Computer Science Network (CSNET)

CSP. *See* commerce service provider (CSP)

current information on Web, WEB 202–208

D

database, search engine, WEB 164–165

DAV. *See* Web Distributed Authoring and Versioning

Dean, Howard, WEB 97–98

deep Web Information stored in a Web site's database and accessible only on dynamic Web pages. *Also called* hidden Web; invisible Web, WEB 191

Defense Advanced Research Projects Agency (DARPA). *See* Advanced Research Projects Agency (ARPA)

Deleted Items folder (Outlook Express) The folder in Outlook Express that temporarily stores deleted e-mail messages until you permanently delete them.

Outlook Express, WEB 101

deleting e-mail messages, WEB 81

Hotmail, WEB 137–138

Outlook Express, WEB 114–115

deleting folders

Hotmail, WEB 137–138

Outlook Express, WEB 114–115

demodulation The process of converting an analog signal to a digital signal. APP 27

destination information on Web, WEB 216–219

detaching The process of saving an e-mail attachment to a file location. WEB 76

dial-up The standard telephone service provided by telephone companies to business and individual customers for voice communications that allows users to transmit data by using a modem at a bandwidth of between 28.8 and 56 Kbps. *Also called* plain old telephone service (POTS), APP 27, APP 29

Digital Subscriber Line or Digital Subscriber Loop (DSL) A type of broadband connection that offers transmission speeds ranging from 100 to 640 Kbps

from the user to the telephone company and from 4.5 to 9 Mbps from the telephone company to the user. *Also called* Asymmetric Digital Subscriber Line (ADSL), APP 27, APP 29

displaying toolbars in Internet Explorer, WEB 14–15

distance learning, ADD 8

DNS (domain name system) software A program on an Internet host computer that coordinates the IP addresses and domain names for all of the computers attached to it. WEB 8

domain name A unique name associated with a specific IP address. WEB 8–9

domain name server The Internet host computer that runs DNS software to coordinate the IP addresses and domain names for every computer attached to it. WEB 8

domain name system software. *See* DNS (domain name system) software

dotted decimal notation A method of writing the parts of a 32-bit IP address as four decimal numbers separated by periods. APP 20

download To retrieve a file from another computer and storing in on your computer. WEB 246

download sites, WEB 259–261

downloading e-mail messages using Opera M2, WEB 93

downloading programs, WEB 261–269

Drafts folder Stores e-mail messages that have been written, but that have not yet been sent.

Hotmail, WEB 136

Outlook Express, WEB 101

DSL. *See* Digital Subscriber Line or Digital Subscriber Loop (DSL)

dynamic Web page An HTML document generated by a Web server in response to a user query; the Web server searches a database of information and creates the HTML document based on that search. WEB 190

E

e-health. *See* telemedicine

electrical interference A flow of unwanted electricity in a wire that is induced from the electromagnetic field created by the electrical current flowing through a nearby wire. APP 10

electronic mail. *See* e-mail

e-mail The transmission of messages over communications networks, such as the Internet. WEB 71–144

    address book. *See* address book *entries*

    beginnings, APP 15

    blogs, WEB 97–98

    detaching files, WEB 76

    Hotmail. *See* Hotmail

    messages. *See* e-mail message

    Outlook Express. *See* Outlook Express

    overview, WEB 72–73

    spam, WEB 79, WEB 86–87, WEB 98–100

    viruses in attachments, WEB 75

    Web-based e-mail services, WEB 95–97

e-mail address A unique identifier consisting of a user name and a host name that represents an individual's or organization's e-mail account on a specific Web server. WEB 72–73

    Hotmail, creating, WEB 123

e-mail message, WEB 73–81

    attachments. *See* attachment; saving attached files

    blind courtesy copy (Bcc) line, WEB 74

    body, WEB 73, WEB 74, WEB 76

    commonly used acronyms, WEB 78

    courtesy copy (Cc) line, WEB 74

    deleting. *See* deleting e-mail messages

    downloading, WEB 93

    emoticons, WEB 78

    filing. *See* filing e-mail messages

    filtering, WEB 79

    forwarding. *See* forward

    header, WEB 73

    Hotmail. *See* Hotmail

    From line, WEB 75

    To line, WEB 74

    netiquette, WEB 77–78

    Outlook Express. *See* Outlook Express

    printing. *See* printing e-mail messages

    queuing, WEB 78

    quoted, WEB 80

    receiving. *See* receiving e-mail messages

    replying to. *See* replying to e-mail messages

    sending. *See* sending e-mail messages

    signature, WEB 76–77

    storing, WEB 79, WEB 94

    Subject line, WEB 74, WEB 75

e-mail program. *See* mail client software

emoticon A text-based symbol used in e-mail and chat rooms to convey humor or emotion. WEB 78

encryption A way of scrambling and encoding data transmissions that reduces the risk that a person who intercepts the Web page as it travels across the Internet will be able to decode and read the transmission's contents. WEB 17

    Internet Explorer (IE), WEB 37

    Mozilla Firefox, WEB 56

Engelbart, Douglas, APP 21

entertainment on Internet, APP 8–9

Ethernet, APP 27

ethics of sharing audio files, WEB 237

evaluation version. *See* limited edition

Expand button, Opera, WEB 90

exploratory question An open-ended question that can be difficult to phrase and for which it can be difficult to determine when you find a good answer. WEB 156

extranet An intranet that permits access by selected outside parties. APP 17

e-zine A Web-based electronic magazine. WEB 239

F

fair use A provision in the U.S. copyright law that, among other things, allows students to use limited amounts of copyrighted information in term papers and other academic reports. WEB 21, WEB 230–232

Fast Ethernet, APP 26, APP 27

favorite (Internet Explorer) The URL of a site you have visited that is saved in a special folder in Internet Explorer so you can later return to the site easily without having to remember the URL or search for the page again. WEB 15

Favorites feature, Internet Explorer, WEB 28–30

    creating new folder, WEB 29–30

    moving existing folders into new folders, WEB 31–32

fiber-optic cable A type of cable that transmits information by pulsing beams of light through very thin strands of glass; fiber-optic cable transmits signals much faster than coaxial cable does, is immune to electrical interference, and is more durable than coaxial cable, but it is harder to work with and is more expensive. APP 11

file

    compressing and decompressing, WEB 269–272

    types, transferring using FTP, WEB 246–248

file compression program A program that decreases the size of one or more files and saves them in a single file. WEB 270–272

file decompression The process of restoring a compressed file to its original state. *Also called* file expansion, WEB 270

file expansion. *See* file decompression

file extension, FTP, WEB 246–248

file transfer mode The way in which files are transferred using FTP, usually binary or ASCII mode. WEB 246

File Transfer Protocol (FTP) That part of the TCP/IP protocol set that includes rules for formatting, ordering, and error-checking files sent across a network. APP 16, WEB 9, WEB 246–275. *See also* FTP *entries*

    compressing and decompressing files, WEB 269–272

    connecting to FTP servers, WEB 248–250

    download sites, WEB 259–261

downloading programs, WEB 261–269

file transfer modes, WEB 246

file types and extensions, WEB 246–248

full-privilege, WEB 252

levels of access for FTP servers, WEB 250–253

navigating FTP sites using Web browsers, WEB 253–256

public directories, WEB 252–253

tracing Internet routes, WEB 272–275

filename, WEB 10

filing e-mail messages, WEB 79

Hotmail, WEB 136–137

Outlook Express, WEB 112–114

filter A feature in an e-mail program that examines the content of an e-mail message and then moves that e-mail message into a designated folder based on criteria defined by the user. WEB 79

filter, search, WEB 180

Firefox. *See* Mozilla Firefox

fixed-point wireless A technology for connecting residential and small business computers to the Internet that is similar to that used by wireless LANs. APP 29

folder

cache, WEB 16

creating in Hotmail, WEB 136–137

deleting. *See* deleting folders

reorganizing Favorites in, WEB 31–32

Folders list (Outlook Express) A list of folders in Outlook Express for receiving, saving, and deleting e-mail messages.

Outlook Express, WEB 101

footer, Page Setup dialog box, WEB 36

form of Web resources, WEB 193

forward The process of sending a copy of a previously sent or received e-mail message to another recipient. WEB 79–80, WEB 93

Hotmail, WEB 135–136

Opera M2, WEB 93

Outlook Express, WEB 111–112

Forward button The button you click on a toolbar in a browser to move forward through the session's history list.

browser windows, WEB 11, WEB 12, WEB 15

forward slash (/), URLs, WEB 10

frame A part of a Web page that appears in its own window within the main Web page window. WEB 16

freeware Software that is available to users at no cost and with no restrictions on its use. WEB 261

From line That part of an e-mail message header containing the e-mail address of a message's sender. WEB 75

FTP. *See* File Transfer Protocol (FTP)

FTP client program A program that transfers files between a computer and an FTP site. WEB 248–249

downloading, WEB 262–265

FTP server. *See* FTP site

FTP session profile The collection of information that identifies a person's user name, password, and the address of an FTP site. WEB 265–266

FTP site A server that stores files and processes requests for those files using the FTP protocol. *Also called* remote computer; FTP server, WEB 246

connecting to, WEB 248–250

levels of access, WEB 250–253

navigating using Web browser, WEB 253–256

Full Screen (Internet Explorer) The browser view in Internet Explorer in which the menu bar is no longer visible and a smaller version of the Standard Buttons toolbar appears at the top of the screen. WEB 24

full-privilege FTP The type of FTP access granted to a user with a user name and password for the FTP site. WEB 252

full-text indexing A method used by some search engines for creating their databases in which the entire content of included Web pages is stored in the database. WEB 165

G

GB. *See* gigabyte (GB)

Gbps. *See* gigabits per second (Gbps)

Gecko engine The browser rendering engine used in Netscape Navigator, the Mozilla browser, and the Mozilla Firefox browser. WEB 17

GIF. *See* Graphics Interchange Format (GIF)

Gigabit Ethernet, APP 26, APP 27

gigabits per second (Gbps) A measure of bandwidth; 1,073,741,824 bits per second (bps). APP 26

gigabyte (GB) A unit of measure for file sizes; it is 1,073,741,824 bytes (8,589,934,592 bits). APP 26

Gmail A Web-based e-mail service powered by Google that is used to send and receive e-mail messages. WEB 96–97

Google Maps, WEB 217–218

Gore, Al, WEB 98

graphic. *See* image; saving graphics to disk

graphic Web page, saving to disk

Internet Explorer, WEB 41–42

Mozilla Firefox, WEB 62–63

graphical transfer process indicator (Internet Explorer) An element of the Internet Explorer status bar that indicates how much of a Web page has loaded from the Web server.

Internet Explorer, WEB 23

graphical user interface (GUI) A way of presenting program output that uses pictures, icons, and other graphical elements rather than text only. APP 22–23

Graphics Interchange Format (GIF) A file format for graphics images that is widely used on the Internet for storing images that have only a few distinct colors, such as line drawings, cartoons, and simple icons. WEB 232

group An address book entry consisting of two or more e-mail addresses. WEB 74. *See also* address book *entries*

grouping operator. *See* precedence operator

GUI. *See* graphical user interface (GUI)

H

header, Page Setup dialog box, WEB 36

heading tag An HTML tag that instructs the Web browser to display the tagged text as a title. APP 22

health care information, locating and evaluating, ADD 4–5

Health on the Net (HON), ADD 4

Help facility, Mozilla Firefox, WEB 58–59

Help system, Internet Explorer, WEB 37–38

hidden Web. *See* deep Web

hiding toolbars in Internet Explorer, WEB 14–15

history list A file in which a Web browser stores the location of each page you visit as you navigate hyperlinks from one Web page to another. WEB 15

    Internet Explorer, WEB 32

    Mozilla Firefox, WEB 52

hit A Web page that is indexed in a search engine's database and contains text that matches the search expression entered into the search engine. Search engines provide hyperlinks to hits on results pages. WEB 160

Home button A button on a Web browser's toolbar that returns the browser to the Web page that opens when the browser is started. WEB 11, WEB 12, WEB 13–14

home page (1) The main page that all of the pages on a particular Web site are organized around and to which they link back or (2) the first page that opens when a particular Web browser program is started or (3) the page that a particular Web browser program loads the first time it is run. Home pages under the second and third definitions also are called start pages. WEB 7. *See also* start page

    default, changing in Internet Explorer, WEB 33–34

    default, changing in Mozilla Firefox, WEB 53

    returning to, using Internet Explorer, WEB 33–34

    returning to, using Mozilla Firefox, WEB 52–53

HON (Health on the Net), ADD 4

hop A connection between two computers as a file travels across a network. WEB 272

host computer A computer connected to the Internet on which users have accounts that are identified by user names. *Also called* host name, WEB 73

host name *See* host computer

HotBot, WEB 203–204

Hotmail A Web-based e-mail service powered by MSN.com that is used to send and receive e-mail messages. WEB 95–96, WEB 119–143, WEB 133–134

    address book, WEB 138–142

    creating accounts, WEB 120–129

    deleting messages and folders, WEB 137–138

    filing and printing messages, WEB 136–137

    forwarding messages, WEB 135–136

    receiving and reading messages, WEB 132–133

    replying to messages, WEB 134–135

    sending messages, WEB 129–132

    Sign Up page, WEB 122

    signing into account, WEB 125–127

    viewing and saving attached files, WEB 133–134

HTML. *See* Hypertext Markup Language (HTML)

HTML anchor tag A tag that enables Web designers to link HTML documents to each other. WEB 5

HTML document A text file that includes HTML tags that indicate how a Web browser should format the text. WEB 5

HTTP. *See* Hypertext Transfer Protocol (HTTP)

hybrid search engine directory A Web site that combines the functions of a Web search engine and a Web directory. WEB 168–172

hyperlink. *See* hypertext link

hypermedia link A connection between an HTML document and a multimedia file, such as a graphics, sound clip, or video file. WEB 7

hypertext A system in which text on one page links to text on other pages.

    origins, APP 21

hypertext link Instructions that point to other HTML documents or to another section of the same document. *Also called* hyperlink; link, APP 22, WEB 5–7

    hypermedia, WEB 7

    hypertext. *See* hypertext link

    navigating between using mouse in Internet Explorer, WEB 27–28

    navigating between using mouse in Mozilla Firefox, WEB 47–48

Hypertext Markup Language (HTML) A language that includes a set of codes (or tags) attached to text that describes the relationships among text elements. APP 22, WEB 5

hypertext server A computer that stores HTML documents and lets other computers connect to it and read those documents. APP 22

Hypertext Transfer Protocol (HTTP) The communication protocol used to transfer Web pages from a Web server to a Web browser. WEB 9

I

ICQmail, WEB 97

identity of Web resources, WEB 192

IETF. *See* Internet Engineering Task Force (IETF)

image

    saving. *See* saving graphics to disk on Web, WEB 232–236

IMAP (Internet Message Access Protocol) A protocol for retrieving e-mail messages from a mail server. WEB 72

Inbox folder The folder in which e-mail messages received from the mail server are stored. WEB 101, WEB 136

Inbox page, Hotmail, WEB 128–129

Inbox window

    Outlook Express, WEB 101

    Thunderbird, WEB 83, WEB 85, WEB 87

inclusion operator. *See* precedence operator

index.html The default name for the HTML document that serves as a Web site's home or main page. WEB 10

information resources on Internet, APP 4–7, WEB 201–240

    audio, WEB 236, WEB 237–239

    citing Web research resources, WEB 227–229

    copyright issues, WEB 229–232

    current information, WEB 202–208

    finding businesses, WEB 220–221

    finding people, WEB 222

    future of electronic publishing, WEB 239

    health care, ADD 4–5

    images and graphics, WEB 232–236

    library resources, WEB 223–225

    maps and destination information, WEB 216–219

    news, WEB 209–212

    privacy concerns, WEB 222

    text resources, WEB 225–227

    video, WEB 237

    weather reports, WEB 213–215

Integrated Services Digital Network (ISDN) A type of DSL that allows data transmission at bandwidths of up to 128 Kbps. APP 27, APP 29

intellectual property, A general term that includes all products, both tangible and intangible, of the human mind. WEB 229

interconnected network A general term for any network of networks. *Also called* internet, WEB 4

Internet A specific worldwide collection of interconnected networks whose owners have voluntarily agreed to share resources and network connections.

    business activity, APP 8

    commercialization, APP 24–25

    communication, APP 4

    entertainment, APP 8–9

    etiquette, WEB 77–78

    growth, APP 18–20

    information resources, APP 4–7

    new structure, APP 19–20

    origins, APP 12–18

    overview, WEB 4

    software, APP 4–7

    tracing routes

        business activity, WEB 272–275

internet. *See* interconnected network

Internet2 A network being developed by a group of universities and the NSF that will have backbone bandwidths that exceed 1 Gbps. APP 28

Internet access provider (IAP). *See* Internet service provider (ISP)

Internet Archive, WEB 227

Internet Connection Wizard dialog box, WEB 103

Internet Corporation for Assigned Names and Numbers (ICANN) The organization that since 1998 has been responsible for managing the most commonly-used top-level domain names on the Internet. WEB 8–9

Internet Engineering Task Force (IETF) A self-organized group that makes technical contributions to the Internet and related technologies. It is the main body that develops new Internet standards. APP 17, WEB 281

Internet Explorer. *See* Microsoft Internet Explorer

Internet host A computer that connects a LAN or WAN to the Internet. APP 18

Internet Message Access protocol. *See* IMAP (Internet Message Access Protocol)

Internet Protocol (IP) A part of the TCP/IP set of rules for sending data over a network. APP 15

Internet Protocol address. *See* IP (Internet Protocol) address

Internet Security properties dialog box, WEB 23, WEB 24

Internet service provider (ISP) A firm that purchases Internet access from network access points and sells it to businesses, individuals, and smaller ISPs. *Also called* Internet access provider (IAP), APP 25

Internet Worm A program launched by Robert Morris in 1988 that used weaknesses in e-mail programs and operating systems to distribute itself to some of the computers that were then connected to the Internet. The program created multiple copies of itself on the computers it infected, which then consumed the processing power of the infected computers and prevented them from running other programs. APP 18

intranet A LAN or WAN that uses the TCP/IP protocol but does not connect to sites outside the host firm or organization. APP 17

invisible Web. *See* deep Web

IP. *See* Internet Protocol (IP)

IP (Internet Protocol) address A number that uniquely identifies each computer connected to the Internet, usually expressed as a series of decimal numbers separated by periods. APP 20–21, WEB 8

IP version 4 (IPv4) The IP addressing system currently in use on the Internet that uses a 32-bit number to label each address on the Internet. APP 20

IP version 6 (IPv6) The IP addressing system approved in 1997 as the protocol that would replace IPv4; IPv6 is more secure and has more than a billion more addresses available than IPv4. APP 20

iRider A Web browser developed by Wymea Bay that is designed for power users. WEB 19–20

ISDN. *See* Integrated Services Digital Network (ISDN)

ISP. *See* Internet service provider (ISP)

J

JANET. *See* Joint Academic Network (JANET)

Joint Academic Network (JANET) An internet established by U.K. universities. APP 16

Joint Photographic Experts Group (JPEG) A file format for graphics images that is widely used on the Internet for storing images that contain many colors and few sharp edges, such as photographs and continuous-tone art. WEB 233

JPEG. *See* Joint Photographic Experts Group (JPEG)

junk mail Unsolicited e-mail messages sent to large numbers of people to promote products, services, and in some cases, illegal or illicit items or services. *Also called* spam; bulk mail; unsolicited commercial e-mail, WEB 79, WEB 98–100. *See also* spam

   Thunderbird, WEB 86–87

Junk Mail folder (Hotmail) A folder in Hotmail that stores e-mail messages from senders that you specify as bulk mailers, advertisers, or any address from which you don't want to receive mail. WEB 136

K

KB. *See* kilobyte (KB)

Kbps. *See* kilobits per second (Kbps)

Kerry, John, WEB 98

kilobits per second (Kbps) A measure of bandwidth; 1,024 bps. APP 26

kilobyte (KB) A unit of measure for file sizes; it is 1,024 bytes (8,192 bits). APP 26, WEB 75

L

LAN. *See* local area network (LAN)

legal issues, sharing audio files, WEB 237

library resources on Web, WEB 223–225

limited edition A restricted version of a program that provides most of the functionality of the full version that is for sale. *Also called* evaluation version, WEB 262

link. *See* hypertext link

LISTSERV Software for running mailing lists on IBM mainframe computers. APP 16

local area network (LAN) Any of several ways of connecting computers to each other when the computers are located close to each other (no more than a few thousand feet apart). APP 9–10, APP 17, WEB 4

local computer The name given to a client when it connects to an FTP site. WEB 246

Location bar (Firefox) The toolbar in Firefox into which you can enter URLs directly.

   Mozilla Firefox, WEB 45–46

location operator A Web search engine operator that lets you search for terms that appear close to each other in the text of a Web page. The most common is the NEAR operator. *Also called* proximity operator, WEB 180

locking In WebDAV, the process that prevents users from simultaneously editing files. WEB 281

log on The process of identifying yourself to a computer with a user name and password. WEB 250

logical operator. *See* Boolean operator

login, anonymous, WEB 251

lossy compression A file compression procedure that erases some elements of the graphic; the greater the level of compression, the more graphic detail is lost. WEB 233

M

Mail button, Opera, WEB 90

mail client software An e-mail program that requests mail delivery from a mail server to the user's computer. *Also called* e-mail program, WEB 72, WEB 81–94. *See also specific programs*

Mail panel, Opera, WEB 90

mail server A hardware and software system that determines from the recipient's e-mail address one of several electronic routes on which to send the message. WEB 72

Mail tab (Hotmail) A Web page in Hotmail that contains a list of message that you have received and provides options for working with e-mail messages. WEB 128

Mail tab, Opera, WEB 91

mailing list An e-mail address that takes any message it receives and forwards it to any user who has subscribed to the list. APP 16

Manage Folders page, Hotmail, WEB 136–137

MapQuest, WEB 216

maps on Web, WEB 216–219

margins, Page Setup dialog box, WEB 36

Mars Student Imaging Project (MSIP), ADD 8

Maximize button The button on the right side of the title bar in a program window that maximizes the size of the window to fill the screen when clicked. WEB 12

MB. *See* megabyte (MB)

Mbps. *See* megabits per second (Mbps)

megabits per second (Mbps) A measure of bandwidth; 1,048,576 bps. APP 26

megabyte (MB) A unit of measure for file sizes; it is 1,048,576 bytes (8,388,608 bits). APP 26

Memex A memory-extension device envisioned by Vannevar Bush in 1945 that stored all of a person's books, records, letters, and research results on microfilm; the idea included mechanical aids to help users consult their collected knowledge quickly and flexibly. APP 21

menu bar The top row in a program window that provides a convenient way for you to execute typical File, Edit, View, and Help commands and specialized commands for the browser that enable you to navigate the Web. WEB 11, WEB 12, WEB 13
   Internet Explorer, WEB 24

message body The content of an e-mail message. WEB 73, WEB 74, WEB 76

message header The part of an e-mail message containing information about the message's sender, recipient(s), and subject. WEB 73

message list (Outlook Express) A list of summary information for each e-mail message in the currently selected folder in Outlook Express.
   Outlook Express, WEB 101

Message page, Hotmail, WEB 132

meta tag An HTML element that a Web page creator places in a Web page header to inform Web robots about the page's content. WEB 164

metasearch engine A tool that accepts a search expression and transmits it to several search engines that run the search expression against their databases of Web page information and return results that the metasearch engine consolidates and reports. WEB 173–175

Microsoft Internet Explorer (Internet Explorer) A popular Web browser program. WEB 11, WEB 22–42
   entering URLs in Address bar, WEB 25–27
   FTP site, WEB 254
   Help system, WEB 37–38
   hiding and showing toolbars, WEB 24–25
   hyperlink navigation using mouse, WEB 27–28

main program window, WEB 22
market position, WEB 17
menu bar, WEB 24
printing Web pages, WEB 34–36
program window, WEB 11–13
returning to previously viewed Web pages, WEB 28–34
saving Web pages. *See* saving Web pages in Internet Explorer
Standard Buttons toolbar, WEB 23
starting, WEB 22–23
status bar, WEB 23–24
Web page security, WEB 36–37

Microsoft Outlook Express (Outlook Express) An e-mail client program. WEB 100–119
   address book, WEB 115–119
   configuring e-mail, WEB 102–104
   deleting messages and folders, WEB 114–115
   filing messages, WEB 112–114
   forwarding messages, WEB 111–112
   printing messages, WEB 114
   reading messages, WEB 108
   receiving messages, WEB 107–108
   replying to messages, WEB 110–111
   sending messages, WEB 104–106
   viewing and saving attached files, WEB 108–110

MIDI (Musical Instrument Digital Interface) An audio file format that stores digital information about each element of a sound, including its pitch, length, and volume. WEB 236

MILNET (Military Network) That part of ARPANET, created in 1984, reserved for military uses that required high levels of security. APP 16

MIME (Multipurpose Internet Mail Extensions) A protocol specifying how to encode nontext data, such as graphics and sound, so you can send it over the Internet. WEB 72

Minimize button The button on the right side of the title bar in a program window that minimizes the window to its button on the taskbar when clicked.
   browser windows, WEB 12

mirror site A replica of an existing server that provides an alternate location for downloading files. WEB 272

modem Abbreviated form of modulator-demodulator; a device that converts a computer's digital signal to an analog signal (modulation) so it can travel through a telephone line, and also converts analog signals arriving through a telephone line to digital signals that the computer can use (demodulation). APP 27

modulation The process of converting a digital signal to an analog signal. APP 27

Morris, Robert, Jr. APP 18

Mosaic The first program with a GUI that could read HTML and use hyperlinks in HTML documents to navigate from page to page on computers anywhere on the Internet; Mosaic was the first Web browser that became widely available for PCs. APP 23, APP 24, WEB 17

moving. *See also* navigating
   Favorites folders into new folders, WEB 31–32

Moving Picture Experts Group (MPEG) format A series of compressed file formats for storing video and audio files on the Web. WEB 237

Mozilla, APP 24

Mozilla Firefox (Firefox) A stand-alone Web browser developed by the Mozilla open source project. WEB 11, WEB 43–64
   Bookmarks Sidebar, WEB 44
   cookies, WEB 56–57
   FTP site, WEB 255
   Help facility, WEB 58–59
   hyperlink navigation using mouse, WEB 47–48

Location bar, WEB 45–46

Navigation toolbar, WEB 45–46

printing Web pages, WEB 54–55

program window, WEB 12–13

returning to previously visited Web pages, WEB 48–53

saving Web pages. *See* saving Web pages in Firefox

starting, WEB 43–44

Web page security, WEB 55–56

Mozilla project, WEB 17

Mozilla Suite A combination of software applications that the Mozilla open source project developed. The suite consists of a Web browser that runs on the Gecko engine, an e-mail client and newsreader (Mozilla Messenger), an HTML editor (Mozilla Composer), and an instant messaging chat client (ChatZilla). WEB 17–18

Mozilla Thunderbird (Thunderbird) A stand-alone e-mail client program that is part of the Mozilla open source project. WEB 82–89

MP3 file. *See* MPEG Audio Layer 3

MPEG. *See* Moving Picture Experts Group (MPEG) format

MPEG Audio Layer 3 MPEG format's audio track; files in the MP3 format are somewhat lower in quality than WAV format files, but they are 90 percent smaller.

   ethical and legal concerns regarding sharing audio files, WEB 237

   file format, WEB 237

   legal file distribution, WEB 238–239

MSIP (Mars Student Imaging Project), ADD 8

MSN Hotmail Plans page, WEB 121

MSN Maps and Directions, WEB 217

Musical Instrument Digital Interface. *See* MIDI (Musical Instrument Digital Interface)

My Docs Online, WEB 278

N

name space management In WebDAV, a feature that lets a developer copy, move, and rename files on a server. WEB 281

NAP. *See* network access point (NAP)

NAT. *See* network address translation (NAT) device

natural language query interface An interface that allows users to enter a question exactly as they would ask a person that question. The search engine analyzes the question using knowledge it has been given about the grammatical structure of questions and converts the natural language question into a search query. WEB 165

navigating

   hyperlinks, using mouse, WEB 27–28, WEB 47–48

   returning to home page using Internet Explorer, WEB 33–34

   returning to previously visited Web pages. *See* returning to previously visited Web pages

Navigation toolbar (Firefox) A toolbar in Firefox that contains buttons for commonly-used Web browsing commands.

   Mozilla Firefox, WEB 45–46

NCP. *See* Network Control Protocol (NCP)

NCP (NetWare Core Protocol), APP 15

Nelson, Ted, APP 21

netiquette The set of commonly accepted rules that represent proper behavior on the Internet. WEB 77–78

Netscape Navigator The first commercially successful Web browser, Netscape Navigator. APP 24, WEB 17

NetWare Core Protocol (NCP), APP 15

network A structure linking computers and other devices together for the purpose of sharing resources such as printers and files. WEB 4. *See also* Internet

   client/server, APP 9–10

   commercial interest, APP 17–18

   connecting computers, APP 10–12

   e-mail. *See* e-mail; e-mail messages

   interconnecting, APP 16–17, WEB 4

   LAN, WEB 4

   new uses, APP 16

   WAN, WEB 4

   wireless, APP 11–12

network access point (NAP) The points at which local portions of the Internet connect to its main network backbone. APP 19

network address translation (NAT) device A computer or piece of network hardware that converts private IP addresses into normal IP addresses so that packets originating within a subnet can be transmitted on the Internet. APP 20

network backbone The long-distance lines and supporting technology that transport large amounts of data between major network nodes. APP 16

Network Control Protocol (NCP) A set of rules for formatting, ordering, and error-checking data used by the ARPANET and other early forerunners of the Internet. APP 15

network interface card (NIC) A card or other device inserted into or attached to a computer that allows it to be connected to a network. APP 9

network node, APP 10

network operating system Software that runs on a server computer that allows client computers to be connected to it and share its resources. APP 9

network place In Windows, a shortcut to a connection to a Web site, FTP, network location (such as a local area network), or online storage provider. WEB 284–286

New Message page, Hotmail, WEB 130

New Message window, Outlook Express, WEB 105

news on Web, WEB 202–208

news search engine A Web site that allows searches of the content of current news stories in multiple publications and wire services. WEB 211–212

news stories, finding on Web, WEB 209–212

NIC. *See* network interface card (NIC)

nickname An abbreviated name, such as "Mom," that represents an e-mail address in an address book for an e-mail program.
address book, WEB 81

node (network node) Each computer, printer, or other device that is attached to a network. APP 10

Norton AntiVirus, WEB 256, WEB 257, WEB 258

NSFnet, APP 16

O

objectivity of Web resources, WEB 192

OC. *See* optical carrier (OC)

octet An 8-bit number. This term is often used instead of "byte" by persons working with computer networks. APP 20

online storage services, WEB 275–286
    collaborative authoring, WEB 280–286
    providers, WEB 276–280

ontology A set of standards that defines, in detail, the relationships among RDF standards and specific XML tags within a particular knowledge domain. ADD 9–10

open architecture An approach that allows each network in an internet to continue using its own protocols and data transmission methods for moving data internally. APP 15

open-source software Software that is created and maintained by volunteer programmers; the software is made available to users at no charge. APP 24

Opera A Web browser program that is not widely used, but is becoming more popular. WEB 18–19

Opera for Mobile An Opera software program that gives users of mobile devices a fully functional Internet browser. WEB 19

Opera M2 An integrated e-mail client program that is part of the Opera Web browser. WEB 90–94

optical carrier (OC) A type of leased telephone line that uses optical fiber. APP 28

orientation, Page Setup dialog box, WEB 36

Outbox folder (Outlook Express) The folder in Outlook Express that stores outgoing e-mail messages that have not been sent.
    Outlook Express, WEB 101

Outlook Express. *See* Microsoft Outlook Express

P

Packet Internet Groper. *See* ping (Packet Internet Groper)

packet switching A method for sending information over a network in which files and messages are divided into packets that are labeled electronically with codes for their origins and destinations, sent through the network, each possibly by a different path, and then reassembled at their destination. APP 14

page ranking A method used by search engines to grade (rank) Web pages by the number of other Web pages that link to them so that the URLs of Web pages with high rankings can be presented first on the search results page. WEB 165

Page Setup dialog box, WEB 35–36
    Mozilla Firefox, WEB 54

page tab A way of showing multiple Web pages within the Web page area in a browser. WEB 12, WEB 13

paper size, Page Setup dialog box, WEB 36

paper source, Page Setup dialog box, WEB 36

parsing The work that a search engine does when it analyzes a natural language query to convert it into a search query. The search engine uses knowledge it has been given about the grammatical structure of questions to perform the parsing task. WEB 165

ping (Packet Internet Groper) A program that tests a computer to determine if it is connected to the Internet. WEB 273

plagiarism Use of material (whether it is in the public domain or is protected by copyright) without crediting the source. WEB 231

plain old telephone service (POTS). *See* dial-up

plug-in A program that is a software extension of a Web browser. WEB 236

POP (Post Office Protocol) One of the Internet-defined procedures that handles incoming e-mail messages. POP is a standard, extensively used protocol that is part of the Internet suite of recognized protocols. WEB 72

POTS. *See* dial-up

precedence operator An operator that clarifies the grouping within complex search expressions, usually indicated by parentheses or double quotation marks. *Also called* inclusion operator; grouping operator, WEB 179–180

preview pane (Outlook Express) The area that appears below the message list in Outlook Express and displays the content of the selected e-mail message in the message list.
    Outlook Express, WEB 102

printing e-mail messages, WEB 79
    Hotmail, WEB 136–137
    Outlook Express, WEB 114

printing Web pages, WEB 16
    Internet Explorer, WEB 34–36
    Mozilla Firefox, WEB 54–55
    Page Setup dialog box, WEB 35–36

privacy concerns with white pages sites, WEB 222

private IP (Internet Protocol) address A series of IP numbers that have been set aside for subnet use within LANs and WANs; These IP addresses are not permitted on packets that travel on the Internet. APP 20

Project Gutenberg, WEB 226

properties In WebDAV, the feature that lets a developer store, delete, and revise information about Web pages, including the page's creator and last revision date. WEB 281

protocol A collection of rules for formatting, ordering, and error-checking data sent across a network. WEB 72

proximity operator. *See* location operator

public domain Copyrighted works or works that are eligible for copyright protection whose copyrights have expired or been relinquished voluntarily by the copyright owner. You are free to copy text, images, and other items in the public domain without obtaining permission. WEB 229

Q

query. *See* search expression

question, search, WEB 156–158

queue A file location in an e-mail client in which messages are temporarily stored prior to being sent. WEB 78

QuickTime A browser extension that plays video, sound, music, 3-D, and virtual reality on Macintoshes, PCs, and wireless devices. WEB 237

quoted message That portion of the body of a sender's original message that you include in a reply to the sender. WEB 80

R

RDF. *See* resource description framework (RDF)

reading messages

    Hotmail, WEB 132–133

    Outlook Express, WEB 108

Really Simple Syndication (RSS) An XML file format that makes it possible to share updates such as headlines and other Web site content via a newsfeed, which is simply a file containing summaries of stories and news from a Web log or Web site.

    Opera M2, WEB 94

    Thunderbird, WEB 88–89

Received tab, Opera, WEB 93

receiving e-mail messages, WEB 79

    Hotmail, WEB 132–133

    Outlook Express, WEB 107–108

Refresh button (Internet Explorer) A button on the Internet Explorer toolbar that loads the page that appears in the browser window again. WEB 11, WEB 16

refreshing Web pages, WEB 33

    Internet Explorer window, WEB 11, WEB 16

Reload button (Firefox) A button on the Firefox toolbar that loads the page that appears in the browser window again. WEB 12, WEB 16, WEB 52

reloading Web pages, WEB 16

    Mozilla Firefox, WEB 12, WEB 16, WEB 52

remote computer. *See* FTP site

reply An e-mail message sent in response to a previously received e-mail message. WEB 81

    Hotmail, WEB 134–135

    Outlook Express, WEB 110–111

resource description framework (RDF) A set of standards for the XML tags that will be used on the Semantic Web. ADD 9

resource list. *See* Web bibliography

Restore Down button The button on the right side of the title bar in a program window that restores the window to whatever size it was before it was maximized when clicked.

    browser windows, WEB 12

results page Web pages generated by a Web search engine containing hyperlinks to Web pages that contain matches to the search expression entered into the search engine. WEB 160

returning to previously visited Web pages, WEB 15–16

    Internet Explorer, WEB 28–34

    Mozilla Firefox, WEB 48–53

root directory The top-level folder of a file system that contains files and other folders. WEB 253

router A computer on a packet-switching internet that accepts packets from other networks and determines the best way to move each packet forward to its destination. APP 14

routing algorithm The program on a router computer in a packet-switching internet that determines the best path on which to send packets. APP 14

RSS. *See* Really Simple Syndication (RSS)

S

Saved Search folder A mail folder in Thunderbird that, when clicked, searches every folder and message for matches using criteria that you specify.

    Thunderbird, WEB 87, WEB 88

saving

    bookmarks in Mozilla Firefox, WEB 50–51

    Web pages, WEB 16. *See also* saving Web pages in Firefox; saving Web pages in Internet Explorer

saving attached files

    Hotmail, WEB 133–134

    Outlook Express, WEB 108–110

saving graphics to disk

    Firefox, WEB 62–63

    saving graphics to disk, WEB 41–42

saving Web pages in Firefox, WEB 59–63

    saving graphics to disk, WEB 62–63

    saving text to file, WEB 60–62

    saving to disk, WEB 59–60

saving Web pages in Internet Explorer, WEB 38–42

    saving graphics to disk, WEB 41–42

    saving text to file, WEB 39–41

    saving to disk, WEB 38–39

scroll bar A bar at the right or bottom of a program window that allows you to move through the displayed document or Web page by clicking the scroll buttons or dragging the scroll bars. WEB 12

search engine A Web site (or part of a Web site) that finds other Web pages that match a search expression. WEB 159–177

    databases, WEB 164–165

    directories, WEB 166–172

    features, WEB 165–166, WEB 189–190

    finding news stories, WEB 203–206

hybrid search engine directories, WEB 168–172

metasearch engines, WEB 173–175

overview, WEB 159–162

using more than one, WEB 162–164

search expression The word or phrase that you enter into a Web search engine; an expression might include instructions that tell the search engine how to conduct its search. *Also called* query; search question, WEB 159

search filter A Web search engine feature that allows you to eliminate Web pages from a search based on attributes such as language, date, domain, host, or page component (hyperlink, image tag, title tag). WEB 180

Ask Jeeves, WEB 183–185

Google, WEB 186–188

search question. *See* search expression

searching the Web, WEB 155–196

Boolean operators, WEB 178–179

complex searches. *See* complex search

evaluating Web research resources, WEB 191–195

filters, WEB 180

search engines. *See* search engine

search expression operators, WEB 179–180

strategy, WEB 158–159

types of questions, WEB 156–158

wildcard characters, WEB 180

security

encryption, WEB 17, WEB 37, WEB 56

Internet Explorer, WEB 36–37

Mozilla Firefox, WEB 55–56

Security indicator button, WEB 36, WEB 55

security indicator button A small picture of a padlock that appears at the right edge of the status bar at the bottom of a browser window that you can double-click to check some of the security elements of a Web page; the button will display as either an open padlock icon or a closed padlock icon to indicate whether the Web page was encrypted during transmission from the Web server.

Internet Explorer, WEB 36

Mozilla Firefox, WEB 55

security zone (Internet Explorer) Classification levels of Web page security risk in Internet Explorer.

Internet Explorer, WEB 23

Semantic Web A next-generation Web that facilitates automated computer-to-computer communication in which the computers understand the meaning of the communication and can act on it. ADD 9–10

semantics The meanings of words. ADD 9

sending e-mail messages, WEB 78

Hotmail, WEB 129–132

Outlook Express, WEB 104–106

Sent Items folder (Outlook Express) The folder in Outlook Express that stores copies of sent e-mail messages. WEB 101

Sent Message Confirmation page, Hotmail, WEB 131

Sent Messages folder (Hotmail) The folder in Hotmail that stores copies of sent e-mail messages. WEB 136

server A computer that accepts requests from other (client) computers that are connected to it and share some or all of its resources, such as printers, files, or programs, with those client computers. APP 9

domain name, WEB 8

hypertext, APP 22

Web, WEB 4, WEB 5

SGML. *See* Standard Generalized Markup Language (SGML)

shareware A program that you can use during an evaluation period, usually for free. When the evaluation period ends, you must either uninstall the program or pay a fee to its developer to continue using it. WEB 261

signature One or more lines in an e-mail message that provide more detailed information about the sender (such as his or her name, address, and phone number).

e-mail message, WEB 76–77

sign-in page, Hotmail, WEB 120

signing into Hotmail account, WEB 125–127

SMTP (Simple Mail Transfer Protocol) One of the Internet-defined protocols that determines which path an e-mail message takes on the Internet. WEB 72

software

DNS, WEB 8

Internet, APP 4–7

open-source, APP 24

software agent An intelligent program that can read Web page tags to determine the meaning of the words in their contexts and authorize actions based on its understanding of those words. ADD 9

spam. *See* junk mail

specific question A question that can be phrased easily and one for which the answer is readily recognizable. WEB 156

spider. *See* Web robot

sponsored links A link that appears on a search engine results page because an advertiser paid to have it placed there. WEB 161

Standard Buttons toolbar (Internet Explorer) The toolbar in Internet Explorer that includes buttons to execute frequently used commands for browsing the Web.

Internet Explorer, WEB 23

Standard Generalized Markup Language (SGML) The document description language on which HTML is based. APP 22

start page The page that opens when a Web browser program is started or the page that a particular Web browser program loads the first time it is run. *Also called* home page, WEB 8

starting
Internet Explorer, WEB 22–23
Mozilla Firefox, WEB 43–44

static Web page An HTML document that exists on a Web server. WEB 190

status bar The bar at the bottom of a browser window that includes information about the browser's operations, usually, the name of the Web page that is loading, the load status (partial or complete), and important messages, such as "Document: Done"; some Web sites send messages as part of their Web pages that are displayed in the status bar as well. WEB 11, WEB 12, WEB 13
Internet Explorer, WEB 23–24

stemming In an online search, the use of the root form of a word to find results containing the root word and its variations, which are created by adding standard endings to the root word. WEB 165

stop words A common word, such as and, the, it, or by that most search engines (even those that claim to be full-text indexed search engines) omit from their databases when they store information about Web pages. WEB 165

storage services, online. *See* online storage services

storing e-mail messages, WEB 79
Opera M2, WEB 94

strategy for Web searches, WEB 158–159

streaming transmission A technique for transferring large sound and video files on the Web in which the Web server sends the first part of the file to the Web browser, which begins playing the file immediately, and while the browser plays the file, the server sends the next segment of the file. WEB 237

subject guide. *See* Web bibliography

Subject line That part of an e-mail message header that gives a brief summary of the message's content and purpose.
e-mail messages, WEB 74, WEB 75

subnetting The use of reserved private IP addresses within LANs and WANs to provide additional address space. APP 20

SuperPages.com, WEB 220–221

Switchboard, WEB 222

T

T1 connection A high-bandwidth (1.544 Mbps) data transmission connection used as part of the Internet backbone and by large firms and ISPs as a connection to the Internet. APP 28

T3 connection A high-bandwidth (44.736 Mbps) data transmission connection used as part of the Internet backbone and by large firms and ISPs as a connection to the Internet. APP 28

tag A markup code that tells the Web browser software how to display text. APP 22, WEB 5

TCP/IP A combined set of rules for data transmission; TCP includes rules that computers on a network use to establish and break connections, and IP includes rules for routing of individual data packets. APP 15

telehealth. *See* telemedicine

telemedicine A way of providing medical care for consumers through the use of telecommunications technology. *Also called* telehealth; e-health, ADD 6–7

Telnet A protocol that lets users log in to their computer accounts from remote sites. APP 16, WEB 9

Temporary Internet Files folder (Internet Explorer) The folder within the Windows folder in which Internet Explorer stores copies of Web pages you have recently viewed. WEB 33

text resources on Web, WEB 225–227

text Web page, saving to file
Internet Explorer, WEB 39–41
Mozilla Firefox, WEB 60–62

Thunderbird. *See* Mozilla Thunderbird

title bar The bar at the top of a program window that shows the name of the open Web page or document and the program

name; you can double-click the title bar to resize the program window quickly.
browser windows, WEB 11, WEB 12

TLD. *See* top-level domain (TLD)

To line That part of an e-mail message header containing the message recipient's full e-mail address. WEB 74

Today tab (Hotmail) The Web page that first opens when you log on to your Hotmail account and includes current information about the day's current events, your mailbox, and appointments that you have scheduled using your calendar. WEB 128

toggle A type of control used to switch between two options or states, similar to a push button on a television set, that you press to turn it on and off. WEB 24, WEB 45

toolbar, hiding and showing in Internet Explorer, WEB 14–15

top-level domain (TLD) The last part of a domain name, which is the unique name that is associated with a specific IP address by a program that runs on an Internet host computer. WEB 8

tracert Short for "trace route," a Windows program that shows the hops between your computer and a remote computer. WEB 273–275

transfer progress report (Internet Explorer) A section of the status bar in Internet Explorer that presents status messages, such as the URL of a page while it is loading, the text "Done" after a page has loaded, or the URL of any hyperlink on the page when you move the pointer over it.
Internet Explorer, WEB 23

transfer protocol The set of rules that computers use to move files from one computer to another on an internet; the most common transfer protocol used on the Internet is HTTP. WEB 9

Transmission Control Protocol (TCP) A part of the TCP/IP set of rules for sending data over a network. APP 15

Trash Can folder (Hotmail) The folder in Hotmail that temporarily stores deleted messages until you delete them permanently. WEB 136

twisted-pair cable A type of cable made by twisting two or more insulated copper wires around each other and enclosing them in another layer of plastic insulation; used by telephone companies for years to wire residences and businesses. APP 10, APP 11

U

UCE (unsolicited commercial e-mail). *See* junk mail

Uniform Resource Locator (URL) The four-part addressing scheme for an HTML document that tells Web browser software which transfer protocol to use when transporting the document, the domain name of the computer on which the document resides, the pathname of the folder or directory on the computer in which the document resides, and the document's filename. WEB 9–10
  entering in Address bar, WEB 25–27
  entering in Mozilla Firefox Location bar, WEB 45–46

UNIX, WEB 246

unsolicited commercial e-mail (UCE). *See* junk mail

upload The process of sending a file from your computer to another computer. WEB 246

URAC Health Web Site Accreditation, ADD 4

URL. *See* Uniform Resource Locator (URL)

Usenet newsgroup, APP 16

user name A unique name that identifies an account on a server. WEB 72–73

User's News Network (Usenet) newsgroups A network that allows users to post information and responses to that information. APP 16

V

video on Web, WEB 237
viewing attached files
  Hotmail, WEB 133–134
  Outlook Express, WEB 108–110

virtual library A Web site that includes resources similar to a physical library. WEB 175–177. *See also* Web bibliography

virus A malicious program that causes harm to a computer's disk or files. WEB 75

virus definition. *See* virus signature

virus detection software A program that regularly scans the files on a computer and files being downloaded to the computer and compares them to a signature that known viruses carry. *Also called* antivirus software, WEB 256–258

virus pattern. *See* virus signature

virus signature A sequence (string) of characters that is always present in a particular virus. *Also called* virus pattern; virus definition, WEB 256

W

WAN. *See* wide area network (WAN)

Wave format (WAV) A file format jointly developed by Microsoft and IBM that stores digitized audio waveform information at a user-specified sampling rate and plays on any Windows computer that supports sound. WEB 236

Weather Channel, WEB 213, WEB 215
weather reports on Web, WEB 213–215

Web bibliography A Web site that contains a list of hyperlinks to other Web pages that contain information about a particular topic or group of topics and often includes summaries or reviews of the Web pages listed. *Also called* resource list; subject guide; clearinghouse; virtual library, WEB 175–177

Web browser Software that lets users read (or browse) HTML documents. APP 22, WEB 4, WEB 11–14
  available choices, WEB 17–20
  downloading FTP client programs, WEB 262–265
  FTP using, WEB 249–250
  navigating FTP sites, WEB 253–256

Web client A computer that is connected to the Web and runs a Web browser that enables its user to read HTML documents on Web servers. WEB 4, WEB 5

Web directory A Web site that includes a listing of hyperlinks to Web pages organized into predetermined hierarchical categories; some Web directories have human editors who decide which Web pages will be included in the directory and how they will be organized, other Web directories use computers to perform these tasks. WEB 14, WEB 166–167

Web Distributed Authoring and Versioning (WebDAV or DAV) A protocol that is a standard extension of the original HTTP 1.1 protocol used to transfer Web pages over the Internet. Because HTTP has built-in features that provide security and other desirable features during file transfers, it provides collaboration features on the Internet. WEB 280–284

Web log. *See* blog

Web news directory A Web directory that includes a hierarchical list of links to online news sources. WEB 209

Web page An HTML document and its associated files that are stored on a Web server and made available to other users through their Web browsers. WEB 6
  copyright law, WEB 21
  previously visited, returning to. *See* returning to previously visited Web pages
  printing, WEB 16, WEB 34–36
  refreshing, WEB 33
  reloading, WEB 16
  reproducing, WEB 21
  saving. *See* saving *entries*
  security, WEB 36–37
  stopping transfer of, WEB 16

Web page area That portion of a Web browser window that displays the contents of an HTML document or other file as a Web page.

   browser windows, WEB 11, WEB 12

Web resource

   identity, WEB 192

   objectivity, WEB 192

Web robot A program that automatically searches the Web to find new Web sites and update information about old Web sites that already are in the database. *Also called* bot; spider, WEB 160

Web search engine A Web site (or part of a Web site) that finds other Web pages that match a word or phrase entered by a site visitor. WEB 14

Web server A computer that is connected to the Web and contains HTML documents that it makes available to other computers connected to the Web. WEB 4, WEB 5. *See also* server

Web site A collection of HTML documents stored on a computer that is connected to the Internet.

   evaluating quality, WEB 193–195

   growth of number of, APP 25

   organization, WEB 7–8

   recently modified, finding, WEB 207–208

Web-based e-mail services, WEB 95–97

Weblog. *See* blog

Webmaster The person or group given the responsibility of managing a server or network; the webmaster usually assigns users passwords and user names, and establishes their level of access to the network. WEB 21, WEB 252

white pages directory A Web site that lets you search for names, addresses, and telephone numbers of individuals. WEB 222

wide area network (WAN) Any of several ways of connecting computers to each other when the computers are located more than a few thousand feet from each other. WEB 4

wildcard character A character, usually the asterisk (*), used to indicate that part of the term or terms entered into a Web search engine has been omitted. WEB 180

wire service An organization that gathers and distributes news to newspapers, magazines, broadcasters, and other organizations that pay a fee to the wire service. WEB 209

wireless network A way of connecting computers to each other that does not use cable. Instead, a wireless network uses wireless transmitters and receivers that plug into network interface cards (NICs). APP 11–12

WordPad, copying text from Web page to, WEB 40–41

World Wide Web (WWW) A subset of the computers on the Internet that are connected to each other in a way that allows them to share hyperlinked HTML documents with each other. APP 21–25

   overview, WEB 4–5

WWW. *See* World Wide Web (WWW)

X

Xdrive Technologies, WEB 276–277

Y

Yahoo!, WEB 167–168

Yahoo! Briefcase, WEB 278–279

yellow pages directory A Web site that lets you search for information about businesses, including their names, addresses, and telephone numbers. WEB 220–221

Z

zip archive A collection of one or more compressed files. WEB 270

zip file. *See* compressed file

Task Reference

TASK	PAGE #	RECOMMENDED METHOD	WHERE USED
FTP, WINZIP, AND WINDOWS TASKS			
Anonymous login using command-line FTP	WEB 251	Type anonymous, press Enter	FTP
File extensions, view in Windows Explorer	WEB 247	Start Windows Explorer, click Tools, click Folder Options, click the File Types tab	Windows
File(s), compress using WinZip	WEB 270	Start WinZip, use the WinZip Wizard to enter the filename for the compressed file(s), select the folders and/or files to compress, click Zip Now	WinZip
File(s), decompress using WinZip	WEB 271	Double-click the .zip file, select the location to extract the file(s) to, click Unzip Now	WinZip
File, download using an FTP client program	WEB 267	See Reference Window: Downloading a File Using an FTP Client Program	FTP
Internet route, trace	WEB 273	Click the Start button, click Run, type command, click OK, type tracert and the URL to trace, press Enter	Windows
Network place, create	WEB 284	Start Windows Explorer, click My Network Places in the Folders list, click the Folders button on the toolbar, click Add a network place, use the Wizard to select a network location	Windows
Web Publishing Wizard, start	WEB 281	Start Windows Explorer, select the folder to publish, click the Folders button, click Publish this folder to the Web, select a service provider	Windows
HOTMAIL TASKS			
Attached file, save	WEB 133	See Reference Window: Viewing and Saving an Attached File in Hotmail	Hotmail
Attached file, view	WEB 133	See Reference Window: Viewing and Saving an Attached File in Hotmail	Hotmail
Contact, add to address book	WEB 138	See Reference Window: Adding a Contact to the Hotmail Address Book	Hotmail
Contacts list, open	WEB 139	Click the Contacts tab on the MSN Hotmail - Inbox page	Hotmail
File, attach	WEB 130	Click the Attach button, click File, click the Browse button, locate and double-click the file, click OK	Hotmail
Group add to address book	WEB 140	See Reference Window: Adding a Group to the Hotmail Address Book	Hotmail
Hotmail account, set up	WEB 120	Start your browser, connect to the Internet, go to the Hotmail home page, click the Sign Up button	Hotmail
Hotmail, start	WEB 120	Go to the Hotmail home page, log on to your account	Hotmail
Mail folder, create	WEB 136	Click the Mail tab, click the Manage Folders link, click the New button list arrow, click Folder, type the name of the folder, click OK	Hotmail
Mail folder, delete	WEB 138	See Reference Window: Deleting a Hotmail Folder	Hotmail
Mail, compose	WEB 129	Go to the Hotmail home page, log on to your account, click the New button list arrow, click Mail Message	Hotmail
Mail, delete	WEB 137	See Reference Window: Deleting an E-Mail Message Using Hotmail	Hotmail

TASK	PAGE #	RECOMMENDED METHOD	WHERE USED
Mail, delete permanently	WEB 138	Open the Trash Can folder, click the Empty button, click OK	Hotmail
Mail, forward	WEB 136	See Reference Window: Forwarding an E-Mail Message Using Hotmail	Hotmail
Mail, print	WEB 137	Select the message, click the Print View button, click the Print button	Hotmail
Mail, read	WEB 132	Log on to your Hotmail account, click the Mail tab, click the sender's name for the message in the Inbox	Hotmail
Mail, receive	WEB 132	See Reference Window: Using Hotmail to Receive Messages	Hotmail
Mail, reply to all recipients	WEB 135	See Reference Window: Replying to a Message Using Hotmail	Hotmail
Mail, reply to sender	WEB 135	See Reference Window: Replying to a Message Using Hotmail	Hotmail
Mail, send	WEB 129	See Reference Window: Sending a Message Using Hotmail	Hotmail
Mail, spell check	WEB 131	Click the Tools button, click Spell Check	Hotmail
MICROSOFT INTERNET EXPLORER TASKS			
Address book, open	WEB 116	Click the Addresses button	Outlook Express
Attached file, save	WEB 108	See Reference Window: Viewing and Saving an Attached File in Outlook Express	Outlook Express
Attached file, view	WEB 108	See Reference Window: Viewing and Saving an Attached File in Outlook Express	Outlook Express
Contact, add to address book	WEB 116	See Reference Window: Adding a Contact to the Outlook Express Address Book	Outlook Express
Favorite, move to a new folder	WEB 31	See Reference Window: Moving an Existing Favorite into a New Folder	Internet Explorer
Favorites bar, open	WEB 28	Click the Favorites button	Internet Explorer
Favorites folder, create	WEB 29	See Reference Window: Creating a New Favorites Folder	Internet Explorer
File, attach in New Message window	WEB 105	Click the Attach button, locate and double-click the file	Outlook Express
Full Screen, change to	WEB 25	Click View, click Full Screen	Internet Explorer
Group of contacts, add to address book	WEB 117	See Reference Window: Adding a Group of Contacts to the Address Book	Outlook Express
Help, get	WEB 37	See Reference Window: Opening Internet Explorer Help	Internet Explorer
History list, open	WEB 32	Click the History button	Internet Explorer
Home page, change default	WEB 33	See Reference Window: Changing the Default Home Page in Internet Explorer	Internet Explorer
Home page, return to	WEB 33	Click the Home button	Internet Explorer
Internet Explorer, start	WEB 22	Click the Start button, point to All Programs, click Internet Explorer	Internet Explorer
Mail, compose	WEB 105	Click the Create Mail button	Outlook Express
Mail, delete	WEB 114	See Reference Window: Deleting an E-Mail Message or a Folder in Outlook Express	Outlook Express

TASK	PAGE #	RECOMMENDED METHOD	WHERE USED
Mail, delete permanently	WEB 115	Open Deleted Items folder, click the message summary of the message to delete, click the Delete button, click the Yes button	Outlook Express
Mail, forward	WEB 112	See Reference Window: Forwarding an E-Mail Message Using Outlook Express	Outlook Express
Mail, move to another folder	WEB 113	Drag the message from the message list to a folder in the Folders pane	Outlook Express
Mail, print	WEB 114	Click the message summary, click the Print button, click the Print button again	Outlook Express
Mail, read	WEB 107	Click the message summary	Outlook Express
Mail, receive	WEB 107	See Reference Window: Using Outlook Express to Send and Receive Messages	Outlook Express
Mail, reply to	WEB 111	See Reference Window: Replying to a Message Using Outlook Express	Outlook Express
Mail, send	WEB 104	See Reference Window: Sending a Message Using Outlook Express	Outlook Express
Mail, send and receive	WEB 107	See Reference Window: Using Outlook Express to Send and Receive Messages	Outlook Express
Mail, spell check in New Message window	WEB 106	Click the Spelling button	Outlook Express
Mail account, set up	WEB 102	Click Tools, click Accounts, click the Mail tab, click the Add button, click Mail, follow steps in the Internet Connection Wizard	Outlook Express
Mail folder, create	WEB 113	Right-click the folder in which to create the new folder, click New Folder, type the name of the folder, click OK	Outlook Express
Mail folder, delete	WEB 114	See Reference Window: Deleting an E-Mail Message or a Folder in Outlook Express	Outlook Express
Outlook Express, start	WEB 102	Click the Start button, point to All Programs, click Outlook Express	Outlook Express
Program, download using a browser	WEB 262	See Reference Window: Using a Browser to Download a Program	Internet Explorer
Start page, return to	WEB 33	Click the Home button	Internet Explorer
Toolbar, customize	WEB 25	Click View, Toolbars, Customize	Internet Explorer
Toolbar, hide or show	WEB 25	See Reference Window: Hiding and Restoring the Toolbars in Internet Explorer	Internet Explorer
Toolbars, lock or unlock	WEB 25	Right-click toolbar, click Lock the Toolbars	Internet Explorer
URL, enter and go to	WEB 26	See Reference Window: Entering a URL in the Address Bar	Internet Explorer
Web page graphic, save	WEB 42	See Reference Window: Saving an Image from a Web Page to a Disk	Internet Explorer
Web page text, save	WEB 40	See Reference Window: Copying Text from a Web Page to a WordPad Document	Internet Explorer
Web page, change print settings	WEB 35	Click File, Page Setup	Internet Explorer
Web page, check security	WEB 36	Click the security indicator button	Internet Explorer

TASK	PAGE #	RECOMMENDED METHOD	WHERE USED
Web page, check security elements	WEB 36	Click File, Properties, and then click the Certificates button or double-click the security indicator button	Internet Explorer
Web page, move forward to in history list	WEB 32	Click the Forward button	Internet Explorer
Web page, preview	WEB 36	Click File, Print Preview	Internet Explorer
Web page, print	WEB 34	See Reference Window: Printing the Current Web Page	Internet Explorer
Web page, refresh	WEB 33	Click the Refresh button	Internet Explorer
Web page, return to previous in history list	WEB 32	Click the Back button	Internet Explorer
Web page, save to disk	WEB 39	See Reference Window: Saving a Web Page to a Disk	Internet Explorer
Web pages, move between using hyperlinks and the mouse	WEB 27	See Reference Window: Navigating Between Web Pages Using Hyperlinks and the Mouse	Internet Explorer
FIREFOX TASKS			
Bookmark file, save to a disk	WEB 51	See Reference Window: Saving a Bookmark File to a Disk	Firefox
Bookmark, save in a folder	WEB 50	See Reference Window: Saving a Bookmark in a Bookmarks Folder	Firefox
Bookmarks folder, create	WEB 49	See Reference Window: Creating a New Bookmarks Folder	Firefox
Bookmarks Manager window, open	WEB 49	Click Bookmarks, Manage Bookmarks	Firefox
Cookies, delete	WEB 57	Click Tools, Options, click the Privacy icon, click the plus sign next to Cookies, click the View Cookies button, select a cookie, click the Remove Cookie button	Firefox
Cookies, manage	WEB 56	See Reference Window: Managing Cookies in Firefox	Firefox
Help, get	WEB 58	See Reference Window: Opening Firefox Help	Firefox
History list, open	WEB 52	Click Go, History	Firefox
Home page, change default	WEB 53	See Reference Window: Changing the Default Home Page in Firefox	Firefox
Home page, return to	WEB 52	Click the Home button	Firefox
Print settings, change	WEB 54	See Reference Window: Using Page Setup to Create a Custom Format for Printing a Web Page	Firefox
Program, download using a browser	WEB 262	See Reference Window: Using a Browser to Download a Program	Firefox
Start page, return to	WEB 52	Click the Home button	Firefox
URL, enter and go to	WEB 45	See Reference Window: Entering a URL in the Location Bar	Firefox
Web page graphic, save	WEB 62	See Reference Window: Saving an Image from a Web Page to a Disk	Firefox

TASK	PAGE #	RECOMMENDED METHOD	WHERE USED
Web page text, save	WEB 60	See Reference Window: Copying Text from a Web Page to a WordPad Document	Firefox
Web page, check security	WEB 55	Click the security indicator button	Firefox
Web page, move forward to in history list	WEB 52	Click the Forward button	Firefox
Web page, print	WEB 55	See Reference Window: Printing the Current Web Page	Firefox
Web page, reload	WEB 52	Click the Reload button	Firefox
Web page, return to previous in history list	WEB 52	Click the Back button	Firefox
Web page, save to disk	WEB 59	See Reference Window: Saving a Web Page to a Disk	Firefox
Web pages, move between using hyperlinks and the mouse	WEB 47	See Reference Window: Navigating Between Web Pages Using Hyperlinks and the Mouse	Firefox
WEB TASKS			
Business listings, find	WEB 220	See Reference Window: Finding Business Listings on the Web	Web
Complex search using AltaVista	WEB 181	See Reference Window: Conducting a Complex Search Using AltaVista	AltaVista
Complex search using Vivísimo	WEB 189	See Reference Window: Obtaining Clustered Search Results Using Vivísimo	Vivísimo
Current news stories, search	WEB 211	See Reference Window: Searching Current News Stories	Web
Filtered search using Google	WEB 186	See Reference Window: Conducting a Filtered Search Using Google Advanced Search	Google
Filtered search using Ask Jeeves	WEB 183	See Reference Window: Conducting a Filtered Search Using Ask Jeeves	Ask Jeeves
Local area map, find a	WEB 217	See Reference Window: Finding a Local Area Map on the Web	Web
Meta-search engine, use a	WEB 174	See Reference Window: Using a Meta-Search Engine	Web
Natural language query using Ask Jeeves	WEB 165	Type question into text box, click Search	Ask Jeeves
Travel destination information, find	WEB 218	See Reference Window: Obtaining Travel Destination Information	Web
Weather forecast, find	WEB 214	See Reference Window: Finding a Weather Forecast	Web
Web directory, use	WEB 170	Click a category link, click a subcategory link	Web

TASK	PAGE #	RECOMMENDED METHOD	WHERE USED
Web research resource, evaluate	WEB 193	See Reference Window: Evaluating a Web Research Resource	Web
Web sites that have been modified recently, find	WEB 207	See Reference Window: Finding Web Sites that Have Been Modified Recently	Web
White pages listing, search for your	WEB 222	See Reference Window: Searching for Your White Pages Listing	Web